BOOKS BY ANNA BOWMAN DODD

CATHEDRAL DAYS, 1887
THREE NORMANDY INNS, 1902
FALAISE, THE TOWN OF THE CONQUEROR, 1904
IN THE PALACES OF THE SULTAN, 1906
THE AMERICAN HUSBAND IN PARIS, 1908
IN AND OUT OF A FRENCH COUNTRY HOUSE, 1910
ON THE KNEES OF THE GODS, 1911
HEROIC FRANCE, 1915
UP THE SEINE TO THE BATTLEFIELDS, 1923

CHARLES MAURICE
PRINCE DE TALLEYRAND

Charles-Maurice de Talleyrand

Eighteenth Century School of Art
(Supposed to be by Prud'hon)
(Collection of Comtesse Jean de Castellane.   Never
before reproduced)

Charles-Maurice de Talleyrand

Eighteenth Century School of Art
(Supposed to be by Prud'hon)
(Collection of Comtesse Jean de Castellane.   Never
before reproduced)

TALLEYRAND

The Training of a Statesman

1754—1838

BY

ANNA BOWMAN DODD

With 42 Illustrations

G. P. PUTNAM'S SONS
NEW YORK — LONDON
1927

134534

TO THE MEMORY OF
MY FATHER
STEPHEN MANN BLAKE
BORN IN FRANKLIN, MASSACHUSETTS, 1812,
TO WHOM I OWE MOST OF THE BEST
THINGS IN MY LIFE

PREFACE

AS many quotations in the present volume are made from Talleyrand's *Mémoires* the following history of these much-discussed *Mémoires* is given as found in the preface and notes of the edition edited and published by the Duc de Broglie in 1891, issued by Calman-Lévy.

The Duc de Broglie in his preface gives the following account of the origin of the *Mémoires:*

Talleyrand made a Will leaving all his papers to the Duchesse de Dino, on the condition, however, that none of them should be published before thirty years had elapsed, from the time of his death. If the Duchesse de Dino were to die before Talleyrand's decease, the ownership of the papers (or memoirs) was to pass to Monsieur de Bacourt.

After Talleyrand's death, in 1838, the papers became the possession of the Duchesse de Dino, but she died in her turn, on September 29, 1862—*i.e.*, six years before the time fixed by the Will for the publication of the papers, and they (the papers or memoirs) passed into the hands of Monsieur de Bacourt.[1]

In the lifetime of the Duchesse de Dino, Monsieur de Bacourt had apparently undertaken the work of preparing

[1] Monsieur de Bacourt had been Talleyrand's Secretary for some years, up to the time of his death.

Talleyrand's *Mémoires* for publication, and had almost finished the task of making a complete copy when death overtook him on April 22, 1865.

According to a Will left by Monsieur de Bacourt, the *Mémoires* were not to be published until 1888—a period of fifty years after Talleyrand's death: until that time the *Mémoires* were to remain in the hands of two Trustees— Messieurs Chatelin and Paul Audral. Of these two gentlemen, Monsieur Chatelin died first, his place as Trustee being taken by his son, Monsieur Chatelin, Jr., while Monsieur Audral, having died in 1889, left the publication of the *Mémoires* to his co-Trustee Monsieur Chatelin, Jr., and to the Duc de Broglie.

The Duc de Broglie further states that the edition which he presents to the public has been printed from the copy written by Monsieur de Bacourt, and in his handwriting; the First Book of the *Mémoires* was certified as being authentic by the Duchesse de Dino and by M. de Bacourt. The Second and Third Books were also certified to be veracious copies of the original by Monsieur de Bacourt. As he died before the Fourth Book was fully completed, this latter Book bears no testimony.

In spite of the above assertions that the copies made of Talleyrand's memoirs were exact copies of the original documents, the more famous historians and critics are of the unanimous opinion that the memoirs (or papers) left by Talleyrand have been greatly modified, that certain pages have been omitted, and many statements changed.

ANNA BOWMAN DODD.

PARIS, 1927.

CONTENTS

PART I

vii

CONTENTS

PART II

STORY OF TALLEYRAND'S MARRIAGE—THE LATER YEARS—
CONVERSION AND DEATH

ILLUSTRATIONS

TALLEYRAND

PART I

THE TRAINING OF A STATESMAN

CHAPTER I

I

CHARLES-MAURICE DE TALLEYRAND-PÉRI-GORD was born in Paris, on the second of February in the year 1754. His father at the time of his birth was nineteen and a half years old, his mother, being by six years the senior of her husband, was in her twenty-fifth year. The house in which the future famous statesman first saw the light of day, No. 4 rue Garancière, still exists. On the very day of his birth, the babe Charles-Maurice was baptized in the parish church of Saint-Sulpice.

Saint-Sulpice and its parish were to have a curiously determining influence in the fate which awaited Talleyrand. It was at Saint-Sulpice that Talleyrand's parents—Charles-Daniel, Comte de Talleyrand, and Alexandrine-Marie-Victoire-Eléonore de Damas d'Antigny—were married on the twelfth of January, 1751. It was at the Seminary of Saint-Sulpice, close to the church, that Talleyrand was to pass seven most trying and rebellious years, during his novitiate for the priesthood.

On the day of his marriage the young Comte Charles-Daniel de Talleyrand was but sixteen years of age, while the bride was twenty-two. By the death of his father—the Marquis de Talleyrand-Périgord, Comte de Grignols,

Colonel of a Normandy regiment, who was killed at the siege of Tournai—as the eldest of seven children, Charles-Daniel, at the age of eleven years, found himself to be the head of the family. The marriage of a youth of sixteen was the more easily possible in the eighteenth century because of the name he bore. Mademoiselle d'Antigny, having passed the first blush of her bloom—since early marriages for young girls was the accepted rule of the period —bowed to the decision of her parents with ready grace. The marriage, as it chanced, was a happy one, in an age when conjugal felicity was so rare as to be deemed a bourgeois condition.

II

In pre-revolutionary days a great name was as important as was distinguished birth coupled with wealth. The Talleyrands asserted their former possession of sovereign rights. As early as the 12th century, the Comtes de Grignols, Princes de Chalais, had reigned as independent princes. As descendants of these Comtes de Grignols, Princes de Chalais, Talleyrand's parents proudly insisted on tracing their pedigree from Hélie V who was sovereign lord of Périgord. In the thirteenth century, the name of Talieran or Tailleran was transferred to a younger son. The Talleyrands were descended from this latter branch of the family, while the head of the clan bore the title of Prince de Chalais, from a great estate in Périgord, recently inherited. *Ré que Dieu* (only God above us), was their motto. There were all the traditions of an age-long race bound up in the descendants of the famous Comte de Périgord—of him who could dare to cry out to his King, Hugues Capet, "Qui t'a fait roi?" in answer to the King's insulting query—whom de Périgord and other great nobles had raised to power—"Qui t'a fait Comte?" The heady wine of his new elevation had worked over-quickly in Capet's veins. Eight hundred years later, the descendant of that mediæval king-maker put one of Capet's descendants—a Bourbon, Louis XVIII—on the throne. Talleyrand thus took his revenge on Dame Fortune, the impecunious situation of his family having forced him into the priesthood. Louis XVIII's elevation to the throne, after the fall of Napoleon, as all history records, was largely due to Talleyrand's offices and influence.

The pecuniary circumstances of Talleyrand's family were as a pricking spur. As a bride, Madame de Talleyrand had brought a small dot of fifteen thousand francs to the family fund. When her second child, Charles-Maurice, was about to be born, so reduced were the resources of his parents, Madame de Talleyrand was forced to make an appeal to her mother for the bare necessities of her confinement. The customs of the age came to the aid of highly born parents; to women of the people was entrusted the offspring of indigent nobles. The exact date of the babe, Charles-Maurice, having been put out to nurse is a debatable point: earlier historians assert he was taken direct from the baptismal font to the house of a poor woman, in the street then known as the rue St.-Jacques, this street being then situated in a suburb of Paris. Later authorities state that it was during the first year of his birth that he was sent *en pension* "into the country."

It was there, possibly, in a mean house, that the misfortune of his life befell Talleyrand. The neglected child was to meet with a serious accident, a servant of the house having let him drop. His own statement records that he had fallen when mounting a chest of drawers. The result was the same—he was lamed for life. A cousin of Talleyrand's—l'Abbé Comte Maurice de Périgord—asserted that Talleyrand had been born lame, and that in the Talleyrand family there had always been a club-footed member.

To whatever cause Talleyrand's misfortune is to be attributed, it changed the course of his destiny. The crippling of those twisted feet—"ses griffes," as Comte Molé in his famous *Mémoires*, recently published, cruelly calls Talleyrand's lower members—this his lameness not only robbed him of the rank, as the head of the family, due to him by birth, but Talleyrand's character was to be warped and his very nature altered, by his bitter resentment at having been thus victimized by Fate, and by his parents. His elder brother, Alexandre-François-Jacques, born in 1752, died at five years of age. By right of birth, Charles-Maurice would thus have been (after his father's death) head of the family; unable, however, to bear arms, because of his infirmity, his parents decided to waive his right and transferred the headship to a third son—named Archambauld-Joseph—born in the year 1762. For this act Talleyrand never forgave his father and mother. In later life, when touching on this period of his childhood, he could never refer to their decision without bitterness. The same note of resentment is dominant in all his recorded or written statements relating to the neglect of his parents in his earlier years. Again and again he comments on his loneliness, on the apparent and systematized abandonment of which he was a victim, and from which he so greatly suffered.[1]

[1] M. G. Lacour-Gayet, in a recent article on "L'Enfance de Talleyrand" in the *Revue de Paris*, August 16, 1926, refutes the attacks made by Talleyrand in his

In the house of the poor people to whom his parents had confided him, the years went on. Charles-Maurice was to reach his fifth year before any change came to mark a red-letter day in his more or less painful existence. For painful it was. As late as the year 1758 the child might have been seen hopping about on one leg, or shuffling courageously on both feet, one foot, the right one, being noticeably shorter than the other. The small face already showed pathetic lines of suffering, never so moving as in the very young. An interest keener than pity would have been felt by any intelligent observer. There was an arresting attraction in the boy's bearing and manner which compelled attention. The ease and grace of gesture, the strong wilful eyes with their look of mingled daring and yearning, and the voice, with its accent of instinctive refinement, marked this child as one separate and apart from his mean surroundings.

The features bore the unmistakable stamp of race. The eyes, grey blue, were quickened with life; the nose, slightly tip-tilted—an upward incline supposed to indicate a certain tendency to irreverence and quick wit—gave the little face a piquant expression. Talleyrand's enemies, later in his career, derisively characterized this expression as being "insolent"—"un retroussé insolent" is Sainte-Beuve's characteristic touch when describing Talleyrand's nose, in

---

Mémoires regarding the treatment of his parents. The distinguished historian quotes from letters shown him by an aged member of Madame de Talleyrand's family, to the effect that Talleyrand's mother writes, in certain letters, of her anxiety caused by the pains in the child's legs, and in others, of the doctors who had been consulted and of certain appliances which had been tried. Such acts would be the very least which could be shown to an infirm child by a parent. The above-mentioned letters not having been fully quoted in M. Lacour-Gayet's article, the author of the present historic record adheres to the testimony accepted by those historians whose authority, thus far, has been undisputed. The present volume having been completed before the appearance of M. Lacour-Gayet's interesting contribution, it has been impossible to note the above contention more at length.

the great critic's memorable, and blasting, portraiture of
the great statesman.

The stars, in their courses, in the year 1758, were working for the neglected child's liberation.[1] In the distant
province of Périgord, in an ancient château, there lived a
great lady—Talleyrand's great-grandmother—la Princesse
de Chalais. The unseen, mysterious influences which
controlled Talleyrand's earlier life had suddenly decreed
that the child Charles-Maurice was to leave the suburb of
St.-Jacques and to be taken to the Château de Chalais.
Whatever may have been the reasons which determined
this happy change in Talleyrand's career, it was the true
beginning of his extraordinary future life: for at Chalais he
was to begin to live. Up to this time he may be said merely
to have existed. Talleyrand was to enter into the milieu
to which, by right of birth and condition, he belonged.

III

The title of Prince de Chalais was one proudly acclaimed
by the Talleyrand family. Historically, the de Chalais'
antedated the dynasty of the Capetians. It was the descendants of this branch of the Comtes de Grignols who
asserted their claim to sovereign rights, as Comtes de Périgord. The bearer of the title in Talleyrand's childhood—
the venerable Princesse de Chalais—was worthy to transmit
so great a name. In every sense of the word she was a
grande dame. She was descended from the de Mortemart
family, famous for their cleverness and their apt wit. She

---

[1] In a rare volume, *L' Album Perdu*, by Henri Delatouche, a visit to the rue St.-
Jacques recorded: Le Bailli de Périgord wishing to make the acquaintance of his little
nephew, found him in a deplorable condition "in the village where he was more or
less forgotten." He discovered him in a field covered with snow, chasing swallows,
with his *frère de lait*, his foster brother, one as ragged as the other.

THE TALLEYRAND COAT OF ARMS

possessed the art of conveying speech through striking and lively phrases. This was an art which may be said to have been "the natural language of the family." Talleyrand went to school early, therefore, to the best and most finished of social adepts. "Les formes d'une politesse digne et sans morgue" were his models in conversation and in manners, during these formative years.

The journey from Paris to Bordeaux, in the mid-eighteenth century, was a trip of seventeen days' duration. For a safe accomplishment of the expedition, Charles-Maurice had been placed under the care of a woman with the awe-inspiring name of Charlemagne—a devoted retainer of the de Talleyrand family.

The two travellers proceeded, by diligence, from Bordeaux to the Château, where Charles-Maurice was to experience the first emotional surprise of his life. He made an amazing discovery. One of his family, he found, was possessed of a heart. The Princesse de Chalais fell in love with her great-grandchild, at first sight. She took the forlorn little cripple to her arms and she kept him there. Her pity, her sympathy, her affection swept the child with an enveloping flood of tenderness. The Princess's devotion was the magic touch which was to awaken that responsive chord of affectionate attachment which Talleyrand, later in life, was to show to several women, to one or two men, and more particularly—a devotion laced with the fiery spark of passion—to his niece by marriage, the Duchesse de Dino.

The influences of a certain state kept up at Chalais were Talleyrand's first lessons in both the refinements of decorum and of beauty of surroundings.

What a change was this ancient abode contrasted with the humble, squalid house, in the suburb St.-Jacques!

Wherever the boy looked, color, beauty, splendor in some form, met his eye. Tapestried walls, rich in animated scenes; portraits of dead and gone ancestors, the very chairs and tables told the story of past reigns as significantly as did the pictures of his ancestors—those warriors and courtiers lining *salles* and *salons*. In such great rooms this impressionable boy must have realized, in some measure at least, the high place to which, by right of birth, he belonged.

An elaborate training in the social graces was soon acquired by this born aristocrat. Talleyrand must be taught how to enter a room, how to bow with grace, how to kiss a lady's hand, and also how to wear with elegance and ease the little satin coat, the laces, the embroidered vests, and the sword which a child in his day, inheriting a great name, must carry. The future courtier, whose supreme grace of bearing and whose *grand seigneur* air were to be remarked in all the Courts of Europe, was already in training.

The social and mental atmosphere of Chalais were to influence Talleyrand's future life and career. He was at last breathing an air of grandeur. He did not need to await the influences of Court life at Versailles. He was at a better, a more finished school. The graces of refinement in speech and manners of those who surrounded him far surpassed, in distinction, the models introduced by the du Barry at Court—models which, a few years later, were to set so pernicious an example to the youth of the day.

IV

Talleyrand's tribute to his great-grandmother, in his *Mémoires*, and his reflections on the benefits derived from these early associations at Chalais, are eloquent proofs of what resources of love and affection lay in the depths of his better nature.

I pleased her; she taught me what I had not yet experienced—tenderness. She was the first person related to me who showed me affection, and she was also the first who gave me the happiness that comes in loving. May mercies descend upon her! Yes,—I dearly loved her. Her memory is still dear to me. How many times during my life, I have mourned her. How often I have realized with bitterness, the inestimable price of a sincere affection coming to one from one's own family. When such an affection is close to you, it is a great consolation in the sorrows of life. If it be at a distance, it is a repose for the mind and heart, and a dwelling place for thought.

The time I passed at Chalais made a profound impression on me. The first object which strikes the eyes and hearts in childhood often determines the nature of the child and gives to character tendencies followed in the course of life.

I really owe to these early years the general spirit animating my conduct. If I have shown affectionate sentiments, even tender ones, without their being too familiar; if I have shown a certain superiority unmarred by haughtiness; if I respect elderly people, it was at Chalais, it was at my grandmother's where all the fine sentiments which the province felt for my relations inspired me with like feelings. . . .

Talleyrand further confesses:

the souvenirs of all I saw, of all I heard, in this early period of my life, are to me of peculiar sweetness. "Your name," those about me repeated daily, "has always been venerated in our country. Your family," was affectionately said, "has always, in all ages, been related to some one of our house. It was your grandfather who gave us this land—it was he who built our church . . . my mother's cross was given her by Madame . . . good trees do not degenerate . . . you will be good, will you not?"

Talleyrand's future career is an answer to that somewhat illusive hope. In reviewing his long past—at eighty —what answer did Talleyrand himself give to that disturbing question?

These few years at Chalais were the happiest of Talleyrand's childhood and youth. When old, disillusioned, embittered, having tasted of every cup a brilliant and successful life could proffer, he would revert to those years as a man turns to a beloved image—to this image of his childhood reflecting candor, innocence, and the heart of a child warmed by affection. How many of these lovely and lovable qualities he was to leave behind, one by one, as he passed life's milestones!

Talleyrand wrote his *Mémoires* in his own great Château of Valençay, in his eightieth year. The fragrance of his "grand-maman's" love and tender care appear to have remained as fresh as though he had visited her but the day before.

V

We can picture the scenes presented at Chalais in the long winter evenings. Close to the burning logs in the deep chimney, the Princess sat, enthroned in her deep Louis XIV fauteuil. The flames would pick out the threaded silver and woven flowers in her brocaded gown. Grouped about the venerable Châtelaine there were her friends, elderly nobles, many of whom, as courtiers, had figured at the levées of Louis XIV. Their old faces would still wear rouge. Their ringletted wigs would brush their embroidered coats, and the rich laces, falling over the wrinkled hands, would tremble, in excited moments of talk.

These her friends, who formed her little court, doubtless

LOUIS XIV'S BEDCHAMBER AT VERSAILLES

talked as old men delight in talking. They would relate the part they had played in the "great Reign." Talleyrand would be made to see, through the stories told and the chief scenes relived of the life and times of Louis XIV, this history of a time already past. These elderly men would extol the precocious cleverness of the boy-King who —at twenty-three—already knew the "business of Kings." We can almost hear the tones of the old quavering voices rising to enthusiasm as the story was told the boy, of how Louis XIV took the reins of government from Mazarin's grasping, crafty hands. For Louis already had felt within him "l'étoffe de quatre rois et d'un honnête homme."

The great figures of that apogee of France's splendor must have been made also to pass, as a living pageant, before Charles-Maurice's wondering eyes and mind. Mazarin, Colbert, Louvois, Turenne, Vauban—what a company of giants in capacity and intellect!

Remote from the glamour of Court life, these ex-courtiers would see the France of their own day already at grips with financial and political ruin. The weakness of the King, Louis XV, was loudly, fiercely deplored. It was on the white back of the Pompadour whose reign was not yet ended, on which was laid the chief burden of the miseries from which the kingdom was suffering. It was she, the voices would cry, whose misrule was rushing France to the edge of the abyss towards which the country was heading.

The favorite's lavish expenditure in costly furniture, in bibelots, in book-bindings, in porcelains, and in interior decorations—what was not her extravagance costing the exchequer? Her follies and the King's indifference between them were digging the grave which was to entomb France's glory, her prosperity, and, above all else, her credit.

The talk of these elderly courtiers was like living the history, past and present, of France, instead of reading it. Talleyrand's precocious intelligence made a certain caution necessary. His head doubtless pillowed against his great-grandmother's knee, before the Chalais fire, on a winter's evening—the boy would drink in the talk of his elders as earth drinks moisture for nourishment. The soil was ripe—it was then virgin soil. Charles-Maurice's mind was as an unwritten page. There had been no cramming of dull text-books. There had been no muddling of a young mind, whose cleverness already was noted, one of singular and tenacious memory, with innumerable facts and tiresome lessons—facts and lessons forgotten as soon as learned. The living speech he heard sank deep.

VI

In one of the most striking chapters of Talleyrand's *Mémoires*, he paints for us the pictures of the life led at Chalais. They are presented with veracity and artistic perfection. The light shed on the provincial, yet aristocratic milieu is as soft and tender as that of a Claude Lorrain landscape.

The manners of the nobility in Périgord resembled its old Châteaux; they had a something at once great and stable; light scarcely penetrated, but it came in softened tones. With useful deliberation progress was made towards a more enlightened civilization.

Talleyrand goes on to reproduce a true *genre* picture of a scene which took place after Mass, every Sunday. His "grand'mère"—as the child loved to call his great-grandmother—"because it seemed to bring her nearer"—took her seat in a vast hall called "the apothecary." In her velvet chair, with a black lacquered table in front of her, Madame de Chalais sat, receiving the poor of the parish who needed medical help. Various unguents, the prescriptions for which were a part of the Chalais inheritance, were ranged on shelves. Every year the curé of the village and the surgeon prepared these remedies. The health of the Chalais peasants must indeed have been robust to resist the united efforts of the son of God and of the village surgeon-barber.

Talleyrand tells us his place "by right" was close to Madame de Chalais. In her elaborate Sunday apparel, this great lady must have been an imposing spectacle. Her gown was of silk, trimmed with ribbons. A "cascade" of ribbons and knots on the sleeves; cuffs with large patterns; a tippet; a bonnet or cap with a "butterfly"; and a black coif tied under her chin—was a costume which lent a certain dignity to its confession of old age. Madame de Chalais was then in her sixty-eighth year.

The patients, meanwhile, had been ranged in line, in an outer room. One by one they were ushered in. Two Sisters of Charity inquired the nature of the trouble, or of the wound, from which the visitors suffered. The unguent best suited to cure, or to dull the pain, was then prescribed.

Talleyrand proceeds solemnly. The solemnity, indeed, with which he narrates these reminiscences proves the tender reverence their memory recalled. It was Madame de Chalais who, having heard the nature of the complaint and having prescribed the specific remedy, indicated the place where the preparation for it was to be found.

Another feature of this little ceremony was typical of those far-away days. Madame de Chalais held, in her

Château, as has been stated, a diminutive court. It was composed of several old noblemen who had retired to their domains. Those who found at the Château de Chalais the charm of that distinction and elegance they had left behind at Louis XIV's Court, were the devoted attendants of the Châtelaine's Sunday charities. And it fell to the rôle of one of these valetudinarians to seek the bottle on the shelf which Madame de Chalais designated; and to still another old gentleman to bring a certain bureau drawer filled with linen. Talleyrand is careful to tell us he "held one piece" while his grandmother cut the desired bands and compresses. Presently followed gifts of herbs, of wines, and of certain drugs presented with encouraging and comforting counsels, tendered by the charitable donator.

What a charming and homely picture! The whole atmosphere enveloping this older, simpler life breathes kindly virtues, and a recognition of the humanitarian tie binding those highly placed, to their dependents. As one passes to-day such great châteaux, in certain remote parts of France, which are for the most part closed, one has the sense of deserted temples where once reigned priests of the cult of kindness and women whom a child could reverence.

CHAPTER II

I

THE years of this all-too-brief happiness, of calm, and of growth at Chalais were soon to end. The powers which ruled the destiny of Charles-Maurice decided he was to leave the Château. He was to go to the Collège d'Harcourt. Again he started forth on the long journey, to end it in Paris. Was it a malicious stroke of fate that, in this city, where, later, the genius of Talleyrand was to play so great a part in the making of France's history, where calumny and hate were to track him, he should have descended at the rue d'Enfer—the street named Hell?

Not one of his family appeared to greet the desolate child, on his arrival. An elderly valet awaited his descent from the coach. During the journey of seventeen days the boy must have been warmed by the thought of finding a mother's smile, at least, to welcome him. He might even have hoped to make the somewhat unduly retarded acquaintance of that elusive father who as yet, according to Talleyrand's own statement, had never laid eyes on the boy. Talleyrand's record of his experiences is the following:

I was struck by this sudden entrance into school without first having been conducted to the home of my father and my mother. I was eight years old, and the paternal eye had not

17

yet rested upon me. I was told, and I believed it, that this precipitous arrangement had been caused by some extraordinary circumstance. I followed the route I was to take.

These lines, and the cruelty of this parental treatment, one followed by design—as Talleyrand was to learn later on—need no commentary. Here are the facts—stark and staring. What effect this indifference and neglect was to produce, will be seen, later on. If the three years at Chalais had released strains of tenderness in Talleyrand which, for the few he loved, were to nourish "an arid nature," as the Gulf Stream warms an icy Atlantic, the treatment of his family, all through his youth and manhood was to aid in the development of those traits of character which, in their ultimate results, have made his name, for certain practices, a byword among men.

The bitterness which, in later life, was to sculpture those telltale lines in the downward curving lips of the great states-man—lines revealing disillusion—this disenchantment began when, looking for a mother's embrace, the boy was confronted with a valet's servile smirk. This singular, and, as Talley-rand was to discover, this "systematic" parental neglect was to be still more brutally emphasized. During the boy's school course at Harcourt, he fell ill of the most dangerous and dreaded of all maladies. He was seized with a bad attack of small-pox. Although his tutor at once informed the family of the gravity of the illness, the sole recognition of the serious situation, by his parents, was—the despatch of a sedan chair!

In his *chaise-à-porteurs* the lad was carried to the house of a nurse employed by a certain Doctor Lehoc. The treat-ment of the disease was such, at the time, that more died of it than of the disorder. The patient was quickly put to bed, thick bed-curtains were tightly drawn, a huge fire was built, and the fever "was excited by very active hot drinks." As Talleyrand adds, with his caustic humor, "in spite of this incendiary régime which killed a great many people, I grew better, was cured and was not even marked."

With singular generosity, Talleyrand states in his *Mémoires* that he was told, later in life, that this extraordinary and seemingly unnatural attitude of his father and mother was in reality part of a plan. They knew he must be trained for the priesthood—a vocation for which he showed little aptitude. Were they to see him too frequently, they doubted their own courage to force him, against his will and desire, to continue in the path which, for imperative family interests, and his own, they had chosen for him. Talleyrand adds: "This fear" (on their part) "is a proof of their tenderness for which I am grateful."

In expressing so magnanimous a sentiment, Talleyrand was entirely sincere. All his life long he showed a considerate attitude towards his family, rare in any age, and doubly rare in the times in which he lived. He could state with a commendable restraint of feeling; "I may say, once for all, that I am perhaps the only member of a large and distinguished family who never in his whole life had the good fortune to spend even a single night under the same roof with his parents," yet he could also admit:

The little interest taken in me, in the way I was sent to school, and other painful impressions, saddened me. I felt helpless and always thrown upon myself. I will not complain of having to suffer so early in my life. To it I owe a capacity for serious reflection and calm judgment in misfortune which pleasurable impressions would never have given me. It is, therefore, not without a certain sense of satisfaction that I look back upon the past. Since then I have come to the conclusion that my parents, after having decided, for family reasons, to devote me to a profession for which I had not the slightest inclination, were afraid of not having the courage to carry out their plans if they saw me too often.

In writing of these his earlier years, Talleyrand constantly reverts to his loneliness during this period of growth, to his sense of having been abandoned, and to his being thrown entirely on his own resources. He confesses that certain memories evoked bitter feeling—those particularly which related to the apparent neglect and indifference of his parents.

The testimony of all his contemporaries supports the point of view taken by Talleyrand in his *Mémoires*. A friend of Mirabeau's, Dumont, a Swiss writer, asserts:

I heard him (Talleyrand) say many times that, despised by his parents as a disgraced creature who was good for nothing, he had contracted in his childhood a taciturn and dull disposition; he had never slept under the roof of his father and mother; they forced him to renounce his right of primogeniture in favor of his younger brother.

Again, Talleyrand states, in narrating his having been taken from the Collège d'Harcourt to go to Rheims, to be with his uncle who was Coadjutor of the Archbishop of Rheims, that

I did not go to my parents before my departure, and I say it, having said it once, and I trust not to be forced to think of it again, that I am perhaps the only one of distinguished birth and belonging to a numerous and estimable family who has never, for a single week of his life, known the sweetness of finding himself under the paternal roof.

LOUIS XV
Photographer: Levasseur, in Paris

In these his celebrated *Mémoires*, begun in 1815–16—
during the Restoration, when much against his will and
desire, he found that the scepter of power and influence,
which had enabled him to seat Louis XVIII on the throne,
had been taken from him, an act of ingratitude entirely in
consonance with the character of the King—Talleyrand
began, in his enforced leisure, to write a record of his life.
The earlier chapters deal with his life and career up to 1815.
At the period of his devoting himself to this task, he was at
the zenith of his intellectual vigor.   He was sixty-two years
of age.   He had attained, on two recent great occasions,
to the apogee of his career.   During the occupation of
the Allied armies in Paris—1814—the Czar of Russia was his
guest.   When the grave question of Napoleon's fate hung in
the balance, the restoration of a Bourbon King was decided
by Talleyrand's famous phrase:—"The Bourbons represent
tradition."   At the Council of Vienna (1814–15) with diplomatic subtlety and consummate art, he had turned the
tables on the matured plans of Metternich, Castlereagh, and
the other negotiators; by breaking up the unity of the Allies,
who had agreed to ignore and despoil France, he succeeded
in securing greater advantages for his country than he had
conceived possible.   To suppose that such a master-mind
would wilfully present to the world a portraiture of his
parents as untrue as it was malicious, is difficult to believe.
That Talleyrand may have wished to prove that certain
influences and the lack of parental care and affection led to
his committing acts he regretted, is more than probable;
but a bitterness so keen as to be felt in all its intensity on to
old age, must have been caused by actual and prolonged
suffering.

II

During the years spent at Harcourt, Charles-Maurice was given formal permission to make the acquaintance of his questionably sensitive parents. Once a week he was taken by l'Abbé Hardi—one of his teachers—to dine with his parents. His comment on these visits is illuminating: "On leaving, I heard regularly the same words:—'Be good, my son, and try to please Monsieur l'Abbé.'"

During these weekly visits, the boy, according to his own statement, was left in complete ignorance of his future destiny. His father maintained absolute silence on the subject. Talleyrand's enlightenment as to his future vocation was to come through the circuitous route of gossip. "Certain vague references to the matter, I heard about me, were the first warnings I received."

In spite of such alarming rumors, the years Talleyrand spent at Harcourt were not altogether unhappy. This college of the mid-eighteenth century had no pretensions to the arduous toil demanded by the French lycées' curriculum of our day. Yet the boy worked diligently, and by his progress in Philosophy, won a degree as Master of Arts.

I might have been a successful scholar; my natural bent led me to think so, and I notice that this opinion is almost universally shared by my schoolfellows. The little encouragement given me, for fear I should become too clever a young man, is the cause that the first years of my life were spent in a rather dull and insignificant manner,

is Talleyrand's own estimate of his accomplishment at this College.

The financial methods of the College must have been of a singularly lax order, since Talleyrand's parents omitted to pay the Abbé Langlois—young Charles-Maurice's preferred instructor—for his four years' tuition. The first funds received by Talleyrand, when he was in possession of a settled income, were, in part, directed to the payment of his former teacher, l'Abbé Langlois.

At his college Charles-Maurice de Périgord made rapid strides. His successes were brilliant. It was the age when punishment literally followed the crime, however slight the crime might be. He frequently narrated the story of his having been forced to submit to the sting of the whip:

My pride as a nobleman [he said] revolted at such an indignity. I escaped from the college and I hoped that the intervention of my father would spare me this humiliation, but on the contrary he said, "*Monsieur mon fils*, one of our ancestors, Henri de Talleyrand, Comte de Chalais, became the favorite of Louis XIII because the King remembered that in his youth your ancestor had allowed himself to be whipped in his place."

III

An agreeable surprise had awaited Talleyrand at his first meal in the refectory; he found a boy friend. A boy with a smile, with wide-open eyes, and an engaging simplicity of nature, sat beside the new scholar. The two looked each other over, as boys do. The smiles broadened. An intimacy was to follow, one of long duration, to last, really, as long as life. Auguste de Choiseul-Gouffier was the nephew of the famous Minister, Duc de Choiseul, then in power. Later in life, Talleyrand's friend was to become Ambassador at Constantinople, under Louis XVI, and Minister of State under Louis XVIII. The two friends were to be more or less constantly in touch during Talleyrand's eventful career. He refers to him as "a charming boy who shared, and still shares, all the cares, pleasures, and dreams of my life."

In the duration of this friendship with de Choiseul-Gouffier we may find one of those anomalies apparently at variance with the accepted conception of Talleyrand's character. Napoleon said of him: "He had a gentle bearing; one that attached one to him." Talleyrand's few friendships, though never touched by the flame of ardor, were tenacious. Few as were his intimates, he rarely lost sight of either the men or the women for whom he had really cared.

IV

Talleyrand's parents—and his uncle, Alexandre-Angélique de Talleyrand, Coadjutor to the Archbishop of Rheims,—decided in parental conclave that Talleyrand was to spend a year at a great ecclesiastical court. He was to be taught and to be shown the splendors attainable by becoming a son of the Church.

There was design, and one well thought-out, in sending this boy of twelve to make his best bow before his uncle, Alexandre de Talleyrand.

The young scholar was no ordinary boy. Although his parents saw him so infrequently, yet his reluctance to enter the priesthood was well known to them. A character already showing decidedly dominating traits was to be bent and influenced. Appeals to certain tastes and propensities hereditary in the grasping Talleyrand family were to be made.

Charles-Maurice was to be presented, at this court of the Archbishop of Rheims, with an object lesson. He was to be dazzled by splendor. He was to see a road opened wide

A BALLET AT VERSAILLES

before him, one leading to one of the most stupendous anomalies ever presented to human eyes.

The dignitaries of the Church of that day outrivalled, in magnificence and extravagant ways of living, the princes of the blood. Bishops in the eighteenth century could afford to maintain a scale of expenditure which even the descendants of kings found ruinous. These princes of the Church had superb private residences, such as Hautefontaine and Saverne. With eight hundred thousand livres income, in those days when money was money, one could spend royally.

It is difficult for us in our day to reconstruct, imaginatively, the magnificence of such semi-royal domains. Still more would it be difficult for us to conceive of a bishop —say of Bayeux, or even of an Archbishop of Paris—living the life lived by the great prelates of Rheims or of Strasbourg in the eighteenth century.

At their Châteaux, these *grands seigneurs* kept open house. Tables were laid for fifty or a hundred guests. In the language of our day, these sons of the Church denied themselves nothing. They had the fairest, the cleverest, the most noted women of their day as mistresses. The time was spent in hunting, in arranging great fêtes, in rehearsing comedies, in organizing horse-races, or in listening to concerts sung or executed by the best artists, from Paris. When these princes of the Church travelled, they passed lesser men in a coach with four, or even six horses. They had their outriders and guards, the latter in gay liveries, like other great noblemen. To what better uses could an Archbishop of Rheims put his vast revenues?

Madame de Rothe, who owned Hautefontaine, as all the world knew, was the Archbishop's niece. What situation more acceptably justified itself than that a niece should receive and "keep house" for a pleasure-loving uncle? Yet all the world knew, and all the world closed its indulgent eyes to, the true relations existing between the two.

With fat abbey lands to feed their purse, Bishops and Archbishops, under Louis XV's negligent rule, had attained indeed to semi-royal state. They had Versailles as a model for both luxury and vice. The scale of living was on the same plane of expenditure. Fêtes, gaieties and amusements, which ended only to begin anew, such gaieties brought nobles and ecclesiastics from the four corners of France. Great country estates belonging to Church dignitaries starred the kingdom with princely Châteaux which revolutionaries, a quarter of a century later, were to mark for destruction.

V

In such a life as Talleyrand was to see at Hautefontaine, in the mid-eighteenth century, and in the Archiepiscopal palace of Rheims, there was every element of seduction in beauty, in grandeur, and in sensuous enjoyment capable of exciting the seeds of ambition to push forth their growth in Talleyrand's susceptible nature. Talleyrand was to see Rheims in all the splendor of its mid-eighteenth century perfection. Rheims then was wearing its regal robes.

The Hotel de Ville, its windows framed in lacy sculptures, still housed the famous library. The Basilica of the eleventh century, with its Romanesque, Gothic, and Flamboyant additions and restorations, recalled the noble proportions of churches when faith was as real as it was absent from episcopal palaces seven centuries later. There was the lovely House of the Musicians—intact; there were streets packed close with dwellings each one of which would have given tourists of to-day a thrill of delight.

Above all other centres of attraction there was the famed Cathedral, in its Gothic perfection. Its deeply recessed, sculptured portals were the home of shifting lights. "Le Sourire de Rheims" was then as a promise of life to come, in its fixed beatitude. The figure of Christ—"Le beau Dieu"—in the North Portal, could then still be seen bending, as he seemed to be actually giving His benediction to the just and to the unjust. Angels, martyrs, saints, holy virgins and the Holy Mother were as an army in nobly-worked stones to move hearts to turn to the life beyond.

When Talleyrand's wondering eyes surveyed these glories, his ears might still be ringing with the music made by the musicians at the Archbishop's dinner of the night before. There had been, possibly, a hundred or more guests, seated at the long tables. Thousands of candles had shed a diffused, softened light on necks as white as were the powdered heads. Princes, *grands seigneurs*, bishops, learned men and women famed for their beauty, whose names are now become a part of history,—in such a frame was the great scene set, a scene which was to teach a lad the valuable lesson of the advantages to be gained, by climbing to high place. The steps to be taken to attain the prizes led one, it was true, to a seminary of priests. But behold the captivating resultant!

Talleyrand was consciously or unconsciously profoundly influenced by these splendors—by this presentment of how life could be lived, once a priest, in grand ways. His future life and career abundantly proved the lesson had not been lost.

At least one keen-eyed, clever recorder of the time divined something of the young Charles-Maurice's moral torment. Madame de Genlis, who was a guest at some of these festivities, had been attracted by the handsome lad's bearing. "He was already in his soutane," she narrates in her *Mémoires* "although he was only twelve or thirteen years old. He limped a little, he was pale and silent, I found his face agreeable and what struck me was his air of an observer." One can picture the clever boy holding up the silken robe, the tilted nose Isabey was to paint later, lifted, in amused or scornful derision, above the muslin cambrics of his *rabat*.

Neither self-mockery nor scorn could help Talleyrand. The cassock of the priest was to be his shirt of Nessus. It clung to him all his life. Through the manifold changes of his career, through his many sartorial transformations, the skirts of the black soutane, if objectively invisible, were ever present to the mind of the world.

VI

The struggle between Talleyrand's true instincts, between his love of freedom, his latent longing for the full development of the stirrings within of his intellectual powers, and the growing taste for the luxuries and sensuous enjoyments promised by following the vocation chosen for him—this struggle had begun. It was to culminate in a moral crisis, a few years later.

In this preparatory school of ecclesiastical luxury, nothing was left to chance. The boy's senses and his imagination were not only to be appealed to by the magnificence of the court life at Rheims—for court life it was;—his clever young mind was also to be infected by the contagion of suitable, of educative reading. The books placed before him were carefully chosen. The *Mémoires* of Cardinal de Retz were given into his hands. Another illustrious Cardinal—Ximénès by name, famous for his great activities —and Archbishop Hincmar's remarkable career—such were the recorded examples of supple, adroit, intriguing churchmen given to the youth who was to tread in the road that was to lead, perhaps, to Rome.

Had Talleyrand not already proved himself possessed of unusual mental powers, as well as strength of will, of purpose, why were all these methods employed to dull the nobler nature, to twist and bend it to his parents' cruel designs? Why must will and purpose be tortured to meet parental decisions? Chief among all other influences, in this year's residence at this ecclesiastical court, was the sceptical spirit of the age. Irreligion had become as much the fashion as had the modes of wearing of powdered locks and of lace ruffles.

Religious beliefs, any form of religious austerity, even in convents or monasteries, were so rare as to be a matter of gossip. Philosophical discussions, the airing of the most advanced ideas of the day, on every topic, from love to the history of religions—such heretical doctrines were subjects of universal conversational treatment by bishops, as well as by the laity. Irreligion had so spread its dissolving power, among the lower orders of the people, that a barber could exclaim, to prove how closely he followed the fashion of thinking as set by his patrons:—"I'm nothing but a *carobin*, but I have no more religion than others."

However lax the religious belief, the King still went to mass. The world of unbelievers, from Archbishops and courtiers to the common people, followed suit. With ecclesiastics, religious observances and ceremonies were obligatory. They must earn their incomes. Sceptics, atheists even, certain priests and bishops might be, but the pomp and ceremonial of church rites must be observed.

Form ruled the world. It was good form to have one's child baptized; one could only be married by a priest; one could not die, respectably, unless extreme unction was administered. Even Talleyrand, himself, though he had broken the solemn vows of his investment as Bishop, bowed to that last sacramental form of purification, before dying. He ultimately made his peace with the Church.

On all the great fête-days, cathedrals and churches were crammed to suffocation. About the Holy Sacrament cardinals, bishops, priests, the great State Orders, in their resplendent robes, clustered as close as though their spirits were fully in unison with their devout postures. All the Court would be on its knees, as the Host was lifted. Troops presented arms, and cannon thundered.

The length of the Mass, indeed, could be agreeably shortened. The book of the day, the licentious novel, or the more scandalous Memoir, could easily be hidden by a large muff, or by clasped hands. To be seen at Mass was proof enough of one's faith and obedience. What Talleyrand actually saw, of the loose living of the day, of the wide breach between belief and practice, was masked by such rigid observance of etiquette, of traditions, of refinements in correct bearing, that eyes must be keen indeed which could pierce beyond these social screens.

As a visitor noted one night, "on arriving at Hautefontaine, one was persuaded the Duc de Guéméné was the lover of Madame de Dillon" (the niece of Madame de Rothe). "After a six months' residence, one was convinced there was nothing in it." So corrupt, so wanton were the morals, at this latter end of Louis XV's reign, that unless society wore the corselet of such conventional rules the rotten carcass could no longer be held together.

In this ecclesiastical world Talleyrand lived, more or less, for a year; its influences were to be seen during his entire life. Since vows could be so lightly observed, why honor them at all? Since great riches could be obtained at the expense of the State, by posing as a priest, why not go direct to State funds, and take, by the really less offensive and hypocritical methods of speculation, what might be the basis of one's fortune? When one was in power, with capacities which could be usefully directed to helping weaker nations—such as Saxony, for example, against stronger ones, Talleyrand may have argued—what real difference was there between preferring, as gifts for such favors, shining gold instead of diamond-trimmed snuff-boxes? What difference, indeed, was there between such well-earned benefits, and the giving, through Court influence, of fat abbayes to Archbishops who ground down the poor to support their ecclesiastical state? From the point of view of pure justice, the balance was surely all in favor of Talleyrand's manner of conducting foreign affairs, as seen from Talleyrand's peculiar point of view. His year of life at Hautefontaine must therefore be considered for what it was meant to be. It was training. Rheims and Hautefontaine did their work, and thoroughly; their lessons of corruption and unbelief sank into the lad's receptive mind, and were to be lasting in their effects. Talleyrand's parents had planned wisely, according to their debased standards. Hautefontaine was a part of the system which was to break down opposition. It did more. For Rheims and Haute-

fontaine were to begin what the influences of the social
and political world of his day were to complete—the wreck-
age of the frail frame of Talleyrand's more purely moral
structure.

Youth is the time of life when we are most honest. I did
not then understand what it was to embrace one profession
with the intention of following another . . . to join the Church
in order to become Minister. It required too great a knowledge
of the society which I was entering, and of the times in which I
was living, to regard this as a matter of course.

In the above phrases Talleyrand gives, in a brief summary, Taine's theory of the determining influence of milieu
on character.

VII

After his year at Rheims, Talleyrand found himself
transferred to the Seminary of Saint-Sulpice. The latter was
the religious and educational college of future priests.

This decision to force Talleyrand into the priesthood
was as much in conformity with the customs and traditions
of that rigidly-ruled, yet amazingly lax world—in point of
morality—of the eighteenth century, as were its laws. No
career, to a cripple, save the priesthood, offered either a living or possibilities of advancement. Prizes were there,
ahead of one, to be had by passing through the door of a
Seminary. Wealth, power—who knew? the flaming scarlet
of the Cardinalate fluttered before the eyes of ambitious
parents. And to Talleyrand's parents, being among the worldly wise, every one of these "possibilities" became realities, as
it happened. For did not Napoleon proffer Talleyrand the
Hat—an offer refused by the then powerful statesman whose
eating anxiety it was, at that time, that the world should
forget that he had ever been a priest?

Madame de Talleyrand does not figure among the eighteenth century historic *dames galantes*. She had, however, a distinct vocation; she was an adept in those refinements of intrigue and finesse which ensured courtly favor. Since the King was the fountain-head of all gifts, it behooved indigent heads of families to be as close to the flowing of the beneficent stream as possible. The Comte de Talleyrand, the future statesman's father, held a position at Court: he was an attendant, a "Menin" as such noble servitors were called, of the Dauphin. [1] The Comtesse de Talleyrand, by right of birth and of marriage, had her own entrées. This privilege was as industriously worked as though the Court were as insensible as a gold mine, instead of being susceptible to a woman's charm. That Madame de Talleyrand possessed an exceptional element of charm, both in manners and speech, her son was to discover when finally he made her acquaintance—a semi-intimacy which did not occur until he had entered early manhood. The talent of knowing whom to sue, possessed by certain members of Talleyrand's family, resulted in an astonishing record of success. Almost every member of the family found himself endowed with some prize;—rich abbayes, episcopal preferment, some tidy nest in government employ, or an assignation of some great estate, fell to the share of the needy younger sons. The Court cornucopia, full of favors, poured its abundant stream of gifts into the lap of the necessitous family. Talleyrand owed much of the success of his future financial fortunes and questionable operations to this talent of knowing whom to interest.

[1] Comte d'Artois, brother of Louis XVI, when he introduced his "attendants" to his young wife, said, "ce sont mes gens."

CHAPTER III

I

TALLEYRAND having ended his course at College, the doors of the Seminary of Saint-Sulpice in Paris swung behind him. They closed on several things not as objectively visible as was a limping lad in a cassock. Talleyrand may be said to have lost his sincerity as well as the credulity and simplicity of his boyhood. Hautefontaine and Rheims had done their work. That world of dissolute courtiers, of irreligious bishops, of philosophical priests and of frail women had destroyed the boy's faith in men's honor and in women's virtue.

With what a sceptical smile must the youth Talleyrand have listened to the learned theological treatises voiced in a serious and devout manner, by the Sulpician professors! Their monastic example of penance and renouncement of worldly ambition—with what indifference must Talleyrand have viewed such appeals to a saintly life! His year of initiation at the episcopal court at Rheims had taught him, as he believed, in what mockery were held both religious belief as well as the practice of religion, by those vowed to their service. Abandoned, practically, by his parents; with no centre of affection outside of the walls of his prison to develop the more tender side of his nature, and with no future before him save the priesthood—a vocation he more and more hated—each year which Talleyrand spent at Saint-Sulpice but intensified his spirit of bitter resentment.

It is recorded that he remained for weeks, even for months, without conversing with his fellow students. He seemed absorbed in sad thoughts. Habits of reflection were thus insensibly developed, and powers of abstraction which, in his later career, were to be among the secrets of his success. He himself states:

I had no possible means by which to defend myself. I was alone; all those who surrounded me had been taught to talk the same language to me, and did not allow me to perceive any way by which to escape the plan my parents had made for me. My tired mind resigned itself. I allowed myself to be led to the Seminary of Saint-Sulpice.

To one of the few to whom Talleyrand confided some of the bitterness and despair which the prospect of his future destiny engendered—to Monsieur de Béthisy, future Bishop of Uzès—Talleyrand cried: "They intend to make me a priest; well! well! you will see that they will make of me a *sujet affreux*—a bad lot. But I am lame, a younger son" (which he was not), "there is no way of escaping my destiny." In his extreme old age, Talleyrand, when evoking these earlier memories, spoke with the same accent of bitter resentfulness. He never forgave nor forgot the wrong done him, by being thus forced to enter the priesthood.

The above promise which Talleyrand gave was strictly adhered to; its prophetic import was carried out, and in certain later actions with such scandalous disregard of what may be termed an elementary sense of honorable dealing as to furnish his detractors with proof of his being

indeed, a *suject affreux*. Talleyrand's moral deterioration
dated from his year's visit to Rheims and to the seven years
spent in the Seminary. What should have been a school
of virtue, a sanctifying process, became to Talleyrand's
rebellious spirit, a nursery of cynicism, revolt and unbelief.

II

The famous Seminary of Saint-Sulpice and its surroundings presented a very different aspect to the one familiar to
the world of to-day.

Renan's description of the Seminary is well known.
This institution of the XVIIIth century then covered the
whole extent of the great Place, where now we find only the
monumental fountain, the Seminary, and the Church. The
sombre pile, the dull, brown building known as the Seminary
of Saint-Sulpice is one of the dreariest structures in modern
Paris. Almost all the beauty of the original enclosures
disappeared with the Revolution. Chief among them,
and the most celebrated for its architectural perfection, was
the chapel built by Lebrun, considered to be a masterpiece.

In Talleyrand's day, in this less closely-built part of
Paris, the famous Seminary of Saint-Sulpice was a great
ecclesiastical convent and Seminary in one. The church we
now see, built by Servandoni, with its colonnade rising beyond the monumental fountain—the latter also designed by
an Italian, Visconti—was only one of the many religious
structures embellishing the great Square.

Renan's entrance into Saint-Sulpice was about seventy-
five years (1843) later than that of Talleyrand. Renan
states that "if one wished to see, in our day, that which best
recalls Port Royal, the old Sorbonne, and in general the
institutions of the old clergy in France, it is there one must

LA DUCHESSE DE DINO

go. . . . Everything is old in Saint-Sulpice save the surrounding walls and the furniture."

Custom and traditions change little in old countries. They survive revolutions.

The account Renan presents in his *Souvenirs d'Enfance et de Jeunesse* might well stand as representative of the life lived in the Seminary, in Talleyrand's day. In the study of theology Renan found that "Theology resembles a Gothic cathedral; it has grandeur, immense empty spaces, and the same lack of solidity." What "spaces" in which to promenade the sceptical indifferentism of budding genius!

Talleyrand, however, paid an eloquent tribute to the benefits resulting from the study of religion. In his memorable address in praise of the Comte Reinhard, delivered before the Academy of Moral and Political Science, in March, 1838, he states that in Monsieur Reinhard's choice of a professon—that of diplomacy—his former studies in theology had "happily prepared him . . . had given him that power and suppleness of reasoning which one finds in all that has come from his pen."

III

Talleyrand was to experience no more "cordiality," at first, among his Professors and their pupils than did his gifted successor in unbelief: "Conversations are elevated and dignified; but each knows little of the other, and the heart remains cold. . . . The directors have a certain breadth of view, they are good . . . their government is little felt," was Renan's record. Such Talleyrand found to be the general atmosphere of the famous Seminary.

Of the four virtues which Renan asserts were taught by the Sulpician professors—poverty, modesty, politeness, and

the rule of a good morality—Talleyrand can only be said
to have practised one. It was the easiest of all with which
to conform, since he possessed the heritage of fine manners.
There were other qualities and gifts which his priestly
training did develop. The "extreme civility"—that true
French civility of an older day—had been preserved as a
tradition at Saint-Sulpice. What may be termed additional
ornaments to Talleyrand's natural courtliness were a certain
grace of ease and a highly finished perfection of poise and
bearing due to the years spent at the Seminary.

Talleyrand's command of language, his oratorical talent,
the lucid and luminous treatment of difficult and tortuous
questions of statecraft, which were among his many and
recognized gifts, were so many proofs of his indebtedness to
his Saint-Sulpice professors. As an intellectual, Talleyrand
could not fail to respond to the methods taught by masters
in the art of mental training. In his subtle processes of
reasoning, as in his mastery of dialectic skill, Talleyrand
proved the value of such educational influences.

If Talleyrand, all his life long, rebelled against his having
been forced into the priesthood, he proved the breadth of
his understanding by his commendable lack of resentment
towards those who had been his instructors. There was no
bitterness in his attitude towards the Church. As long as
he lived he "multiplied his good offices towards Saint-
Sulpice," as Monsieur Lacombe so justly notes in his history of *Talleyrand the Man.*

He spoke of his professors and teachers at the Seminary
with admiration. He showed for certain among them,
when in trouble, a tender, protecting care during the Revolution. In later years Talleyrand "took a sort of pride in
proving his sympathy for Saint-Sulpice." There was an

element of grateful remembrance for the teaching therein received. This feeling was not unmixed with his recognition of the real merits of some of the self-sacrificing, noble men who were his teachers.

Talleyrand's tribute to the value of the training given at the Seminary gave a decided shock to the solemn members of the Institute—forty years later—when he stated that the study of theology was the very best schooling for the career of a diplomat! As Minister of Foreign Affairs, under Napoleon, he himself proved the truth of this assertion. Certain knotty questions, relating to the forms of worship, being under discussion when the Concordat was being framed, it was Talleyrand, and not the Roman negotiators, whose cleverness and dexterity solved the difficulties which confronted those engaged in the writing of this important document. Talleyrand, consciously or unconsciously, was influenced indeed, all his life long, by his priestly course. An out and out sceptic in matters of religious belief, Talleyrand never avowed himself an enemy of the Church. He adhered to catholicism, as a necessary organizing religious power. While he appeared to disregard religious dogma and religious observances, he proved his belief in the virtues of a faith he no longer practised. France was essentially a Catholic nation, a Catholic country. There was no safety for either King or ruler or government which did not take cognizance of the profound religious basis of the French people.

When at his Château de Valençay—where he was happiest, after the more fitful fever of life had spent its course—Talleyrand would gather about him churchmen of all grades. "I have seen Cardinals, Bishops, and simple

village curés in his house. . . . I have seen the Bishop of
Rennes spend months at Valençay, and Abbé Bourlier—
Bishop of Evreux—staying at the Hôtel Talleyrand, in
Paris"—thus wrote his niece, the Duchesse de Dino, to
l'Abbé Dupanloup (May 10th, 1839).

Talleyrand was never more gracious, more brilliant
than when in the company of churchmen. His care that no
word should be uttered in their presence which might give
offence, was well known. During their stay in his house,
the service and life were so arranged that these guests lived
"with the same liberty and holiness" as they would were
they within their own gates.

Talleyrand's quarrel was against his fate, in a word,
and not against the Church, as such. The abuses of the
Church's power—ah! that was another matter.

IV

During the long years of Talleyrand's education as
priest, like all men of genius, he was a voracious reader. The
fine library which Cardinal Fleury had left to Saint-Sulpice
was Talleyrand's chief distraction, as it was his intellectual
delight. His reading was on extraordinarily broad lines:
philosophy, history, geography, and the lives of the great
men of the past were his preferred subjects. Napoleon, in
his youth and young manhood, had shown a like passion for
reading. When poor and hungry, he was nourished by
any good book he could lay his hands on. He came to his
extraordinary state as the re-organizer of a France in ruins,
armed and equipped by the long hours spent in the study
of classical history, of Plutarch's Lives, of Montesquieu's
L'Esprit des Lois, and of the history and laws governing
France. Napoleon and Talleyrand served many years of

apprenticeship in thus more or less insensibly preparing for
their future great careers. Only men thus armed maintain
power.

Such books, and such uses of the stolen hours spent in the
chapel of the Sorbonne in which to brood, to reflect on life,
and on his coming vocation, are revealing. Talleyrand
was forging his future armor. He was accumulating a
store of intellectual ammunition. His craving for a wider
learning than could be had through a purely priestly training was to stimulate comparison, to provoke his powers
of assimilation, and to perfect his analytical finesse. His
seven years of confinement in the Seminary, with the annex
of its fine library, were the true nursery of Talleyrand's
genius.

Talleyrand confesses his taste for less sober and more
dangerously stimulating literature than philosophy. He
also developed a relish for the travels of pioneers and of
adventure in strange lands. This latter predilection, insensibly, may have influenced his journey, later, in 1794, to
America.

Talleyrand said to the Duchesse de Dino, in his later life:

I was so unhappy that I hardly spoke to anyone during my
first two years in the Seminary. I lived silently and alone,
spending the recreation hours in the Library, where I sought and
devoured the most revolutionary books I could find. I fed my
mind with histories of revolt, of seditions, and of revolutions in
every land. I was indignant against society. I could not understand why, because I had been afflicted with an infirmity from
childhood, I should be debarred from occupying my natural
position.

This state of revolt and his sense of isolation led to the
inevitable result: he fell in love. The record of this, his

first love affair, reads like a bit of gay romance lighting the dreary study of the tomes of ecclesiastical lore. In his *Mémoires* Talleyrand writes of this love episode with all the indulgence and delight common to elderly men who rehearse the pleasures of their youth.

He had found his inamorata at prayer, in the chapel of Saint-Sulpice. It was as suitable a place as any for a priest in training to be in—but his eyes should have been on his Prayer-book rather than searching for the charms of female attraction. The kneeling figure of the young girl is presented in pleasing phrases: assiduous in her devotions, she seemed oblivious of the unremitting devotion of another order—in the fixed gaze of the black-robed figure near by. Talleyrand found, apparently, much to admire in the piety of others, were such piety garbed in the added graces of beauty, simplicity, and modesty. His own attendance on the chapel services became the chief "office" of the day.

A happy chance brought about a meeting which was to end in intimacy. The idyll began under the chapel porch. The skies were kind. During the service, one afternoon, a rainfall had succeeded to the bright day. The young girl appeared to hesitate to expose her hat, with its ribbons and flowers, to the downpour. The gallant young novice promptly proffered his umbrella and his escort.

That their conversation might be prolonged, Mademoiselle Dorinville[1] begged of her rescuer to mount with her the steep, dark stairway leading to her tiny apartment, in the rue Férou.[2] Thus happily begun, the acquaintance rapidly

[1] The young girl's name was Dorothée Dorinville. She was known at the Théâtre Français as Lucy, or Lurzy. Later in life Talleyrand was to have other and more enduring associations with the name of Dorothée.

[2] The old Hôtel at rue Férou is still to be seen in excellent state of preservation, with its interesting sculptured façade, in its quiet court.

attained to the stage of closest companionship. Taciturn
Talleyrand could begin to exercise those seductive arts
which, in later years, were to make his conquests furnish
copious pages to his biographers.

In his first experience in the realm of love, Talleyrand
brought to his mistress the naïveté, the rushing tenderness,
and the passion of youth. There is, indeed, a somewhat
obscure story of a former brief adventure which had had no
further development. There is also a very scandalous one
narrated by certain historians, one which rests on no more
solid foundation than malicious gossip.

Between this young actress—for Mademoiselle Dorinville was playing subordinate parts in the theatre—and
this Charles-Maurice still in his teens, the intimacy was
the stronger because of its being built, not alone on mutual
attraction, but also on sympathy. Both confessed to the
wrong done them by fate and fortune. Mademoiselle
Lurzy or Lucy was forced by her parents and her poverty to
earn a precarious livelihood in playing second-rate parts at
the Théâtre Français. Talleyrand dilated on his own prescribed and hated fate—that of a future priest. Both
indeed were poor, but there were all the riches of the continent of love to explore.

Talleyrand's mistress was pretty. Her historians deny
her the dower of brains. "I never noticed that she was not
clever" (Je ne me suis jamais aperçu qu'elle manquât
d'esprit), Talleyrand confesses, somewhat naïvely, later
on. Talleyrand had wit to lend; he could afford to live
on the capital of his own cleverness.

> Tout son charme est dans la grâce;
> Jamais rien ne l'embarrasse;
> Elle est bonne et toujours rit.

Elle dit mainte sottise,
A parler jamais n'apprit.

Béranger, in his sonnet to "Jeannette," might have inscribed it to "Lucy" since he painted a picture of this young actress in more attractive colors than have the historians.

Whether Talleyrand's Superiors were cognizant of this liaison, carried on for a period of two years or more, is not stated. The Church at times closes its wise eyes, remembering the frailties of human nature. The cassock, in those days of easy morals, did not always clothe beings of spotless purity. The love-affair was known, although Talleyrand's visits to the near-by rue Férou were as secretive as possible.

A marked change in Talleyrand was noticed during this episode, by both his Professors and his companions. The desperate mood of revolt and his longing for silence and isolation—this phase had passed. His fellow-students found in him an unsuspected charm of manner. They delighted, as did his Superiors, in the brilliant conversational powers which were, later on, to conquer the world of his day and to embalm his fame in lasting attractiveness.

V

Some of the Professors with whom Talleyrand was most closely associated were firmly convinced of his complete unfitness for the priesthood. Their clear-sighted views were communicated to his family. Again the family influence prevailed. His uncle, the Coadjutor at Rheims, listened to no warnings. Talleyrand was to go on with his training.

Talleyrand left the Seminary of Saint-Sulpice with the reputation of possessing superior intellectual powers.

He was forced to spend some time at the Sorbonne, in order to obtain his degree. Sainte-Beuve, who never departs from his deprecatory critique of Talleyrand unless forced to do him reluctant justice, asserts that Talleyrand's thesis, which he called *Tentative*, was a remarkable production. Curiously enough, it was dedicated to the Virgin Mary.[1]

Talleyrand was barely twenty when he came to the decisive moment of his life. The face Prudhon[2] has painted must somewhat have changed to one of fuller maturity, of more accentuated features. Talleyrand had already met life at first-hand. He was now to feel the iron hand of fate forcing him to an unwilling surrender.

Ere he was ordained priest, it is more than certain that the soul of Talleyrand, as well as his conscience, was still capable of precipitating tragic revolt.

The evening before he was to take his priestly vows, his friend, Choiseul-Gouffier, found him in the greatest distress. Talleyrand confessed to the anguish of mind which was consuming him. He saw before him, with the luminous blaze of reality, all the morrow was to bring to him. Once the irrevocable vows were taken, he was forever to be set apart from the rest of mankind.

A priest! . . . As a priest, he could never possess true freedom. Mind and soul must wear fetters. More than ever, with mature development, Talleyrand realized how unfitted he was, by nature, and by his perhaps accepted

---

[1] When lying on his death-bed, in acute suffering, Talleyrand's young niece, Pauline, whom he called his "guardian angel," hung around his neck a medal of the Blessed Virgin, and after his death, two medals of the Immaculate Conception were found in his purse.

[2] See *Frontispiece*. This picture of Talleyrand painted when young is unsigned. It has been attributed to both Greuze and Prudhon.

and recognized spiritual poverty, for the vocation imposed on him.

Haunting his tortured mind there were the gnawing doubts, the demoniacal spectres of scepticism. How vow one's life to the practice and teaching of beliefs already, for him, half dead? Would the cloak of simulated piety always be at hand? Must deceit, must hypocrisy, be the real officiants of his priestly service?

Crushed, utterly overwhelmed with the poignant sense of the awful fate before him, never as yet as acutely visualized, Talleyrand gave way to a paroxysm of despair. His friend, Choiseul-Gouffier, found him in tears. Talleyrand's future life was to prove what the drying up of that source of emotion was to cost him, since he was capable of experiencing at this period, at least, not only the full bitterness of his fate, but a fierce rebellion against the forces he felt himself too weak to oppose. His will-power, which later was to develop into one of the dominant traits of his nature, had been temporarily sapped. Seven years' training in the Saint-Sulpice Seminary had not been conducive to the development of independence of character.

Other influences pressed about him, from all sides; the counsel of his parents and the hard school of his childhood, as well as the dissolving lessons which Rheims and Hautefontaine had taught, had their rebound. Force of resistance and the will *to be true, to be free*, had been bent and broken. Talleyrand's education now bore its fruits. He was to go on, consciously practising dissimulation. He lacked the virility of soul which could have saved him. True friend that he was, Choiseul-Gouffier besought the man in agony before him to "put the bitter chalice from his lips before it was too late." Arguments, and persuasive ones, followed. But to no avail. The replies were broken, but assured now, which he gave his friend—"he could not go against his mother's supplications," he said, her entreaties were more insistent than ever, he was weary of battling with the forces which were arrayed against him, all his world was rushing him to take the one and only step and, since no other career was open to him, his poverty being no crutch on which to lean, he must indeed tread the one path in which he could be helped by those in the seats of the strong.

On the morrow, on a dreary December day, the eighteenth of the month, Talleyrand took his final vows. He was ordained priest in the chapel of the Archbishopric, at Rheims (1779).

VI

Talleyrand's uncle—Alexandre-Angélique de Talleyrand-Périgord—had arranged for his nephew's ordination in the chapel of the Episcopal Palace. The former Coadjutor was now Archbishop, Duke of Rheims. This Prelate who, during the Restoration, was made Cardinal and Archbishop of Paris, in later years had a weight on his conscience. For if "Talleyrand was a priest, he could say to himself that it was his fault." It was he who had urged Talleyrand's coming to Rheims when he was a lad of twelve, that he might be properly impressed; it was he who had overcome the objections of his Professors at the Sorbonne, when they expressed grave doubts as to Talleyrand's fitness for the vocation chosen for him, against his own will and desire. At the critical moment of his ordination, when Monseigneur de Beaumont had purposely delayed Talleyrand's admission to the priesthood, more and more unconvinced of his religious inclinations, it was again his uncle, the Archbishop, who planned for Talleyrand's taking of the final vows. Later, his uncle was to make him Vicar-General as well as a Canon of his Cathedral.

When this elderly prelate, a sincere and devout Christian, was to see Talleyrand turning his back on his own order, during the Revolution; when the Archbishop was still further to be shocked and outraged by his nephew's attack upon the rights and property of the clergy; when the latter's future career, as a diplomat, as Minister, had placed the name of Talleyrand as one among the great statesmen of history, the soul of the elderly Archbishop of Paris was heavy within him. No earthly fame or glory could counterbalance Talleyrand's sins against the Church. As a mitred Bishop, he had outraged the Church by consecrating priests excommunicated by the Pope; still a Bishop, unreleased from his vows as an anointed Bishop—since release there was none, under the laws of the Holy Church—Talleyrand had married. Great as was his fame, yet as man, what crimes and what vices were not laid to his charge! The wise and gentle Professors of the Sorbonne had had keener insight into their clever, but sceptically-minded pupil, than had the Archbishop.

Heavy indeed was the weight of remorse that lay on the soul and conscience of Alexandre-Angélique de Talleyrand-Périgord, the later Cardinal and Archbishop of Paris. By his influence and persuasion he knew that he had been largely instrumental in the losing of Talleyrand's soul. That soul, at least, before it passed into eternity, he felt, must be saved.

The old Cardinal's prayers had been unremitting for Talleyrand's abjuration of his errors, during his own long life. On his deathbed he bequeathed to his successor—Monseigneur de Quélen—the burden he had carried for nearly half a century. Remorse had bitten, indeed, deeply into his soul.

While the Cardinal lay dying—1821—Talleyrand, himself old, weary, daily visited his uncle. What were the topics broached between the ex-Bishop of Autun—this unfrocked priest, the married, the once excommunicated churchman, the now world-famous statesman and diplomat, even then, in his old age, perhaps the most celebrated Frenchman of his day—what were the topics discussed between Talleyrand, Prince de Bénévent, and this aged ecclesiastic who was carrying the heavy weight of useless regret into the dark valley of death?

CHAPTER IV

I

IN a private Hotel in the Faubourg St.-Germain, there dwell some of the more distinguished descendants of the Talleyrand family. Two pictures in the dining-room of this interesting house rivet the gaze. They are hung on the tinted walls so that they face one another. One of the pictures is a portrait of Talleyrand as a young man of nineteen or twenty.[1] On the opposite wall hangs the famous portrait, full length, of Talleyrand, by Prudhon, as he appeared at the age of fifty-four, painted after the Treaty of Erfurt.[2]

The juxtaposition of these two canvases produces an extraordinary impression. It is a sensational one. Between the two presentments of this remarkable man, one can image, in the mind's mirror, all the currents and the influences which changed the gay youth into the grave, self-restrained and imposing *grand seigneur* of fifty-four. The broad stream of a great life rolls between the two. The face of Talleyrand, in his youth, is captivating in its expressive ardor; the pose of both face and figure show energy and a going forth to life with curiosity and zest, yet with a certain guarded eagerness.

[1] See *Frontispiece.*   [2] See illustration facing page 448.

50

This youthful portrait is perhaps the most revealing of all those which have come down to us. There is fascination in the picture of this youth of eighteen or twenty who looks out at one through the blue eyes—the grey-blues that are the sign of power. The brow is already the home of intellect; it is broad, high, and slightly rounded. The features are delicate, finely chiselled, and the general expression is one of finesse. The mouth betrays a certain formative process; the underlip is in-drawn, as though the years of solitude and loneliness already had forged the armor of self-restraint and self-repression. The pallor of the face is indicative of a precocious knowledge of life and of a premature expenditure of both physical and mental forces. This pallor is also confession of Talleyrand's physical limitations, for here are no robust, vigorous features flushed with the ruddy tints of the young men of his world who hunted, played *paume*, fenced, or who could indulge in healthful equestrian exercise. The face is the face of a youth who has lived already and too deeply and too young—of one who has lived through the passions and the intellect.

This was the face that was soon to be as well known in Parisian salons as it had been at Saint-Sulpice. Essentially Parisian at this period—this pallor of Talleyrand's was the complexion of many of the fast livers of the day. The successive changes in Talleyrand's physical equipment could have been noted, by a contemporary, for the succeeding sixty-four years of his life.

II

Priest though he was, Talleyrand was now free. Both Saint-Sulpice and the Sorbonne were a part of his past.

He had passed indeed, and forever, beyond the stage of compulsory educational obedience. He already felt within him the prescience of unused powers. He proposed to lose not a moment of his time. His intellectual resources and personal attractions must aid him in forging his way to high fortune. At this decisive turning in his life, he proved he was possessed of the true spirit of his caste. In other words, he understood the soul of his century. The dull life of a parish priest was one not to be thought of; there were no glittering rewards, no great prizes to be won in following the humble career of a true, sincere son of the Church.

There was another road opened wide before him. It was dazzling in its brightness; every one of its by-paths was alluring. It was the road that led to society, and later on, to the Court and, through its favors, to episcopal honors. In such worlds he could hope to forge his way. The prestige of his birth and name would surely lead to place and to riches. Since he must play the game, he would play for big stakes.

His romantic history was not unknown. The custom of placing younger sons, or those unfitted to take the headship of great families, in the priesthood, was too frequent a method of disposing of such for Talleyrand's fate to evoke either sustained pity or surprise.

His name alone would have secured his entrance into the higher ranks of society. The immediate successes attending the young Abbé's appearance at Court and at the more famous salons were due, however, to Talleyrand's personality. He was a marked man from the outset of his career. He carried with him the secrets of that charm which conquered Mirabeau, as it did Napoleon, and, as it did later, the Czar of all the Russias. Talleyrand's bearing was distinction itself. He even "limped with grace." Apart from these physical advantages, his manner was one to be envied. It had the ease and the gentleness which are the heritage of the finest breeding. No one could approach Talleyrand, once his character was formed, without realizing that one was in the presence of a great gentleman. This fact alone would explain his personal success with such an infinite variety of human beings. Such bearing and such a manner ensure instantaneous conquest.

Talleyrand did not trail his cassock along the polished floors of the salons of his day. "L'Abbé de Périgord," as he was called, dressed the part in the fashion of the hour. Greuze painted him in a blue coat, white waistcoat, and flesh-colored knee-breeches.[1] His neck was enveloped in a high and fine lawn cravate. It was in such gay apparel that the youthful Abbé made his entrance on the stage set for pleasure. Leaning on his cane, with his graceful limp, and his enigmatic smile, he was accepted from the outset as an interesting personality.

Talleyrand had a remarkable sense of the value of costume and of scenic effect. It has been said of him, that as Minister, he was never as imposing nor as impressive en deshabillé, in his dressing-room, as in full court-dress. Few great men are. Louis XIV alone seems to have remained Olympian, in appearance, even in his night-cap.

Talleyrand was to take, as part of his training for his future career, the lessons presented in the society of which he now became a distinguished member.

He made his entrance on this great scene at the plastic period of his youth. When he died, at the age of

[1] This portrait is to be seen in the Musée de St. Omer. It forms a part of the collection known as the Teil Collection. See illustration facing page 62.

eighty-four; when a new world had come into being; when manners and men, with the pruderies of Louis-Philippe and his exemplary but austere Queen, had brought in codes of morality and conventionality which were like a strait-jacket to the flighty, irresponsible spirit of French *joie-de-vivre*—with Talleyrand, in the year 1838, there passed away the last superb representative of the century which had bred fine manners, the art of conversation, and that peculiar quality of enjoyment which is born of lax morality.

III

In the Paris, and at the Palace of Versailles, on the day of Talleyrand's début, there were twenty-five thousand men and women who practised but one industry—that of amusing themselves. The whole stage of life was set with this sole object in view.

In a hundred years men can be trained to do almost anything. In a little less than sixty years, Louis XIV had taught the world how a King and his Court could turn life into a prolonged pageant—into a tourney of pleasure.

Louis XIV proved himself to be the greatest royal stage-manager the world has ever seen. He set the stage magnificently. There was Versailles—that superb archi-tectural pile, as long as a long street, to house his own splendor. There was Marly, with its air of intimacy, its fountains and statues set, as was Versailles, in the midst of forests and verdure, so that Nature was in conspiracy with the architects to give a sylvan setting to their master-pieces. There were Fontainebleau and Saint-Germain to which to journey, to hunt, to rest, if only to be freed, for awhile, from the sound of the chisels which, at Versailles, never ceased to scrape during that long fifty-four years' reign, after the death of Mazarin.

These palaces were palaces in every sense of the word. Goldsmiths, upholsterers, cabinet-makers, artists—every branch of industry and of art was pushed to the extreme of inventive originality and of artistic achievement to decorate and to embellish these royal domains.

It was not enough to have ceilings beautifully gilded and painted; not enough to have every canopy and chair a work of art—so great was their beauty that they were fit to be shown, as well as to serve as models, in the museums of our own generation; it was not sufficient for so fastidious a connoisseur as was this "Sun-King" to find each room, each salon, set like a scene of a stage where the cost of the setting was not considered, and where each and every object on consoles, on mantels, and on inlaid tables must be a genuine masterpiece—an incomparable bibelot from Sèvres or from Saxony—the King must link hands with Nature; he must have flowers—flowers wherever he looked—his delicate, voluptuous taste being prodigal of sentimental inspirations. Below the balconies of his mistress of the period, this lover of women planted jasmin and other odorous vines. He himself, in his beloved Versailles, preferred richly scented shrubs and flowers.

The scene was, indeed, splendidly set. Those who were to people the palaces, to decorate the great parks and forest glades, these privileged beings were soon in training. Louis XIV's courtiers, in the richness of their dress, in their display of jewels, of fine equipages and of semi-royal residences, in town and country, must live up to the scale of as expensive, and of as extensive, a *mise-en-scène*.

If the gondolas which floated in the canals of Marly

must be "red, green, white, blue or the¦ color of the dawn";
if their furnishings must be Genoese velvets, Bruges satins,
brocades from Lyons, and silk fringed with gold, what must
be the gowns, coats, hats, plumes and jewels of those seated
therein?

In order to present to our minds what the Terraces of
Versailles were like, in the eighteenth century, we must
picture to ourselves the spectacle made by the gilded coaches
and sedan chairs, by the brilliance of the gold or silver-
wrought brocaded skirts and coats; by the delicate laces of
jabots and wristlets; by the square-shaped diamond buckles
on the red-heeled shoes; by the exquisitely embroidered
vests; and by the great plumed felt hats, with their purple,
or pink, or grey, or scarlet feathers nodding and dancing
against the blue of the sky. The constellations of the stars
were not so brilliant as was this glittering mass of uniforms,
costumes, liveries, painted vehicles, plumes, jewels and
glistening silks and satins. The sun's rays, playing on
such scenes, made one think of an Oriental bazaar rifled
of its gorgeous stuffs and gems.

With all the splendor—what discomfort! Courtiers
cramped in two tiny rooms in the Versailles attics; the cold,
in winter, so great, that the water froze in the glasses set
for the royal table; and always, day in and day out, the
"mécanique" of the Court must be observed. There were
the King's *petit* or *grand lever;* there was Mass; waiting,
standing on one's feet, there were hours spent in the ante-
chamber; there was the hunt to be followed at just such an
hour, however early, or a walk on the Versailles Terrace of
hundreds of these doomed but servile nobles, to swell the
grandeur of a pomp-loving and exacting sovereign. There
was no real leisure, no happy-go-lucky pleasure for those

living under his despotic rule; the real business of life was centred in one passion—that of begging for preferment.

"Who is that nobleman?" asked the President, of Mesmer. "A pillar of the ante-chamber" was the answer.

What a life! And what soul-eating boredom! "I see a great many fêtes at the French Court, but no gaiety," writes honest Madame Palantine. Madame de Maintenon's cry is the more piercing: "Do you not see that I am dying of sadness, having attained to a fortune no one could possibly have imagined?" "If I could only make you see the ennui that devours the great, and the trouble they find in filling their day!"

There was one sole resource, one way of killing the universal malady of boredom. The gaming table was the opium of these courtiers. They played as the drunkard seeks his dram, courting oblivion, though to play meant ruin.

In fifty years, Louis XIV had taught the powerful French nobles a lesson which Louis XI, with all his craft, had not thought of. Louis XIV prepared the ultimate ruin of the French nobility, as a power, by setting them examples of extravagant expenditure and high play, and by pushing them to the extremes of luxury.

His successor, Louis XV, on his accession, had found the stage of his sovereignty superbly set. The Olympian figure which once had filled so grandly the scene, dwarfing all others, was gone. The rigid rule of the autocratic Maintenon was ended. The dullness, the dreariness of a reign which had lasted too long, of whose stiff etiquette all were tired, one where routine had taken the place of devoted service and indifference of admiring homage—this dull Court was remembered only to be criticized or ridiculed.

IV

After Louis XV, "Le Bien-Aimé," as his loving people had called him in the earlier years of his rule, had reigned nearly sixty years—from 1714 to 1774—we shall see, through Talleyrand's eyes and those of his contemporaries, what this spoiled darling of the gods and men had done with his inheritance. In Talleyrand's youth and young manhood, the King had sunk to the lowest point of his degrading and unashamed immoralities.

Louis XIV had built up the temple of royalty to house and adorn the glories of France. Through his liaison with the du Barry, with this "fille de rien," Louis XV had debased the prestige of royalty to the lowest level. He had parted even with all semblance of shame. His own people had the decency their King lacked; they shuddered with horror at the story of how the du Barry, excited by champagne, had broken the window of the Œil-de-Bœuf, at Versailles.

What a lesson for ambitious men was the one which the King taught his youthful subjects at Louveciennes! It was during this year—the last of the great days of Bourbon splendor—that he took much of his pleasure at the "boudoir-palace."

The extravagance of the favorite, her lavish expenditure in creating the model little palace of the day, was the talk of every coterie in Paris. It was criticized and satirized by every friend Talleyrand met in the salons he frequented.

This "boudoir-palace," of which not a wall remains to-day, built in the incredibly short period of three months, was at once a temple of art, a palace of enchantment, and a boudoir where the King might feel at ease.

One must go to the Memoirs of the day, and to the

MADAME DU BARRY

By Mme. Vigée-Lebrun

Goncourts' résumé of the magnificence of this wonderful dwelling, to gain an approximate idea of the wanton waste of treasure spent to embellish and adorn this miniature residence.

In the gallery of the Louvre you may see the vestibule, which was used as a dining-hall, reproduced by Moreau. The room was alive with color. The marble walls were intersected with Corinthian pilasters, whose capitals, bases and stems were gilded bronze. In one of the four tribunes, the courtesan's own band played, during dinner. The mirrors, framed in gold, reflected the living forms of the seated women, with their flat, wavy coiffures, the alabaster of their powdered necks, and the pink of their rouged cheeks. The courtiers beside them, with their brocaded coats, laces and jewels, made an harmonious blend with the delicate finery of the ladies' elaborate attire. Behind these living shapes, there were the four motionless, fixed forms of the women carved by Pajou, Lecomte and Moineau—startlingly real on their gold-garlanded marble pedestals.

All other objects, as well as the interior decorations, were equally splendid. At Louveciennes the service was of gold, and the porcelain the finest and most exquisite which Sèvres could produce.

Noiselessly, tirelessly, in and out of the gilded doors, passed the regiment of serving men. The lackeys wore liveries of blue or crimson velvet; their boots were of soft leather, white-topped, while their swords beat the measure of their steps, clinking at their sides.

Zamore, Madame du Barry's little negro, so often reproduced in the prints and pictures as train-bearer to his mistress, wandered from one guest to another. His bulky little frame was decked out in velvet and laces. With his woolly head enveloped in a large silk turban, the tall feathers would prick the bare arm or shoulder of a guest who had kept a dainty bit for the little horror—such attentions being a subtle flattery to the favorite.

Zamore, with his black and white "animal eyes," made the scene complete. For with him, as in an old-time tragedy, "enters Traitor." It was he who betrayed Madame du Barry to the "sans culottes," on her return from England, during the Terror.

As the centre of all these diverse elements, of these various human ornamental figures, on two of those seated at the long tables, eyes were constantly turned. The softened lights lent an added beauty to the still youthful, to the supremely lovely face seated beside the King. Louis XV, at sixty-four, had preserved his air of mingled dignity and grace. The face, with its worn features, showed signs of age, but the carriage of the head, the poise, and the bearing of the figure were instinct with that aspect of guarded aloofness which kingship develops.[1]

[1] The life-like bust in the lower gallery at Versailles reproduces this haughty distinction of the King, with astonishing fidelity.

CHAPTER V

I

"HE who did not live before 1789 has never known the sweetness of life," was Talleyrand's own oft-quoted tribute to the delights of living, in these last years of the eighteenth century.

Fêtes, love, the hunt, balls, taking part in comedies; passing from the boudoirs of Paris to the Châteaux where the round of gaiety swept its lively whirl—such was the life lived during the reign of Louis XV and in the earlier years of the reign of Louis XVI.

Voltaire's résumé of the real meaning of this eighteenth century life was paraphrased in the amusing summary :

That the gods established kings for the sole purpose of giving Fêtes every day—always presuming that they be diverting; that life is too short to make any other use of it; that lawsuits, intrigues, wars, quarrels between priests, which devour life, are absurd and horrible things, that man is only born for joy, and that the "superfluous" must take first rank, among the absolutely necessary things.

The society of the latter part of the eighteenth century practised this rule to the letter. The one occupation of life was to amuse one's self, and in devoting one's self to that pursuit, to amuse others was included in the amiable code.

The charm of the eighteenth century, in its unequalled and unsurpassable social attractions, through the Memoirs and letters of the period, has been transmitted to our day. As an ideal of certain phases of human intercourse it still maintains the magic of its example. This perfection was gained at the expense of the higher moralities. Duties, responsibilities—these were ignored. Pleasure was king. The system for a training in festive gaieties demanded the atrophy of natural affections involving sacrifice. Illicit relations—love in a word outside of marriage—must be the torch to light the festival of life. These "dancing souls" must be bound by no fetters.

This uninterrupted dissipation of forces demanded vigorous constitutions. "We shall kill the Dane. It is impossible to survive the life he lives here. Every day there are balls, opéra-comique, comedies in every royal house to which he goes," wrote blind Madame du Deffand. The "Dane" was the young King of Denmark.

The above might serve as a record of Talleyrand's life during the last year or two of the reign of Louis XV and of all the earlier period of Louis XVI's reign.

Wherever life was gayest, loosest, fastest, Talleyrand and his two chosen intimates, Comte Louis de Narbonne and his boyhood friend, Auguste de Choiseul-Gouffier, were to be seen. The pace was indeed killing; but for years it was never relaxed. So far from "killing" any one of the three, each one of these dissipators of life's forces lived to serve under Louis XVIII, Talleyrand's later robust physique carrying him far into the next century, his life only ending in the year 1838.

These three young men were to be met so constantly in

PORTRAIT OF TALLEYRAND

By Greuze.　Musée de Saint-Omer, Collection Teil

each other's company as to be called "the Inseparables."
They were all of the same great world of great families.
The bond of youth, of high spirits, and an unslaked desire
to drain the cup of pleasure to its last drop united them,
as it was to carry their friendship on to old age.
They were linked, also, by interests common to those who
were seeking place. They had favors to ask of those in
power. They counted on certain personal attractions, on
their assured standing among the highly born, on their heritage of a noble name, and, without avowing the gift, on their
talent for intrigue, to push them far on the broad highway
to success. Both de Narbonne and de Choiseul-Gouffier had
inherited a certain fortune, which they dissipated. Of the
three, their contemporaries would have prophesied the
swiftest run in the race to fortune's goal, to the fascinating
Comte Louis de Narbonne.

The Comtesse Blennerhassett, in her *Life of Madame de
Staël*, summarized her characterization of Narbonne as
being "brave, amiable, magnificent and dissolute." We
are to find him, later, a prominent figure in the next reign.
During the Revolution he is to be seen in the front rank.
Narbonne had had a singular history. One of the King's
daughters, one of those unmarried women whose quarrels
made their little courts during the lifetime of their father
Louis XV, and of their nephew Louis XVI, centres of intrigue
—the more attractive of the four, Madame Adelaïde, had
had a love affair. She had become enamored of her
chamberlain, Comte de Narbonne-Lara. The child born
of this violent passion, in 1755, in the duchy of Parma, then
governed by one of her married sisters, was the now young
and gifted officer and courtier, Comte Louis de Narbonne.
He had been brought up as his father's legitimate son.

Nattier represents the Princesse Adelaïde in his accustomed manner. His royal model is seated, her voluminous gown forming billows of silken waves below a diminutive waist, cramped in the triangular corsage of the period. The fine oval of the face shows the features delicate, but inexpressive. The hands are exquisite, as should be royal hands vowed to useless inactivity. The open scroll, below the uplifted finger, symbolizes the love of music, the sole distraction, save intrigue, gossip and tobacco, of the four sisters. Beaumarchais was to win his entrance to court favor and to find in such circles certain models for his revolutionary *Mariage de Figaro* through the Princesses' delight in music; for Beaumarchais was proficient in other arts than that of an ironic and humorous presentment of the follies and the spirit of his time.

Louis de Narbonne was a year younger than Talleyrand. Although they were constantly seeking each other's society, Talleyrand's perspicacity had pierced through the veil of Narbonne's charm and grace of manner. He knew him and understood him, but he felt in him a certain lack of depth, of weight; he was not to be trusted as was his boyhood friend, Choiseul-Gouffier.

Of the three young men, Narbonne's chance of winning high place seemed, indeed, the one most assured. Gossip relating to his birth, far from being considered an obstacle to winning fortune's favor, appeared to be his security for such advancement. His ease in obtaining entrance to the "little court" of his unrecognized but true mother— Madame Adelaïde—was the open door to all other privileges.

Choiseul-Gouffier was more than ever Talleyrand's friend. The latter, probably, came as near to loving him as he did any man. The self-contained, the commonly undemonstrative, Talleyrand wrote to him in the following enthusiastic vein, from one of the Châteaux where he was visiting: "How we miss you here—you—so noble, so high-spirited, so popular."

Talleyrand could surpass almost any writer in conveying delicacy of sentiment or in confessing real affection, when he chose. In his tribute to his friend, in his *Mémoires*, we find a note of sincerity which charms as well as surprises.

The character of Monsieur de Choiseul is noble, good, confiding, sincere. He possesses a loving nature, he is easy and also forgets easily. He is a very good husband and father [this was written after de Choiseul-Gouffier's marriage] although he is never with his wife nor with his children. He has friends, he is fond of them, but he is quite content not to see them. Affairs fill only a small part of his time; he has created for himself occupations which suffice him. His exquisite taste and his erudition, which he devotes to art, place him among the most useful and distinguished of Amateurs. . . .

Monsieur de Choiseul is the man whom I have most loved.[1]

The very spirit of the end of the eighteenth century breathes through every line of this clever characterization.

Talleyrand was to lose sight of his friend for some years. Yet, in renewing their intimacy, he found the man

[1] Choiseul-Gouffier was the French Ambassador to Turkey at the time Lord Elgin took the metopes of the Parthenon to England. The French Ambassador was a *fin connaisseur* in all matters relating to art. His classic work *Voyage Pittoresque en Grèce*, in two volumes, illustrated by Hilaire and Casas, is probably the most "sumptuous monument erected to Hellenic glory" (René Puaux). Monsieur Puaux, in his admirable article in *Le Temps*, Aug. 20th, 1926, states: "Choiseul-Gouffier was *persona grata* in Turkey, and could have obtained all the *Firmans* (concessions) he wished. But this *grand seigneur français* could not dream of tearing out the metopes of the Parthenon, or lame the exquisite portico of the Ereichteion or to separate a Caryatide from the admirable group of her sisters."

the same as the boy he had loved in their college days. The smile, one which Choiseul-Gouffier kept through life, was born of a frank, generous and easy-going nature—of everything, in a word, which Talleyrand was not.

Choiseul-Gouffier's later successes were to come to him less from courting favor than from finding honors proffered him. His semi-indifference, his known honesty, qualities which then seemed as lost as a lost art, won him both friends and consideration.

Among the cleverest of all the more sagacious courtiers of the day, who would have seen in Talleyrand, "this gay young abbé"—adroit, insinuating, and brilliantly endowed as he was—of whom it was said, a few years later, that he "dressed like a coxcomb, talked like a deist, and preached like an angel"—who would have seen in him the future great statesman, the man who was to seat a Bourbon on the throne, who was to prepare the fall of Napoleon at Erfurt, who was to make France victorious at Vienna, where the Powers had assembled to humiliate and despoil her, and who was to finish his great career as Ambassador at the English court at the age of eighty years?

II

Although Paris was the centre of an unceasing round of gaiety, the country residences of France, whose style and whose splendor Louis XIV had made the fashion—these furnished marvellous opportunities for carrying on the war against ennui.

There is not a residence where the birds of passage of the *beau monde* do not take their flight, to dance, to hunt, to talk, to take part in comedies. One can follow the passage of these brilliant birds, from one aviary to another; they remain a week, a month, three months, spreading their wings and their plumage.

This company of "birds" did not give all of their time to preening their fine feathers, to the twittering of gossip, or to purling forth love notes. Some of these great Châteaux were dangerous nests of intrigue.

Such a nest was Chanteloup. It was at this famous Château Talleyrand was to receive his first lessons in the art of conducting great affairs—among other lessons. He owed his frequent invitations to Chanteloup to his friend, Auguste de Choiseul-Gouffier—the latter being the ex-Minister's nephew.

No life of the time would be veracious, as a picture, without including an account of Chanteloup. The life lived there, and the causes influencing the influx of the hosts of visitors, are revealing. The Duc de Choiseul and his court at Chanteloup—for a minor court it was—were symptomatic. The dissolving elements preceding the Revolution are plainly discernible in this revolt of society against the reign of the du Barry.

The Château life of certain Princes of the Blood and of famous nobles was even more significant of the times than was the life in Parisian Salons. The most frequented roads in France were not those which led to Versailles; they were the travelled ones which took the Court and nobles from Marly, Fontainebleau and Versailles to Chanteloup. Like the Pied Piper of Hamelin, de Choiseul had carried his world away with him. He had virtually emptied the Court.

Horace Walpole wrote: "It is an entirely new spectacle for France to see a disgraced minister become the object of veneration and respect; it is as unusual to see a king become unpopular—which in this country is synonymous with having become *démodé*—out of fashion."

This was indeed the epoch of "triumphant exiles." Certain houses, such as the Prince de Condé's Château, under Louis XVI, during the duke's short exile, and Chanteloup— these residences were the real courts. No more startling proof of the decline of the Bourbon power, of the crumbling of authority, and of the scoffing indifference of the nobility could be given than the flight to such Châteaux.

III

The Duc de Choiseul, after his long reign, as Minister under Louis XV, had retired to Chanteloup, his beautiful country estate. His disgrace had been due to the hate of Maupeou. The du Barry, the reigning favorite, having been well trained by de Choiseul's political enemies, had tossed in the air those historic oranges, as she had cried: "Saute Praslin! Saute Choiseul!" The amusing little comedy effected its aim. The *lettre de cachet*—long delayed, since Louis XV was attached to the wittiest, cleverest and most brilliant Minister of his long reign—was finally signed.

Choiseul took his defeat with the calm and dignity of the *grand seigneur* he was, both by birth and nature.

The people of Paris, however, were of a different mind and temper. In the favorite Minister's disgrace, they saw but one clear truth; he had been treacherously sacrificed by the King, to the whim of the hated favorite.

The flame of indignation rose to dangerous heights. It spread with the swiftness of all popular movements. The streets surrounding the ex-Minister's hôtel, and the house itself, were besieged. High and low—princes, dukes, ladies of the most exclusive worlds were mingled with shop-keepers,

with *dames de la Halle*, and with that frothy scum of the
slums which rises to visibility on the occasion of turbulent
demonstrations.

Choiseul, in disgrace, was the symbol of the vicious
King's enslaved passion.   The Minister's public triumph
was the voice of the people, of their alarmed consternation.
It was also a precursor of that fury of maddened passion
which precipitated the Revolution.   The people's outburst
may be said to have been the prelude to the Revolution,
hence its interest from the historic point of view.

Choiseul, who appeared to have all France behind him,
its opinion, the press, the salons, even "Ferney"
(Voltaire's home in Switzerland), had indeed emptied the
Court; he now ruled France as never before.   He who, in the
days of his power, had made war, had signed treaties, and
had prepared the martyrdom of Marie-Antoinette by intriguing for her marriage to the loutish boy-heir, Louis:—
he whom Catherine II called "le Zébre de l'Europe,"—he
who had conducted the car of his destiny with "reins made
of the ribbons depending from a mistress's robe"—this
creation of a Pompadour now reigned in a world of his own.

IV

Those swinging coaches rolling out of Paris and Versailles, whose occupants filled the country Châteaux, were
the objective sign of the abandonment of the King.   Isolated
with his mistress in her boudoirs, Louis XV began what
Marie-Antoinette more innocently was to achieve through
favoritism and her love of pleasure—the contempt of the
people for the Bourbon rule.   It was rather the "outsiders"
who consciously or unconsciously were beginning the fateful
rule which was to end in the Terror.   Criticism, denunci-

ations of the King's weakness and blindness, of the intrigues going on under the King's very nose, of the terrifying state of the nation's finances—such criticism and denunciations were the fomenters of insurrectionary forces. Conversation, liberated from the tyranny of Court espionage, rose on wings of freedom to heights of audacity impossible in the stifling Versailles atmosphere.

The new philosophic ideas; Rousseau's startling theories of the necessity for a return to Nature; the publication of his *Contrat Social;* Voltaire's last book or play; Paine's *The Rights of Man;* the mounting cry of distress and revolt among the peasants; the catastrophic state of the finances of the king- dom, with the further plunge towards the abyss of ruin precipitated by the wasteful excesses of the du Barry—all such topics and subjects which are now the history we learn and read were the daily conversational bread of the cleverest talkers—save the Greeks—ever seen on our planet.

The Duc de Choiseul was himself the leading spirit, the animator of this brilliant, discursive talk. His violent, repeated attacks on the favorite—Madame du Barry—were a natural, but a most mistaken policy. She had been instrumental in causing his banishment. To hold her up to ridicule, to deplore her extravagances, above all, to point, with an eloquence all the more effective as it was largely inspired by revenge, to her influence on Louis XV, was but human.

The statesman, however, should have refrained from this lowering of the prestige of the tottering Bourbon rule. Every one of de Choiseul's invectives, each of his stinging attacks on the du Barry's history, character, and power, were carried on the wings of gossip to the whispering galleries of Versailles, and from the Palace to the streets.

ÉTIENNE-FRANÇOIS, DUC DE CHOISEUL (1719–1785)

Choiseul's animosity was one of the fagots that helped to light the revolutionary conflagration.

V

The portrait we see of the famous Minister hanging on the walls at Versailles does not carry with it that persuasion of conquering charm which the Memoirs and letters of the day record. In the forward, bending figure the artist has caught something of the abounding vitality which characterized his sitter. The face is the face of the changeful, easy-going, clever courtier and of the sensuous and sensual man of the century which loved a man rather for his defects than for his virtues. The artist has indeed rendered that *joie de vivre* with which de Choiseul was endowed.

One gift above all others the ex-Minister did possess— one above all others to be envied—he carried joy with him wherever he went.

One of the habitués of Chanteloup—Cleicken—caught the very spirit of this contagious quality. "Never have I known a man who knew as did he, how to irradiate his surroundings with joy and content. When he entered a salon he fumbled in his pocket from which he seemed to draw an inexhaustible abundance of gaiety!"

Gaiety!—ah—the magic word! Possessing the gift one has been given, at birth, the touchstone of success.

The Minister who lost to France Canada, Sénégal, Minorca, and a part of the Antilles, and who could sign the treaty which shut the door of Canada on France by lightly crying—"good—we go—and now it will be England's turn"—this man was then the idol of the hour, as he had been the delight of the King and the Court.

It is true de Choiseul acquired Corsica, which was "looking for a master." France also was looking for a master, in 1796. And a young man with a worn and sallow face and the ringletted hair of the Directoire "picked up with his sword the crown of France which he had found in the gutter" and placed it, later, on his own head. What might have been France's, or Napoleon's, fate, had caprice made de Choiseul disdain the acquisition of Corsica?

Such was the man and Minister who was to be a star of brightness to dazzle and to charm young Talleyrand. How resist such a combination of talents? Who would not have been swayed by the magic of the ex-Minister's presence?

VI

Chanteloup itself—the beauty of its forests and glades— the setting of the Château, with its palatial air of stately magnificence in its frame of verdure and great spaces— such a princely residence was proof of the wisdom of securing vast revenues through whatever channel the Pactolian stream may have flowed.

Everyone worth knowing knew the story of de Choiseul's great fortune. It was not a pretty story. But what a fortunate ending had the tale!

In de Choiseul's earlier days, he was known as the Marquis de Stainville. He had been the lover, and the lover "éperdument aimé," of the clever but not noticeably beautiful Duchesse de Gontaut. Married at sixteen to a man nearly sixty, Madame de Gontaut, during her liaison with de Stainville, was delivered of a son. This son was de Lauzun, afterwards to be known as the Duc de Biron.

This unexpected birth in the family was received with the greatest joy. The elderly Duc de Gontaut was too

grateful, at this unhoped-for gift of an heir, to make unpleasant personal reflections. The babe was received as a
tardy recognition by Providence of the necessity for continuing the distinguished name of Biron. The duke's
gratitude extended to the man who had made him legally
a father. Later on, de Stainville—Duc de Choiseul—was
to be his brother-in-law. Relations in this extraordinary
world were, to say the least, strangely, but not unaccount-
ably, mixed.

The mother of the gift-babe, though dying, had arranged
that her lover should not lose by her sacrificial end.

At nineteen, spent by her birth pangs, the Duchesse
summoned to her deathbed her young sister, Louise-
Honorine Crozat du Chatel. Louise was twelve years old.
The dying woman had been the greatest of Parisian
heiresses. To ensure her fortune going to her lover, the
Duchesse made her sister—virtually still a child—swear to
marry the Marquis de Stainville. The child solemnly gave
her promise. What a scene for such a painter of dramatic
situations as was Balzac!

The engagement was fulfilled to the letter. Louise-
Honorine married her sister's lover, at the age of fifteen.
She brought to her husband a life-long adoration and
120,000 livres' income. Of the consecrating passion vowed
him, de Choiseul made light; he could show to "the child I
married" respect, but the fortune she brought him was
literally worth its weight in gold to him, as compared to the
rare beauties of a mind and soul he alone failed to appreciate.
Choiseul, naturally, was *grand seigneur* not only in action.
He could throw to his wife the flowery phrase "her virtue,
her agreeableness, *her feeling for me* have communicated
a happiness to our union superior to the advantage of her

fortune." It was paying the greatest of debts with the common coin of words.

What potency has virtue? The lovely little Duchesse—clever, endowed with every grace of mind and nature—was treated with that indifference which immoral men feel for moral rectitude.

Such were the examples, at this the most influential of social centres, which were set before one of the keenest, most impressionable minds among the youth of the day. If the King's Court at Versailles was a "sink of iniquity," the glamour of the life at Chanteloup only served to heighten the value of successful achievement at the expense of the most elemental morality.

But who talked of such tiresome qualities as virtues or morality in those still gay days of the seventies and eighties of the eighteenth century? Pleasure was king. Rousseau's fatiguing theories might darken other days and skies. At Chanteloup the sky was the color it should be—azure blue—the color of love and gaiety.

Libertinism became almost obligatory in a society where fidelity in marriage was regarded as an unpardonable eccentricity. "Hide your love of your husband, my dear," was the counsel of a wise old prelate to a young wife who had not sufficiently disguised her affection for her spouse, during their stay at a certain Château. "All the vices are permitted here save that of married felicity," he had added.

How deeply resented were any infractions of the rule of the correct tone still lives in the biting apostrophe of the Duchesse de Guiche to her husband. "You are making a great fuss over a very little thing. Your father was much better company," was her scornful reply to her husband's angry reproaches; for the Duchesse's lover, Joseph Archambauld

de Talleyrand (Talleyrand's brother), having been surprised in her room by the duke—the flight of the adorer to
the balcony not having been sufficiently rapid—the outraged
husband had sought the questionable solace to his wounded
vanity by fighting a duel with his rival.

Parents and relatives even, in this singularly corrupt
world, were so impregnated with the prevailing spirit of the
age that Monsieur d'Argenson could say of a young, gifted
niece, as lovely as she was clever, "We hope she will give us
a great deal of sorrow."

The life Talleyrand led at this period was about to give
much "sorrow" to his parents. His excesses in gaming and
in loose ways of living were soon to make him notorious.

The oldest roué of the Court—the Duc de Richelieu—
could whisper in Louis XV's ears, always widely opened to
hear scandalous gossip—"That young Abbé, Sire, will go
far; he will surpass me." It was at the age of twenty that
"l'Abbé de Cour" was to earn this unenviable reputation.

VII

Earlier in life, at Rheims and at Hautefontaine, Talleyrand had seen the scenes set for costly entertainment, by
the princes of the Church.

At Chanteloup there was another, an even livelier life
led by the innumerable guests who came to—and less
readily left—the hospitable Château. Some of the guests
spent weeks—others made visits of a year or more. In those
days servants had not learned that they, and not their
patrons, were masters. Hospitality, and one practised on
as great a scale as was possible in the seventeenth and
eighteenth centuries, rested on a base of servantalia whose

foundations were slowly undermined by the principles preached, during the Revolution, of *The Rights of Man*.

All that was most noted, brilliant, learnèd and gayest in the salons of Paris and Versailles must be seen and heard at Chanteloup.

Among frequent visitors at the Château were l'Abbé de Périgord, the Duc de Lauzun, his lovely but neglected Duchesse, the irresistible Chevalier de Boufflers, the Abbé Delille, Madame du Deffand, the Duc's domineering but clever sister—the Duchesse de Grammont—and how many others! What an audience to hold and to charm!

The winter evenings in the salons, before the great logs burning in the deep chimneys—what incentives to prolonged conversations such a background offered! Fresh from the day's hunt in the forests of the Château, the men surrounding their hosts had the quickened wits of those who had lived all day in the open.

At the gaming tables, or in the cushioned fauteuils, one would see a circle surrounding the Maréchale de Luxembourg, each listener waiting to catch a witticism one might carry back to Paris; or there would be the pallid face of blind Madame du Deffand in her lace cap, her expressive hands in air, seated in a deep "tonneau"—that barrel of a chair into which Horace Walpole's long, lean face was to protrude to hear this noted wit expend her cynical charm. [1]

For so distinguished a guest as was this international celebrity, every precaution had been taken by her hosts; none of her habits must be changed. In the salons, as in

[1] When Napoleon was starting for his campaign in Russia he ordered the proof sheets of the famous correspondence of Madame du Deffand and Horace Walpole to be put into his carriage. "Je m'ennuie en route; je lirai ces volumes et j'écrirai de Mayence ce qu'il y aura a faire." Some suppressions it was thought by his critics should be made. *Books of Character*, Chatto & Windos, London.

her bedchamber, she was to find those famous *tonneaux* which kept her free from draughts. Writing to Voltaire, Madame du Deffand paid, and handsomely, her debt of gratitude for these considerate attentions. "I can say with truth that this visit was the most agreeable time of my life."

Watching all those distinguished guests, listening to the sparkling conversations, adding his own witticisms, one would have seen Talleyrand's clever, youthful face, his wary glance taking in the gay scene, as his recording mind and grand manner were to reflect to later generations, the vanished charm of this century of joy and license.

Among the many other visitors there was Walpole's niece "who must see Chanteloup." There was Madame de Mirepoix, who had besmirched the family escutcheon by "presenting" the *fille de joie*—the du Barry—at court, in order to pay her own gambling debts.

There was witty, malicious Madame de Coigny (formerly Duchesse de Fleury), Lauzun's love at one time—who sang, who never seemed to cease from singing. It is to be hoped that Lauzun, who was caught in the chains of her enchantment, was a good listener. But where stop? All Paris, all Versailles, at one time or another, during the years of de Choiseul's exile, passed through the salons of Chanteloup, or abode within its hospitable walls.

With as great a multitude of guests in the great house, the perpetual resident of the Château—the little hostess's most devoted friend and admirer, l'Abbé Barthélémy—confesses he had lost his head.[1] "Ah—Mon Dieu! What a lot of people, what cries, what a noise, what piercing laughter, what a smashing of doors, what rascally tricks,

[1] The Abbé Barthélémy was the author of *Le Voyage du jeune Anacharsis.*

what voices, arms and feet in the air, what screams of laughter at billiards, in the salons, in the music room where the spinet is!"

The Duchesse de Fleury must have been among those who contributed to this "noise." She had a volubility of ideas and words, such a heat in conversation that, as Walpole said to her, "I fear you will ignite us all, and one day that we shall all be consumed in your flames." And he added, with his caustic dryness, "But what does one do with that at home?"

It was in such a school that the youthful Talleyrand was to receive his perfected social training. Already an adept in making his cleverness and his wit serve him, both wit and brilliancy were here to acquire an added finish. He already cultivated, young as he was, the art of telling silences. Talleyrand's silences were indeed pregnant with meaning. He could condemn an action, refute an argument, and damn a reputation by the lifting of an eyebrow, or by a glance which was at once impertinent or aggressive, yet one which could be eminently discreet. Added to these facial attractions, he possessed a sang-froid, a power of self-control which dismayed the timid and impressed his superiors. He had, in a word, a discretion beyond his years.

He was careful to carry his intellectual advantages with a negligent air; he was even more careful to restrain his wit to light thrusts. In this over-civilized, extravagantly critical society, to be extreme in anything was esteemed a crime; all must be smooth and gracious.

Talleyrand's debt to his host—the Duc de Choiseul—was not confined to the hospitality he received at Chanteloup. One among the many lessons which the duke inculcated, was never forgotten by the future Minister of Foreign Affairs:

In my department [Choiseul used to say to the young people], I always made others work more than I did myself. It is no use burying yourself under a mass of papers; you must be able to lay your hands on subordinates who can get at the pith of them, and then you will have time enough and to spare. For a statesman, a nod, a gesture, a change of punctuation, should be sufficient. His proper place is in the world; in his office he learns nothing.

This teaching was not lost on Talleyrand. He was to practise this economy of force and energy in every office he subsequently held—a manner of conducting great affairs little understood by lesser men who ridiculed such methods.

In the famous *Toilette de Monsieur de Talleyrand*[1] which has made the tour of the world, the malicious author, Comte Molé, thus stigmatizes the great statesman's own manner of "conducting public affairs":

As his valet was presenting his master with the second sleeve (of his vest)—the one which was the most difficult to adjust, since Talleyrand, between pushing his arm through the first and second sleeve invariably began to walk about, to gesticulate, to narrate or to treat of some affair—such moments were the busiest and the most laborious of his day.

His detractor goes on to state:

. . . At the Council of Ministers and at diplomatic Conferences, he listened, wiped his face, and said nothing. As for the time he spent at the Ministry! he passed it in signing "papers," indulging at the same time in making fun of d'Hauterive or of some other of his employees whom he used as the butts of his

[1] *Le Comte Molé—Sa Vie, ses Mémoires.* Edited by Le Marquis de Noailles. Vol. 3. Librairie Ancienne Edouard Champion, Paris, 1923.

raillery . . . In affairs, he can be serious, but never grave. Without confidence in his fortune (luck) or in his own power, incapable of prolonged meditation or of interior work, *he has none of the qualities of a statesman.*

Such flippant criticism and the malice which animates the author need no comment.

Monsieur de Bacourt, who was Talleyrand's secretary while the Prince was Ambassador in London, recounts

that M. Talleyrand rarely wrote a whole despatch: his portfolio was filled with a great variety of little memoranda and phrases. When the question which corresponded with these notes presented itself, such memoranda were confided to a secretary, and M. de Talleyrand gave a general idea of the way the document should be treated, and told him how and where the phrases he added should be introduced. The despatch was reviewed by M. de Talleyrand who gave it a final rendering which went to prove that it came direct from the Ambassador and not from his secretaries. M. de Talleyrand faithfully observed this rule—"that a superior should never do anything which a subaltern could do for him,"—a rule given him when at Chanteloup, by the Duc de Choiseul.[1]

[1] Sir Henry Lytton Bulwer's *Essay on Talleyrand*, p. 338. See Bulwer for "Mission in England."

CHAPTER VI

I

WHILE waiting for Fortune to throw him a lucky number, Talleyrand, in his "breakfasts" at Bellechasse, was courting, and was being courted by some of the leading minds of the day. As Talleyrand's successes in the great world became more and more assured, the wits and the more brilliant men of his time sought his company.

In a modest house which he had taken in the rue de Bellechasse, in Passy, it became the habit and the fashion for certain of his friends to meet, for the usual morning cup of chocolate. Those quiet rooms, whose furnishings betrayed the intellectual tastes of the occupant, with the many books scattered about, became a noted social resort, soon to be known as a veritable centre of gaiety, of wit, and of animated conversation. The fare at these breakfasts was, at once, of the most restricted and yet of the richest order. A cup of chocolate—and the brightest wits in Paris—what could one want more? Such nourishment offered late in the morning, was of sufficiently magnetic attraction to entice thither both the youth and the best brains of Paris—that city of brains.

One might have been up all night; one might have been

making the tour of half a dozen salons; one might have lost
or won at cards; or one might have quarrelled with one's
mistress, or have been in the first radiant morn of forming
a new passionate attachment—always the best of all moments, it is said, in a liaison—yet that early morning walk
to Bellechasse drew one as a loadstone attracts the magnet.

The cool of the fresh day renewed one's spent forces.
The unfrequented streets of Passy were like a quiet hand
pressed on one's languid pulses. The host awaiting his
guests—l'Abbé de Périgord—was the most fascinating, the
wittiest, and the most inscrutable of *charmeurs*. His wit
would be the grindstone which would put a new edge on one's
dulled mentality; his cynicism would bite like an acid into
one's frayed energies; his cleverness and communicative
gaiety would be the spark to set ablaze the minds of the
noted men gathered about him. Above all other attractions
was the certainty of hearing discussed the very latest
novelty in ideas. The opinions of the day were tossed
about as balls are flung and caught.

II

The men gathered there, most of whom were "rich in
youth, in imagination, and in ideas"—this group, over their
cups of chocolate, discussed, indeed, every topic, repeated
every bit of scandal, invented new epigrams, read their
madrigals, and elaborated schemes of government in that
easy conversational tone which was the *bon ton* of the age.

My room, where they met every morning [Talleyrand writes
with a certain lingering pleasure in his *Mémoires*], and where they
found any kind of breakfast, presented a singular contrast. We
talked of everything with the greatest liberty. Subjects were
treated with the wit and in the fashion of the day. In these talks

there was both pleasure and instruction, and, in truth, ambition also, in perspective. Those were excellent mornings whose pleasures I could even now enjoy. One wished to know everything, to pass judgment on everything.

Thus wrote Talleyrand, at eighty years of age.

Louis de Choiseul, Duc de Lauzun, Panchaud, Borthès, l'Abbé Delille, Mirabeau, Champford, Laureguais, Dupont de Nemours, Rulthière, de Choiseul-Gouffier, Louis de Narbonne—all these men, many of them to become famous as time went on, met together constantly and always with pleasure. La Fayette (intimacy with Talleyrand came a little later), Mirabeau, Mathieu de Montmorency, Narbonne, and Talleyrand alone would have made any reign illustrious. Superior to all of these in point of personal charm, of brilliant conversational talents, and of that caustic wit so greatly appreciated in the pre-revolutionary days, in that eighteenth century society, were de Narbonne and Talleyrand.

We are to see these two young noblemen and their friends, none of them as yet playing a prominent rôle on the historic stage, appear and reappear in all the scenes which were to determine the future destinies of France.

III

With such a group of brilliant minds and thinkers assembled in Talleyrand's rooms, conversation ranged indeed over a wide field of thought.

The arts, letters, and the more purely intellectual tendencies of the age were by no means neglected. What a wealth of subjects, indeed, was offered to the younger, to the more impressionable minds of this group. There were the rise and decline of Voltaire's tragedies, and the amusing envy of the latter towards every writer whose talent showed promise of success—towards Marivaux, Nivelle de la Chaussée, Sabatier and de Belloy.

Voltaire's genius was already leading the mind of his day. "He gave to the human mind a great impetus." Even then, around that gossiping breakfast table in Passy, every one of these young men may unconsciously have realized how Voltaire's dauntless courage, power, and audacity were preparing the way for intellectual and political freedom. There were some among the group of Talleyrand's friends who remembered that Ninon de Lenclos, having "divined" Voltaire, though she knew him only as a boy, had left him money in her will.

Voltaire himself was to "divine" Talleyrand. When he was old in years, but as young in mind and as quick in discernment as at thirty, Voltaire had laid his hands on Talleyrand (then twenty-four) blessing him; Voltaire "blessing" Talleyrand would have formed a fitting subject for Hogarth's ironic presentment.[1]

Galland's translation of *Les Mille et une Nuits* (1704)— *The Arabian Nights' Entertainments*, the Oriental novelty— was among the oft-quoted books, one preserving its eternal freshness.

The new modes of thought, the revolutionary ideas introduced by such thinkers as Rousseau, by Voltaire in his later works, by Diderot, d'Alembert, Marmontel and Condorcet, were as so many torches to light and to inflame the excitable minds of those seated about the Bellechasse breakfast table.

[1] Michaud, who recounts this scene, years later, gives neither date nor place. L. G. Michaud, *Histoire politique et privée de C. Maurice Talleyrand*, 1853.

In Talleyrand's day, the fermentation of the new ideas accelerated the driving power of thought. The minds of the younger men, who were to play conspicuous rôles in the coming tragic days of Louis XVI's reign and of the Revolution, were being influenced for life, by the new ideas and ideals which were to usher in the new age.

The intellectual effervescence excited by the *Contrat Social;* by the new doctrines of freedom, of conscience, and by the theory of Paine's *The Rights of Man* were a heady intoxicant. The effect of the new theories—modern for those days—on education; the mental excitement induced by Rousseau's theories; the revelation of the joys to be experienced in natural emotions and in the beauties of nature as presented in *Émile* and in *La Nouvelle Héloïse,* can only be imagined, perhaps even thoroughly understood, by those of us born in the mid—or latter—end of the nineteenth century. Such works as Strauss's *Life of Jesus;* Renan's *Vie de Jésus* and his subsequent volumes on the Apostles, then startled the world by their boldness and historical criticism. The uprooting presentment of life and its development by Wallace, Bain, and particularly by Darwin's *Origin of Species,* the theory of evolution, and the epoch-making works of Herbert Spencer and of Tyndal's and Huxley's scientific discoveries, were each and all as wonder-working revolutions in the nineteenth century as were the daring ideas and the theories of Voltaire, Rousseau, Paine, and the Encyclopædists, in Talleyrand's time.

IV

From the political and national point of view, what a tragic situation France presented to these gifted men who loved her!

Of all the topics that most stirred these friends, the condition of France, the intellectual as well as the political and international status of the country were paramount subjects of absorbing interest.

The new ideas, at first floating about as more or less vague theories, were assuming formidable shapes, with their more definite and precise tendencies. The serious danger they presented to the existing State, as well as to the privileges of the nobility and to the power of the clergy, were being more and more apprehended, dreaded, fought and denounced by those most interested. Such ideas were also exploited, encouraged, and applauded by the ardent believers in the new doctrines.

It was well enough to allow philosophers, thinkers, and men of letters—it was maintained by conservative men—to entertain their leisure with dynamic political theories. The dream of individual liberty, the interesting topics of the rights of man, of political liberty, and the dangerous speculations recorded in Rousseau's *Contrat Social* were themes suitable to the intellectual diversion of clever men.

The advocates of the new ideas were reminded that there were, unfortunately, other ears opened to receive the doctrines. There were those who had appetites more eager to learn of relief from real suffering than were the well-born, who, being comfortably housed and well-fed, could afford to toss revolutionary theories about as lightly as the du Barry had tossed her oranges. Hunger brings a keen edge to whet intelligence. The people in France, as every one knew, were already experiencing the pangs of semi-starvation. The ministers who succeeded de Choiseul saw ruin ahead.

France, from having been the most dreaded, the most envied of all nations, was now, in these later years of Louis

XV's reign, experiencing the scorn of Europe. The rise of
Prussia and Russia, as first-class powers, and the alliance of
Austria with these two nations, was the first death-knell to
France's prestige. The partition of Poland by the three
powers was a felonious proceeding, one executed with
extraordinary duplicity. Austria had played the rôle of
traitor to France since Marie-Thérèse, the Empress of
Austria, had willingly aided and abetted Prussia and Russia
in ignoring the interests of France.

The war, later, between Russia and Turkey destroyed France's commerce in the Levant. The consequences, resulting from these disasters, had been the loss of
France's political, as well as her military, status in Europe.
These great changes were seen to be only a part of the causes
of the visible crumbling of France, as a foremost power.
The map of Europe had been re-made, with France now
practically ignored. She had become a negligible quantity.

This shifting of imperial power soon brought about
alarming consequences.

The loss of trade in the Orient had crippled revenues.
Where was any Minister of Finance to find sums to supply
the royal demands on the Exchequer? The continued lavish
expenditure of the King; the enormous sums spent by the
Pompadour, and now by the du Barry, on their establish-
ments; the maintaining of the several Courts of the Dauphin,
of the Princesses, and of the Princes of the blood had long
since drained the state funds. There were also all the
royal residences to be kept up.

When Terray, in 1770, became Controller General, the
faults and failings of previous bad financial administrations
proved a further burden to him. His ministry had inherited
a debt of sixty-three millions for the year 1770, one hundred

and ten millions for the year before, and one hundred and
fifty-three millions in 1769 which had been "anticipated."
The King had left Terray free, with his usual indifference,
to bring to the situation the resources of his talent. But
what could talent do against such a sea of debt?

V

The Jesuits, the clergy, and the group of the political
leaders—d'Aiguillon, the Duc de Richelieu and their followers—were in possession of power. History tells us what disasters their policy and the rule of "Esther" (Madame du
Barry) and the Jesuits brought to France and the next reign.

On as observant a mind as Talleyrand's, the plots and
plannings of the Jesuit party must have made a profound
impression. Versed as he was in ecclesiastical lore, con-
versant as he was in the habits of thought and in the dis-
ciplinary processes of Jesuitical educational training, Talleyrand's own future methods—in certain later State transactions which have won him an unenviable reputation—
must be directly traced, I think, to the examples set before
his young eyes at twenty, at the Court at Versailles.

We catch one glimpse of how preferments were carried
on at Court, in the oft-quoted witty réplique of Talleyrand's
in the salon of Madame du Barry, one evoked by his
consuming desire for advancement.

Talleyrand, it appears, had been assiduously courting the
du Barry, during the last year of her reign as favorite. He
found himself in excellent company, since among those
suing for court influence were the Empress of Austria,
Marie-Thérèse, her most trusted Minister—Mercy—the
Archbishop of Paris, the Jesuits and their leaders, the Duc
de Richelieu, and the Comte d'Aiguillon.

COMTESSE DU BARRY

La Tour

When Talleyrand's hour came, for the coveted admission to Madame du Barry's salon, at Versailles, he had found it crowded with a number of young noblemen.   The beautiful room resounded with laughter.   The merriment of these young gallants was the less restrained since, to their most audacious sallies, Madame du Barry responded with anecdotes which pushed the conversation to the limit of indecency.

The topic which was found most fruitful of excited debate was the slight resistance offered by the women of the day to amorous proposals.   One disconsolate *roué* had summarized the ease with which conquests were made in the *mot* which became historic—"that nowadays no man could plume himself on having had luck."

In spite of the animated discussions which filled the air with the clash of mingled derision and laughter, one voice, Madame du Barry noticed, was silent.

L'Abbé de Cour, as Talleyrand was called at that time, was seen moving about on his insufficient feet, going from one picture to another, from one table covered with costly trifles to the next.   He seemed engrossed in thought; and the character of his rumination did not seem to tend to his enlivenment.

On being asked by his hostess the reason of his moody pre-occupation, Talleyrand replied, in a caustic tone, that "it seemed easier to have all the women one wished than to possess a single good abbaye."[1]

The next morning, the story proceeds to narrate, as the King assisted at Madame du Barry's toilette—one of the peculiar customs of those more intimate days—the favorite, in her effort to amuse the "unamusable King," remembered

[1] *Talleyrand et la Société Française.*   Loliée, p. 27.   Emile Paul, 1910.

the *Abbé de Cour's* clever epigram. The King laughed. Talleyrand, according to Loliée, would have won his "good abbaye" direct from the hands of royalty, had not a more despotic sovereign than a Bourbon king claimed Louis, "le Bien-aimé,"—for within the year Louis XV had ceased to live.

The gift of "a good abbaye" by the new King—Louis XVI—was due to his Majesty's desire to fulfil the purpose of his predecessor.

CHAPTER VII

I

AS though to give to the world of Talleyrand's youth the final lesson of the vanity of all things human, a malicious Fate grouped about Louis XV's deathbed the very passions which had made his reign a byword and a mockery. Hypocrisy, lust, and vice hovered about the chamber as evil shapes haunt delirium.

The rumor of the King's illness at Trianon reached Paris on the night of Wednesday, April 29th, 1774. The city, as a city, listened languidly. Louis le Bien-Aimé having become Louis the Hated, his people had but one prayer—that this might be the last of the illnesses of a king who had brought France to the verge of ruin.

King Louis XV, about to mount his horse to follow the hunt, had suddenly felt an attack of weakness. Abandoning the idea of riding to the hounds, he courageously followed the hunt, in a coach. He even supped at Trianon, as usual. At first, the doctors were persuaded the indisposition was but a slight attack of erysipelas. Grave symptoms shortly announced the real nature of the malady. The King had an aggravated case of small-pox.

Ill as was Louis XV, the first surgeon of the King—La Martinière—forced the sick man to rise and to go to Versailles. "It is at Versailles the kings are ill," he cried. The King, tottering, too weak to stand, was carried to his coach.[1]

At the Palace, during the thirteen days of the progress of the disease, some of the most extraordinary situations it is possible to conceive were enacted.

The King's daughters, who had never seemed to be penetrated by feelings of especial tenderness for their father, were suddenly possessed by a fury of self-sacrificing devotion. No one but they must minister to the dying monarch. Though their lives must pay the penalty—since the Bourbons had stood out against inoculation—none others—save one—were admitted to the chamber that had the odor of a charnel house. Madame du Barry proved as great a devotion. When Mesdames left the infected rooms, at night, the one human being who could stir the King's feverish pulse to heightened beat, crept in to take their place. She sat out the night beside the all-but-unrecognizable "France," as, in her gayer, more abandoned, moments Madame du Barry had disrespectfully called her lover.

Little by little, the scenes which succeeded each other in that chamber of infection became the common talk of every street corner, of every salon in Paris, and of all France. There were fourteen medical men, every one of whom had the right to examine the King. There were six doctors, five surgeons, and three apothecaries. The King showed his tongue to each of the fourteen at any hour of the day. His pulse must also be felt by each one of his medical attendants.

When the gravity of the disease became known to him, Louis was restored, for a moment, to the consciousness of what, as King, he knew was before him. He told his mistress

---

[1] Another version is that it was the Abbé of Versailles who insisted on the King's going to Versailles—"It is there, Sire, that kings die," he said.

she must leave the Court "so as not to repeat the scandal of Metz,"[1] for the King realized he must receive the sacraments and that he must make his confession—he who had not been to confession for thirty-eight years. He must also order the ceremony of Le Viatique. The dying monarch, therefore, must put away the dear object of his passion. To receive absolution he must make the greatest of sacrifices. He could not face God until he had given heroic proof of his repentance.

The very next morning, in giving "the order," he requested that Madame du Barry should be sent for, again. "She is gone, sire," replied la Bourde, his valet. "Where?" "To Rueil." "Ah, she is gone already!—the end, then, must be near."

II

Around the royal bed conflicting ambitions, desires, fears and pseudo-pietistic fervor now battled.

With the expulsion of the favorite, the clergy, the Archbishop of Paris at their head, felt their own great hour had come. The King had proved himself "Le Roi très Chrétien." His last hours, therefore, belonged to the Church.

With the departure and fall of the du Barry, the Ministry, however, knew its own death-knell was sounded. It summoned all its forces to avert the dread hour. To the last, d'Aiguillon fought for his place. Even after the Ministers had been dismissed, he felt all was not lost. He invited a large concourse of guests to his house, to evening coffee, to prove how secure he felt. To the last, the duke was to show himself to be, indeed, a "galant homme."

[1] When Louis XV, as it was thought, was dying at Metz, his mistress, Madame de Chateauroux, was ordered peremptorily to leave the town.

As he owed his elevation to the manœuvres, so well learned, of his intelligent pupil—Madame du Barry—he proved he knew what was due to her, now she had been exiled. He sent her to his own Château at Rueil, in a hired coach. The duchess, his wife, and the du Barry's sister-in-law, attended her.

Meanwhile, in that loathsome chamber, Death—endowed with power to prove to kings how soon they may become a mass of corruption—was hastening to end the struggle. The fight for control between the "Out-Bars" (the Ministers) and the clergy, the "In-Bars," was being fought with the ferocity and the trickery of cunning. The quarrels went on for days between the party of the Ministers, the Jesuits, and the intimates of the mistress. These latter —strange and fearful anomaly!—were all scheming against the administering of the Sacraments. Once this most solemn of rites was accomplished, the King would be publicly known to be a dying man. With his death, the powers vested in the Ministry and the Jesuits came to an end. Those who no longer believed in anything, in God or Devil; those who believed in everything, including the Devil, hell and damnation, all fought with the desperation of passion intensified by the knowledge that time for winning the battle was shortening.

In the end, the sceptics and the long-nourished hate of the de Choiseuls and their clique, won. The King was dying.

The last of the Bourbons to reign, in the true sense of the word, gave the order for the ceremony of the Saint-Viatique. For this supreme act of contrition there was displayed the pomp of the great religious and Bourbon court ceremonial. Troops were under arms. The royal Guards and the hundred Swiss Guards lined the entire distance from the King's chapel to the great court of the Palace. The military line swept on; mounting the grand staircase, it came to a halt only at the bedchamber of the dying King. The Cardinal of Saint-Aymon, surrounded by bishops in their vestments, the pontifical scarlets blending with the softer violets, preceded by the clergy of the parish of the chapel, were followed by the Dauphin, his two brothers, the princesses, and the grand officers of the Crown and the Ministers. This group, in its turn, left the open court. The Cardinal and the clergy moved slowly up to the royal chamber, accompanied only by those who had been exposed to the dread infection.

As the Cardinal, under his dais, was seen devoutly bending over the Sacrament, and as the drums beat their stirring music, the sun, on that April morn, rose to flood the imposing spectacle with its glory. It was six o'clock in the morning.

Another light, as the procession moved on—one paler, more vacillating—shone against the bloom of dawn; candlelight played its feebler yellows on the gold-wrought vestments, on the pale cheek of the Dauphin—so soon to be king—on Marie-Antoinette's dimmed eyes, blinded by tears, and on all those courtiers' and Ministers' faces. What passions, fears, dead hopes, crushed ambitions, and gleams of triumph could have been read by the faint glow of the taper each mourner carried!

Those who were without the death-chamber could now gaze on the swollen, bronzed face—unrecognizable, awful to look upon, in its disfigured horror—of the last of the autocratic kings of France.

Marie-Antoinette, as she knelt at the door of the King's

chamber, gazed on this dread face. Did the memory of that terrifying vision haunt her, among other visions, in her long nights in the Conciergerie?

III

Two days later, when the single candle, placed on the window-sill of the dying monarch's room—the signal agreed upon—at last announced death had come, the valets and coachmen who had been waiting for the signal, hurried to take the putrid body to its last resting place. The coach was followed for a certain distance, on to Saint-Denis, by some guards and servants in livery, by the Grand Aumônier and by some of the clergy. This latter part of the escort went as far as the Place d'Armes, at Versailles.[1]

A few guards and servants, therefore, alone escorted the remains of the once "beloved" King, to the church of Saint-Denis. The real funeral dirge, sung by the people, along the route, was no dirge, but a derisive shout. They mocked, in ribald cries, the two ruling passions of the King's too-long life—love and the chase. "Voilà le plaisir des dames! Voilà le plaisir!" and there rang out, in imitation of the hunting call, "Taiaut! Taiaut!"

At the very instant at which the candle had been extinguished on that palace window-sill, a curious sound, as of an army in motion, might have been heard. Through the corridors and great rooms of the Palace of Versailles—struggling, pushing, rushing, heedless of whom they hurt or trod on—the Court of the dead King was hurrying to greet the live one.

---

[1] In his will, dated January 6th, 1770, Louis XV had given orders for his obsequies: "I forbid all the grand ceremonies at my funeral, and I command that my body be carried to Saint-Denis in the simplest form possible." *Louis XV intime*, Comte Fleury. Librairie Plon, 1899.

"Le roi est mort—vive le roi!" Madame de Noailles was the first to cry, as she sank on her knees before the King.

Louis, now XVIth of the race, stood—troubled, awkward, yet with a new-born dignity—before his kneeling subjects. Marie-Antoinette, her eyes blinded with tears, was clinging to his arm. "We are so young—may God help us!" was Louis' prayer for the bearing of that burden, which was already crushing him—"for they have taught me nothing!"

CHAPTER VIII

I

WITH the new reign, great changes were to come to Talleyrand. He was to feel the mounting of new hopes, the elation of the freshened energies which came in with the young King and Queen's elevation to the throne. He was also to have the "First dish of his great Fortune" served to him.

Talleyrand was to accompany his parents to Rheims. His father had been given the signal honor of being one of the three notabilities who were to carry the sacred vessel of the Ampula—the vase which contained the holy oil—for the anointing of the King.

In the spring of 1775, Talleyrand and his parents therefore, went to Rheims for the Coronation. It appears that at this time his father and mother were seriously troubled by their clever son's dissipated habits, by his loose, gay life, and his continued rebellion against his vocation. The ceremonies of the Coronation were to give fresh spectacular proof of the high honors which the Church offered her sons.

Talleyrand was once more in Rheims. He was to view it with new eyes. He was to see the city aflame with color. Tapestries, rich silks, and brocades hung from every balcony, rising and falling with the lilt of the wind, as though in salute. Above the draped windows, all that was young and fair, as well as the old and bent, were crowded together, to welcome their King. To the stirring music of drums, trumpets and silver-tongued flutes, there rose the shouts and applause of the thousands gathered below the white necks and bent heads of the ladies, in the balconies and windows.

The sparkling sunshine lit up this richly-decorated city, the golden light harmonizing tapestries, the gowns of the townsmen, their nodding plumes, and the picturesque costumes of the crowd in the streets.

The King and the King alone, it appeared, was to be the central figure of the imposing ceremony. Marie-Antoinette was to feel the first prick of the hostility of the Court, at these coronation festivities. An old custom had been revived; the Queen was to have neither escort, nor was she to figure in the official programme. Such was the decree issued by Marie-Antoinette's enemies, who were already sufficiently powerful to enforce its acceptance.

Popular enthusiasm, popular curiosity, and patriotism decided otherwise. The thousands who had come to Rheims to witness the crowning of their King were far more eager to see this young and lovely Queen than to look upon "heavy Louis."

Marie-Antoinette, with her ladies, had entered the city at night. She was met, in every street she passed, by shouting voices. Peasants and citizens crowded the thoroughfares. Moonlight lent its magic lighting; on those upturned faces, saluting their sovereign, the light blent rough-featured country-folk and stern-faced Rémois countenances. The youthful Queen, who bent down to receive this touching, spontaneous homage, must have won every heart. Her subjects looked on 'a radiance doubly enhanced by the moon's tender bloom.

On the morrow, at the Episcopal Palace, the nobility of Picardy, of Champagne and of Lorraine were assembled in the great rooms, to greet Marie-Antoinette. The slight intended, and carried out by the Master of Ceremonies, had turned into a triumph.

II

If Marie-Antoinette had entered the city without escort, the preparations for the King's reception were of the most elaborate description. Those who had assisted at the coronation of Louis XV considered the Sacre of the young King Louis XVI to have surpassed the former ceremony, in splendor.

The Cathedral itself was decked as a bride. Gothic architecture, in the artificial worlds of the eighteenth century, was considered as being barbaric. All of the nave which could be hidden was hung with the tapestries which are still among the glories of the Cathedral's treasures. The choir was surrounded by a high wooden enclosure, of Corinthian design, richly ornamented with reliefs in gold. Statues and torch standards decorated the openings into the tribunes. The Throne was hung in violet velvet embossed with the emblematic *fleur de lys*.

"La belle journée que celle du Sacre!" cried Marie-Antoinette: "I shall never forget it!" Beautiful indeed was this Sunday in May. It was seven o'clock in the morning. A stream of light swept the lower part of the Cathedral's perfect nave.

Talleyrand, as did the hundreds assembled there, saw the Queen, in the Tribunes, as she sat enthroned in her youth—

MARIE-ANTOINETTE
Madame Vigée-Lebrun
In the Museum of Versailles

her appealing youth—with her royal mien of mingled haughty pride and girlish elation. Surrounded by her ladies, erect, controlled, she was superb in the beauty of her high health and the flush of her eighteen years. Beneath the mound of her towering feathers Marie-Antoinette merited, at this solemn moment, as much the compassion as she was to win the admiring, the even passionate homage which her subjects gave her in the early years of her reign. There were no tears now, in those full, blue eyes; there was triumph and gladness, and the exaltation of royal pride in this accomplishment of the rite which made her Queen. For this high place had she not been educated and trained? Had she not left her home and family? Had she not suffered, already, as woman, one not yet wife,[1] the indifference of a husband who as yet was none? Louis might be a disappointment as a man; as a King—that was another matter. Marie-Antoinette was every inch a woman.

In a day when royalty was only second, in majesty, to God Himself, she, in common with the canons who sat draped in their hoods in the stalls, and in common with the Court awaiting their new monarch with trembling breath—all bent in homage to this advancing, youthful successor of Clovis.

III

Talleyrand's keen eyes were to witness the crowning of the last but one of the Bourbon kings. Charles X (the Comte d'Artois, Louis XVI's brother) was to be crowned at the great Cathedral. Neither Louis XVIII nor Louis-Philippe were crowned at Rheims.. Napoleon had the sword of Charlemagne brought from Rheims, placing the iron

[1] *Mémoires.* Madame Campan.

crown himself on his head—a gesture which may be said to have been characteristically Napoleonic.

Who among those who knew the youthful Abbé de Périgord could have divined that thirty years later, it would be this slim, pale-faced Abbé, with his sceptical smile and recording glance, then transformed into the middle-aged, powerful Minister, who was to seat another Bourbon on the throne? Did the sacerdotal splendors of the scene before him kindle enthusiasm in that youthful soul? Or did the future deputy of the National Assembly already turn his cool, indifferent gaze on the pomp and magnificence deployed, in the long ceremonial, with the cynicism of one nurtured in the school of Voltaire and of the Encyclopædists?

That Louis XVI never awakened sympathy or the magic of attraction, in Talleyrand, can easily be inferred from his later political attitude toward his King. Yet here, at this solemn moment of his crowning, the youthful, ungainly figure of the monarch was to be seen at its best.

Louis XVI entered the Cathedral between the two bishops of Laon and of Beauvais. Preceded by the Archbishop, the music of the marching orchestra filled the lofty arches. The Constable of France, holding high the royal sword, walked in front of the King.

Louis' heavy features had an unaccustomed air—that of struggling to assume a semi-conscious majesty. His natural awkwardness of motion was enhanced by the weight of the superb Coronation robes—the long crimson vestment that was laced with gold, and by the trailing silver robe that fell from the shoulders. Of the six Princes of the blood who followed the youthful monarch three of them, as in a Shakespearian tragedy, were to have their predestined rôles. The Comte de Provence was to be Louis XVIII;

the Comte d'Artois was to be King Charles X; and the Duc d'Orléans was to play, as the future intrigant of the family, the part of traitor.

The endless ceremonial of the Coronation services reached its climax as the King, seated in his chair, was lifted high above the heads of all, by the Bishops of Laon and Beauvais. They asked the assembled multitude if they willingly accepted Louis XVI as their sovereign. This was a part of the ceremony that may very well have been a survival of the tribal Gallic days, or of the earlier inauguration of the Kings of France which had been only a civil ceremony. To receive the homage of the army, the King was lifted upon his shield. Pépin, in order to render his crowning more respectable, introduced a religious ceremony.

IV

Louis was now King indeed. He had been publicly acclaimed as ruler of his people. The further ceremonies of the crowning of French monarchs proceeded. Louis took the oath of fidelity, in Latin, to his people, the Archbishop girding his Majesty with the spurs and the sword. Next, the King "espoused his people" with the ring, and later, gloves were handed to him, symbols both of his intimate union with those whom he was to govern. A dozen peers, six Princes of the blood, and six Princes of the church, moved forward. The crown of Charlemagne having been presented, the twelve Princes held the famous iron crown above the King's head. It was the privilege of the Grand Aumônier actually to place the crown on the King's head. This final act was the enthronement—the exaltation of the monarch to the right to rule.

After the Mass was ended, suddenly, the tribunes, the

stalls and the King's and the Cardinal's thrones, filled but a moment before, were emptied. The long cortège headed by the King continued to move onwards, by a covered way, to the Archiepiscopal Palace. Only the people were left, now crowding the emptied spaces—was this possession also symbolic of all that was to follow?

Talleyrand was to end the great day at the evening banquet where were assembled the notables of the Court, the Clergy, the Magistrates, and all that was most prominent in birth and family, in Rheims. Among all other pleasures which the ceremonies of the Coronation brought him, he formed lasting friendships with the Duchesse de Guise, the Duchesse de Fitz-James, and the Vicomtesse de Laval. The latter lady married Mathieu de Montmorency-Laval. "My acquaintance with several women, remarkable in different ways, whose friendship never ceased to give a charm to my life, dated from the Coronation of Louis XVI."[1]

Talleyrand was the same age as Louis XVI. Both were born in 1754. One might have thought his participation in these moving ceremonies, the human sympathy aroused by the sight of these two young people assuming so gigantic a task as that which lay before them, in shouldering the kingdom's awful responsibilities—one would have imagined that so touching a sight might have moved him to vow devotion to those who were in such dire need of true hearts and clever brains.

In the earlier days of the Revolution, we are to find Talleyrand neither ignorant of the dangers assailing the King and the throne, nor unmindful of his duty in attempting to avert such dangers. Later on, it is true, he showed a

---

[1] *Mémoires du Prince Talleyrand*, Vol. 1, p. 17.

brutal front to the monarch's solicitations; he had come to believe Louis utterly incapable, and was completely disillusionized.

The accepted conception of Louis XVI has been proved to be erroneous, in several particulars: heavy, awkward, brusque, even brutal at times, he was capable of great tenderness. He passionately loved the queen, once she was his wife: he loved his people—his first act as King being to command the distribution of 200,000 francs to the poor of Paris. "Take the sum from my private purse, should the needs of the State suffer from my gift." He had that rare quality in a sovereign—goodness of heart. The happiness of his people was an obsession with him—this weakness "not to afflict his people" being one of the causes of his irresolute conduct, during the Revolution. His knowledge was extensive: he knew history, geography, and in politics his ideas were, for a King, extraordinarily large. He spoke English and German, reading Clarendon's account of the death of Charles I in the original. In conversation he could surprise his listeners by his caustic wit; his common sense—so often superior to that of his councillors—might have averted many calamities had he been less timid—less given to a fatal hesitancy.[1]

[1] *L'Ancien Régime.* Brentano. Arthême Fayard et Cie., Paris, 1926. pp. 546-7.

CHAPTER IX

I

WITH the close of the reign of Louis XV, the actual youth of Talleyrand came to an end. In that artificial age, a young man of twenty-one or twenty-two was considered to be a full-fledged adult. Talleyrand was to enter on a new phase of life; his true life as priest was to begin. He was chosen to fill important posts, as administrator. His advancement, along clerical lines, if not rapid, was continuous. The first gift of substantial benefit came from the young King; at the end of September, 1775, Louis XVI gave to l'Abbé de Périgord the sinecure of the Abbaye of Saint-Denis, in the diocese of Rheims. This Abbaye yielded a revenue of 18,000 livres— Talleyrand's first settled income.

While still enjoying the advantages of the sinecure of the Abbaye, Talleyrand was appointed by his uncle, then Archbishop of Rheims, Vicar General of his cathedral (December 19th, 1779). Six years later he was created a Canon of the Cathedral of Rheims, in the year 1785.

It was at his uncle's Archiepiscopal Palace at Rheims that Talleyrand, in the year 1783, met Pitt.[1] The two

---

[1] An earlier date is given; Pitt is mentioned as having gone to Rheims when Talleyrand was there for a year as the guest of his uncle, the Coadjutor.

young men were then mutually attracted.   Pitt had come to
France to improve his knowledge of the French tongue,
and Talleyrand talked French to the Englishman, while
Pitt gave lessons to his friend in English.   The friendship
was put to the test of sincerity in 1792, on the occasion of
Talleyrand's going on his first Mission to England.   Pitt
refused to refer to the earlier relationship;—the revolutionary outburst in France having cooled Pitt's ardor
for France and Frenchmen.   It was Pitt, who, in 1794, was
to compel his former friend to take flight, to America.

At the age of twenty-six, Talleyrand was to rest his foot
on the first step of the ladder which, eventually, was to lead
him to his extraordinary future career.

The 10th of May, 1780, the province of Tours designated
Charles-Maurice de Talleyrand-Périgord to be nominated
as their choice for one of the Agents du Clergé.   "At this
period of his début, when it was important he should be
talked about, he did not have the nonchalance which he
was to practise later on in his more mature years."[1]   Zealous in the discharge of his duties and in the exercise of all
those services relating to the affairs of the clergy, Talleyrand
gave signal proof of his remarkable abilities as administrator, as well as his talent for organization.   His zeal,
competence and ardor evoked high praise from his superiors.
He who later preached the doctrine of the old Greek, "In
nothing be overzealous"—*pas trop de zèle*—brought to his
work such warmth of enthusiasm as to elicit the indulgent and
smiling, if somewhat cynical, remark, from clerical lips: "It is
youth—with more experience it will pass."

The amount of work Talleyrand performed while Agent
Général of the Clergy, and the powers he displayed in so

---

[1] *Talleyrand et la Société Française.*   Fréderic Loliée, p. 66.   Emile Paul, 1910.

many different directions, won him the esteem and admiration of his superiors.

Talleyrand's life and career may indeed be divided into two distinct and widely contrasting periods. From the time of his nomination as Agent Général of the Clergy to his return from America, in 1796, Talleyrand proved himself to be an energetic force. His activities in the service of the Church, and later, of his country, in the National Assembly, in his missions to England, and in his repeated, if futile, efforts to "make money" in America—in this period, between his twenty-sixth and his forty-third year, Talleyrand showed an energy, a resourcefulness and an ardor in the pursuance of his duties and in the execution of his designs which were in marked contrast with his later indolent, seemingly careless, even at times, reprehensibly lazy methods of conducting great affairs. His later manner was in fact, doubtless, largely an assumed one. Apparent indifference, backed by power, proven ability, and a world-wide reputation is imposing. In reality, Talleyrand's nature led him insensibly to economize effort, once his foot was firmly placed on the ascending ladder of success. He was incorrigibly indolent when no great issues were at stake.

Sainte-Beuve's estimate of him in the earlier years of his administrative career is the following: "He was not quite the same man before his fortune was made as he was afterwards. I see him much livelier in the former period; he gave himself more readily; he was anxious to win good opinion."[1]

He took pains to court the society of such grave and reverend men as Turgot, Malesherbes, Lamoignon, and also

[1] Sainte-Beuve. *Nouveaux Lundis*, Vol. 12, p. 20.

others who were politically important, such as de Maurepas,
while busy with his own exacting duties as Agent.

The sudden change of *l'Abbé de Cour*, of more or less
scandalous amours, the frequenter of the gayest salons and
of less reputable resorts, into the "zealous young priest,"
produced an amazed surprise only among those who had not
followed Talleyrand's processes of development. Each
year had given a keener edge to his more and more clearly
outlined ambitions. Since he must forge his way to success
through ecclesiastical preferment—the only road opened to
him—he entered on his course in earnest. In this new post
of Agent Général his activities were incessant. He interested himself in certain forms of popular education.
The whole diocese of the kingdom was studied; new plans
were presented for better methods—methods which, later,
bore fruit; during the Revolution, educational reform was
one of Talleyrand's chief hobbies.

It was in view of these proven abilities that the clergy
caressed the hope of seeing in this "zealous young priest
one of the future lights of the Church." On that memorable
day, during the Revolution, when Talleyrand rose in the
Assembly to propose that all the rights and privileges of the
clergy should be abolished, the Church experienced a rude
awakening to the true character of this hoped-for "light
of the Church."

Realizing that the spoken word carries weight and
influence, Talleyrand took to preaching. As he intended
to be a bishop, to study oratorical effects was essential.
That he "preached like an angel" is the sole record of the
effects his sermons produced. There is none other, not a
single sermon having been preserved. Even Talleyrand's
intuitive powers could not divine the rôle he was to play, a

few years later, in the National Assembly. The pulpit had
served him, he then found, as a rehearsal of the effects he
was to produce in the Tribune.

Among the many charitable efforts made, while serving
as Agent Général of the Clergy, Talleyrand showed his
interest in the poor, their wants, and hardships—a care
which unquestionably influenced his future work in the
National Assembly. Pozzo di Borgo—the Ambassador[1]—
who knew Talleyrand well, in later years, proved his knowledge of the statesman's life and character when he said to
Sir Henry Lytton Bulwer: "That man made himself great in
always siding with inferiors (*les petits*) and in helping those
who had most need of him." In those days, it was unusual
for a man born a noble, with such a name as was Talleyrand's, even when in holy orders and in the exercise of his
duties, to go out of his way to interest himself, for example,
in the re-marriage of poor Breton women, widows of fisher-
men who had disappeared. He also attacked the evils
resulting to the poor from the royal lottery; he proposed
that the clergy should purchase the lottery, that thus
it might be suppressed. This ardor of reform, in the latter
instance, is the more interesting in view of the later attacks
on Talleyrand for his own indulgence in gambling.

II

During the years preceding his nomination to the see of
Autun as Bishop, during his bishopric and while he was
the Deputy of his diocese to the National Assembly,
Talleyrand's intimate life was a crying scandal. He was as

---

[1] Charles: André—Comte de Pozzo di Borgo—a Corsican and an enemy of Napoleon. Later, under the Czar Alexander I he was made ambassador to Paris, in the
reign of Louis XVIII.

much married as a priest had no right to be, since he was not only living, openly, with a highly connected and beautiful woman, but he was also known to be the father of his mistress' child.

This famous liaison with the young and lovely Comtesse de Flahaut dates from the year 1782–3. Gouverneur Morris, in his Diary, gives an interesting account of his own meeting with Madame de Flahaut, at Versailles. The meeting took place in the salon of Madame de Cabanis. It was presumably she who gave Morris the following facts relating to Madame de Flahaut's history:

She was at this time in the glory of her youth and attraction, with possibly a touch of sadness about her and certainly a rare sympathy, which, added to her thoroughly trained mind, with its decided philosophic cast, gave her an uncommon power over men. Hers had been a strange life. Married at fifteen to the Comte de Flahaut, then quite fifty—who had denied himself no excess of dissipation—she found herself coldly neglected. The Abbé de Périgord, who had performed the marriage ceremony for her, became her friend, companion, and instructor, for she owed to him the training of her intellect. He became the father of her only child, who was named Charles, really after the Abbé.

A more authentic record of this, the most famous save one of Talleyrand's liaisons, has recently been given by Lord Kerry.[1] As the great-great-grandson of Charles Auguste, Comte de Flahaut de la Billarderie, Lord Kerry's descent from this latter nobleman—the son of Talleyrand and his mistress—enabled him to give to the world some valuable, trustworthy information. In this volume it is

[1] *The Secret of the Coup d'État,* edited with an Introduction by the Earl of Kerry and a study by Philip Guedalla. G. P. Putnam's Sons, 1924.

stated that Adèle Filleul was seventeen years of age when she was married to Charles-François, Comte de Flahaut, who was past fifty. The marriage was one, it is surmised, of pure form. Adèle had gone from the Convent to the altar; her husband appears to have been as indifferent to the seductive charms of his youthful wife as others found them to be irresistible.

Shortly after her marriage, Madame de Flahaut lived a lonely life. Talleyrand conceived for the neglected young wife a passionate attachment; and, for a time, at least, this passion was reciprocated. The lovely and talented Adèle, however, was as susceptible to the influence of the corrupt age in which she lived as was her lover. She could not escape the temptation to exercise the effects of her wit, cleverness, and charm on others rather than solely on him who, presumably, had been the first to profit by her slight regard for the seventh commandment.

Talleyrand and his mistress were to have the not uncommon experience of passing from the *tepidarium* of passion to the *fridigarium* of indifference. Lord Kerry states that Talleyrand quarrelled with the mistress whom he had so passionately admired—yet during the greater part of his life he remained in close touch with the son, and from time to time, during many years, he and Madame de Flahaut, later known as Madame de Souza, were to meet. One can, indeed, state that Talleyrand "placed" his son, since he it was who procured for the young man his first nomination under the Republican Government, when Talleyrand was Minister of Foreign Affairs, in the Directoire. Flahaut's letters to his mother also prove that Talleyrand, when Minister of Foreign Affairs, under the Emperor Napoleon, continued to interest himself in the career of the young man, "never ceasing to help him by his counsels and advice," such undisguised devotion being significant proof of his sincere attachment to his son.

Talleyrand's liaison with Madame de Flahaut lasted six years. The heat of the passion, though sensibly diminishing with the years, still drew them together, in daily meetings. The intimacy, when at its height, was so universally admitted it ceased to be a matter of gossip. The relationship of the son—Charles—to Talleyrand was taken for granted by all the society of the day.

III

The further history of de Flahaut, Talleyrand's only semi-recognized son, reads like a story of romance. He was to serve in the 5th Dragons under Louis Bonaparte—brother of the First Consul: he was to follow Napoleon himself to Moscow, and to become his aide-de-camp. Napoleon appears to have shown the young officer marked confidence, entrusting him with difficult missions, quasi-diplomatic in character.

After the Emperor's abdication, de Flahaut was without a post. But he flew to Napoleon's side during the Hundred Days. He was with him the entire day at Waterloo. He followed him to la Malmaison during the dark days of Napoleon's stay in the Château where, as Consul, Napoleon had spent so many happy hours. The presence of Queen Hortense may have been as drawing a magnet as was that of the fallen Emperor.

Flahaut would hardly have been the son of his father had he not followed his example along other roads than those which led to advancement. Flahaut's fine physique, attractive appearance and his seductive manners had brought him many successes in the Courts of Love, during Napoleon's reign. Among other conquests he had won the heart of Hortense, wife of Louis Bonaparte—then King of Holland. Lord Kerry's interesting article in the *Revue de Paris* (September 15th, 1924) states that while this liaison was suspected, at first by a few, in the end it became a matter of public gossip. Flahaut and Hortense both left France in 1815. Flahaut proved the nobility of his character in the protection he gave to his *amie*, who with neither crown, friends nor money had received, in July, an order to quit France—immediately. Hortense was able to reach her destination in Switzerland, where she had a house. Flahaut was arrested at the Swiss frontier. Fouché's secret police had orders to prevent any plots being hatched by Napoleon's step-daughter and de Flahaut. The frontiers of Switzerland being barred, through the endeavors of his mother—then Madame de Souza, the wife of the Portuguese Minister to Paris—he obtained a passport for England. He arrived in England in 1815. The marvellous luck which seems to have followed de Flahaut throughout his whole career awaited only a chance, apparently, to serve him.

Charles de Flahaut was thus once more a refugee in England. As a child, he had fled with his mother to escape from the horrors and dangers of the Terror: Madame de Flahaut's friends of the days of 1792–3, now in 1815 received him warmly. Lord Wycombe, Madame de Flahaut's former admirer, had exerted himself to make his former flame's exile as agreeable as possible. As the son of Lord Landsdowne—Talleyrand's intimate friend—Lord Wycombe had opened the most exclusive doors to Adèle de Flahaut. Her son profited by his mother's success as a reputed beauty, wit and celebrity—her novel, *Adèle de*

Sessange, having brought her both money and fame in 1792.

Flahaut, twenty years later, was to be seen as an intimate at Holland House. Lord William Russell and Lord and Lady Grey were among his friends.

It was through Lord and Lady Grey that he met Miss Margaret Elphinstone, only daughter and heiress of Admiral Lord Keith. As Admiral of the Channel Fleet, Lord Keith had expended most of his best energies in defeating Napoleon's plans; he had had his labors, at last, rewarded by "receiving" himself the fallen Emperor at Plymouth, and sending him, under escort, to Saint-Helena. And here was this prospective son-in-law—not only a passionate lover of his hated enemy, but a Catholic—and an illegitimate son of one whose history was anything but savory—a man, also, who had been the lover of Napoleon's step-daughter and who was the father of a son by her! The proposition was preposterous, from Lord Keith's point of view. Lord Keith thought to have found in the Regent's animosity to Napoleon and all connected with him, an influence to sustain his own position stronger than that of parental opposition. Flahaut could hardly be favorably considered from the Regent's point of view, since it was the policy of the English Government to maintain amicable relations with the restored Bourbon monarch—Louis XVIII.

Miss Elphinstone's determined attitude, however—she being a young woman of exceptional character, very deeply attached to the handsome and charming Frenchman, aureoled for her with a romantic history—finally carried the day.

Even after the marriage, Lord Keith refused to receive the married pair. Later, his Lordship, in his turn, fell a victim to de Flahaut's charm of manner and to the elevation of his character.

In the end, it appears that it was the happy fate of this illegitimate to win out, along the lines of success. Flahaut was sent as Ambassador Extraordinary to Berlin. This was probably again through Talleyrand's influence. Curiously enough, when the father was Ambassador to England, de Flahaut, during the latter's absence, wished to fill his place. Later on, in 1840, Flahaut was sent as French Ambassador to Vienna, where he remained seven years, until the revolution of 1848.

The far-reaching effects of this liaison of Talleyrand and Madame de Flahaut is of peculiar interest, not only in relation to its later influence, through de Flahaut's son, on French history, but eventually, in the curious link established, through Talleyrand's grandson—the Duc de Morny—with our own American history.

The letters of Madame de Souza, Madame de Flahaut, and those of her son, discovered in the archives of Lord Kerry's family, reveal hitherto unknown details of the birth and history of de Morny. Through these details we learn that long before Hortense was separated from her husband—King Louis (Napoleon's brother whom he made King of Holland)—the attachment between the Queen and de Flahaut had begun. Auguste de Morny was the son born to the lovers. The secret of this birth was jealously guarded. An obscure couple, Jean Hyacinthe Demorny and his wife, recognized the little bastard. Among the de Flahaut archives the Will of this elder Demorny figures, in which he left his supposed child all his possessions, which probably were only nominal. The tutelage of the child was given to Monsieur and Madame de Souza, the latter being his grandmother. Not only did Madame de Souza find in her love and devotion to her grandchild the chief delight of her later

years, but Monsieur de Souza, her husband, "appeared to be
strangely attracted by the charms of his wife's illegitimate
grandson."

Morny's history was to be as dramatic in character as
was that of his known-to-be, though unacknowledged,
father. It was far more important, from the historic point
of view. As Duc de Morny, the name of the obscure foster
parents was ennobled by the change of the particle. While
de Morny was pursuing his education in Paris, he met his
father's family. Flahaut's clever wife—Madame de Flahaut—had a breadth of nature as unusual as was her
able and capable mind. On a visit to Paris of Monsieur
and Madame de Flahaut with their children (in time, five
daughters were born to them) the young Auguste de Morny
not only made the acquaintance of his step-mother and his
half-sisters—but he was considered, eventually, as forming
one of the family. He lived for months with them in
England, visiting in English country houses, where the
verdict was all in favor of the inherited Talleyrand and de
Flahaut charm and cleverness. Morny's subsequent history
as soldier, financier, diplomat and man of fashion, during
the second Empire, is too well known to need re-stating.
The great part he played in putting Louis-Napoleon on the
French throne earned him the title of "King-maker." The
duke's influence on all the more important political and
financial policies of France, during his half-brother's reign,
until his death in 1865 proves the inheritance in direct line,
of the debt owed to his famous ancestor. Talent, and
talent of no secondary order, the Duc de Morny possessed.
Genius, save in exceptional cases such as that of Lord
Chatham and of his equally great son William Pitt, seems
to be the rarest of all transmissible qualities.

Morny's financial foresight was not as keen in the unfortunate and notorious "Jecker affair," as it had been in his speculations in the Deauville dunes, which eventually brought him in a fortune. The Swiss Bankers, Jecker de la Torre & Cie., had launched a huge loan to the Mexican government, based on the security of Mexican bonds worth seventy-five millions of francs. When the bankruptcy of this audacious venture came to pass, under Juarez's government, the Duc de Morny was found to be implicated. America's hostility, at the outset, to Napoleon III's invasion of Mexico, was unquestionably envenomed by her capture of the compromising letters addressed from Europe to the Banker Jecker—letters in which Jecker, writing to Conti, names the Duc de Morny as an "associé" in the disastrous enterprise, stating that the Duc was to receive thirty per cent of the profits.[1]

In the history of these two illustrious descendants of Talleyrand—of his only known son and grandson—we may trace the heritage of some of the more remarkable and salient characteristics of their famous progenitor. Flahaut is seen to possess the gentler qualities of Talleyrand's nature, those qualities he showed to a few women and to fewer men; allied to this tenderer side, Charles de Flahaut's character was ennobled with the stuff of heroism and of heroic devotion, as shown by his fidelity to Napoleon, in the troublous Hundred Days. Flahaut's care and protection of Hortense, when exiled, deserted by all who had courted her in her prosperity, prove the chivalric quality of his nature. Enterprising and ambitious, de Flahaut was endowed with capacities which enabled him to fill every post with honor and ability.

[1] *Le Duc de Morny.* Marcel Boulenger, p. 128. Librairie Hachette.

In the Duc de Morny's character we seem to discern a different strain.   There is a blend of the adventurer in the pliable, supple politician, who organized the *Coup d'État*, in the man of affairs, in him who founded Deauville, speculating in lands (more fortunate than his famous ancestor —when in America) as he did in Mexican values. [1]

Something of the delicacy and bloom of the *grand seigneur* inheritance appears to have been brushed away by coarser adventurous affiliations.   Morny is the precursor of the modern man of affairs—*plus* the politician.   He had in him the stuff of a born leader of men.

[1] *Le Duc de Morny*.   Marcel Boulenger.   Librairie Hachette.

CHAPTER X

I

IN spite of Talleyrand's crowded life during the years since leaving the Seminary up to the time of his nomination as Bishop, he never lost sight of the main object set before his calculating, far-seeing vision. Sensuous and sensual man of pleasure as he was, he did not permit his liaisons, nor his gaieties, nor duties to blur the outlines of the goal in view.

If Talleyrand sought and craved at this period, ecclesiastical distinction, his secret longing for a "riche abbaye" was influenced both by greed and ambition. He needed funds. He sought advancement along the lines of his order, since he saw no other doors open through which he could push his fortunes. As such doors were stretched wider and wider before him, one by one the sacerdotal vestments, it is true, were to be dropped. As during the years preceding his Bishopric, when he was a priest, he never for a moment proposed to deprive himself of any one of the joys of life, so when he entered the political arena, even the memories—as well as the duties and spiritual responsibilities involved by his consecration as Bishop—seemed to fall away from him, as a veil is rent. To the Church and the world, however, the Bishopric, so ardently desired, hung as

120

an intervening barrier between Talleyrand as he wished to be considered, after the Revolution—that is, as being freed from the yoke of his vows—and the priest whom the Church and the world could never forgive for having broken those vows.

It was in the turbulent year 1788, when the rising fury of the people against Marie-Antoinette was beginning to show alarming symptoms, that "The Second Dish of Talleyrand's great fortune" was to be served him. This, his elevation to a Bishopric, was accompanied by one of those ironic turnings of the wheel of chance which were so often, seemingly, to push Talleyrand's fortunes—and in the end, in view of his after-life and career, were to bind him forever to a hated past.

Talleyrand learned of his elevation to the Episcopal throne of Autun with mingled feelings of bitterness and of hopeful assurance. This somewhat obscure Bishopric was not in any sense the fulfillment of his ambitious designs. There had been, for a certain time, the glittering promise flashing before his eyes of as great a distinction as the Cardinal's Hat. The story of Talleyrand's possible elevation to the cardinalate, at the age of thirty-four, is a diverting one.

The personages concerned in the affair were the Comtesse de Brionne, the King of Sweden, and Marie-Antoinette. As a secondary *dramatis persona* there was Comte Mercy, the Austrian Ambassador to the French Court.

Madame de Brionne was a clever and brilliant woman. She was in active correspondence with Gustave III, King of Sweden. This monarch was eager to keep in closest touch with France and French philosophy. Among Madame de Brionne's friends she numbered Grimm, Bachaumont,

Frederic II, the Princesse de Lambesc, and others among the intellectual lights of the day.

The Comtesse particularly delighted in Talleyrand. His grand air, his wit, and his cynicism—all these graces had captivated her.

Knowing the Abbé's vaulting ambition, Madame de Brionne entered into the lists to advance his fortunes. She wrote to Gustave III proposing that His Majesty should use his influence with Pius VI to invest l'Abbé de Périgord— as Talleyrand was then called—with a Cardinal's Hat.

That such a request should be made was entirely in keeping with the methods employed in this age when woman's influence was supreme. Talleyrand, all his life long, owed much to women. His warmest friendships were among brilliant and charming women. During the sixty long years of his social life as "l'homme du canapé" he exercised the magic of his personal attraction. The man who courts women's society, who gives time and expends both intellectual and social energy in the capture of their favor, invariably succeeds. Talleyrand's infirmity, in the salon, was no crutch; it served as an effective aid to prolonged conversations. While more restless men wandered about, from one centre to another, *l'Abbé de Cour* was as often as not a permanent fixture. His seat beside the divinity of the moment was conceded, as by right. He was the "prudent fixture" whilst others were the "imprudent movables."

II

Pope Pius VI, it appears, was on the point of acceding graciously to the Swedish King's request, when, from a totally unexpected quarter, violent opposition was encountered.

Marie-Antoinette, working through Comte Mercy, her ally and confidant, addressed an energetic protest to the King of Sweden's request. Madame de Brionne had taken the side of the de Rohans in the disgraceful "Affaire du Collier"—that fatal intrigue of Cardinal de Rohan's to win Marie-Antoinette's favor. Furious at the undeserved infamy this scandal had brought upon her, the Queen revenged herself on all those who had sided with the de Rohan party. She persuaded Mercy to protest against a Frenchman's receiving the honor of the Cardinalate. She insisted it was Austria's turn to obtain the coveted elevation.

Pius VI was a tolerant Pope—one disposed to grant any reasonable favor. He had lent a kindly interest to Gustave III's proposal. He was willing enough to number so clever and brilliant a man as Talleyrand was reputed to be, among his Cardinals. He listened to the voice of Austria's advocate with as smiling a mien.

The Queen had had need of all her influence to nullify the possibility of the project becoming a reality. Yet King Louis was no more friendly than was she, in furthering the proposal. The ten or twelve years of the life led by Talleyrand in Paris salons, and elsewhere, had told against him, and seriously.

There were more serious charges. Talleyrand had continued to frequent houses of ill-fame and doubtful, so-called clubs. He knew men of known unorthodox views, and others whose reputations, like their fortunes, had long since become a lost possession. At the house of Madame de Genlis, it was known that Talleyrand passed entire nights at her gaming tables. His various liaisons, notably the one now the talk of Paris,—and the all but acknowledged paternity of his son by Madame de Flahaut—

such an infraction of the outward appearance of morality which a priest should observe, told heavily against him.

An even more serious charge than his love affairs was the fact of his having only recently trafficked in the public funds.

Under Calonne's ministry, Talleyrand had made large profit out of reprehensible financial operations. Having known the minister—Monsieur de Calonne—for some years, he had used his influence to induce the latter to open the doors wide to certain speculations. This abuse of confidence alone would have revolted so upright a nature as was that of Louis XVI. This dishonorable action, however, was not the only deflection from the true angle of right conduct one could lay to l'Abbé de Périgord's account.

The King reproached the priest not only for the levity of his worldly conduct, as well as for the unconcealed manner in which he had carried on his liaisons, but also for his open indulgence in gambling. It was the scandalous notoriety due to the indulgence in these several passions which had lost to Talleyrand, a short time before, the post of the Bishopric of Bourges, one to which he had ardently longed to be nominated.

In later life, these errors of his younger days gave to Talleyrand some distressing memories.

At the age of eighty he more or less confessed himself to his niece, the Duchesse de Dino. [1] The talk had drifted to the past—to his, Talleyrand's, past. He admitted that certain memories haunted him, troubled his mind. On Madame de Dino's questioning his reason for some of the acts he had committed, he answered:

"I really cannot give you a sufficient explanation, it

[1] *La Vie Privée de Talleyrand*, Vol. I, p. 183. Bernard de Lacombe Plon Nourrit, Paris, 1910.

happened at a time of general disorder, when nothing seemed of importance, neither one's self nor others. You cannot tell how men can go astray in an epoch of social decomposition."

Talleyrand could thus soothe his too-lately awakened conscience with the anodyne of philosophic reflections. Epochs of social decomposition are, in truth, the test of character. Weak or mediocre natures succumb to the temptations offered by the dissolution of social laws. Strong characters are braced by the forces arrayed against them.

It was Talleyrand's misfortune to have passed his youth in the most corrupt courts France has ever witnessed. The few pillars of rectitude his character could show had been bent and broken under the influences of his time.

III

Referring to the loss of the rich prize of the Bishopric of Bourges Talleyrand wrote to his friend, de Choiseul-Gouffier:

All this time I have been at Rosny I have been anxious about your position and full of disgust at my own. Here is the Arch-bishopric of Bourges given to the Bishop of Nancy, and the Bish-opric of Nancy to l'Abbé de la Farre. And now, what will happen? I see no chance of any new movement for a long while in the clergy. . . . Nothing that I desire turns out as I wish: my friend, I am not in a lucky moment. But things will change—I shall wait.

Waiting was one of Talleyrand's great assets in life. "Let time do its work" was one of his favorite axioms, borrowed, perhaps, from Macchiavelli.

The Bishopric of Autun, from Talleyrand's point of view, was indeed a serious downfall from the great posts to which he had aspired. To find a Cardinal's Hat slipping away, one to be replaced by a Bishop's mitre, and that one not the Mitre of the Bishop of Bourges but of Autun, was a deception a true Christian might accept as spiritual discipline—a spiritual state difficult to imagine as being even conceivable of acceptance to Talleyrand's sceptical mind.

The clergy were strongly in favor of his nomination to the Bishopric. They pleaded his youth and the frailty of human nature as palliatives of his light conduct; they also brought forward, as proofs of Talleyrand's fitness for the post, the debt the clergy owed him for the admirable manner in which he had conducted the affairs of his administration, as Agent Général. They instanced the eloquent letter, by l'Abbé de Périgord to the Holy Father, deploring the abandonment of monastic life. The Abbé's friends among the clergy went so far as to insist on the soundness of l'Abbé de Périgord's "orthodoxy."

Still the King held out. If he had opposed the Pope's intention of placing the Cardinal's Hat on Talleyrand's head, he was even more disinclined to number him among the Bishops of France. On this occasion, at least, the intercession of Talleyrand's family was to prove effectual, one which came at a solemn moment, and in dramatic fashion.

The recognition by the reigning monarchs of France of the de Talleyrand-Périgord claim, as a family, to "Cousinship" with the Bourbon dynasty, was signally emphasized by the visit of the King—Louis XVI—to the bedside of Talleyrand's dying father. Louis Philippe was to prove the same regard for this ancient house, when Talleyrand was near his end.

The timely and serious illness of the abbé's father— Comte Charles-Daniel de Talleyrand-Périgord—worked the miracle of a softening change in the King's attitude. On the occasion of the King's visit to the dying man, the Comte's personal request for his son's elevation to the Bishopric prevailed. The King gave his consent to Talleyrand becoming Bishop of Autun.

To the Church of France, as well as to the people of Autun, it was announced "that the King, well informed in regard to the good life, habits, piety, doctrines and other virtuous and recommendable qualities attributable to Sieur Charles-Maurice de Talleyrand-Périgord, Vicar General of Rheims, has accorded and given as a gift the bishopric of Autun on the 10th day of the month of December, 1788." [1]

It would be difficult, I think, to determine which of the two, the King as donator of this Episcopal gift, or the recipient, had the less liking or pleasure in the whole transaction. Louis XVI knew every word of the above document to be false. Talleyrand felt he had been cheated—not only of the Archbishopric of Bourges, but later, of the highest of all ranks in the Church, after that of the Holy Father himself— of the Cardinalate—through the joint influence of the King and the Queen. He, on his part was neither grateful nor was he satisfied with this inferior see of Autun. Chief among its objectionable features was the fact that the see was a poor one—a consideration paramount to Talleyrand's grasping nature—the revenues being only 22,000 livres. The one mitigating circumstance, in softening the new Bishop's disappointment, was the promising feature of sure promotion; the Bishop of Autun was considered to be in direct line of succession for the rich Archbishopric—one of the richest in all France—of Lyons.

[1] *Archives Nationales.*   Noted in *Talleyrand Evêque d'Autun,* Lacombe, 1 Vol., Perrin et Cie., 1903.

IV

According to the ecclesiastical rule, l'Abbé de Périgord, before attaining to the Bishop's mitre, must pass a certain prescribed period of time in retreat. In the solitude of the Seminary of Issy this man who, since his childhood, had always hated his vocation, and who had persistently proved by his worldly and dissolute life how light a chain he considered his vows to be, was supposed to pass days and nights in prayer, in fasting, and in acts of contrition.

In the quiet Seminary of Issy[1] were to be enacted scenes typical of Talleyrand's past, his present, and his future career. He was to submit himself to the rigors of his retreat with as light a conscience as he was to take his new vows; yet, since the Bishopric was at last in full sight, he felt he must conform to the necessary, religious observances. He was to shock, even to outrage, by his irreverence and inattention, his spiritual director—l'Abbé Ducloux. Monsieur l'Abbé confessed that never before in all his experience had he been confronted with so difficult, so distressing a situation. In the midst of his most earnest attempts to lift the future Bishop's soul to spiritual heights, in would rush a bevy of frivolous worldlings from Paris. These visits would seem to have been solicited by *l'Abbé de Cour*, as though he had begged to be protected from the dreary exordiums of the priests about him.

For the later ceremony of his sanctification, Talleyrand convoked not a single member of his family. He was confirmed as Bishop by Louis-André Grimaldi, Bishop (and Count) of Noyon, and by the Bishops of Saint-Dié and of

---

[1] The Seminary of Issy was a dependency of the Seminary of Saint-Sulpice. It was at the former Seminary, according to Renan's *Souvenirs de Jeunesse*, that the novices passed their first two years' training for the priesthood.

PORTRAIT OF TALLEYRAND AS BISHOP

AN ASSIGNAT

Paper money of the Revolution

Béziers. The ceremony took place in the chapel Saint-Sauveur, in the Seminary, January sixteenth, 1788.

L'Abbé Hugon, a Sulpician, who attended the new Bishop as acolyte, narrated, fifty-five years later, to Ernest Renan at Saint-Sulpice, that Talleyrand's attitude during the entire length of the impressive ceremony was most reprehensible; he was cold, indifferent, abstracted and went through the necessary gestures of his part like an actor who knew his rôle, but who played it mechanically.

V

Autun, in the latter part of the eighteenth century, was a far more primitive, more parochial city than is the one we may see to-day. It was then, as now, a little city of narrow, slanting streets which seemed to lead one, insensibly, to the hill on which the Cathedral uprises, its fine towers nobly outlined against the blue of the clear Autun skies.

From whatever angle or site one views the city, the Cathedral is the dominating, the central objective. The Church of Rome, wherever it may have erected its buildings and in whatever country, has ever had the instinct of choosing situations. The picturesque beauties of nature, the charm of even romantic surroundings have been auxiliaries intelligently considered as adding to the attractions of convents, monasteries, parish churches, and cathedrals.

Originally planned as a Byzantine Basilica, the Cathedral has undergone successive changes. These modifications were influenced by the varying taste in architectural modes. The first radical alteration in the primitive structure was due to Cluny models. The now famous porch, one of the most imposing in Europe, and one of the most original in conception, opening on the central portion of the church, was

planned on a grandiose scale. The perfection of this porcn is
unsurpassed, in its breadth of dimensions and in sobriety
of detail, by any other in France.

The impression produced is one of mingled awe and
delight as one mounts the steps of this wide stone edifice—
for edifice it is—in its harmonious completeness. It was
originally projected, indeed, as an exterior church where the
poorer victims of illness or disease could perform their
devotions without entering the Cathedral proper. The pre-
valence of contagious diseases in those earlier centuries,
made such isolation obligatory.

The site for the construction of the Basilica of Saint-
Lazare was determined by the munificence of a gift. In
the twelfth century faith was the inspiring, the illuminating,
and passionate sentiment pervading all classes. To endow
a church, to build a monastery, to erect a cathedral worthy
of being the sacred receptacle of the bones of a Saint, or
of a martyr, were commonplace actions, in those days.
The manner of giving differs in different ages. In our day,
benefactors unconsciously obey the practical, utilitarian
spirit pervading modern life.

In the twelfth century, the bones of a Saint could inflame
passionate ardor in the devout. A duke considered that the
sacred relics of Saint-Lazare must be enshrined in a receptacle sufficiently imposing to honor such holy remains.
Hence for eight centuries France has gloried in one more
architectural masterpiece.

If Talleyrand had shown indifference by his bearing at
Issy, and by his air of being entirely out of the scene, spiritu-
ally, during what should have been the deeply moving hour
of his consecration as Bishop, he lost no time in taking
possession of his see. Though he made no haste to perform

the duties of his high office, in person, he was to prove remarkable aptitude for controlling his diocese—at a distance.

VI

Talleyrand could now indulge in the vast projects which filled his ripened mind and those inspired by his voracious ambition. Twenty-two thousand livres a year, could not yield, in state and expenditure, what eighty-eight thousand livres enabled an Archbishop of Rheims to enjoy. At least, the Bishop of Autun could live a larger life in Paris —and—he could order a coach.

The purchase of this coach—a superb one, it appears—is the first proof history records of Talleyrand's indulgence in display. As we are to learn, shortly, to what use he was to put this resplendent carriage, we are led to infer Talleyrand kept it in Paris.[1] In the narrow Paris streets therefore, we may imagine Talleyrand's clever aristocratic face, looking out of the windows of the richly decorated vehicle of the period, with its velvet cushions and its lackeys, the latter hanging, like additional decorative adjuncts, on to the long worsted straps.

The new Bishop regaled his intimates with the story of how he had silenced the coachmaker's importunate demands for payment. To the poor man's oft-repeated question:— "When can I hope to be paid?" Talleyrand would laughingly narrate—"I answered:—'You are very curious, my friend.'" The coach, it is true, was eventually paid for, but not until constant use had more or less worn threadbare the velvet of its cushions.

Talleyrand was launched at last, on the long highroad of his extraordinary fortune. His contemptuous compliance

---

[1] Talleyrand's residence, in Paris, at this time was in the rue de l'Université— supposed to be No. 95.

with the obligatory rites and ceremonies of the Church he must serve, proves his skeptical attitude toward all things religious. His cleverness and ability in his administration of the possessions of the Church—as Agent Général—demonstrated his talents of order and administrative ability. The governing of his episcopal see, from a distance, asserted his independent attitude towards church discipline. He was to make his Bishopric serve him as the Revolution and the four succeeding reigns were to serve him, since he used each in turn for advancement, for the winning of high place, and eventually, for the accumulation of riches, while always, as he asserted proudly, serving the best interests of his country.

The titles now added to his own were to typify the ascending scale of his career;—l'Abbé de Périgord as Bishop of Autun was to be known as Comte de Saulien, as Baron d'Issy-Lévêque, Lucenay, Grosme and Touillon. As Deputy he was called the Bishop d'Autun; as Minister of Foreign Affairs under Napoleon he became Prince de Bénévent. [1] Posterity embalms his fame as the noted wit and great statesman more simply as—Talleyrand.

VII

The manner in which the future minister and statesman treated the new rôle he was to play as Bishop was typical of much that was to follow. Talleyrand was now thirty-four years of age. His character was formed; its outlines were etched with the precision which maturity brings to strong natures; and his world, both social and ecclesiastic, had already pronounced their judgment on his cupidity, his abilities, his cleverness, his wit, and his exceeding personal charm.

[1] During the Restoration and until his death he was called Prince de Talleyrand.

His talent for organization was immediately proven by the lengths to which he went, in at once setting his Bishopric in order. It was still from Paris he gave the necessary injunctions. Talleyrand, like a general, apparently, felt he could best observe the execution of his command from a distance,—the distance, preferably, being that between the Paris of its last best days, and obscure Autun.

A certain Simon de Grandchamps, invested with the functions of Grand Chantre of the Cathedral, was to take possession, in the name of the Bishop, of the see. Talleyrand instructed his delegate to confirm the Grand Vicars chosen by his predecessors in their titles; he further nominated several Vicaires-Généraux, some officials, and a secretary. After this, such time as he could spare from his busy and absorbing Parisian life, he gave to the writing of remarkable letters.

The first of these pastoral letters which Talleyrand sent to his diocese was to forestall many others in the astute knowledge they proved of men and of their impressionability. In one of these letters he quoted St. Paul's epistle to the Romans: "I am impatient to see you." This impatience, it is true, was to be experienced rather by his parishioners than by their Bishop. It was by means of his letters that his diocese was to be kept in a state of growing interest and curiosity—was to be impressed in a word, as were certain Eastern nations, by the increased prestige of invisible authority.

All the resources of Talleyrand's insinuating grace of style, of his caressing ways of flattering human egotism, and of his knowledge of just how to touch the emotions without falling into bathos—here are the secrets revealed in his letters, writ large for all to judge of the consummate art of one of the greatest of artists in conveying sentiments in which he did not believe.

He begins his first pastoral letter with the unctuous phrase:

Since the day when, our very dear Bretheren, the choice of His Majesty called on us to live among you, each moment we could repeat what Saint Paul wrote to the Romans—"Testis est Deus quod sine intermissione memoriam vestri facio!" Yes, suffer that we should use this expression. Our very dear Bretheren, you have become our beloved and unique occupation.

There are several lines of delicate and flattering assertions, such as that "All our thoughts, all our wishes, all our sentiments, go out to you." . . . "All events, all objects have taken on a new aspect, are of a more vivid interest, seen now in connection with this diocese so highly esteemed for the admirable qualities of its inhabitants—a diocese so precious to religion of which it is one of the earliest conquests." There are certain pages in these epistles in which he introduces a sentimental note. He refers to his father's last moments—to the latter's longings to have his son made Bishop of Autun,—to the fact that Autun was his mother's birthplace, and to the happiness that came to his dying father when he was assured that his beloved son was indeed to be anointed Bishop "of our beloved diocese. . . ." "Enfin, après le moment fatal, c'était au milieu de vous, c'était dans la patrie de ma mère que ma douleur aimait à se réfugier et qu'elle semblait se promettre quelques consolations."

It is to be proved if hypocrisy ever wore a robe of more finely woven phrases.

The peroration of this letter was a masterpiece of artful appeal to his parishioners' affection and to their piety.

Religion teaches us that every perfect gift comes from on high: that it is only the help of the grace that Divine Goodness dispenses, which permits us worthily to fulfill our vocation. Unite then all your prayers—you who pray for the happiness of this diocese—you above all—pure and innocent souls—sheltered from the world and its sad errors—let your days be filled with a holy communion with God . . .

This letter was read in all the parishes of the diocese. It produced an immediate and unanimous sentiment of enthusiastic devotion to the new Bishop. The echoes of Talleyrand's dissolute life which had floated down from Paris, which had shocked the more devout Christians in these remote, provincial, religious centres—the alarms created by such gossip were dissipated by the apostolic earnestness of the Bishop's letters.

A number of the priests in the diocese were Sulpicians and others were Oratorians. These stern fathers of the Church, indeed, were less easily moved by fine phrases than were their parishioners. Talleyrand had in his quiver certain honey-tipped arrows which touched the vital parts of these doubting "brethren." His training as Agent Général stood him in good stead. The ability, sagacity, and judgment with which he proceeded to administer and to govern his diocese, from Paris, greatly impressed his detractors. The dinners given at the Bishop's Palace were on such a scale of splendor as appealed peculiarly to the sons of a Church indulgent to lovers of good wines and dainty dishes.

CHAPTER XI

I

UP to early March, 1789, Talleyrand had not as yet paid his visit to his see. He was following intently the drift of the momentous change in public opinion and in the political world.

While giving the time necessary to the composition of the above admirably phrased epistles, Talleyrand's life and thoughts were absorbed in interests as far away from "the unique occupation" of his diocese as though Autun and the Autunois were a part of the planet Mars. In point of fact his thoughts, wishes, and sentiments were centred in very different spheres of interest. Paris was in the ferment of that political upheaval which, in this year 1789, was to begin the tragic epoch of France's new birth. All Paris, as were all thinking men, were being convulsed by the quaking of premonitory fears, hopes, tremors and the wildest fancies. Those invincible forces which precede revolutions were making themselves felt. No one—least of all the King—knew what, if anything really helpful or salutary, was to happen. Yet everyone—the common man sipping his coffee at a café, or the cleverest talkers in the salons, all were conscious that some great changes were in the air. Talleyrand, cleverest among the clever, was holding his ear close to that murmurous whispering of the man in the narrow streets, as he did to the talk in the most exclusive salons.

He was living, intensely, the exciting social life which preceded these earlier years of the Revolution. There was a ferment, not only of philosophic and of revolutionary ideas and theories which seemed to permeate the very air of Paris in those fateful days, there was also a certain impending dread, a dumb sense of prescience. Men and women everywhere in France were possessed by a mounting fever of excitement.

The talk in Paris, in the salons, had begun to be swept from the more shallow currents of gossip, of love-making, of discussing the last fête and planning for the one to come—this trifling had been rushed on to the broader seas of grave discussions.

The state of France was such as to engross the attention and to increase the apprehension of every thinking mind.

The throne, everyone felt, was tottering. The incredible series of mistakes and errors of conduct committed in the fifteen years' reign of the young King and Queen had kept all France, at first, in a state of amazed astonishment, to be succeeded by one of condemnation, and, among the people, of relentless bitterness and hatred—directed principally against Marie-Antoinette.

There was, indeed, nascent revolution in the air. Great changes had come, since the early days of the new reign, in the eventful years from 1787 to 1789.

Marie-Antoinette, through her inordinate love of pleasure; her extravagances; her interference in the government of the Kingdom; her known Austrian intrigues; her devotion to her favorites—first to the Princesse de Lamballe, later to the Duchesse de Polignac and to all the de Polignac family

—the devotion of the Queen to these her intimates, to the exclusion of the powerful clique of great ladies she had alienated by her favoritism; the libels and scandals resulting from her indiscreet adventures in seeking pleasurable diversions with her brother-in-law, the Comte d'Artois; and the still more serious and disastrous "Affair of the Diamond Necklace"—that abominable machination of an adventuress playing on the credulity of the Duc de Rohan—all these errors and scandals had resulted in Marie-Antoinette's being as hated as once she had been loved.

Paris, the whole country, was oppressed by a poignant sense of approaching disaster. Misery, want, financial depression and financial deficit were as so many warning fingers pointing to something ominous—to a sinister shape that seemed to be lurking in shadows—to the spectre which was daily assuming more and more definite outlines.

In the midst of the turmoil and of the general state of perturbation, Talleyrand felt his own hour had come.

Not only are we to see Talleyrand entering at last, in dramatic fashion, on the great historic stage, playing a prominent part as a decisive factor in some of the early revolutionary upheavals and changes, but in his after life, like the stormy petrel, Talleyrand was to be found at his best when the battling elements about him were fiercest. His coolness, his sang-froid, his powers of rapid penetration, of quickened mental decision, following fast on concentrated control of intellectual energies, made his conclusions, in moments of critical difficulty, of commanding force.

II

During the years 1787 and 1788 Talleyrand had contracted an intimacy first with Mirabeau, and later with

Necker. Both of these famous men were greatly to influence Talleyrand's future life.

Talleyrand was to have one of those curiously interesting experiences with Mirabeau not unusual between men of genius.[1] They were to be enamored of each other's talents, charmed by each other's wit, and to be drawn together by certain traits of character—a resemblance which both would most violently have resented. After falling into each other's arms, they were to tear each other to pieces. The story of their intimacy and of their rupture might have been that of a love affair.

In the two famous letters which Mirabeau wrote—one to Calonne, and the other to a friend—we may see the zenith of this spasmodic friendship descend to the nadir.

Mirabeau, writing to Monsieur de Calonne, then Minister of Finance, thus recommends his friend, l'Abbé de Périgord:

Monsieur l'Abbé de Périgord joins to a very real and experienced talent a profound circumspection and proved secrecy. Never can you choose a man who is more to be trusted, more piously devoted to the cult of gratitude and friendship, less envious in participating in the glory of others, more convinced that such fame should redound to the renown of the man who knows how to conceive, and who dares to execute.

Such an introduction produced the most desirable of results. Calonne, in his fatuity and weakness, may be said to have laid the corner-stone of all the Talleyrand fortunes. As we have learnt, he initiated the priest so thoroughly into the secrets of financial operations that the latter was

[1] *Mirabeau.* Louis Barthou, 1900. Hachette & Cie., Paris.

enabled to speculate, to great advantage, in the state funds.

A year later, Mirabeau is seen treading the thorny path of bitter disillusion. He writes to a friend—to d'Antreignes: "I am hoping this man" (Talleyrand) "is not known to you. . . . Through the history of my misfortunes I was thrown into his hands . . . and I still have to use discretion with this vile, avaricious, low and intriguing man." The whole story is that of one clever man using his talents to score against another clever man. One cause of the quarrel is said to have been Mirabeau's having written disparagingly of Talleyrand from Berlin, where he was playing the rôle of political observer.

Mirabeau, in other words, was in the foreign secret service, a post it appears, Talleyrand's efforts had secured for him. Talleyrand revenged himself by furnishing interesting information to the Minister—Calonne—relating to certain phases of Mirabeau's previous shady career.

The balance in that recriminatory battle swung round in Talleyrand's favor. Impressed by the Abbé's cleverness, Calonne furthered Talleyrand's pressing suit for the Bishopric of Autun.

The future Bishop owed a debt to Mirabeau far more weighty than the latter's recommendation to Calonne. Mirabeau was the first among men of talent to impress Talleyrand with the great advantages to be reaped in following a diplomatic career. We are to see the results of this influence in Talleyrand's subsequent journeys to England.

III

Monsieur Necker, the famous Swiss Minister, who had succeeded Calonne, had been called and recalled to the

MIRABEAU

ministry to attempt the impossible task of rehabilitating French credit.

Necker was a powerful stimulant to Talleyrand's growing desire for a more profound study of the laws governing finance. He went to school to the clever Swiss Protestant. Having learnt, as he thought, all he could from that source, he criticized him as being "a stranger—a bourgeois of a small republic, of a religion which was not that of the majority of those of the nation, full of himself, surrounded by flatterers . . . of mediocre talents . . ." etc. Yet, later on, in the more turbulent days of the Revolution, he, together with the American, Gouverneur Morris, was to be constantly in touch with Necker. To this Minister whom he, Talleyrand, considered "was the last who should have been chosen to fill as important a post as was that of a Minister of France, at so critical a time"—to Necker, Talleyrand owed much. It must be admitted that to those to whom Talleyrand owed most, in point of enlargement of ideas, of breadth of vision, and of expert knowledge in certain branches of statescraft and finance, he showed little or no gratitude. The aridity of Talleyrand's nature was shown particularly in his political relationships. His affections appear to have been carefully trained to expand only in the direction of family or sensuous drawings. He was an economist in matters of the heart.

He quarrelled with Mirabeau; he abused Necker; later, he was to desert and to denounce, even to vilify "ce brigand" Napoleon—as he called the victorious young general whom he had courted, and the Emperor whom he had served. Yet to each one of these men—two of whom towered above Talleyrand in the loftier stature of their genius—he stood deeply in debt for guidance, enlightenment, or for in-

numerable favors. Such debts should have been paid, at
least, by the discretion of silence, since gratitude was a coin
not in use in the Talleyrand mint.

Michaud, publicist and historian[1]—a contemporary of
Talleyrand, who hated him as only a passionate clerical and
royalist can hate one who was to go over to the people in the
National Assembly—asserts boldly that Necker and Talleyrand were the closest of friends in the eventful year 1788, and
that the planning and furthering of the convocation of the
famous Etats-Généraux was actually their joint work.

It is certain that this recall of Necker to power was a
popular motion. Parisians, particularly, received the
nomination with enthusiasm. Much—too much—was expected of Necker's proven abilities. Already the pinch
of hard times was fastening its grip more and more fiercely
on all classes. Commerce and industry were at a standstill.
Suffering was abroad in the land.

IV

Among the many other reproaches levelled at the King
was his having financed the military aid rendered, in earlier
years, to the Americans in their war of Independence.

The exalted state of mind which animated La Fayette,
Rochambeau, and all the clever, ardent enthusiasts who
had followed those heroic young noblemen across the seas
to help Americans fight for Liberty—above all to fight
England, the real motive for the French Court's participation in the war—this enthusiasm had long since passed.
After the Peace of Versailles, in 1783, with England's

---

[1] *Histoire Politique et Privée de Charles-Maurice de Talleyrand*, par L. G. Michaud,
Bureau de Biographie Universelle, Paris, 1853.

recognition of the United States and the end of the war, France was liberated from fear of English enmity. But French coffers had been emptied of their millions. The deficit in the budget of 47,000,000 of francs had been largely due to the 40,000,000 given to America. The people of France, now freed in their turn from the spectre of war with England, would have preferred their millions to the "empty gain of freeing strangers."[1]

The motion, therefore, of the Notables to convoke the States-General was acclaimed as the coming sure remedy for all the several ills from which the State was suffering. Alas! the State—being sick beyond all remedies—was to try one cure after another, until the Terror was to prove that the delirium of anarchy must precede a return to healthier conditions.

As soon as the convocation of the Etats-Généraux was decided, December 27th, 1788, Talleyrand's quick working mind discerned the immediate utility to which he could put his neglected see. He must be sent to the Assembly as a deputy, and by his diocese, and at once. The ripening of his political abilities, his ambition to take a first place among the political leaders of his country, the directive forces of his nature—passions which were more ardent when they had as an arena the Tribune or the Ministerial Council than when confined to the boudoir—all of these forces and passions were in play. The consummate art with which he was to charm his provincial flock and the pains he took to win his seat as deputy were proof of how completely he was in control of his masterful abilities. His quick decision to be nominated as Deputy to the Assembly was as a lightning flash illuminating the road before him—the road of his destiny.

[1] See Addendum No. 1.

V

Once his plan formed, active preparations were made for immediate departure from Paris.

His fine coach was seen rolling along the French high-roads. Precautions to announce the arrival of Monseigneur l'Evêque had been carefully taken.

On the twelfth of March, 1789, before dawn, all the bells of Autun were chiming their clamorous tongues. The streets were packed with the curious-eyed, impatient, enthusiastic Autunois. What emotions, what exciting sensations awaited these provincials in looking, at last, on the face of this noted man—about whom there were so many strange, even terrible stories! Now that he was before them, now that they could see how great a nobleman he looked—how superb was his coach, how grandly he sat, smiling, as he gave his blessing with such grace and readi-ness—surely those sad gossips, the Parisians, were envious of so noble a man and Bishop! His pastoral letter had prepared, indeed, the way for his triumphal entry.

In the Episcopal Palace, when Talleyrand, later on in the day, awaited the Canons who were to come with the Cross and Holy Water, he must have presented a regal figure. In his canonicals, in his violet robes and filmy laces—his brilliant face lighted with the gleam of conscious power, of purpose, Talleyrand must have seemed the incar-nation of both temporal and spiritual pomp—if not of piety.

Talleyrand neglected none of the means necessary to obtain his election as Deputy. The lessons taught at Hautefontaine of the importance of carrying out to the last duty the obligatory religious ceremonials of such a charge as was his, had not been forgotten. The services of his

Cathedral were performed with exemplary zeal. One would have given much to have had a pictorial presentation of Talleyrand seated on his Bishop's throne, wearing his pontifical robes with the grace of which he was master, his face beneath the mitre reflecting an expression at once impressive, serious and inscrutable. His training at Saint-Sulpice and at court enabled him to assume, with perfect art, the bearing necessary to enhance the desired effects.

On one occasion Talleyrand wished to officiate pontifically. It was on the day of the Annunciation, at High Mass. He did not succeed, with his customary grace and efficiency, in performing the offices. His lameness caused him to stumble, and his inexperience to commit blunders. Ridicule is what no Frenchman, even a genius, can endure. Hearing the amused comments of certain of the officiants near by, the Bishop never again attempted, at Autun, to say High Mass.

In the gardens of the episcopal palace, other devout and more effective poses were presented to his unsuspecting prelates. Under the uncertain April skies Talleyrand could be seen, at fixed hours, walking, with bent head, beneath the tender greens of the timid spring foliage, an image of piety, reading his breviary, as he paced the well-kept paths.

His priests and canons were not only to be impressed with the devout religious attitude of their new Bishop, Talleyrand was careful to appeal to less strictly spiritual sentiments.

The frequent and stately dinners given at the Palace were the talk of the brief day of Talleyrand's Bishopric, and they were remembered long after as having been among the benefits and pleasures of their Bishop's reign. Oratorians and Sulpicians alike deplored the loss of so Mæcenian a Bishop.

At these dinners, the talk was skilfully turned to dwell on parochial affairs relating to certain needs and desires, such as might be beneficial to the rule of the diocese. As host, Talleyrand brought to these banquets the art and charm which, as courtier and as the finished man of the world, he possessed to perfection. How could provincial priests, or even clever Jesuits—co-students with Talleyrand at Saint-Sulpice—but be won to the point of enthusiasm by the display of so much intellectual brilliancy and social *savoir faire*, coupled with the proof of their Bishop's devout piety? Talleyrand played his part to perfection. A good Bishop, he was considered also to be an ideal candidate.

Talleyrand proved he possessed the knowledge of the right means by which to conquer the hearts of the less critical devout. He canvassed with skill and an unremitting zeal. He went personally among the people; he talked familiarly with the Autunois mothers and their daughters, wisely with the men, asking that their desires be made known and he aroused, both as future Deputy and prelate, praises and loyalty wherever he went.

On the second day of April, 1789, he was elected by a large majority, as Deputy of the clergy of the Province of Autun. Having accomplished the great object in view, the real Talleyrand was about to reveal himself.

The fine coach was once more to flash across the French high-roads. Autun had ceased to be of use. It had accomplished the chief purpose for which Talleyrand considered it had been destined.

The time chosen for this abrupt departure brought consternation to the souls of his admirers and advocates.

On the very day of Easter, on the twelfth of April, without
waiting to preside at the sacred offices of the day, Talleyrand
mounted the steps of his coach and drove away.

Before Talleyrand passed into the open country, he was
driven through, at least, one of the noble Roman Triumphal
Arches still standing in Autun.   One wonders if he took heed
of the lesson taught by these memorials of Roman pomp, of
her power, and of her vanished glory.   Cæsar too was ambitious. He had come to Gaul and to this ancient town of
Autun to help her to fight her enemies, as he was later to
conquer Gaul itself that he might pave the way to Roman
supremacy.   It was his fate to be stricken down at the base
of a column, as he had stretched forth his hand to grasp
the royal sceptre.

The towering arches are still there in the Autunois
streets, after two thousand years.   And through them, at
every turn of the wheel, as Talleyrand swept on and on,
he, too, went on to his fate.   Each milestone was to mark
one further departure from the life he had hated, from the
vocation he detested. As he had dropped, one by one,
his beautiful Bishop's robes to don his travelling apparel,
Talleyrand was to free himself one by one, as he thought,
from the chains which had fettered him.   In his subsequent
career as Deputy; as the priest who was to present the Bill
to the General Assembly for the confiscation of the properties of the clergy; as the emissary sent to England to attempt
to make certain treaties; as the *émigré* who was to take his
flight from the horrors of the Terror, first to England and later
to America—Talleyrand, as he believed, was to put further
and further away from him both priesthood and his Bishopric, as he also was to loosen the bonds and vows which
held him to the Church.   The Church, however, refused to

release from his vows the consecrated Bishop, and while the statesman is the imposing figure which dwarfs the Bishop, yet the laces and violet robes of the latter seem still to cling about the court costume of the Minister.

Talleyrand never saw the youth who was to spend a few months at Autun on his way from Corsica to school—and whom, as the Victor of Arcole, years later, he was to divine, to court, his belief in Napoleon's "star" as the coming man being one of the forces that led Napoleon to strike the decisive blow on the 18th Brumaire. The destinies of these two men were to be strangely interwoven and as dramatically sundered.

CHAPTER XII

I

ON his return to Paris, Talleyrand found he was in ample time to take part in the opening ceremonies of the assembling of the States-General, on the first of May. Hence his haste. Autun, its Bishopric and its episcopal duties could not weigh in the balance against the stirring drama to be enacted at Versailles. On this scene of political action he was to make his mark, at the outset.

The Etats-Généraux served him for his first entrance on the world's stage. He made his début as a political force in the National Assembly. However vaulting a man's ambition might be, however vast the conception of the rôle he considered his talents might enable him to fill, no setting could be imagined which could provide so spectacular an ensemble as did that of La Salle des Menus Plaisirs and the Jeu de Paume. A signal proof of Talleyrand's genius was his immediate recognition of the vast possibilities the arena presented, wherein the fiercest passions were to be fought out until the struggle ended in a welter of blood. Hitherto, Talleyrand's talents had won for him more or less local fame, as his charm and his wit had conquered the court and society. In less than a year after the opening of the Assembly of the

149

Three Orders, Talleyrand's name was known from one end of Europe to another. Far distant America was to learn that this new star, risen above the political horizon, was coupled with that of La Fayette, Mirabeau, and Sieyès.

Certain aspects of the earlier contentious spirit animating the Assembly must be understood, in order to enable one to estimate the part played by Talleyrand, in the great drama.

Paris, as was the whole kingdom, was stirred to its remotest centres by the meeting of the Three Orders— the Clergy, the Nobles, and the People. Eleven hundred and fifty-five deputies, of whom six hundred were the People's deputies, were to be united at Versailles. The whole country was animated by a profound spirit of reform.

The people believed that, at last, energetic measures were to be taken to rescue France from its miseries; the exactions of the "privileged classes" (the clergy and the nobles), the extravagance of court expenditure, the intolerable burdens, the unjust taxes and the imposition of unpaid work for the State, such as *la taille*, etc.—burdens which made the life of the poor a grinding slavery—would cease.

The convocation of the States-General, which was the prologue to the Revolution, was brought about, in part, by the weakness of Calonne and by the incapacity of the King to grasp results. Necker, after leaving the Ministry in 1781, was succeeded by four more or less incompetent ministers. Joly de Fleury was perfectly insignificant, but he was liked by the Parliaments. Monsieur d'Ormesson, unlike the King, was conscious of his mental limitations. He was conscious, also, of his "thirty-one years" as being inadequate, from the point of view of experience, of assuming so grave a task as the governing of France then presented. The end of his brief reign of seven months saw him in quick retreat.

Then came Calonne, he who treated "affairs" (of state) "as though they were pleasures and pleasures as though they were affairs." With such aptitudes to suit the ideal of what a Minister of Finance should be, his abilities, his charm and his known capacity for work appealed to such questionable judges of State affairs as were Marie-Antoinette, the de Polignacs, and the Comte d'Artois. The King would have preferred Loménie de Brienne, Archbishop of Toulouse, as Minister. The despotic rule of those greater church-men—Cardinals de Richelieu and Mazarin—were dread warnings of what befell a King who took prelates for Ministers—warnings the King then heeded.

Calonne's Ministry precipitated the crisis whose causes had been prepared by the reigns of Louis XIV and Louis XV. Chosen by the court, true courtier that he was, he followed ruinous court examples. He encouraged, he did not lessen, greater excesses in prodigality. He must please the Queen. He bought St. Cloud for Marie-Antoinette, who had always longed to possess it. He promised inexhaustible riches to the nation—with an empty treasury. He imposed rigorous taxes, while having to face the Parliaments which refused to execute the royal decrees He courted men of finance, "whom he permitted to exploit the distress of the nation." Talleyrand profited by this laxity on the part of the Minister of Finance. Calonne had resorted to one device after an-other to arrest the impending doom of State bankruptcy. He bought Mirabeau's venal pen. He tried certain plans of his abler predecessors—Colbert's, Vauban's, Machault's, and Turgot's. Calonne finally had recourse to a plan of Necker's.

"What you are proposing to me is a receipt of Necker's," said the King. "Sire, we do not possess a better one"—replied his supple Minister.

Mirabeau had one to proffer. Even his giant intellect could neither grasp nor divine that which the measure he boasted later, as having been suggested by him to Calonne, was to bring about. "Convoke the Notables," was the famous Tribune's remedy for the state of collapse into which Calonne's mismanagement and excesses had brought State affairs.

The King accepted the suggestion with joy approaching rapture. If one hundred and forty-four Notables, among them six or seven non-privileged members of the Third Order—the Tiers Etat—could not find a solution for the disorders of the State, then none could, was his conviction. In any case, his, the King's, responsibility would be shifted. He could sleep now, on both ears—"sur les deux oreilles." And sleep was as necessary to this lover of the chase—the King's ruling passion—and to this King of a voracious appetite as is the gratification of other passions to other men.

The Notables made the embarrassing discovery of the extent of the nation's debt. Before that stupendous problem they confessed their own incapacity. Only one solution was possible. The States-General must be convoked, a decision to assemble which body was to result in precipitating the very ills and conflicts which it was hoped would be averted. In bringing face to face the Three Orders of the Kingdom, the chasm separating the interests, traditions, and ambitions of the Nobles, the Higher Clergy, and those of the People,—this divergence was to be revealed, with appalling results.

II

The lists, in what was to be the dramatic engagement between the King, the Clergy, the Nobles, and the People, were now open.

There was the King still secure, as he supposed, in full power of exercising and enforcing his monarchical supremacy. There were the Clergy and the Nobles entrenched in their age-long prerogatives of privileges. There was the Nation, now conscious of its rights, conscious also of its needs, wants, desires and ambitions. The Nation was more powerful than either King or Nobles, being more enlightened, inspired by a loftier ideal, and alone possessing the wealth—that wealth which the Nobles, when they possessed it, had dissipated, and without which the King could do nothing.

The real battle of interest was to be fought out between the Clergy and the Nobles, on one side, and the People, on the other. The King was to be sacrificed on the altar of the people's hate of monarchical rule.

It was in such a mêlée of opposing interests, ambitions, and of the fierce strife for authority that Talleyrand was to prove his talents, as politician and orator. In the arena of the first gathering of the Assembly, in La Salle des Menus Plaisirs, and later in the Hall of the National Assembly, he was to begin that career of political activity which lasted from this, his thirty-sixth year, on to his old age, in 1834. Talleyrand was to be plunged, at the very outset, into the sea of conflicting interests, into the vortex of passionate revolt, which ended in the doom of autocratic monarchical rule in France.

To Talleyrand as to other astute profound minds, the

dissensions in the Kingdom had long been known, studied, and their causes analyzed; their possible effects had been more or less accurately gauged. As happens in all cataclysmic upheavals, however, the virulence of popular passions is a force none can rightly predict. That France should go to the lengths of a sanguinary Revolution, should prove its ferocity, its savage cruelty, and should exult in practices which made her name execrated by all Europe and America—who could conceive of a France thus transformed?

III

Had the Fates, in derisive humor, ordained an assembling of the forces of the Kingdom whose convulsive conflict was to shake France to its foundations, the scene could not have been more superbly set. All the actors—or their representatives—were to be seen in gala costume, on the two festal days. The curtain of the coming tragedy was lifted on spectacular splendor.

Gouverneur Morris's description of the scene of the opening ceremonies is as graphic as it is full of movement and color.[1]

On Sunday, May 3rd (1789), the court and clergy of Versailles awaited the result of the audience to be given to the deputies, on Monday. A superb day dawned, "a heavenly day," Talleyrand says. The beautiful lawn of the Palace was crowded with groups of gaily dressed officers and high dignitaries of the Church, each wearing the brilliant tokens of his rank. Ladies decked in the brightest colors and wearing the gayest smiles, talked and sauntered about, or sat on the stone benches along the alleys, beneath the delicate spring foliage.

[1] *Diary and Letters of Gouverneur Morris,* edited by Anne Cary Morris. 2 Vols. Charles Scribner's Sons, 1888.

In striking contrast to these were the groups of the members of the Third Estate—the Tiers-Etat—shunned as if they bore the seeds of pestilence among them. They talked in whispers, hurriedly and earnestly—they never smiled. Their costume of black hose and short black cloaks, to which they had been condemned by the old sumptuary laws and which denoted the plebeian, made the contrast even greater. Proudly they carried themselves in this dress, but on their faces were care and gloomy forebodings, and a sudden ominous silence fell upon them whenever a stray member of the noblesse happened to pass near.

Above the laughing, chatting groups of the Nobles, and of the glum-faced members of the Tiers, in a balcony of the Palace, there sat, like a queen in a faery story, Marie-Antoinette among her ladies—"A bevy of beauties all in high spirits, discussing the pageant of to-morrow, which to them had an added interest as being solely spectacular." The fact that the Salle des Menus Plaisirs was lighted from above, and that thus both beauty and costumes would be set off to utmost advantage, was the feature of the coming festivities which stirred to enthusiasm both the Queen and her friends.

IV

On a clear May day, the first of the month, at mid-day, there sounded through the streets of Versailles a cry that rang out in stentorian tones: "De Par le Roi!" Heralds in violet coats enriched with golden *fleurs-de-lys*, superbly mounted, preceded by a company of Hussards and trumpeters, marched through the streets of Versailles. The trumpets' vibrant notes having ceased, the King's orders were given.

The opening of the Etats-Généraux was proclaimed.

Talleyrand was to be a part of the imposing ceremonies of the "presentation," May second, and also of the parade of the Three Orders through the city streets, to the Church of Saint-Louis.

Grave mistakes marked the two ceremonies. With that contemptuous disdain of the people, inherent in the concept of autocratic majesty, the King's "subjects"—the People— were made to feel their separateness from the other two Orders. The Clergy and the Nobles on the day of their presentation to the King were received by his Majesty in his cabinet. The doors were widely opened for the Clergy; half of the door was closed, as the Nobles appeared. The King's bed-chamber was esteemed to be good enough as an audience chamber in which to receive the deputies of the People. Although the striking difference shown in the reception of the Three Orders was in the order of established tradition, the Tiers Etat were not the same subjects, nor were they of the same temper as were their ancestors, when under the rule of Louis XIV. They made their plaint heard: they intimated to the King "how painful were such marked differences for the party which was the truly national one of the Three Orders." The hint of power in the appeal was neither understood nor apprehended.

As the long line of the deputies passed before the King, not a word was uttered; once only did the monarch break his ungracious silence. "Bonjour—bonhomme" said dull Louis to a Breton in peasant's garb—to "Père Gerard" who has gone down in history as the one representative who evoked this negligent recognition from his King. It was the fate of Louis XVI to go through life cursed with moral near-sightedness. He could never see nor seize the psychological moment. He could have won over every one of those weary, nerve-strung, resentful subjects had he had the humanity of François I or the bonhomie of Henri IV.

The second scene of the great Act passed off with greater éclat, but with no improvement in the regard shown for the Third Order.

Four days later, the Versaillais housewives were busy. Every house must prove its joy—its spiritual ecstasy. For the Holy Ghost was to be invoked: its light must descend on those destined to bring order to the distracted kingdom. The Châteaux and hôtels of the Nobles—those long grey façades now in our day so sad-faced,—were resplendent with hanging tapestries and gorgeous velvets, as the streets themselves were to blaze with the glory of the great procession.

The Fête of the Saint Esprit had drawn all Paris, all the surrounding country, and even inhabitants of far-distant cities to congest every nook and corner of Versailles. Roofs were as peopled as were the windows; the latter could be had at the cost of three louis.

In his cloth of gold mantle, holding his taper in his strong, flexible hand—one that could turn so dexterously locks and screws—Louis passed from his chariot to lead the procession into l'Eglise Saint-Louis. Marie-Antoinette, seated among the Princesses, made the note of jeweled splendor. As she passed beneath a certain window, she lifted sad eyes to a sickly-faced boy, reclining on a mound of cushions. As the Queen smiled, the child caught the smile and answered it, for it was the Dauphin, brought from his sick bed to see the procession. He was to die within the month, at Marly.

There were certain faces in the long cortége on which curious, critical eyes were fixed. Mirabeau's rudely modelled features, the face pock-marked, the head leonine, the frame massive—on Mirabeau's "insolent ugliness," many eyes centred. Among the Bishops, Talleyrand's aristocratic countenance, with its inscrutably aloof yet suave expression, rose above his violet robes: his limp became doubtless more and more pronounced as the length of the march continued. The Duc d'Orléans, known later as Philippe Egalité—the traitor of the royal family—was loudly acclaimed as "L'Ami du Peuple"—the enemy of "l'Autrichienne."

Marie-Antoinette, as she left the coach to enter the Cathedral—to sweep by in the grace and dignity of her imposing carriage—for her and the Princesses there were no welcoming shouts. Instead, a hissing murmur gathered force, one that came from a group of women, "Vive le Duc d'Orléans!" was the insult, and the first of those hoarse cries which were to hurl curses at the Queen, on the fifth of October. The King, as he followed the Queen, appeared not to have heard the women's blast of hate. Did the hate, the angry scorn in the cry account for Marie-Antoinette's sudden reeling—for a faintness which made an instant's halting necessary—that her ladies might sustain her?[1]

The procession of the court and the Etats-Généraux was headed by the King's household, by his pages, his écuyers and—his falconers! These latter, a survival of mediæval hunting days, were to make their last public appearance as was, indeed, the King himself as an autocratic sovereign, in these few months before the Constitution was voted.

On the return to the Château de Versailles, in the royal carriages, there sat the King and his brother, the Comte de Provence. Twenty-five years later, the latter was to be

[1] *Marie-Antoinette Reine.* Pierre de Nohlac, Calman Lévy, Paris, 1900.

known as Louis XVIII. The successor of this future
monarch was to be the then sensual, pleasure-loving and
frivolous Comte d'Artois—the first among the royal princes
to emigrate, when he heard the terrifying rumble of revolutionary cries. He was to reign as Charles X, as the "pious
King," after his mistress, Madame de Polastron, dying,
had "given" him to her confessor,—"Je vous le donne"
had been her last words. The two Ducs d'Angoulême and
de Berry were both to have their names figure in the pages of
the Bourbon Restoration. The forces which were to play
their part in the tragedy of the coming years—forces which
were to decide the future of France till our own day, and
long after—were now assembled. The *deus ex machina*
of the restoration of Bourbon power was the limping prelate,
to whom doubtless not a thought was given by the King and
his brothers.

Gouverneur Morris was to see the procession on the day
following this gay sight, from a window, in the company of
Madame de Flahaut. The chattering, laughing groups in balconies and windows, who were looking on the scene below as
though it were a play, ignorant of what lay in the womb
of time, seeing in the long dun-colored mass of the Third
Order, as they marched gloomily past, the tiresome, dull
note in the brilliant pageant, who among the cleverest
could divine that these were to be the future rulers of
France?—the Samsons whose strength was to bring down
the Temple of Bourbon power?

The pageant was moving on. "The Nobles glittered in
gorgeous dresses and orders. The Bishops, superb in violet
robes, were followed by their humble curés in modest garb.
The Commons in black mantles, very plain, and hats without feathers," was Morris's description.

V

The opening ceremonies of the Etats-Généraux followed immediately. The memorable scene was set with a spectacular magnificence unknown to those of us living under Republican forms of government.

The gathering of the King, the court and the Assembly was held in the Salle des Menus Plaisirs. The Hall was impressive with its majestic row of columns, its decorative frieze and elaborate cornice. The King's throne was between the columns, rich in "its opulent drapery of violet velvet and embroidered *fleurs-de-lys*." Below the throne was a smaller one—that of the Queen. The rank of royal princes and court dignitaries was defined by those who had rights to armchairs, to stools, or to settees. In the semicircle of the great Hall, on uncomfortable benches—"with neither cushions nor backs"—on these seats, just opposite to the throne, the People's representatives were seated. They were crowded closely together; and on their right the Nobles and the delegates of the Clergy faced the latter group.

The scene, as an ensemble, was brilliant. As though the last display of Bourbon splendor had sentient conscience of its coming doom, all that the long centuries had accumulated of riches, of contrasts in magnificence of apparel, or had developed of courtly dignity in presentation, was there to impress eye and sense. The King in his royal robes; the Queen in her coronet, flashing jewels and dancing plumes; the royal Princes in their gold-embroidered coats and orders; the Nobles in their satins, and velvets, their hats crowned with white feathers, near enough to the semi-regal capes—violet or crimson—of the prelates, to strike a con-

ROBESPIERRE

Painter unknown—Musée Carnavalet

trast—this blaze of gems and colors but brought into stronger relief the drab, sombre mantles and coats of the 560 deputies of the People.

There was one of these deputies who was not in the least dazzled. His hate of riches, his rage against the oppression of authority, against "injustice to the humble, the poor," was now like a consuming fire, as he faced this "idolatry of Empire." In spite of "his blue eyes, his blond hair, and his large shoulders," Maximilien Robespierre was repulsive. He was small, thin, with an air at once cringing and authoritative. He had a sinister eye. His short hose, worn nearly threadbare, his black velvet coat—recently dyed—and his clean shirt were covered by his lawyer's robe. The only objects of apparel to suggest the care and luxury with which Robespierre the "elegant" among the Terrorists (arch-fiend of them all) was to adorn his person in four short years, were his silk stockings. He had come up to Paris, as deputy from Arras, with ten louis as his sole fortune, lent by a friend of his sister's. With Fleury, a farmer, with Petit, a laborer, with Payen, a cultivator— Robespierre made his entrance into Versailles in as humble a vehicle as he was to leave Paris in 1794—in the "tumbril" which took him to the scaffold.

VI

In the great Hall des Menus Plaisirs, in a clear strong voice, the King addressed the vast audience. He gave His Majesty's welcome to the Etats-Généraux; his speech was short and to the point. "Protestations of love and veneration" rose up from the auditors. The Keeper of the Seals, advancing, knelt at the foot of the Throne to receive the orders of the Sovereign. His violet and crimson costume made a brilliant note of color as he backed his way out, facing the monarch, to take his place among other brilliant robes. He read something no one heard.

He was succeeded by the Minister of Finance, Necker, whose too lengthy report of the Finances seemed to anticipate that eternity in which there is no time. One—two —long hours! Plumed heads turned this way and that; weariness, ennui were written on every face—there was no relief. All must remain—the King on his throne—he and his Queen; the Royal Princes who, at least, were comfortable though bored; those lesser mortals on settees; and the 560 Deputies of the People, pressed as close as sardines in a box, with neither backs nor cushions nor arms—all must sit out these two long hours. Who took notice of the People's deputies? Who could imagine that their having been received in a King's bedchamber, looked upon as social pariahs in the beautiful Park of Versailles—a pleasure park—and crowded on hard benches for hours should have been among so many other wrongs to bring in the reign of these very People?

CHAPTER XIII

I

THE difficulties which had confronted the deputies from the first assembly of the Etats-Généraux were, seemingly, insurmountable. From the outset, the Nobles and the higher Clergy showed the old spirit of the Frondeurs. The two orders resented, and fiercely, any move which might trench on their prerogatives. After the opening ceremonies, the Nobles and the Clergy proceeded to hold themselves and their deliberations apart from the Tiers-Etat.

The Tiers-Etat resisted this autocratic ruling—this assumption of the continuance of exclusive power—with all the vehemence and passion of a power that recognizes its newborn force. All discussions—the latter Order declared—must henceforth be held in public.

Thus two parties were formed, at the very first. While the Nobles and the Clergy clung, with the tenacious obstinacy of age-long, inherited traditions, to their prerogatives, the Tiers-Etat—the people's deputies—had the loftier purposes of reformatory ideals. Leaders among the Tiers-Etat sprang up as though created over night. They made their views and voices heard. They were already marked men; Mirabeau—the giant towering in

163

intellect above all others—Bailly, Sieyès, Etienne, Camus, Le Chapelier, Malouet and others—these clever men saw clearly the route that must be followed. More and more they were affirmative in their insistent demand for a united Assembly which should be representative of the Nation—not one split up into groups. And more and more they proclaimed the pertinent fact that the deliberations, being the affairs of "the Nation," were of collective interest and must therefore be proposed and discussed collectively.

Necker wanted the right to raise loans and to restore financial credit and security. The Tiers-Etat—the Third Order—insisted on the voting being public—"par tête," the Three Orders, the Clergy, the Nobles and the Tiers, all voting and holding their deliberations in common. The Nobles and the Clergy, having already separated themselves from the lower Order, asserted their determination to examine separately the various motions proposed, and after such deliberation, a reunion of the Orders might convene for common discussion.

The two older Orders refused to yield to the pressure put upon them; nor would they heed Talleyrand's warnings as to the consequences of their obstinacy.

One of the more obscure members of the Tiers-Etat, one Legrand by name, deputy from Berry, had proposed, boldly, that the Etats-Généraux should proclaim itself as being the National Assembly—L'Assemblée Nationale; this act contained in itself the whole force of the Revolution. For by degrees the National Assembly, growing bolder and bolder, finally asserted its supreme rights to deny to the other two Orders their independence; the latter, it was voted, could neither legislate nor oppose the deliberations of the Assembly. The Tiers-Etat went still further. The King himself was not to be permitted to interfere with the National Assembly's decrees.

The People (the Third Order) again addressed an invitation to the Nobles and the Clergy to join the Assembly to concur in the great work which was to procure the regeneration of France. The Deputies next solemnly swore to what Bailly declared to be "An imposing and religious act." "You swear and promise to fulfil with fidelity the functions with which you are charged?" "We swear and promise" was the vow made. The die was cast. The King was henceforth only King in name. The People were supreme.

II

Talleyrand, at first, was entirely opposed to the reunion of the three Orders. The vehemence, the exaltation of the spirit in the Assembly, terrified him. He was essentially the man of order, of compromise, of moderate measures. The tide was too strong, however; he was swept along to a final decision.

With that clarity of vision so marked a characteristic of his genius, seeing the irreconcilable character of the Assembly, Talleyrand thereupon bent his energies to accomplish some form of compromise. In a brilliant discourse he supported the contention of the Tiers. Talleyrand's eloquence carried the day. This going over to the people by as highly placed an aristocrat as was the Bishop was the latter's first bold announcement of the stand he intended to take. It was at once understood as a revolutionary departure from the ranks of his class. The Tiers acclaimed his adherence with enthusiasm.

The Clergy, after Talleyrand's appeal, and also after

hearing the Duc d'Orléans' proposition to reunite the three Orders, went over to the Tiers-Etat. Headed by the Archbishops of Bordeaux, Aix and Vienne, the Bishops of Châtres, Coutances and Rodez, one hundred and forty of the Clergy took their seats beside the People's deputies. Further conciliatory measures having proved abortive, to induce the Nobles to join the Tiers-Etat, Mirabeau announced that Sieyès had an important motion to present. The latter declared that the Nobles having refused all overtures of conciliation, they, the Tiers-Etat, must now "sortir d'une trop longue inaction"—must end a too prolonged inaction.

By the force of Talleyrand's irrefutable arguments, the final reunion of the Three Orders was accomplished. Although later, in his own *Mémoires*, he was blandly to deny this notable act, such commentators on his life as Sir Henry Lytton Bulwer, as Michaud, a contemporary, and Ferrières all confirm the truth of his participation in the momentous accomplishment.

III

During the conflict between the Nobles and the Clergy, and the People's deputies, Talleyrand was greatly alarmed at the stand taken by the King and the court. The Queen, the Comte d'Artois and the de Polignacs had used all their powers of persuasion to provoke the King to reprisals. Louis XVI was not of that quality of mind which faces a crisis as brave soldiers face cannon. He commanded several regiments of Swiss and German nationality to protect him from the necessity of coming to any decision.

Talleyrand made a desperate venture. He decided to

warn the King of the abyss towards which his indolent policy was precipitating the monarchy. Realizing that the King did not perceive the gravity of the discussions and dissensions going on in the Etats-Généraux—discussions which resulted in their being merged into the National Assembly—Talleyrand made a request for a private audience.

The court was at Marly, in deep mourning for the little seven years' old Dauphin. The answer given was that the Comte d'Artois would receive Talleyrand and his two friends, the Vicomte de Noailles and the Comte d'Agoult.

Talleyrand had always shown a strong liking for the Comte d'Artois—"Je l'aimais" he confessed. The meeting took place at midnight in the Château at Marly. The King's brother was in bed. Talleyrand approached the bedside, and pled, in an impassioned and lengthy speech, for a more vigorous policy to "save the Country, the King, and the Monarchy."

What was chiefly needed, he asserted, was an immediate display of firm, resolute royal power. Talleyrand announced that he and his friends were ready to ensure such an action by their united efforts and devotion in forming a ministry. The hour, the scene—the desperate plight of both King and People—and all that hung on a mere word to be uttered—can history furnish many other as touching and as momentous situations?

Nothing came of this loyal attempt of Talleyrand's to infuse strength of will and energetic purpose in either the King or his entourage. "C'était un acte de force et la force, il n'y avait autour du roi personne pour la manier."[1]

---

[1] *Translation:* What was needed was a forcible act, and there was no one about the King to wield force.

Discouraged, disabused, Talleyrand, realizing that no strong ministry would be formed, said, "Sous peine de folie, il fallait penser à soi."[1]

IV

In these first years of the Assemblée National Talleyrand appeared to be allied heart and soul with the new movement. To better France, to better its government, to introduce measures to correct abuses, particularly to liberate the people from the tyranny of unjust taxation as well as from seignorial and ecclesiastic exactions—his participation in these momentous changes lent weight to the whole concerted movement. That his devotion to remedy certain abuses was wholly disinterested is perhaps doubtful. The course he pursued, after the bill was voted, of the confiscation of the Property of the Clergy, was colored by that subtle taint of double dealing which was to disgrace some of his later political actions.

Talleyrand's further participation in the onward movement of the plunge towards the revolutionary abyss, more and more revealed his purpose and inflexible design.

His purpose was to wield power. His political ambition was to found a constitutional monarchy. His design was to liberate himself in liberating others. The fetters—those hateful chains which bound him to a life and service everything in him resented as being an enforced slavery—he had every reason to believe might be severed. The ever-growing liberalizing spirit animating the deliberations and

---

[1] In April, 1814, when Baron Vitrolles, by Talleyrand's demand, went to invite the Comte d'Artois to come to Paris (after Napoleon's fall), he said: "Ask the Comte if he recollects the nocturnal interview." The Comte confirmed the story, remembering every detail.

decisions of the Assembly seemed to promise an ultimate emancipation.

Sorel alone[1] among historians considers

that the Revolution and its consequences carried Talleyrand outside of the sphere for which he was destined. . . . Everything under the older régime seemed to mark him as one destined to occupy the first place, in affairs of State. . . . A Bishop at thirty-five, he was born a Cardinal and a prime Minister.

Talleyrand's own conception of his destiny, as proved by his acts, is a direct denial of the famous historian's generalization. A close study of the uses to which he put the progressive stages of the development of liberty, under the edicts of the People's votes, proves incontestably his secret designs. He meant to be free.

His fixed goal was to be a secularized priest—if indeed his deeper design was not to obtain complete Papal emancipation from his vows. When Napoleon offered to make him Cardinal, Talleyrand refused the Hat.

V

Talleyrand and Mirabeau were to be brought daily into closer and closer intimacy during the earlier period of the Assembly. They met on a common basis of political belief and aspiration.

Mirabeau, it is recorded, was to inspire Talleyrand with the conviction that a constitutional monarchy was the true basis of the ideal government for their country. Mirabeau was enamored of English examples, of English orderly, conservative principles. Talleyrand's traditions, his sense of moderation, his longing to carry on French customs

[1] *L'Europe et La Révolution Française*, 8 vols. Albert Sorel. Plon Nourrit, Paris.

in a government purged of autocratic rule—such inherited tendencies and political aspirations met Mirabeau's views at almost every point. Both developed a passionate ardor in pursuance of a policy which should bring about an alliance with England. So far from seeing in her a "traditional enemy," England was France's "predestined ally." During his whole life and career, an alliance between the two countries was Talleyrand's constant and fixed hope. He carried on this his purpose to his seventy-sixth year—when, as Ambassador to England, he accomplished his lifelong design.

If Talleyrand, as orator, did not display Mirabeau's passion, nor rise to the heights of Mirabeau's unique talent, he had certain advantages which the latter did not possess. Mirabeau's oratory could sway an audience by its eruptive eloquence and its volcanic intensity. Talleyrand's imposing form, the perfection of his phrase, the science of his logic and the suavity of his manner would carry his hearers captive by virtue of other attractions. The contrast between the aristocratic aloofness of his bearing and the deep, grave, male voice never failed of its effect; the man of profound thought, of intense purpose was betrayed by that voice which did not seem to belong to the apparently indifferent *grand seigneur*.

VI

In the recorded speeches of Talleyrand as in his diplomatic letters under the Directoire, to Napoleon, those to Louis XVIII and to Louis-Philippe, the sententious phrases do not communicate vibration.[1] Everything is measured, is

[1] *Le Ministère de Talleyrand sous le Directoire.* Edited by G. Pallain. 1 vol., Plon Nourrit, Paris, 1891.

clearly, logically stated.   The language is as exquisite and
finished, in many of these letters, as is the cutting of a Greek
intaglio.   The admiration Talleyrand's written words excite
is that induced by one's delight in perfection.   Perfection,
like virtue unsoftened by charm, however, leaves one cold.

What the magnetism of voice, what the grace of gestures,
harmonious and expressive, may have added to the finished
phraseology of Talleyrand's speeches in the Assembly, can
only be inferred.   He took rank, at the outset, as among
the leading orators in that day of blazing oratorical splendor.
We may therefore presume the subtle charm of his unique
personality made vibrant words which on the printed page
fail to quicken a pulse beat.

His mature intellectual grasp of political situations;
the lucidity and power with which he could present revolutionary ideas and reforms, in his speeches to the Assembly;
the influence he wielded with the foremost leaders of the
period; his independence and daring in taking up positions
which he believed to be those which would further his own
advancement as well as his policy—this combination of
mental equipment allied to astute political foresight made
it possible for Talleyrand to forge his way to pre-eminent
leadership, at his first appearance in his new rôle.

If he did not possess the strength of soul, nor the *je ne sais
quoi* of the sublime in Richelieu's genius which lifts a man above
even the first rank, he [Talleyrand] displayed as great a breadth
and sense of development, all the suppleness, all the expediency,
all the fertility of the author of the Peace of the Pyrenees,

is Sorel's eloquent tribute to Talleyrand's talents.

Talleyrand, indeed, appears to have been wanting in the
first, last, and greatest essential of great oratory—that

magnetic attraction which can overleap the barriers of either
the footlights of the stage or the bars of a tribune. His
magnetism was of a more intimate order. To the hour of
his death he captivated as malicious a spirit as was Comte
Molé. His magic was chiefly effective in Council or in
the tête-à-tête.

Talleyrand's activities in furthering great reforms persisted. Nominated to the Direction of the Department of
Paris, the place left vacant by Mirabeau, he proposed a
scheme for the broadening and popularization of public
education. This latter was one of his hobbies, as had been
his hopes of establishing a National Bank, on a solid basis.
He was violently opposed to the reduction of interest on the
public debt and to the creation of "assignats"—of paper
currency.

Talleyrand confesses that in order to put these reforms
to a successful issue, he consulted numerous experts, among
them Lavoisier, Monge, Vieg, d'Azir, de La Harpe and
Condorcet. His work in the Assembly and later in the
Department of Paris was incessant, ranging over a wide
field.

It is in the bills Talleyrand proposed in the Assemblée
Générale; in the financial schemes he either originated,
proposed or seconded, that we see Talleyrand's statesmanlike qualities emerging to prove his talents along such lines.
His intimacy with Necker, with Gouverneur Morris, as well
as his intercourse with such men as Condorcet, de La Harpe,
Lavoisier and Mirabeau, were the fortunate fostering influences for the fuller development of his remarkable powers.

Some of his contemporaries saw in Talleyrand's career, a
close following of the policy advocated by the great Tribune.
It is certain Mirabeau's plan, in foreign politics, had been

to propose a great alliance with England. Whether he or Talleyrand had first seen that England was France's "natural ally" has not been made clear. That the necessity of an English alliance was Talleyrand's one unalterable conviction is proven by his using all his powers to accomplish the desired union, when, as Ambassador to London, he was still striving to accomplish a fusion of interests.

CHAPTER XIV

I

THE last public appearance of Talleyrand as Bishop was as dramatic in its setting as were to be the successive changes in his life.

The Bishop of Autun was nominated by the King to celebrate the Fête of the Fédération, at the Champ de Mars —then called Champ de la Confédération. The Fête was to commemorate the taking of the Bastille.

In the setting of this memorable ceremony, July 14th, 1790, there was an impressive grandeur united to an antique simplicity. There was also an uninvited guest, in the shape of rain, which added not a little to the peculiar aspect of the crowd.

In the midst of the Champ de Mars, the Altar of the Country—l'Autel de la Patrie—had been erected. Amphitheatres, vast in extent, had been built by the people, to seat the thousands assembled to witness the spectacle of their King who was to take, like the simplest citizen, the oath of fidelity to the law and to the nation.

The scenes which had preceded the Fête had been as remarkable as those which had been presented during the Middle Ages, in the building of certain of the great Cathedrals. In the year 1790, the people of Paris were fired, not

by religious zeal, but with the fervor of the patriotic cult of
fraternity.   The stir of a great movement—one holding
in its womb nascent forces as yet neither wholly visualized
nor fully ripened—stirred the thousands assembled at the
Champ de la Fédération.   All classes felt the contagion of a
passion which they could neither define nor analyze, yet deep
was the sentient quality of that inner intensity.   Paris—as
has all France—has experienced the exhilaration of other
more violent, more objectively visualized exaltations; but
never perhaps were thousands of French citizens moved by
as pure, elevated and consecrating a fervor as at the celebrat-
ing of the Mass of the Federation.   With this new cult of
a union of hearts, of ideals, of purpose, the world—their
world—was to be re-made.   The heavens were opening on a
new era; this day was to be its dawn.

II

In order to hasten the erection of the amphitheatre, all
Paris had turned laborer.   The vast semicircle must be
raised several feet.   The loose earth in the middle of the
arena not sufficing, the "Plaine de Grenelle" and its adjacent
territory were invaded.   Loads of soil were rushed to the
Champ de Mars.   Every available vehicle in Paris, every
barrow, cart or carriage was sent to the aid of those who
toiled from early morn to late at night, in this pious work
of a People's Festival.   Aristocrats sent their coronetted
coaches, as the humblest citizen contributed his wheel-
barrow—if only for a few hours—to help to erect this Temple
which was to consecrate King and People in united fraternity.

What a motley were the workers!   Young officers, in
their brilliant uniforms, pushing carts along, side by side

with ragged women of the people; from the adjacent convents came monks in their habits to dig spadesful of earth which they flung into barrows trundled by Chevaliers de Saint-Louis; and *filles de joie* could be seen carrying huge pailsful of soil, helped along by powdered lackeys, while ladies bearing the proudest titles, unused to the lightest labor, worked feverishly, with helpless hands, to fill buckets and baskets.

III

On the great day even unkind skies could not quench the enthusiasm of the Parisians, enamored of the new god Liberty. The rain descended pitilessly on the patient thousands who stood out the long hours, undaunted—though drenched. The numerous multi-colored umbrellas added a curious note to the festival, as did the rain-splashed vestments of some of the officiants.

The buzzing voices, the laughter, the songs that rang up from the mighty crowd,—many of those present having come from the most distant parts of France for the great day—these voices and shouts were suddenly stilled. In the midst of a silence that could be felt, so ominous, so sinister seemed the contrast between the clamorous gaiety of a moment before and this frigid welcome, the King and Queen entered the enclosure. The King mounted his throne; not a single voice acclaimed the Sovereign. The drums of the advancing guard broke, in welcome sounds, this portentous silence.

In front of the Ecole Militaire, a Tribune had been built, which extended into the arena in order that the royal family might be nearer to the altar. In this Tribune were seated Louis XVI, Marie-Antoinette, the Dauphin, the young

Lafayette taking the oath at the Champ de Mars

Fête de la Fédération

princess Marie-Thérèse, Madame Elizabeth and the Comte and Comtesse de Provence—the brother and sister-in-law of the King.

Oceans of ink have been needed by historians to describe the fate attending each and every one of those seated in the Tribune.   The King and Marie-Antoinette were to perish on the scaffold; the Dauphin's end, in his prison, has been shrouded in mystery; his young sister, Marie-Thérèse, the only member of her own family to survive the Terror, was to be, as Duchesse d'Angoulême, throughout her life, the most pathetic and the least sympathetic of royal princesses; Madame Elizabeth, the King's staunch, loyal little sister, rising to heroic heights in her devotion to the King and to Marie-Antoinette, must pay for her devotion to her family by mounting the steps of the scaffold; and Talleyrand, who was officiating as High Priest at this revolutionary Fête, was to seat the Comte de Provence, through his influence over Alexander, Czar of Russia, as Louis XVIII on the throne of France, twenty-four years later.

IV

The cortège of sixty Aumôniers, preceded by a detachment of the National Guard, issued from the Ecole Militaire, to be met by l'Evêque d'Autun.   Joined by the Aumônier Général of the Paris National Guard, followed by the sixty Aumôniers of Paris and others of certain districts and departments, the procession made its way to the altar.

All eyes were fixed on the Bishop of Autun.   Superb in his vestments, the aristocratic head held high beneath the towering mitre, the face was seen to be inscrutable— impassive in its immobility.

Before the assembled thousands, the Bishop must perform the difficult feat, with his twisted feet, of mounting the steps of the open air altar. The long silken robes mercifully hid what even his grace in limping could not wholly disguise. Having attained the altar's elevation, with a motion he could command, the Bishop swung the silver censer containing the Holy Water over the vast assemblage, over the guards, the priests, and, with a perceptible gesture of respect, he asperged the King and Queen.

Assisted by two abbés, he then proceeded to celebrate the Mass. His brother Archambaud de Talleyrand was distinctly seen below the altar, by interested spectators, a fact which he indignantly denied at Coblentz, when he joined the two Princes—the Comte de Provence and the Comte d'Artois—then in exile.

The rolling thunder of three hundred drums announced the conclusion of the Mass, and the Bishop next advanced to bless the banners of eighty-three departments.

The final climax of this strange ceremony was the taking of the oath of fidelity to the nation, to the law, and to the King. His Majesty rose, to attest, with a simple sincerity that should have been endurably convincing, his love and loyalty towards his people. The Queen, older, already saddened and chastened by the last years of her tragic experiences, had an impulse as natural as it was appealing.

When the crowd, whose eyes were fixed on the Queen, saw her lift the Dauphin in her arms, holding him before her, as though he were a symbol of the continuity of sovereignty, a thrill of emotion shook the soul of every beholder. Silence had followed the cheers for the King. Not a single voice had cried "Vive la Reine!" The Queen's maternal instinct, in presenting the Dauphin to the crowd, stirred the

primitive source of feeling.   Quick as a lighted torch, the
Latin soul responded.   Plaudits, cries, cheers rent the air.
Hands clutched hands, tears fell unheeded; faces were illumined by a sudden born love and joy.   Only a year later, a
smile from the Queen was to cause Talleyrand and La Rochefoucauld to lose their place in the Department of Paris.

Madame de Staël was present in the following year, at
the same ceremony.   The voices which now cried "Vive le
Roi!" sounded to her like a cry of farewell.

Profoundly moved, she already saw Louis XVI trans-
figured into a martyr. As he mounted the steps of the altar
to take the oath to the Constitution, some children surrounded him.   "One thought to look upon a sainted victim
voluntarily offering himself in sacrifice."

Madame de Staël never forgot the expression of the
Queen's face, with her eyes already dimmed with the tears
she had shed.   The splendor of her toilet and the dignity
of her bearing were in violent contrast to the cortège with
which she was surrounded. This was the last time that
Madame de Staël saw the King and Marie-Antoinette.

In reading this description of the famous author one is
reminded of that other, one of the most classic in literature:

It is now sixteen years since I saw the Queen of France, then the
Dauphiness of Versailles; and surely never lighted on this orb,
which she hardly seemed to touch, a more delightful vision.   I
saw her, just above the horizon, glittering like the morning star,
full of life and splendor and joy.   Oh! What a revolution!
And what a heart must I have to contemplate without emotion
that elevation and that fall.   Little did I dream, when she added
titles of veneration to those of enthusiastic, distant, respectful
love, that I should have lived to see such disasters fallen upon
her in a nation of gallant men and cavaliers.   I thought ten

thousand swords must have leaped from their scabbards to avenge even a look that threatened her with insult.[1]

Alas, where were the "ten thousand swords" which were to flash their glittering light in consecrated devotion to avenge their Queen's detractors? Marie-Antoinette must face the long, slow, tortured steps of martyrdom, on to her calvary, before she could count on a world of unborn generations to be her true defenders—her loyal advocates, and passionate lovers.

V

La Fayette, the hero of liberty, had been the first to take the federal oath.[2] He had crossed the space of ground between the throne and the altar, to lay the point of his sword on the altar table, as he repeated the words of the solemn oath. In a tumultuous chorus, the King and the people then united in swearing to the new covenant. After this moving scene, the Bishop intoned a Cantique. Twelve hundred musicians accompanied the religious song, while from the throats of thousands of the assembled multitude there rose up the chorus of a people who believed this dawn of the new day was to lead to the promised reign of freedom.

As though nature were in conspiracy with the ironic

---

[1] *Reflections on the French Revolution*, Burke.

[2] "La Fayette, who is commemorated by statues and street names in several American cities, scarcely pretended to care about America. His object in placing his sword at the disposal of the rebels, was frankly stated by him as being 'l'abaissement de L'Angleterre, l'avantage de ma patrie et le bonheur de l'humanité' ('The abasement of England, the advantage of my country, and the *happiness of humanity*')." *England.* 1 vol., p. 98. By William Ralph Inge. Ernest Benn, Ltd. London, 1926.

destiny of nations, sheets of rain continued to fall.   Swirling
winds swept the decorated altar of the people, the silken
robes of the Bishop and the laces of his acolytes.   The
relentless downpour drenched the figures of the thousands
seated in the open amphitheatres.   The grim Sisters Three
may well have bent upon the scene their pitiless, prophetic
glance—big as was the future with the monsters of cruelty
which the reign of "the people" was to bring forth, in place
of the "fair day of benignant peace."

The contention has been made that Talleyrand officiating
as Bishop at the Fête of the Federation, was to be considered
solely as being an officiant—that his saying Mass was entirely in consonance with his duties as Bishop.   His personal convictions, his unbelief, were his own affairs.   Monsieur Lacombe takes this post-revolutionary attitude.   A
Bishop, in those sceptical days, would have been of the
same indifferent morality as the deputy, who, querying in
1841 "What is the Chamber?" was answered: "A great Bazaar, where every one barters his conscience, or what passes
for his conscience, in exchange for a place or an office." [1]

Talleyrand announced himself as a philosopher, yet in
spite of his sceptical attitude, he knew the people of France;
the nation as a nation was Catholic.   In these agitated
times, the necessity was the more imperious of the restrain-
ing and uplifting influences of the Church.   Emotional, excitable, impressionable, the effect on the people of this Mass
of the Federation might have important results.   Such may
well have been the reasoning of the man who was so little
of a Bishop and so deep a thinker.   What spoils the logic
of such reasoning is the fact that as an anointed Bishop
Talleyrand, at least, should have observed the outward de-

[1] *The Modern World.*   A Survey of Historical Forces.   Vol. VII.

corum of his sacred office, and not have given history the
chance to record his reported irreverent aside—as he marched
up the steps of the altar—"Pourvu qu'on ne me fasse pas
sourire!" ("If only I am not tempted to smile!").

CHAPTER XV

I

IN the year 1790, Talleyrand considered his bondage to the Church had been severed. The final wrench, from his point of view, was due to a Bill introduced into the Assembly for the Civil Constitution of the Clergy.

Talleyrand's own part in the passing of the Bill cannot be said to have been a glorious one. Known now, acknowledged and admired as one of the most eloquent speakers in the Assembly, the Bishop had been noticeably silent during the protracted discussions relating to this schismatic act, which meant the overturning of the whole organization of the Church, as the monarchical rule over the State had also seen its powers and privileges taken over, one by one, by the Constitution and transferred to the people. The priority of the Pope, the divine right of the Holy Father to exercise control over fifty-three French bishops: His right of confirmation, His supreme power, in a word—that power inherent in the sovereignty of the Pontiff—was voted away. Popular election was to arrogate to itself all control over spiritual matters.

Such a revolutionary measure could not but develop passionate protest. The Pope thundered anathemas. The more aristocratic order in the episcopate fought for the maintenance of what was left of pontifical sovereignty, with warlike obstinacy and noble courage. But the Bill was passed on the 24th of August, 1790. The King must perforce accept the infamous law, his sanction being necessary—mere shadow of royalty that he was!—to the legality of the Bill.

The Bishop of Autun broke the significant silence he had preserved in the Assembly the very day after the royal sanction had been obtained. His oath was among the first to be uttered:—"I swear, with uplifted hand, scrupulously to fulfill my functions, to be faithful to the law, the nation and the King, to maintain the Constitution, and notably the decree relating to the Civil Constitution of the clergy."[1] "Notably!"—the word is pregnant with meaning.

II

The execution of the new law immediately brought about peculiar and anomalous situations. The curés, priests and bishops who were to be ordained according to the secular ruling—who was to consecrate them? A curé, l'Abbé Expilly, a deputy of the Assembly, and a certain Marolles who had been Bishop of l'Aisne—these ecclesiastics found a serious difficulty confronting them. Large groups of bishops and the lesser clergy had bravely stood out against the iniquitous law. Yet neither the abbé nor the newly elected bishop could officiate unless they could be confirmed. To whom could they apply, save to the Bishop of Autun? The latter, it is true, were he thus to usurp the sovereign rights of the Holy Father, had no right whatever, even from

[1] In taking the oath before the King, Louis Philippe, in 1832, prior to his departure for London as Ambassador to the Court of Saint James, Talleyrand whispered,— "It is the thirteenth—Sire!"

the point of view of the newly enforced law, to consecrate priests in Paris, since, nominally, his diocese was in distant Autun.[1]

Regarding himself now as a purely Constitutionalist priest, Talleyrand brushed all feebler obstacles aside. Abbé Expilly and Bishop Marolles were consecrated by him in the church of the Oratory, in Paris.

In those days of incessant change, when new laws made all conditions of life different in the afternoon from what they had been in the morning, La Fayette, on his white charger, leading the troops supposed to control all turbulent elements, was certain to make an impressive appearance, at critical moments.

The services at the Oratory had not passed without La Fayette taking up his customary position. The members of the community had left their house, refusing to be accessory to what, they considered, was a sacrilegious, an infamous act. General La Fayette promptly appeared to take control. His troops were placed within the Oratory. There had been, however, none of the violence feared; and the members of that strange community of Oratorians, "a body where everyone obeys and no one commands," could return, unmolested, to their house, after the ceremony

---

[1] Popular and religious feeling had been at its height during the shock of the passing of the Bill of the Civic Constitution of the Clergy. Some of the clergy who had refused to take the oath as Constitutionalist priests had threatened the Bishop of Autun's life. Talleyrand had been greatly alarmed; he had hidden himself near a church where he was to consecrate two priests; if found, he felt assured of what fate would be meted out to him. He would surely be assassinated. Gouverneur Morris records: "The Bishop of Autun is horribly frightened for his life."

The Bishop had gone to the Louvre to leave in "a black envelope" his Will, making Madame de Flahaut his heir. In consequence of some things he had dropped in conversation, she concluded that he was determined to destroy himself, and therefore spent the night "in great agitation and in tears." Talleyrand had escaped, however, the fury of the outraged priests. (*Diary and Letters of Gouverneur Morris,* Vol. I, p. 385.)

which they considered had been a scandalous desecration of their home.

III

Of the fifty-three French bishops scattered throughout their dioceses in France, only three had followed the Bishop of Autun's open revolt against the rule of Rome. The Bishop of Orléans accepted the civic powers granted by the new bill, resigned his Bishopric and married; de Brienne, newly installed at Toulouse, refused the Cardinal's Hat and was swept into the revolutionary whirlpool; and de Savigny, Bishop of Viviers, was the one who lived to repent; he committed extravagant actions, once freed from Papal obedience. In later years he was to weep, as he made his contrite submission to the Church's authority, after having enjoyed certain carnal delights during his temporary freedom.

Meanwhile, the Pope had taken a stand. His Holiness decreed that those "who had dared to proceed to the consecration of the Constitutionalists" must be immediately deprived of all jurisdiction. Also, "all who had taken the oath of fidelity to the Civil Rights Bill of the clergy must retract, or be likewise despoiled of all their privileges within twenty-four hours."

In the end, Talleyrand found himself excommunicated, among the other priests who had adhered to the Constitution.[1]

This act of Roman Papal power proved to be the determining factor in Talleyrand's subsequent career.

Excommunicated—Talleyrand felt that his chains were

[1] *Talleyrand, Evêque d'Autun,* Bernard de Lacombe, Perrin et Cie., 1903.

practically severed. He considered himself as being secularized. This was Talleyrand's complacent version of Rome's action. It was sustained, however, by a caustic phrase in the Pope's letter. "Nothing more desirable can come to pass than to see him renounce the Church himself, he who, for so many reasons, merits to be thrust out."[1] The language is clear enough.

In March, 1792, the Pope hesitated before launching his full and final decree. He pleaded with the "son whom the Church had carried in its bosom": the aged Pius VI recalled to Talleyrand, whom he singled out as being the "Author of the Schism" (the revocation of the power of Rome over the French clergy), "the inexhaustible patience of the Church";—and finally accorded sixty days for a complete retraction of the sins and errors committed by Talleyrand and other Constitutionalist priests against the Church. The Pope, in these conciliatory measures, proved himself the true Christian, the true father of his "sons" that he was.

The sixty days passed. The bull of excommunication found Talleyrand already out of France. In 1792 he had gone to England—to escape the horrors of the Terror.

The *sécularisation en droit* did not come from Rome until 1802, under Pius VII, when Talleyrand's remarkable work under Napoleon, in the Concordat, won him his long-awaited release—but not absolution from his vows of celibacy as an anointed Bishop.

Talleyrand, though still Bishop in name, was no longer Bishop of Autun. The tie had been rudely severed when Talleyrand wrote to his diocese suggesting that his clergy follow the example set by the sixty ecclesiastics and by their

[1] *Epistolata E. S. R. E.*, 4 des Nones d'Avril, 1791.

Bishop who had taken the oath to the Assembly, as Constitutionalist priests. Passionately Catholic, Roman since Cæsar, in their tenacious loyalty the canons and clergy of Autun with "apostolic boldness" indignantly spurned their Bishop's revolutionary demand. Their courageous attitude excited a determined hostility in the Assembly, as it won a commendatory eulogium from Rome.

Rome's sentence of condemnation relieved Talleyrand from further responsibility—did he indeed feel that any still existed—as executive Bishop of Autun. The tie—one which had held him to Autun for so short a time, yet one which was to take such struggles to break—this tie of officiating as Bishop was ended.

The political emissary as Minister (sub-rosa) to England; the Minister of Foreign Affairs under the Directory and under Napoleon; the negotiator, the subtle, brilliant statesman who outwitted Metternich and Castlereagh in the Council of Vienna; and the aged Ambassador to England, carrying to completion his never abandoned plan for an alliance with England—this the Talleyrand of statecraft and of commanding power had started on his long triumphant career.

IV

Talleyrand is reported to have celebrated his severance from the Church with a cynical levity which was to earn him, in later historic periods, reprobation as severe as has been meted out to some of his baser acts.

He wrote to his intimate friend,[1] the Duc de Biron:

---

[1] "The following letter has been attributed to several persons—even to Louis XVI." *Talleyrand, Evêque d'Autun*, p. 273. Lacombe. The wording of the letter has the ring of certain of Talleyrand's lighter letters: hence I quote it. (Author.)

TALLEYRAND-PÉRIGORD

From a miniature by Augustin, painted when he was named Minister
of Foreign Affairs under the Directory

"Dear Biron—You know of the letter of excommunication, come and console me, and sup with me. Every one will refuse to give me bread and water, therefore to-night we shall only have frozen meats and frappé wines."

During what remained of the year 1791, Talleyrand was to be buffeted by the waves of circumstance. With the death of the Archbishop of Paris, he was to hear of a project to offer him the vacant post, as a Constitutional prelate. Having considered that the chain of obedience to Rome had been snapped by the Pope's bull of excommunication, Talleyrand could see in this new post only the forging of new fetters to the life he felt was now, fortuitously, behind him.

On the offer being actually made, he promptly declined the honor. This refusal to serve in the highest capacity within the spiritual province of the new Constitutionalist government was the last connection of a purely personal nature Talleyrand was to have with the Roman Catholic Church until the hour of his death—at the age of eighty-four.

On learning of this proposed elevation to the throne of the Archbishopric of Paris, Talleyrand was to make a somewhat singular public confession. The necessity he felt, urging him to such an avowal, was occasioned by an accusation launched against him by his enemies. It was stated that it was he himself who had intrigued to be called to the vacant throne of the Archbishopric of Paris.

He was, also, held up to public condemnation as being a desperate gambler. Scandalous stories were circulated relating to the immense sums won by him, in the lowest gambling dens of Paris.

To these venomous aspersions, Talleyrand, pricked to the quick, made the following statement:

I have just read in the *Journal de Paris* that you have designated me for the Archbishopric of Paris . . . some electors have announced to me their wishes, and I consider I must publish my reply.

No—I shall not accept the honor my fellow citizens deign to accord to me.[1]

And after stating, in dignified fashion, his views on the subject of personal liberty, he adds:

It has been spread abroad, together with the announcement of the nomination to the Bishopric, that I had won seven hundred thousand francs at play. . . . Here is the exact truth. In the space of two months, I won, not in public gambling houses, but in society or at the "Club des Echecs" . . . about thirty thousand francs. I establish the exactitude of these facts without attempting to justify them. The taste for gambling has spread in an aggravated form throughout society. I have never liked it, and I therefore the more reproach myself not to have offered sufficient resistance to this seduction.[2]

This statement, which Talleyrand felt incumbent upon him to make public, is in startling contrast to English customs relating to the inviolability of personal liberty. It would have been considered a gross breach of good manners for Fox to have written such a document as Talleyrand asked all Paris—all the world to read. Fox's vice of gam-

---

[1] *Lettres vaux Auteurs de la Chronique de Paris*, 8 Février, 1791, publiée par le *Moniteur Universel*. T. VII, p. 325.

Talleyrand, Evêque d'Autun, Lacombe, p. 257. Perrin et Cie., 1903.

[2] Talleyrand, according to M. Pichot, had three methods of increasing his fortune: Gambling, agiotage, and the gifts or *douceurs* which he received from the great or smaller dignitaries or dynasties whom he served. Talleyrand himself estimated he had received six millions of francs as *donations* from the great powers he had served. His speculations on the Bourse tempted his confession; counselling a friend, he said: "Don't play—I've always played on certain and authoritative tips and it has cost me how many millions!" (*Souvenirs Intimes sur de Talleyrand par Amédeé Pichot*. E. Denter Edition, 1870.)

bling was as violently attacked, in private, by his political enemies, as was Talleyrand's passion for high play. But a man's private life is sacred in England. Talleyrand, it is true, was exceptionally placed, being in the revolutionary swirl of changes. His prominence in the Assembly, his strained position as an excommunicated Bishop, who nevertheless was proposed for the highest seat in the Episcopacy, as a Constitutionalist Archbishop, counted for much in his determination to end the scandalous stories afloat.

In spite of the libels published and the reprobation which Talleyrand's private life had evoked, among his friends and political adherents he was still considered to be the ablest of the Constitutional leaders. Were a difficult situation to arise with any foreign power, it was Talleyrand who was to be chosen to present France's point of view, and to further her interests.

CHAPTER XVI

I

ONE must go to Gouverneur Morris' Diary for some side lights thrown on the screen of the more intimate social and amorous life which Talleyrand led at this time. In these pages we see reflected, as in a mirror, the daily meetings between Talleyrand and his mistress—Madame de Flahaut—Madame de Staël and her friend Comte de Narbonne.

On Talleyrand's return from Autun to Paris, he had formed a friendship with this distinguished American. Morris' financial talents, political acumen and business capacity were to be of benefit to him.

Gouverneur Morris, born in 1752, was two years Talleyrand's senior. It is difficult to imagine two men more dissimilar in character, in their mental and moral training, and in their conception of life. Certain traits they had in common. Both had the aristocrat's social distinction, and both had had severe mental discipline. Talleyrand had had a far wider outlook and a more extensive social experience than had the American. But Gouverneur Morris, as a force, was more finely tempered, of nobler fibre, and was possessed of loftier ideals of conduct. Morris was a precursor of the many-sided, of the more gifted modern Ameri-

GOUVERNEUR MORRIS AS A YOUNG MAN

can men of affairs. Trained as a lawyer, he became a thoroughly practical and successful man of business. Before coming to Paris, he had been a banker, a financier, a soldier, and was one among the framers of the American Constitution. Here were talents and capacities proven, and of a wide range.

A series of anonymous papers on the mischievous effects of the proposal, by the Assembly of New York, to issue paper money, had made Gouverneur Morris' reputation as a financial expert. "The extent of his knowledge of this exceedingly difficult subject" (finance) "surprised his fellow workers, and when the report was read before a large audience of interested persons, he spoke with remarkable force and eloquence." This instant recognition of Morris' talents as an expert in finance was rendered him at the age of twenty-three. As his own, and as Alexander Hamilton's meteoric career proved, there was, or there seemed to be, a super-element of vitalizing power, a Hellenic vibration in the air, at that end of the eighteenth century, which gave to youth the wisdom and the profound, as well as the exact, modes of thought which mature experience alone is supposed to develop.

Gouverneur Morris' unusual capacity, the diversity of his talents, his eloquence, his persuasive manners and his diligence were to prove to be of incalculable service to the Federal cause. At Valley Forge, where the American army, during that terrible winter of 1778, was reduced to starvation rations, when the soldiers were suffering from bitter cold with their uniforms in rags, and when desertions were assuming alarming figures, we find Morris suggesting a practical plan for raising the necessary funds to feed and to clothe the army, as well as to reorganize the forces. The friendship between

General George Washington and Gouverneur Morris, which lasted many years, was then established. Morris' correspondence with the President during the years of his residence in Paris, from 1788 to 1794, and when journeying to England and in European countries, proves his rare insight and political sagacity. The value President Washington attached to Gouverneur Morris' opinion told heavily against Talleyrand, during the latter's stay in America.

II

The important financial and commercial relations between France and America could never have been possible, during the year 1789, unless such relations, at that critical period of America's development, had been in the hands of so accomplished and skilled a financier as was Morris. His friend and cousin—Robert Morris—had been made Superintendent of Finance by the American Congress. Gouverneur Morris was named Assistant Superintendent. Together with his superior, he established the first bank in America. It was called "The Bank of North America." It started its career with the modest sum of four hundred thousand dollars. Morris wrote long afterwards to a friend: "The first bank in America was *planned* by your humble servant."[1]

The second important national debt America owes to Morris' fertile genius was his project for the coinage of the new government. The birth of the "almighty dollar" was actually due to Morris; and the plan for our common coinage, as it is in use to-day, was largely of his devising.

That versatility which was so marked a feature in the

---

[1] *Diary and Letters of Gouverneur Morris,* edited by Anne Cary Morris. 2 vols. Charles Scribner's Sons, 1888.

young men of this great age was shown by Morris' participation in forming the Federal Constitution. His part in the making of that remarkable document was of inestimable benefit.

He vigorously opposed slavery, denounced the slave system, and moved to insert the word "free" before "inhabitants." His denunciation of the slave system was as vigorous as it was prophetic: he termed it "a nefarious system, the curse of Heaven on all the states in which it prevails."

III

Morris was barely twenty when, on completing his studies, he wrote to a friend how eager was his longing "To rub off in the gay circles of foreign life some of the many barbarisms which characterize a provincial education." This was the hope of the future wit and of the accomplished man of the world whose "many barbarisms" were never discovered by the great world of Paris.

Morris' ardent desire to start on a foreign tour was not an unusual aspiration among the more highly gifted young men of this tumultuous period of our country.

The umbilical cord with English traditions, with English literature, and with English life was not as yet completely broken. The stately dignity in manners, the elegance in conversational and epistolary intercourse, as well as the care in dress among the more highly placed Americans were all evidences of the still surviving influences of the Mother Country. The love of the classics, in literature, was a pertinent sign of the ever-continuing traditions in the educational equipment of gentlemen. The practices of Oxford and Cambridge had been transmitted to our own

Queen Anne's College and to William and Mary's College. These colleges had been modelled on the great English Universities.

Morris must wait until the month of November, 1788— seventeen years later than the planning of his youthful project—to depart "from Philadelphia for the kingdom of France," as he wrote to General Washington.

The journey occupied forty days. By the third of February, 1789, Morris was installed in Paris at the Hotel Richelieu, in the rue de Richelieu. In a letter to the Marquis de Moustier, who had been sent as Minister from France to America in 1787, Morris writes: "The more I see of Paris the more sensible I am of your sacrifice in leaving it to traverse a great ocean and establish yourself with a people as yet too new to relish that society which forms here the delight of life."

Morris' purpose in establishing himself in Paris for a term of years had a very definite object. During his connection with his friend and cousin, Robert Morris, both of these eminently practical men had interested themselves in serious business ventures. American tobacco was largely exported to France. Tobacco as well as flour contracts had been entered into by the Morrises. It was felt that a competent business agent should be in France to look after these contracts, as well as to enlarge the business. Gouverneur Morris, being young—but thirty-seven years of age—unmarried, speaking unusually good French for a foreigner, was considered to be the ideal representative.

Morris' commercial, financial, diplomatic and social successes in Paris were largely due to his knowledge of the French language. His clever biographer, Anne Cary Morris, relates that when quite a child he had been placed in the family of a French gentleman, Monsieur Tetar, living in New Rochelle. Once fully launched in French society, Morris complained of "not being perfectly master of French." The length of time which had elapsed since the days when he had spoken no other language, in Monsieur Tetar's household, had naturally diminished Morris' ease in his use of the delicate idiom. He was, however, to reconquer his former fluency and accuracy, and to find no difficulty whatever in using this foreign tongue as a vehicle for his caustic wit and his remarkable conversational versatility.

Various letters to French nobles and to some of the leading public men, which Morris had presented on his arrival, secured his immediate entrance into the most exclusive social and political circles. Strangers were the great novelty in Paris, at this time. They were received with cordiality and even with enthusiasm. Gouverneur Morris' reputation as a financier and as an officer in the War of Independence, soon to be known too as a brilliant and original thinker, added to his aristocratic bearing and handsome face, secured him an immediate personal triumph.

It was into the delectable enjoyment of this "society which forms the delight of life" that Morris was to step at once, in Paris, and almost at a bound, from the still somewhat primitive new United States, into the most highly finished, the most complex, and the most alluringly seductive of social worlds. Talleyrand has phrased its charm in the memorable words:

I have witnessed imperial magnificence; I see each day the establishment of new and rising fortunes; nothing has equalled, in my eyes, the splendors of Paris in the years which ran between the Peace of 1783 up to 1789.

IV

Talleyrand and Gouverneur Morris were to meet almost daily in several of the more famous houses in Paris. The society in this stirring period, preceding the actual horrors of the Revolution, still retained the essential charm which distinguished the salons under the reign of Louis XV.

New elements were introduced, certain radical changes were noticeable, for with these turbulent times the structure which we know as modern life was to see its foundations laid. The Revolution was the cradle rocked by the Furies which nursed the periods succeeding it to full stature.

The life lived in the French salons during the eventful days of this vanishing world was as important an element in one's existence as were any of one's occupations or duties. These reunions were the forerunners of the modern clubs of our day. Men went, in Talleyrand's time, to the salons to hear all the news, to push one's political fortunes, to win or to lose a year's income at play, or to meet the love of the moment or of a lifetime.

Morris found that most of the apartments in the great Hôtels had large wide rooms with boudoirs adjoining, for intimate *causeries*. In winter, there were the big fireplaces blazing with huge logs; at night, thick silken curtains or rich brocaded ones were closely drawn, and on the powdered heads and rouged complexions of the guests hundreds of candles shed a softened light.

After a stormy session in the Assembly, and the long wearisome drive from Versailles over the rough cobble-stone roads; after Talleyrand had had a heated discussion with Mirabeau—for a reconciliation had been effected between the two leaders; after the hours of gaiety in the Palais

Royal, where Talleyrand's enemies maliciously asserted that he was planning, together with the Duc d'Orléans, some of the various plots which were to precipitate the horrors of the dread tragedies of the Revolution—what delectable hours of balm, of renewed vitality awaited one in these beautiful rooms!

V

The recognized social and intellectual centre of all the more celebrated men of the day was the salon of Madame de Staël. She received as often in the house of her father, Minister Necker, as in the Swedish Embassy, in the rue du Bac. Her husband, the Baron de Staël, was then the Swedish Ambassador.

In the attractions of another salon, Talleyrand and Morris were to find a more magnetic charm, for various reasons, than in the celebrated gatherings in the rue du Bac.

There was a different atmosphere in Madame de Flahaut's more modest salon in the Louvre, to the one breathed in the "chambre ardente," as Madame de Staël's more intimate salon was called. The branch of the poplar tree, whose agitated leaves trembled, as she turned and twisted the twig in her beautiful hands, was symbolic of the intellectual tumult precipitated by the prodigious mental vigor of the most brilliant woman of her age. Madame de Staël confessed that the quivering of the leaves was a necessary accompaniment to her thoughts. Above the perpetually active branch there played the fire of her superb eyes —eyes reflecting every phase of the ardor, the passion and the enthusiasm of the one who was called "the Bacchante of the Revolution." Neither exquisitely shaped hands, nor the finest eyes in Europe, nor eloquence, nor genius could draw away either Talleyrand or Morris from the fireside of a lovelier feminine type, of a woman endowed with charm, with wit, and with beauty. Comte de Flahaut, in his wife's salon, appears to have interfered as little with the scenes played therein as though—unlike Shakespearian apparitions—he was conscious of the inefficacy of his ghost-like appearance.

VI

The comedy played so unconsciously, by the three principal actors in Madame de Flahaut's rooms, for the delectation of amused later readers, was replete with the elements essential to the true form of dramatic art. The first principle of this art demands that the personages shall be live human beings and the passions experienced be real. These conditions were fulfilled. There was love in various forms; love (or passion—in those days one and the same) dawning; love in distress; love waning: as there were jealousy, mutual distrust, and self-interest—the latter undisguised and unabashed. Politics played their rôle, and affairs, financial and commercial, were ever recurring *motifs* in the intricate action, until in the end these became the leading ones, as the love notes were sung more and more *pianissimo*.

Not the least among the comic elements in the various scenes, was the lamentable fact that both of the masculine rôles should have been played by men who were lame. Gouverneur Morris had his wooden leg.[1] If the Bishop of Autun "limped with grace" Gouverneur Morris stumped with vigor.

[1] Morris had lost his leg in an accident. While attempting to stop a pair of runaway horses, he was thrown from the carriage. The fall injured his ankle and the bones of his left leg were fractured. In that day of crude surgery, amputation was affirmed to be the only means of saving his life.

Madame de Flahaut had been Talleyrand's mistress for years long enough for the proof of the intimacy to have grown to boyhood. Her son, Charles de Flahaut, her only child, was born on the 17th of April, 1785. At the time this part of Morris' Memoirs was written, he was between four and five years of age.

Gouverneur Morris and Talleyrand were to meet almost daily in Madame de Flahaut's rooms in the old Louvre. This privilege accorded to the de Flahauts, of their residence in the Louvre, was one of those royal favors granted to indigent nobles who had certain charges at Court. The Comte de Flahaut de la Billarderie, the day after his marriage to Adelaïde-Marie-Emilie Filleul, had received the charge of the *Intendant des Jardins du Roi* (Superintendent of the Gardens of the King), and with this post the privilege of a residence in the Louvre Palace. These gifts came through the usual avenues—through court favor. Madame de Flahaut's elder sister had married the Marquis de Marigny, the brother of Madame de Polignac. Hence the nomination of de Flahaut, through the Queen's intercession, who could refuse her favorite none of her demands for her insatiable family. [1]

The intimate intercourse between Talleyrand and Morris, carried on in Madame de Flahaut's salon, was sufficiently diversified in its interests, as he and Talleyrand were interested in many of the same financial schemes. Projects for commercial treaties with America, and plans

---

[1] Many of the great Palaces were filled with such families. When the Revolutionary Terrorists swept through the upper rooms of Versailles and of the Louvre, and other royal domains, they found the apartments as packed with lodgers as though they had been rabbit warrens. Two of those who lived in the old Louvre were not among the dispossessed. Adèle de Flahaut was to flee for her life in 1792. The knife of the guillotine was to make her a widow in 1793.

of Talleyrand for speculation in the American debt were curiously interspersed with intimate domestic details which prove how sophisticated and conventional, in spite of our modernism, our own world has become.

Morris had met Madame de Flahaut at the house of Madame Cabanis, at Versailles. Morris, apparently, had had other meetings with Madame de Flahaut than the one first recorded in his diary on April 3rd, 1789. The weather seemed in conspiracy with fate to render the first rendezvous noted, a disappointment. Morris states:

"I go, April 3rd, to keep an engagement with Madame de Flahaut, to see the paintings, statues, etc., of the Louvre. She is in bed and her brother-in-law is sitting with her. So it appears she has, as she said, forgotten her engagement with me." They meet finally in the Louvre. But Morris confesses that though he returns to her salon "I take my leave and thus a scene, which my imagination had painted very well, turned out good for nothing." Morris, apparently, had conjured up visions of an easy conquest.

VII

Morris continued to find the Louvre salon more and more attractive. On the evening of April 20th, he noted:

I am taking tea in Madame de Flahaut's salon, the Marquis de Boursac comes in fresh from the elections. . . . Madame de Flahaut goes to make her visit of condolence to Madame Gilbert, whose husband, a Neckerist, is dismissed from his place.

Promise to return . . . go to Madame de Flahaut's. Meet the Bishop of Autun. Talk more politics than I ought . . . I go to the Louvre and get Madame de Flahaut to correct my letter to Necker.

Morris had been engaged for some time in forming plans

of finance for France, one of which he had presented to Malesherbes, who seemed pleased with it, as was Thomas Jefferson, then American Minister to France.

By October twenty-eighth the relations between Madame de Flahaut and Gouverneur Morris had reached the state of intimacy.

Go to the Louvre. The Bishop is with Madame; he asked a dinner with her son, who is arrived this day. Quite a family party. He goes away, and I tell her that I am very sorry to have interrupted such a scene. She dwells much upon her child, and weeps plenteously. I wipe away the tears as they fall. This silent attention brings forth professions of endless affection. She means every word of it now, but nothing here below can last forever.

We go together to Madame de Laborde's and make a short visit, the child being in company.

The scene is gem-like in its precision. The light thrown upon the facts that a lover, his mistress, and the innocent offspring are referred to as naturally as though the parties had been blessed by the Church which still claimed Talleyrand as a celibate, is as significant of the easy morals of the day, as is Gouverneur Morris' facile acceptance of eighteenth century amatory relationships. Morris stumping along with his wooden leg; the little lad, presumably, trotting by his side; Madame de Flahaut's tears dried, with her son known to be the son of her lover, all three bent on a visit to a friend, present a picture unique in its simplicity and candor.

VIII

Although Madame de Flahaut asserted she "abhorred politics," and began a novel which afterwards became famous, every fluctuating tremor of opinion, every political move in the General Assembly had its repercussion in the Louvre salon. Morris frankly states he goes there "to hear what is going on."

Talleyrand, as deputy, had his finger on the pulse of that agitated day. The question, for example, of bread—of the feeding of Paris—was becoming more and more the one dominant state problem. Morris, with his commercial interests at stake, wished ardently that Necker would come to an agreement about the terms for "the arrival of flour and for the payment." He states, in his diary:

The Bishop thinks the Assemblée will not meddle. I am sure they will not, because they act only from fear, and will not risk the consequences of being responsible for the subsistence of this city. . . . He says that nobody but M. Necker can sustain the famine and bankruptcy which appear unavoidable. Lafayette asks if he does not think it would be right to prepare a ministry for some months hence. The Bishop thinks it would. They discuss a little character, and, as *par hazard*, Lafayette asks whether Mirabeau's influence in the Assembly is great, the Bishop replies that it is not enormous.

At coming away, the Bishop observes to me that Lafayette has no fixed plan, which is true. With a great deal of the *intrigant* in his character he must be used by others because he has not talent enough to make use of them. . . . A small company at the Louvre; we sup and leave them together, at play. The Bishop d'Autun says the committee have been engaged all this evening with M. Necker in considering how one hundred and thirty millions of paper can be issued with the least inconvenience. The affairs are in a sad condition indeed, and I think they will not mend speedily.

Financial affairs were in so pitiable a state that Necker resorted to the subterfuge of calling upon popular contributions to swell the empty Exchequer.

On the 17th of December the report of the ten commissioners was presented to the Assembly. On the 19th
Morris says:

The Bishop just came from the Assembly. Says they have
passed tumultuously the plan of the committee grounded on the
plan of M. Necker. He seems much dissatisfied with it.

Necker's plan adopted, the Caisse Patriotique was open, and
into it flowed every imaginable thing, of great or small value—
precious stones, articles of jewellery, and "mouches" boxes. The
latter ornaments, some time since, had been abandoned by the ladies. Great ladies sacrificed their jewels, and adorned themselves
with ribbons instead. Madame de Genlis and Madame de Bulard,
to give emphasis to their patriotic feelings, wore pieces of the
stone of the Bastille set in laurel leaves, pinned on with a forest of
ribbons of the three colors. The King and Queen contributed
their share, in gold plates and dishes of great value. A spasm
of generosity possessed all ranks, and rivalled the soldier fever
which for months had been strong, and had filled the streets of
Paris with the most fantastic costumes imaginable, of which
red, green, and gold epaulets were a brilliant feature.

In considering a plan for a national bank proposed by
M. Necker, "one of them took it into his head to move that
every member should give his silver buckles, which was
agreed to at once, and the honorable member laid his upon
the table, after which the business went on again." Morris
goes on to state:

Go to the Louvre where the Bishop d'Autun is waiting for me.
Explain to him a plan which I communicated to Madame for
purchasing facilities in America, in which she is to be interested.
He tells me that, if the advantage is great and the operation
solid, he thinks he can obtain two millions. We are to talk
further. He observes on what I say that the American debt

would furnish a good speculation. I tell him that I am already
engaged in it; that it is so large an object that the junction of
many capitalists became necessary.

Madame being ill, I find her with her feet in warm water, and
when she is about to take them out, one of her women being
engaged in that operation, the Bishop employed himself in
warming her bed with a warming-pan, and I look on. It is curious
enough to see a reverend Father of the Church engaged in this
pious operation.

This is not the only surprise which is to amaze what
remains of provincialism in Morris.

Madame being ill goes into the bath, and when placed therein
sends for me. It is a strange place to receive a visit, but there is
milk mixed with the water, making it opaque. She tells me that
it is usual to receive in the bath, and I suppose it is, for otherwise
I should have been the last person to whom it would have been
permitted. . . .

After dinner (January 13th) go to the Louvre, and find
Madame de Flahaut in deep distress at the idea of leaving Paris.
. . . The Bishop arrives. He has had me elected into a society
here which as yet, I do not exactly know the meaning of; it is,
however, a select one. He expects to get a million for the speculation proposed to Madame.

There are certain scenes of jealousy between the two
habitués of Madame de Flahaut's salon which prove that
Talleyrand had not lost, as yet, the sensibilities of a lover.
"Go to the Louvre. Immediately after my arrival the
Bishop comes in, who seems not at all content to find me
here." Nevertheless, after a discussion about the "million"
Talleyrand had hoped to raise for speculation in the Ameri-
can debt—a plan which proves abortive—he leaves the
American in possession.

A little later on, it is Morris' turn to find his place partly taken as constant admirer, consoler and friend. On his return from a visit to England, he made an unpleasant discovery:

Lord Wycombe *est enniché ici.* I sit beside my fickle friend Madame de Flahaut, and as, luckily, the music always makes me grave, I keep still in the sentimental style.

The bloom, nevertheless, was off the delicate blossom of the relationship. Morris still haunted the house: and the Bishop was, as ever, a daily visitor. But to him also, there seems to have come the frost of indifference. "Visit Madame de Flahaut. It seems to me from appearances, that Lord Wycombe is expected." . . . "Lord Wycombe is established here in the place which I occupied formerly . . . she is a coquette and very fickle."

Like the traditional moth, however, Morris fluttered about the flame, and Talleyrand was not, as yet, wholly cured of his love-malady. "Go to the Louvre, and find Madame has quarrelled with the Bishop, who is jealous of me. In consequence of the quarrel, she is very ill, and surrounded by friends and servants." The quarrel was apparently not of long duration, as Madame de Flahaut announced, a few days later, that she had passed the day with the Bishop whose "leg is hurt."

There were more quarrels and reconciliations between Talleyrand, Morris and the lady. Finer feelings, however, were uppermost in Morris' mind—the characteristic American ones;—for let trouble or adversity come to a woman once cared for and in trouble, and the generous gesture in an American gentleman is instinctive. The tone of the diary suddenly changes. The dread approaches of the revolutionary movement were heard, coming nearer and nearer.

Go from hence to the Louvre. Madame de Flahaut is distressed. She has been in tears all day. After much entreaty she tells me the cause. Her pensions from Monsieur and from the Comte d'Artois are stopped; on that from the King she received but 3000 francs, and must therefore leave Paris. I try to console her, but it is impossible. Indeed, the stroke is severe, for with youth, beauty, wit and every loveliness, she must quit all that she loves, to pass her life with what she most abhors.

What "she most abhors" was, of course, her husband. "Return to the Louvre," Morris states, after having been at the Palais Royal "and sup. I lend Madame 1200 fcs in paper to redeem some gold which she has pawned. I do not expect to be paid."

In January, 1791, Madame de Flahaut made Morris her confidant:

I leave her to receive the Bishop. She drops an expression for the first time, respecting him, which is cousin-germain to contempt. I may, if I please, wean her from all regard for him. But he is the father of her child, and it would be unjust.

Talleyrand's "coolness and cruelty" may possibly be explained as resulting from the characteristics which Morris himself had discovered as being the motive of Madame de Flahaut's attitude towards her admirers. She was indeed a coquette and more inconstant than was Talleyrand. The latter was a lover of women; their society, their affection were a necessity to him. But he had an instinctive dread —one peculiar to all strong, independent natures—of any woman obtaining too strong a hold upon him. Only in his

MME. DE STAËL
By Tavernier

old age did the famous Duchesse de Dino acquire an ascendency over that powerful will. Madame de Flahaut's infidelity would have had its immediate effect on such a nature as was Talleyrand's—one as self contained, proud and inflexible. Resentment, however, was not Talleyrand's way of showing displeasure or wounded pride. Madame de Flahaut was to become a source of anxious care to Talleyrand, during the Terror. He was to meet her and their son, in London, in 1792. She was to flit in and out of his life, from that year, until they met again in Amsterdam, in 1796, on Talleyrand's return from America. Their social relations, after Madame de Flahaut's marriage to the Portuguese Minister, Monsieur de Souza, in 1802, were to continue throughout Talleyrand's brilliant career. Madame de Souza was to be seen at Talleyrand's famous receptions, when all that was most noted and brilliant in Europe passed before the then famous statesman and Minister. Her hôtel was close to his famous "Palace" in the rue Saint-Florentin.

Madame de Staël considered that the attraction of Madame de Flahaut and of her salon had lasted quite long enough. She had done all in her power to attract Morris and Talleyrand to her home. She deemed that Gouverneur Morris, as well as Talleyrand, were guilty of gross neglect of her and of her more brilliant coterie; for as everything was known in Paris, the almost daily meetings of these two friends in Adèle de Flahaut's rooms were looked upon by Madame de Staël in the light of an infidelity. The woman of genius had many of the weaknesses of her sex. She had no patience with those who failed to prove their preference for her above all others. But when could genius prevail against youth enhanced by the added attractions of talent, feminine charm and beauty?

In his diary, Gouverneur Morris gives an amusing account of his introduction to the Necker salon:

The Maréchale de Castries calls and takes me to dine with Monsieur and Madame Necker. In the Salon we find Madame de Staël. She seems to be a woman of sense, and somewhat masculine in her character, but has very much the appearance of a chambermaid. A little before dinner, Monsieur Necker enters. He has the look and manner of the counting house, and being dressed in embroidered velvet, he contrasts strongly with his habiliments. His bow, his address etc; says, *I* am the man. Our company is one half Academicians.

It is to Madame de Staël's contemporaries one must go for generous and even enthusiastic recognition of the great heart that animated one who should have been one of the noblest of women.

Lamartine's tribute is well-known. "Her genius was like an antique chorus in which all the great voices of the drama were fused in a stormy harmony." And Senac de Meilhac's praise: "She would animate a solitude, she would replace a world; in herself she would be the whole world." Her powers of self-sacrifice, her resourceful efforts during the Revolution to save her friends from the knife of the guillotine, her courage in fronting personal danger, and the lavish generosity—both hospitable and financial— she extended to French *émigrés* in Paris, in London and at Coppet, should alone have aureoled with fame a woman on whose brow rested the laurels of an almost unique genius.

She was to prove herself one of the most faithful and devoted of all Talleyrand's women friends. Her admiration for his talents as well as his character was unbounded. "He is a much misunderstood man" was one of her favorite statements, when she heard him attacked. "If Talleyrand's conversation were to be purchased, I should ruin myself," was one of her many tributes to his conversational powers. Yet she herself already, in 1789—before she had won her great European reputation—was cited as the most brilliant conversationalist among women. That there may have been, for a time, at least a stronger tie than mere friendship between Talleyrand and Madame de Staël seems probable. Whatever its nature, it appears to have been a mere "passade," never a prolonged liaison. Madame de Staël's conversation had indeed the thrall of a Circe—like enchantment. Talleyrand and Gouverneur Morris alike were stirred by her eloquence and moved by her power.

Her conquests of both lovers and friends were largely due to this rare union of a rich nature and of an abounding goodness allied to her surpassing intellectual gifts. The greatest men of her age, in all ranks of life—kings, princes, philosophers, men of letters, artists, the most cynical of courtiers, and the most astute politicians—were irresistibly drawn to this woman whose heart was as large as her mind seemed a mine of riches. Her unceasing activity was such that Talleyrand might have said of her as he did of Napoleon: "He who would give that man a little laziness would be the benefactor of the universe."

Some of Madame de Staël's lovers might well have deplored the fact that among so many gifts she did not remember that the art of non-pursuit proves as great a talent as does that of capture.

CHAPTER XVII

I

TALLEYRAND was to find in Mirabeau's illness and death a chance to climb to higher power in the Assembly.

Up to the last moment of his life, Mirabeau had fought—indomitable Titan that he was—to save the State, to save the monarchy. "I am the man for the reëstablishment of the Order—and not for the reëstablishment of the old Order." He was linked to Talleyrand through this common tie of passionate consecration to keep the Revolution from being precipitated into the chaos of anarchy. "The King, the Law, the Nation," such were the watchwords both Mirabeau and Talleyrand strove to make the rallying, the magical words for all true lovers of France.

No one saw more clearly than did Mirabeau the tragic end which awaited the King, unless some form of rescue could be devised to save him and the monarchy.

After the funeral march of the royal family, led by the people who were, later, to be their executioners—after that fatal journey from Versailles to Paris—Mirabeau's prophetic vision had pierced the veil of their future destiny.

On the very day after the King was—practically—imprisoned in the Tuileries, Mirabeau said to Monsieur de la Marck: "The King, the Queen, and with them France itself are lost unless they can get away from Paris. I am occupied with a plan to facilitate their escape." The plan was admirably conceived. It failed, as did all others to save the crown and France.

Mirabeau's well-known negotiations with the Court had also come to naught, as did all the plots to save the persons of the unfortunate monarchs.

The first interview of the famous Tribune with the Queen is picturesquely described by Monsieur Barthou in his admirable "Mirabeau":

Brought back to Paris by violence, spied upon and a prisoner, watched over by hate, and outraged by malignity, the dairy-maid of Trianon was consumed by the desire of how to save her kingdom, her crown, her family, and her life. This man whom she awaited, whom she had despised, and who had maltreated her, would he show her the way to safety—bring her salvation? The scenes of the fifth of October—her guards murdered, her palace invaded, her person menaced, the frenzied populace screaming, yelling—these scenes were before her eyes. She could not chase away the remembrance of such scenes, nor could she, in spite of all that had been told her, disassociate from them the name of Mirabeau. When she saw him, horror and fright possessed her. The shock was terrible. However, she conquered herself. As he talked on, as he spoke, in his caressing voice, of his mistakes and his remorse, of his intentions and his hopes, of his submission and of his respect, in lieu of the monster who had affrighted her, a man of generous nature, a tender-hearted man appeared before her. How could one doubt such sincerity and loyalty, couched in such accents? How could one resist abandoning one's self to the devotion of one who offered, as hostage—his very life? Surprised at finding so much seduction and delicacy allied to such formidable power, she became the woman with all the graces of her irresistible affability, without forgetting what she owed to her dignity as

Queen. On his side the King showed himself simple, resigned to the necessary sacrifices, conciliatory and confiding. Mirabeau, touched, moved, conquered, had cried "Madame—the monarchy is saved!" and according to Madame Campan, he kissed the Queen's hand.

The scene was a touching one. Had the fine sentiments, the mutual attractions, and the spirit of confidence but lasted! The King soon proved his vacillating nature—that fatal weakness of indecision which precipitated the coming tragedies of the end. The Queen, later, continued her intrigues with Austria; and Mirabeau, disheartened and disabused of all confidence in the adherence of either monarch to sane plans, to salutary measures, could but cry again, "All is lost! The people will kill the King and Queen and they will beat their corpses—yes—*beat their corpses!*"

II

Mirabeau did not live to see part of his dire prophecy come true. The idol of Paris and of the Assembly had lived long enough, however, to suffer from the changeable spirit of the revolutionary days. Violently attacked in the Jacobin Club, Mirabeau found himself, on his entrance—one of his last appearances in public—the butt of ridicule and of venomous aspersions.

Lameth accused him with a vehemence unusual in this somewhat mediocre orator. He exposed, with fiery invective, the "errors of his youth, his contradictions, his intrigues, his weaknesses." The attack was greeted with wild applause.

When Mirabeau rose—when he showed his "terrible hure" (his awful jowl)—the frantic audience tried to shout him down. The President attempted to prevent him from even addressing the members.

When Mirabeau finally could be heard, he attained sublimity. Never had any of his improvised speeches been so transcendent in their fiery eloquence. Menaced, persecuted, outraged, he turned on his assailants to rend them, one by one. His stormy powers soared to heights which carried all before him. His enemies, his detractors were cowed before the tempestuous splendor of his lightning flashes. He held his audience at his mercy, and the tribute they rendered the great orator must have rung in his ears as he lay on his deathbed. "I shall stay by you until I am ostracized," he had cried, in the delirium of his magnificent defiance. It was death, and no jury votes of mortals, which was to silence the words of the greatest of the revolutionary orators and statesmen.

"Ah—had you but seen the monster!" Madame de Staël had cried, after hearing one of Mirabeau's greatest speeches.

And now "the monster" lay ill, dying. The excesses of his earlier life, the later drain on the already sapped resources of his superb vitality, and those stupendous efforts which Mirabeau had made in the Assembly to check the dread, precipitous plunge towards anarchy, had left no reservoir of vigor to combat his malady; a short week's illness sufficed to extinguish the glowing torch of life that was Mirabeau.

"Monster" in appearance though he was, and monstrous as had been certain excesses of his youth and earlier manhood—"the wall that separates me from all that I long to accomplish," he had cried in bitter knowledge of what his past had cost him—yet with Mirabeau, the one mighty buttress that upheld tottering monarchy, tottering "Law, Order and the Nation"—this one powerful support fell down when he lay in his coffin.

Knowing the end was near, he had summoned Talleyrand to his deathbed.[1] To the last, the orator of the Tribune was the public man. Talleyrand was to read, in the Assembly, after his death, his speech on the "legality of according divisions (of property) in direct line of succession." The great Tribune must hear all the news, as he lay a'dying; and while he made no secret of his knowledge of what a void his death would bring, he met his end with the smile of a stoic. The god with the feet of clay was gone.

III

Talleyrand's address in the Assembly on Mirabeau's death was couched in simple, lofty style. Amid profound silence, he began:

Yesterday I went to see Mirabeau; a great concourse of people filled the house where I brought a feeling of sadness even more poignant than that felt by the general public. That spectacle of desolation filled the soul with the image of death; it was everywhere save in the spirit of him who was facing the most imminent danger.

He had asked for me. I will not dwell on the emotion excited by several of his speeches. Monsieur Mirabeau, even at this moment was still the public man, and from this point of view, we

[1] The very day he died, Mirabeau said to Talleyrand; "I have here, a great many papers: in them is to be found the honor of my memory: promise me that these papers shall one day be known, and that your friendship will aid in avenging my memory in seeing that these documents are published." (*Correspondence de Mirabeau*, t. 1, p. 256.)

These *Mémoires* were edited by Bacourt who, later with the Duchesse de Dino, was to publish and *modify* Talleyrand's *Mémoires*.

must look upon his last words as a precious relic which has been snatched from the immense prey which death has seized.

L'immense proie que la mort vient de saisir!   The phrase rings in one's ears a century and a half after it rang in those of the silent, awestruck, semi-stunned members of the Assembly.   For now that he was gone, each man who sat there, spellbound by the eloquent tribute paid by Talleyrand to the dead orator, knew there was no one—no one force—mighty enough to replace the prey death had seized.

The breach Mirabeau's death opened in the dike he and Talleyrand had so strenuously tried to build against the advancing revolutionary flood, opened wide to admit Danton; after Danton, Marat; and after Marat, Robespierre.

The Assembly itself was soon to be dissolved—a measure advocated, insisted upon by Talleyrand.   Since the King had accepted the Constitution, Talleyrand's contention was that it had no further *raison d'être*.

CHAPTER XVIII

I

THE first strictly diplomatic mission entrusted to Talleyrand was assigned to him by the Department of Paris and approved by the sovereign. Semi-official though his duties were to be, the King had consented to Talleyrand's being the emissary chosen.

The object of his journey to London was a delicate one. He was to attempt to win from the English Government a promise of neutrality, in case of an attack being made by the French Princes' army on France. The Comte d'Artois, in his exile as *émigré*, at Coblence, and the Comte de Provence—the King's two brothers—were employing their leisure in conspiring against their King. Surrounded by a servile court composed of French fugitives, the two brothers had elaborated a serious and menacing plot. Its object was to dethrone Louis XVI. An army was to be raised with the aid of foreign gold. Foreign troops were to attack France, to crush the Revolution, and once Louis XVI was disposed of, the Comte de Provence was to be acclaimed Regent.

The plot was vigorously fomented by the restless, intriguing French nobles, whose zeal in the project was intensified by the spectre of their failing resources. Although it was more than suspected that the King and Queen were in sympathy with this foreign invasion—for Marie-Antoinette was still in secret correspondence with Austria —the King named Rochambeau and Luckner to the command of the National armies of the North and the Rhine, for immediate action, were the Princes' army to advance.

The situation in France was becoming more and more tragic. New revolutionary leaders appeared. Danton was making his voice heard.

The catastrophic changes brought about by the growing insubordination of the people, their hunger and anger; the irresolution and desperate plight of the monarchy—Louis turning now to this refuge, now to another; the hate aroused by the rumored intrigues of the Queen with Austria; and the loss to the nation, to the Crown,—to all France—of the one tower of strength, in the tottering edifice—of Mirabeau —these conditions were hastening the coming Terror.

War was in the air. In 1790, had patriotic Frenchmen taken up arms, it might have saved the monarchy. Two years later, when it broke out, its immediate effect was to dethrone the King.

II

The time for energetic action had arrived.

The Minister of Foreign Affairs, Monsieur de Lessart, in sending Talleyrand to London that he might exert all possible influence, both at the English Court and with the government, to maintain strict neutrality, in case of France being attacked, felt that were Talleyrand successful, one great danger would be averted.

Here was a mission exactly to Talleyrand's taste. He felt assured of a hearty welcome in London from such friends as Lord Lansdowne and Lord Holland; Fox he had met in Paris; Pitt he had known at Rheims, and already London had become a chosen Mecca for innumerable French fugitives.

Comte Louis de Narbonne, now Minister of War for the space of ten months, had not forgotten his friends in the moment of his elevation. It was he who had assigned Lauzun, Duc de Biron, as Talleyrand's companion. "I imagine, my friend, that a little tour in England would be excellent for your jaundice, and I very much hope that I am not mistaken," was his message to him.

Talleyrand must have started on his journey (January 24th, 1792) with a sense of its being a holiday for the nerves and mind, since his intimate friend—Lauzun—was associated with him.

Who was gayer, wittier, more accomplished in all the ways that made his society one of the delights of life, than Lauzun? His whole existence had been a prolonged festivity. He was the soul of every gathering he attended; he wrote the most charming madrigals; his morning notes— *billets de matin*—had been considered little masterpieces, in the days when life was still a festival; he hunted as well as he danced; and he had changed his mistresses as often as he had his embroidered coats and with as easy a grace. Talleyrand had always delighted in him; at his breakfasts at Bellechasse, at Chanteloup, as in society, Lauzun was among the "Inseparables." Talleyrand spoke of him as being "courageous, romantic, generous, witty." And yet, in the envelope of this seemingly frivolous worldling there was the stuff of the serious patriot. His letters to Talleyrand from Berlin, after leaving the latter to complete the affairs which had taken them both to London, show political sagacity and ripe judgment. In every clever Latin, there is something of both the Greek and the Roman. The Frenchman takes life as the Greek sipped wine, at a banquet: but in more serious matters, nascent political talent changes the light-hearted trifler into a clever politician, and in war, a Gallo-Roman valor and power of endurance electrify the libertine into the soldier of Verdun.

III

Once on the Channel, the two friends had long hours in which to discuss their plans; also in which to relish, with peculiar zest, the novel sense of freedom. The feverish life of Paris; the tumults, the insurrections; the growing danger of a famished, exasperated people; the chaotic state of the government—the Revolution, in a word, with all its horrors and dread possibilities—were left behind. It must have seemed to both of these friends that the fiercest winds were kind, and the angriest waters but a summer sea.

The joint appearance of these two celebrated noblemen in London was a sensational one. Already announcements had been made in the newspapers of the coming of these distinguished visitors. Of the two, Talleyrand inevitably excited the greater interest and curiosity. "Monsieur l'Evêque" as he was called by some of the writers in the press, in semi-derision, had already enough history behind him to stir both the social and the political world.

What would he be like—this brilliantly clever, unfrocked priest? Here was a new variety of aristocratic ecclesiastic: a priest who had renounced his vows, a noble who had joined the revolutionary forces, and about whom the most scandalous stories were afloat—what manner of man could such an one be?

Talleyrand's imperturbable calm, his wit and conversational powers, at any other moment of time, would undoubtedly have conquered London. He was at this time in the prime of his manhood. At thirty-seven, the features of the most enigmatic face in Europe had assumed already that impassive look through whose mask there played the fire of intellectual strength. The voice was strong, virile—a true male voice. And when the face relaxed its guarded aspect, when a tender, playful mood lit up the countenance and gave a peculiarly caressing expression to the dark blue eyes, the accents of that deep tone, in contrast to the charm of the face, struck the ear with astonishing force.

Talleyrand's powers of mind had been greatly developed by the years passed in the political arena. His natural aptitude for affairs had had a chance of fullest play. It is also certain that the fierce opposition as well as the enmity aroused by his daring, and his strength of purpose shown during the Revolution, had fortified both mind and character. He had need of these qualities in the struggle which lay before him, in this London venture.

IV

The reception Talleyrand was to find on his arrival in London was neither cordial nor was it promising. His reputation for lax morality, his speculations in the public funds, added to the part he had played during the Revolution, told heavily against him. His position also was not an accredited, an official one. As a former member of the *Constituante* he could not be named, himself, as either Minister or Ambassador. Perceiving, with his quick insight, that all of his endeavors would prove to be abortive unless the French government were officially represented,

Talleyrand advised that an Ambassador should be accredited to the Court of St. James', and at once. He suggested a certain young nobleman—the Marquis de Chauvelin—who had embraced, with the passion and disinterestedness of youth, the revolutionary cause. Neither the age—de Chauvelin was twenty-five—nor the abilities of such an Ambassador would interfere with Talleyrand's own policy and manœuvres. Chauvelin, in other words, was to be the "Blind" behind which the statesman was to work. Chauvelin, however, was not to present his papers on this, Talleyrand's first mission.

Gouverneur Morris' well-known letter to Washington, March 17th, 1792, is a curious commentary on the later relationship of the two men who had been constantly brought into such close intimacy, in the Louvre salon.

As the Bishop of Autun has now got back to Paris, it may be well to communicate the results. His reception was bad for three reasons. First, that the Court looked with horror and apprehension at the scenes being enacted in France of which they consider him as a prime mover; secondly, that his reputation is offensive to those who pique themselves on decency of manners and deportment; and lastly, as to propagate the idea that he should corrupt the members of the administration. [Talleyrand had boasted unwisely, that he had £40,000 at his disposal.] He also allied himself with leading characters among the Dissenters. He renewed the impression made before his departure from Paris that he meant to intrigue with the discontented.

In spite of Morris' disparaging comments, Talleyrand's "intrigues," or his more forcible, if more secret measures, did result in a semi-success.

By what art he won his triumph over the formidable animosity shown him, by the government and the press, only one or two precise revelations have come down to us. His friendship with Lord Lansdowne and other great noblemen must have been of some help to him, in all his negotiations. It is possible, also, that all of the forty thousand pounds did not return to France with Talleyrand. In all governments, negotiations held in secret are oftentimes the most effective.

The actual offers made by Talleyrand to tempt England to remain neutral were: first, the ceding of the island of Tabago; second, the demolition of the fort at Cherbourg; and third, the advantages which would be given to England in a commercial treaty. The hope of an alliance with England was out of the question in view of George III's attitude towards France, the Revolution, and towards Talleyrand himself. Talleyrand's personal charm, his statesmanlike propositions, and his presentment of his country's needs prevailed, among certain groups. But not at Court. On his arrival, Talleyrand had secured a presentation at Court. The King barely returned Talleyrand's bow. The Queen turned her back on him, while Lauzun was received with all due honors.

V

Talleyrand, whose social *flair* was as keen as was his political insight, had lost no time in a wasting of force. After his reception by the King, he knew that any hope of an alliance of France with England was chimerical. The English nation and national feeling were behind the sovereign and Pitt. The violence and growing fury of the Revolution in France had not only alarmed, but had horrified the staid, sober English mind.

With France in the convulsions of her national upheaval, England felt herself delivered from a dreaded and a more or less hated rival. She could not be expected to be more than human; there was secret exultation among most Englishmen and their leaders in the knowledge that Fate was taking their own revenge in hand. The French participation, with arms, men and money, in the American War of Independence was not forgotten. The mills of the Gods were grinding, and actively, entirely to English satisfaction.

Talleyrand was quick to trace the currents influencing the English mind. He threw himself into the Opposition. He courted Fox, Lord Lansdowne, and was courted, in his turn, by the latter. At Lansdowne House, Talleyrand soon won his place. His imperturbable calm and his air of the finished courtier commanded immediate respect. His manner was found to be un-French, "being a sententious manner; his courtesy, at once cold and distant, with an examining air which formed a sort of defence around this diplomatic personage." This was Talleyrand's armor— the one which he wore in public.

In intimacy, with such enlightened and cosmopolitan Englishmen as Lord Lansdowne, Fox and their coterie, Talleyrand won all hearts by the charm which none other exercised as did he;—"that familiar, caressing attention (charm) full of delicate attentions to please, and amusing others in order to be amused," was one which both the French writer Dumont, and Sir Henry Lytton Bulwer aptly describe as being Talleyrand's supreme gift of attraction.

There were meetings of a different order with the Prime Minister, Lord Grenville. From the first, the English Minister had declared he could have no sort of discussion, nor could he enter into any conversations with an emissary from France whose government had no official representative.

Talleyrand's attempts to ensure England's neutrality were nearly completely frustrated before his departure after his second mission by the scenes enacted on June 20th, in Paris. The King was assaulted by the Jacobin mob. Incensed at the monarch's refusal to sign the bill of deportation of those of the clergy who had refused to take the oath as Constitutionalist priests—this mob in their fury had invaded the Palace. Finding the King alone, in his apartments, the "patriots," flourishing swords, screaming vile curses, threatening sanguinary reprisals, were finally appeased by the helpless King's consent to don the red cockade. To the hoarse chorus of "*ça ira*" the exultant crowd rang in the first triumphant notes of the Terror.

Talleyrand was reduced to a state of helpless despair. His position became untenable. The effect in England of the terrifying scenes at the Palace was promising shipwreck to Talleyrand's achievements.

VI

In March, Talleyrand, realizing the gravity of the situation, took ship for France. He had asked for permission to re-enter France, that he might "explain matters" to the Government.

News travelled slowly in 1792. On reaching the French coast, Talleyrand was met by friends who had driven down from Paris to greet him. The accounts they brought with them of the political situation were more than disturbing—they were alarming. Narbonne, as Minister of War, had been dismissed by the King. "It is surprising to learn that the King is still in a position to dismiss anyone," was remarked by one of those in the coach. Lessart, the

Minister of Foreign Affairs,—Talleyrand also learned—was arrested. Accused as having intrigued with the Austrian Court, he was to be tried before the Court of Orleans.

The changes which had taken place during Talleyrand's absence gave him a fairly clear sense of the coming tragic gravity of the revolutionary crisis. The Girondists in March, 1792, had obtained a decisive victory: in accusing and sentencing de Lessart,—for Danton later on ordered the ex-Minister to be taken to Versailles where, during the September massacres, he was strangled by the infuriated mob—in thus attacking and condemning de Lessart, they had actually accused and sentenced the King and the real enemy of France, who, as they believed, was the Queen. The universal belief that Marie-Antoinette was in direct collusion with Austria to turn the Monarchists in France against the nation, was the "poisoned dagger" the Girondists had launched against her.[1] Louis XVI, having accepted the Constitution, carried out to the letter the rules he had sworn to obey. He planted the dagger in his own bosom; for he had made Dumouriez Minister, with the other Ministers of the same violent and impolitic party.

The result was electrical. The Ministers promptly declared war on Austria. This seemingly mad act—for the French army was known to be sown with corruption, was undisciplined, and had broken out in mutiny, not once, but several times—this act of a despotic faction precipitating France into war, eventually resulted in the dictatorship of Robespierre, the Terror, and later still, in the Directoire which gave Napoleon Bonaparte his chance, through the Consulate, to capture the crown of the Bourbons.

The immediate effect of the call to arms to fight Austria,

[1] *Histoire de France*, Jacques Bainville. Arthème Fayard, Paris.

among other measures, was to send Talleyrand again to England.

Before the Girondists had played their desperate game against Austria—thus forcing her, later, into the Coalition (into the Princes' army)—Gouverneur Morris asserts, in his diary, that it was he who suggested to Talleyrand that he should try to be named Ambassador to Vienna. Such a post would have appealed particularly to the taste and to the aptitudes of the ex-Bishop. The project did not find acceptance with the Ministers of the Gironde.

VII

Dumouriez—now Minister of Foreign Affairs under the Girondists' rule, he who was to be the Victor of Valmy—had another plan. He proposed that Talleyrand should make a second effort to accomplish the almost impossible task of securing England's continued abstention from joining the continental Coalition against France, now become dangerous. Austria having joined the Coalition, the Eastern French frontiers were being threatened.

Dumouriez was the real leader, instigator, and advocate of the war. A small, nervous, excitable man, he was possessed of great personal charm. As a speaker and conversationalist, his outbursts of wit and raillery were so gay and spirited, and so convincing, so eloquent was his ardent enthusiasm, that the unimpressionable King could exclaim, "No one has ever talked to me like that." Dumouriez could appeal peculiarly to both the King and to Talleyrand.

Though a soldier by profession, he had acquired a diplomatic training in passing from the army into secret diplomacy. He had quick recognition of the possible disastrous effect the proclamation of war might have on England. The instructions given to Talleyrand, in his first mission, had been that in order to obtain England's continued neutrality the Low Countries would not be attacked.

France's urgent necessity of protecting her Belgian frontiers must now be made clear, must be fully realized by Lord Grenville's government. Dumouriez felt that he had, in his choice of Talleyrand, the one man in France whose diplomatic talents could continue the work of conciliation which, in his previous mission, he had begun in England. Under the Girondist government, the accelerating movement of the Revolution was undermining the results of Talleyrand's recent efforts. More urgent measures to induce England to remain neutral must be taken.

Dumouriez's plans for the war, on a vast scale, were plans on which he had long meditated: these included the confident deduction that Holland, unsupported by England, would not budge. England's neutrality, therefore, must at all costs be continued. On this neutrality hung all Dumouriez's plans.[1]

Although the Minister of Foreign Affairs for this delicate mission, chose Talleyrand as his emissary, Dumouriez had as little taste for the negotiator as the latter had for this little man with his "common, almost ugly face . . . with the small eyes, and the brusque manners" which, though vivacious, were yet restrained. Talleyrand's keen eye had penetrated the disguise of the soldier of fortune; for cleverly as Dumouriez now wore the robes of a Minister, practising his rôle with the suppleness of one familiar with Embassies, clever, adroit, audacious as he was, "possessing all the resources of great men," yet was he lacking in the essentials

[1] *Histoire de la Révolution.* La chute de la Royauté, pp. 418, 420. Albert Sorel.

of true nobility of character and the long vision of the statesman.

Dumouriez, on his side, distrusted Talleyrand. He also feared his insight and his known talents for penetration and discernment. Yet, the two men had need of each other. The yoke was rendered the lighter by distance.

On this mission, at least, Talleyrand was not to be rebuffed by Lord Grenville's scornful reminder that negotiations could not be carried on with a country which had no official representative at the Court of St. James'.

Dumouriez's letter to his King, dated the 28th of March, 1792, reads:

I design that M. de Talleyrand should depart at once for London, he having already begun a negotiation which he conducted with much skill, of which I will render some extracts to the King. As, according to the decrees, he cannot go with an accredited title to England, I propose to the King that he should be given *un adjoint* (a partner) with the title of Minister Plenipotentiary.

This letter is very significant. Talleyrand was again to carry on a most difficult mission with no official recognition of his status.

The "Ambassade" which Dumouriez had composed as a frontispiece, had Chauvelin as titular Ambassador. Talleyrand was to be the real negotiator. There were several others: Dumont, a friend of Mirabeau's; Reinhard, a theologian from Württemberg "so in love with the Revolution" that he had become a naturalized Frenchman. The theologian's post was that of Secretary to the Embassy; "he possessed a force and a remarkable suppleness," said Talleyrand of him. And there was Garat—Garat whom Camille Desmoulins called the "nightingale" because of his talent as a singer. Garat lived up to his reputation for furnishing melodious entertainment. His true rôle was to contribute unceasing gaiety to the party. "He's a schoolboy on a vacation," Talleyrand cried. He seemed to have no other function.

The new Minister Plenipotentiary—the young Marquis de Chauvelin, a friend of Narbonne's as well as of Talleyrand himself—was one of the Masters of the Robe. He was wholly inexperienced in affairs of State. He was to be "the blind," behind whom and through whose purely official status Talleyrand was to attempt the gigantic task of staying England's armed fist.

Talleyrand's acceptance of a project so seemingly impossible of accomplishment, as was this mission to England, proves his conscious sense of power. He had already measured himself with the English giant statesmen, with Pitt, whose cold shoulder was as significant a gesture as might have been a knock-down; with Fox, on whom he could count, though his power now was limited and his enthusiasm for the Revolution gone forever; and on that statesman of smaller stature—Lord Grenville—he could count, for Talleyrand knew he would, at least, listen to any statement, even though he might refuse assent to the most moving appeals.

Chauvelin had his audience with the King on May 2nd. Talleyrand conducted affairs, while the youthful Ambassador made the official visits. The French Embassy met with a frigid reception at Court, and was received almost "insultingly by the public." England feared French propaganda; she was in no humor to have revolutionary ideas sown on her soil. The first effort Talleyrand made was to dissipate all such unfavorable notions.[1] Talleyrand be-

[1] Sorel, 330 and 385, 387, and see Lolié and Sainte-Beuve.

lieved he knew the dangers and pitfalls before him, in the stony course of English opposition. The roughness of the road he was to tread was to test all the powers of endurance, both moral and mental, of one of the most adroit, persistent, defiant, and unconquerable natures the world has seen. For the course before Talleyrand, first opened to him by his earlier mission to England, was to stretch on from this April, 1792, to the 18th Brumaire—on to the year 1799. These were the years of Talleyrand's experience with adversity. Many of them were lean and bitter years, flecked here and there by transient gleams of brighter fortune.

These missions to England were, in truth, the beginning of Talleyrand's diplomatic life. His skill in negotiating difficult affairs of state; his tact, his mastery of adroit and insinuating persuasiveness, his subtlety and the finished delicacy of a manner which impressed those hostile to Talleyrand the man—this almost unique equipment marked him for his future illustrious vocation. Formed in the school of de Choiseul, with the great traditions handed down by Richelieu and Mazarin, Talleyrand was now versed in the intricacies of difficult Embassy negotiations.

Dumouriez was right in his estimate of Talleyrand's diplomatic equipment. None other could possibly have secured even a few months' respite from English armed enmity. Talleyrand's avowed longing for closer relations, for an alliance between France and England, was a trump card to play, whether it won the trick or not.

VIII

It is interesting to note that in Dumouriez's plans for carrying on the war against the Coalition forces, he was inspired to enforce the acceptance of two projects, both of which, having been in operation in recent times, have greatly influenced the trend of European political and national life in our own day.

Talleyrand's intercourse with the numerous friends he found in London, with the many aristocrats who frequented the gatherings at the house of the Duchesse de Mortemar in Burton Street, for one example—and others—such intimacies and frequentations were instanced as proving Talleyrand's real proclivities and aristocratic preferences. His detractors exulted in sending to the Paris press accounts of his social and of his supposed treacherous activities.

Not only Talleyrand, but Dumouriez, was soon able to gauge the all-but-hopeless task undertaken. The open hostility of the English Court to the new and young French Ambassador was the signal for all those who follow Court signs of disfavor to find everything French, not only obnoxious, but dangerous. All England, in time, became infected with the Court influence. The unwise, the even flagrant audacity of the revolutionary propaganda, with its wild cries of revolt against authority; its radical views; its appeals to the seditious element in England—these efforts of the Girondists to prove the righteousness of their own perverted doctrines, armed English common sense, English pride, and English conservatism against France, and all its revolutionary methods. The fact that the propagandists carried their inflammatory pamphlets into Belgium exasperated English feeling the more. Religious fanaticism and revolutionary zeal have this in common: to prove their belief, their doctrines as revealed truth, they must fight unbelief with the same ferocity as wild beasts fight for their young—and with the same cruel savagery. Talleyrand found it expedient immediately to refute, with indignation, the reproaches levelled by the English press and political speakers, of the propaganda carried on by the French revolutionary parties in England.

IX

After waiting a full month, Lord Grenville deigned, at last, to reply to the various attempts made by Talleyrand through France's accredited Ambassador—Chauvelin—to extort a direct answer to the hopes, and the considered plans proposed for a complete understanding between the two countries. "The disdain and the prudence of the English Minister reduced the official representatives of Dumouriez to purely academic occupations."[1]

Lord Grenville addressed his answer to the French mission through the press:—could insult wear a more gossamer veil? England regretted the war; she promised to respect the treaties; she expressed the desire to remain at peace with France, and she trusted France would do her part in maintaining this peace—"in enforcing respect for His Majesty and his Allies." The latter word might have been a bombshell. But the "Allies" referred to were known to be Prussia and Holland. Dumouriez was even more anxious to remain at peace with Prussia than could be England herself. Prussia, however, was soon to put an end to such hopes; she presently joined the Coalition.

Talleyrand and his inexperienced and sometimes compromising Ambassador had to content themselves with Grenville's published and veiled answer. In spite of having to fight calumny and the attacks of the English press, Talleyrand was to carry back to Paris a semi-victory. Pitt, in reality, was not ready for war. Prosperous as was

[1] *Histoire de France.* La Révolution, p. 354. Ernest Lavisse.

England, British finances were not, as yet, entirely satisfactory; and to make war England must await a repleted exchequer. Having decided on maintaining a strict neutrality, the government could assure France of England's continuing a non-combatant attitude, providing France, on her part, respected the rights of England.

An alliance with England, Talleyrand found to be impossible. Neither Pitt nor Lord Grenville would listen to the Girondists' great diplomatic plan—"to Brissot's, to Clavière's, to Condorcet's project of opposing a league of liberal nations, of France, England, and the United States of America, to the absolutist powers,"—a project which was the forerunner of the League of Nations.

Lord Rosebery states, in his remarkable volume on "Pitt," that no English Minister can ever wish for war. Pitt was more than ever convinced that to keep out of the turmoil of the European conflicts was the sanest policy. He had succeeded in balancing the budget, in diminishing armaments, in bringing to conclusion the law establishing the extension of electoral rights. At as happy a turn in financial and political affairs, a war would imperil the very victories won. War was opposed to his whole political plan. Pitt in truth considered that France and the French Revolution were matters concerning France alone.[1] He doubtless considered also, as did many lesser Englishmen, that the horrors of the Revolution were the judgment of Nemesis: England was never to forget that it was French *louis d'or* which had enabled America to win her independence. England, at peace, could pay off a part of that hate-

---

[1] It is interesting to note that Pitt took the same attitude towards the French Revolution which President Coolidge, and America behind the President, take towards Europe at the present time.

ful and baneful score. Her rival—in commerce as in any possible supremacy in European affairs—was disabled. It was England's moment. France might be a natural enemy. As rival and as a foe she was now out of the running.

Yet Belgium as well as Antwerp had been seized. And France's victorious armies had captured Savoy, Nice, the Low Countries and the Rhine Provinces of Germany. In all of these, the new French institutions were enforced—brutally enforced.

The fatal day of June 20th brought all negotiations to an abrupt end. There had been a concerted plan among the Girondists to push the King to extremes—to make an end of the monarchy. Their chance to accomplish their end seemed to come on the day the King rejected the decree to deport all of the clergy who had refused to sign as Constitutionalist priests. Another concession was also denied: the guard of honor, serving as the King's personal protection, was to be disbanded; in its place 20,000 "Fédérés" were to be at hand to combat a counter-revolution. Again the King found himself possessed of a kingly courage. The decree was not signed, and the Girondist Ministers were dismissed (June 12th). "Monsieur Pitt" as the King was now dubbed, by the revolutionaries, was to be made to pay for his audacity. A popular demonstration being organized, armed with a petition to the Assembly to recall Girondist Ministers, was to find its real theatre of action in the palace of the King.

The scene that followed was an armed action of the people in reply to the guns of the foreign armies.

The "atrocity" of the mob storming the Tuileries; their invasion of the King's private apartments, where he was found, leaning against a window, four faithful grenadiers

LOUIS XVI, DERNIER ROI DES FRANÇAIS,
NÉ LE 23 AOUST 1754,
décapité le 2 Pluviose, l'an 1er de la République.

Parvenu au trône à l'âge de 19 ans, Louis XVI montra un désir sincère d'assurer le bonheur des Français, mais l'influence de ses perfides conseillers rendit ses moyens personnels presque nuls. Sous son regne s'accrurent de beaucoup les prodigalités de la cour. Un déficit énorme dans les finances obligea ce monarque à convoquer l'assemblée des notables, puis les États-Généraux, qu'il tenta inutilement de dissoudre dans la séance royale du 23 juin 1789. L'opinion publique le força d'éloigner les troupes rassemblées autour de Paris, et de rappeler les ministres patriotes qu'il avoit renvoyés. Il parut alors seconder l'élan général vers la liberté, il applaudit à la réforme des abus, et présida la fédération du 14 juillet 1790. Le 21 juin suivant, il s'enfuit avec toute sa famille, après avoir consigné dans un mémoire les motifs de son mécontentement. Il se plaignait, entr'autres choses, d'être prisonnier dans ses états, gêné dans les pratiques de sa religion, et d'avoir été forcé d'approuver la lettre par laquelle il déclaroit aux puissances étrangeres, son assentiment libre à la nouvelle forme du gouvernement. Arrêté à Varennes, ramené à Paris, et conservé cependant sur le trône, il accepta solennellement la constitution de 1791. Accusé bientôt après de favoriser les ennemis du dehors et les princes émigrés, il fut assiégé dans son palais des Thuileries, le 10 août 1792, et enfermé au Temple. Une convention nationale fut convoquée, elle abolit la royauté, et le 13 Décembre, Louis XVI comparut devant elle, pour être interrogé sur les crimes qu'on lui imputoit. Le 26 du même mois, il fut entendu dans sa défense; le 16 janvier 1793, il fut jugé à mort, et il subit son supplice le 21, avec résignation et fermeté. Avec lui disparut une monarchie qui avait subsisté pendant 14 siecles, et qui, dans ses trois Dynasties, avait compté 66 rois. On a publié, après sa mort, un Testament, qu'il écrivit à la tour du Temple, dans les derniers jours de décembre 1792, et dans lequel on remarque ce paragraphe: « Je recommande à mon fils, s'il avoit le malheur de devenir roi, de songer qu'il se doit tout entier au bonheur de ses concitoyens; qu'il doit oublier toute haine et tout ressentiment, et nommément ce qui a rapport aux malheurs et chagrins que j'éprouve; qu'il ne peut faire le bonheur des hommes, qu'en régnant suivant les loix: mais, en même temps, qu'un roi ne peut les faire respecter et faire le bien qui est dans son cœur, qu'autant qu'il a l'autorité nécessaire, et qu'autrement, étant lié dans ses opérations, n'inspirant point de respect, il est plus nuisible qu'utile ».

LOUIS XVI

From a copper print

alone protecting the sovereign from the fury of the demons crowding about his Majesty; and the threatening cries of the savage-faced Marseillais "Fédérés" who were determined that Louis XVI should "cry for mercy"—this outrageous attack on the sovereign's privacy, on his honor, roused Europe to hot anger.   The King's final resignation to submitting to the red cap tendered him seemed to the king-loving people of England an abdication of sovereign rights.   The pathos of the scene was increased by Marie-Antoinette and her children; behind the frail table of the Council Chamber, the Queen conciliated the howling mob by placing on the Dauphin's head the cap that was the symbol of mob-rule.

Neither King Louis nor his Queen could be made to "cry for mercy." The crowd howled its fury, but the Girondist plot had failed. With that failure, the Girondist party was doomed.

The effect of this attack on the person of the King was to arm Europe with a great watchword. The divine right of kings to reign and rule was a tenet which must be upheld.   So far from every throne in Europe feeling a sense of insecurity, menaced by the people of France's intolerable and insolent echoing of the cry of Louis XIV— "l'Etat, c'est moi"—every king and princeling, tightening his crown closer to his head, grasping his sceptre in one hand and his sword in the other, led his troops onward with the cry, "Down with anarchy!"

Such scenes of violence could have but one effect on a law-abiding people.   England had had her lesson in revolutionary excesses.   She had repented of her instructive past; she had no mind to allow insidious, seditious and inflammatory foreign doctrines to sow their pernicious seed.

In England, the French Embassy was in a state of

collapse. How could one fight for a country led by bandits? The very firmness of the King, fronting possible death, holding his own against such mob-rule—his attitude of princely firmness, as unexpected as it was sublime—but added to the appalling situation.

CHAPTER XIX

I

TALLEYRAND recrossed the Channel with a certain feeling of satisfaction: England was to remain neutral. The collapse of all hopes of an alliance was disappointing. In the perturbed state of Europe, consequent on the War of the Princes and their Allies against France, England could enter into no treaties; all she asked, all that Pitt hoped for, was that France would let England alone. That Talleyrand's assurance to France of the determination of the government to preserve strict neutrality was, in reality, in no sense wholly due to his own diplomatic victory is supported by Pitt's remarkable statement at about this time. In February, 1792, after instituting a series of reforms, such as repealing taxes, reducing the number of seamen, and refusing to renew the subsidy for the Hessian mercenaries, the latter states:—"Unquestionably there never was a time in the history of this country when from the situation of Europe we might more reasonably expect fifteen years of peace than at the present moment." [1] So much for the foresight of one of England's greatest statesmen.

Talleyrand had contented himself with the bare fact

[1] *Pitt,* Lord Rosebery. Macmillan & Co., 1919.

that England preferred neutrality to engaging in the war raging across the Channel.

The conditions on his arrival in Paris were not such as to make the news he brought capable of increasing his prestige.

On this, his second return to France, he found Paris in the throes of popular fermentation. The Jacobins were now the virtual rulers of the hour, fighting to oust the Girondists. Talleyrand was received as though he were a suspect rather than as a successful negotiator. He had the premonitory sensation of facing real, immediate danger. His keen political ear could hear the thunderous roar of the Terror before the horror had actually sprung at the throat of France, to hurl her to the bottomless pit.

Talleyrand found the government a farce; the Jacobin Club was attempting to dictate all politics. The Girondists were expending frenzied efforts, not to govern, but to continue to inflame popular passion. Ministers were nominated only to be overthrown. Party strife was paramount. Paris, in a word, was in the chaotic state of anarchy which, like unto a dishevelled, maddened Mænid, was to rush France into the vortex of the Terror.

In such a crazed world to whom was one to appeal, for cool, clear views on foreign affairs? who cared about London, English neutrality, or the English King's surly indifference? Talleyrand might as well have spent his time trying to convert the heathen in Africa as to have used his best powers to discover if England intended to remain neutral. His work, he felt, was all undone. As though this tragic situation were not big with fatal consequences, an even more serious personal defeat must be met, accepted and acted upon.

FÊTE GIVEN AT THE HÔTEL DE VILLE IN HONOR OF THE CONSTITUTION

Owing to the assaults of the Jacobins, the Constitutional Council of the Department of Paris was suppressed. This left Talleyrand without the support, in Paris, of an important official position. The suppression was due to its President the Duc de la Rochfoucauld-d'Enville's having "pronounced a suspension of Pétion and Manuel" (the former the Mayor of Paris, and the latter the Syndic of the Commune of Paris) "for having failed to protect the King from the attack of the mob on June 20th."

A scene hostile to the members of the Department of Paris took place on the Champ de Mars, July 14, 1792. It was the Anniversary of that simulacrum of Fraternity, of the year 1790. It was the anniversary, also, of the taking of the Bastille, in 1789.

As the members of the Department of Paris appeared, shouts, insulting cries rent the air. "Vive Pétion! Vive Pétion!" were the vivas which the angry crowd hurled at the "aristocrats" who had dared to vote down and out the people's Mayor. Talleyrand and a group of his fellow members of the Department were viciously assailed by the shrieking mob. As the little group of noblemen passed beneath the balcony of the Tribune wherein sat the superbly costumed queen—her jewels, the mound of her feathers and the satins of her gown in such contrast to the now lined face, with eyes and lids reddened permanently, as it seemed, by the tears she had shed—Marie-Antoinette, in response to the courteous salute given by Talleyrand and his friends, rewarded their tribute by a sad smile. It was a smile which was to cost Talleyrand and his fellow members dear. It was a hectic moment when every straw was the signal for testing which way the political wind blew. The smile settled the fate of the Department of Paris. La

Rochfoucauld, Talleyrand, and their colleagues were denounced as being Court favorites—enemies of the people.

Pétion and Manuel were re-instated in their offices, by the vote of the Assembly. Such defiance of the authority which had been vested in the Department of Paris, sealed its fate. Its end was accomplished. Talleyrand felt that his position was daily becoming more and more uncertain: all semblance of power, of authority, was taken from him.

II

Talleyrand, Madame de Staël, Madame de Flahaut and Gouverneur Morris were all to live through the terror-striking days of that early August of the year 1792 which was to decide the fate of the monarchy. In spite of the impending tragedy, the lives led by those still in Paris are a curious commentary on the veil which hid the real meaning of the gathering danger from most of the more astute minds.

Although one salon after another was closed; although the emigration had reached such proportions that Paris was practically emptied, those still in the capital wined and dined and flitted from one hôtel to another. Friends met to consult on the best means of escape, were the worst to come. Yet one could walk about in the streets and gardens of Paris, in apparent security.

One can imagine what a range the conversations of those who met daily must have embraced. Every stirring speech in the General Assembly, and later, those heard in the Convention, were commented upon by the deepest and cleverest minds of the day; every dramatic event, in the progressive stages of the Revolution, was brought by the chief actors in the tragic scenes, direct to the "chambre ardente" of

Madame de Staël. The account of the last horror, told by
an eye-witness, would thrill with nervous tremor or appre-
hensive fear those seated about the brightly-lit supper table.

Though some of the guests might find their names on the
dread list on the very morrow, up to the last, society held
its reunions. The salons were the last barriers presented by
aristocracy against mob-rule—a barrier which proved
stronger than had the iron gates of the Palace of Versailles.
"For supper," said the wittiest woman of her day,
Madame du Deffand, "is one-fourth of the chief duty of
man. I have forgotten what are the other three-fourths."

Gouverneur Morris writes, in his diary, on August 3rd,
1792: "I dine at the British Ambassador's. We walk after
dinner to the Champs de Mars where we see a few ragga-
muffins who are signing the petition for the *déchéance*."
"Went to court; nothing remarkable, only that they were up
all night, expecting to be murdered." And on the sixth:
"Monsieur and Madame de Flahaut dine with me. The
Bishop of Autun and Monsieur de Beaumetz are of the
party. The weather is very hot. . . . The public mind is
much better than it was and will mend."

Such was the astonishing state of mind of one of the
cleverest men and politicians in Paris. This was four days
before the dawn of the fatal day when the fury of the Revolution was to be let loose!

III

For the Reds of the Midi had come up from the South,
through the white, blanched roads of Provence. The dusty
grey olive trees had offered scant shelter from the broiling
August sun. The Battalion of the Marseillais had marched
and marched—patriots every one! On July twenty-ninth,

these fierce warriors reached Charenton. "Patriot clasps dusty Patriot to his bosom; there is foot-washing and refection; dinner of twelve hundred covers at the Cadran Bleu—the Blue Dial," writes Carlyle in his *French Revolution*. On the morrow, the Battalion made their entry into Paris.

All along that hot, weary march from Marseilles to Paris, there was to ring for the first time, in provincial as in Parisian ears, the greatest of war songs—*La Marseillaise*. Rouget de Lisle, in the later Revolution of 1830, on hearing his own revolutionary hymn shouted by crazed Parisians, cried:—"Ah-h, it goes badly—they are singing the *Marseillaise!*" Had Talleyrand's, had Morris' ears been fine enough to catch the fatal message the song carried, they too might have cried, "Ah, it goes badly!"

It was to go from bad to worse. On Sunday, the 5th of August, Louis XVI held his last levée. "Never," said Bertrand-Moleville in his *Mémoires*, "had a Levée been so crowded." Within the Tuileries the courtiers wore, for the last time, some of their fine laces, embroidered vests, and beautiful coats. The generals and officers were resplendent in the gay uniforms of the time. Yet many of the nobles were in black. And above both glittering gold-embroidered coats and satin waistcoats were serious, care-worn faces. There were tears in many an eye. The glass windows and heavy doors of the Palace could not keep out the dread shouts of "Déchéance! Déchéance!"—those wild cries of the crowd in squares and streets, yelling for the "forfeiture" to be paid by the King to his people.

The insurrection which the fatalist King did not believe was ripe, was now indeed ripe to bursting. That curious, inexplicable vibration we call contagion was abroad in the air; the thrill of the revolutionary movement was communicated from man to man. How was it started, this contagious spasm which every revolution develops—or of revolutions there would be none?

The oldest courtiers felt that sinister quickening in the hot August air. They had hastened to the Court to lay down their lives, were murder to be attempted. There were seven hundred, young and old, in attendance. The faithful Swiss Guards were there—"steadfast as the granite of their Alps." And the Marseillais were cleaning their guns; for it was not to feast, even meagerly, at a Blue Dial Inn, they had come, but for business.

IV

"The night is beautiful and calm," treacherous Mayor Pétion stated, on his walk to the Tuileries. He was soon to set forth again, "because of the heat in the rooms" was his excuse; because of the King's freezing reception of him being the true reason. For what had this weak-kneed Pétion done to protect the good city of Paris? The city had gone mad.

At midnight—the dread sound! The tocsin sounded. From every steeple in Paris the clanging, noisy tongues rang out their murder-curdling message to the people. As though hypnotized by the very horror the hellish sounds conveyed, the courtiers "who had come to die," if necessary, at the King's feet, remained to count each stroke, to name each bell that bellowed forth from Saint-Roch and Saint-Eustace. From Saint-Germain l'Auxerrois there rang again that noisy clangor which had done its work on Saint-Bartholomew's black day. Robespierre, now become the "elegant" among the revolutionary leaders, was perhaps grimly smiling at his ease, in bed, thinking how well the work was being done for him, for Marat was pulling at one of the bells, working like a sweating blacksmith.

The tocsin had rocked one faction of the irresolute, semi-terrified, semi-exultant members of the Assembly, out, and another one—quite a new one—in. And no man was sure enough of anything, or of himself, or of his followers, or who there was who could head any movement whatever. There was one woman in the street who knew what *she* wanted. It was Thérèse de Mericourt in her riding habit and her helmet, with her sword and her pistols at her belt. She strode the streets for action, and soon found enough to do to satisfy even a Fury.

V

Worn out on the night of the 9th, the King had gone to bed. And—merciful powers of acceptance given to such natures as his—to sleep!

The Queen had eyes wide enough open to see all, to hear all. Even to listen, as the dawn broke, to her sister-in-law, to her "dear Elizabeth," who called her to "Come— see what a lovely sunrise!"

And then, in the ears of all, there was heard the wild, dread shout. The city had found its lungs. "Vive la Nation!" was the new-born cry of a new-born people. The cry was to be repeated, shouted—it was to be signed as real in flowing blood.

The courtiers heard it, looked to their swords and eyed the doors—could they pass? The King heard it, now awake, and with bent head, he came at last to a decision. With resolute heart—"Marchons!" he cried, to the Queen. And march they did, this royal family. Silently, in the conscious dignity of outraged majesty, they walked on and on—through the palace:—the King, whose eyes were swollen, still heavy with sleep! the Queen, whose "Austrian lip, fuller than usual, gave to her countenance something of majesty, which they who did not see her in those moments cannot well have an idea of"[1]; Madame Elizabeth and the two hapless children, and a following of courtier friends —all marched on and on.

The National Guard cried, "Make way!—the King is going to the Assembly!" Way was made. The doors of the Assembly closed on the imprisoned family—until, months later, others doors were opened wide, and broad daylight was to stream on the King's head, for the last time, and later, on that of the Queen. When each went forth to their martyrdom, it was seen that though neither wore a crown, they had exchanged that tinsel of majesty for the glow of an aureole.

There were other martyrs on that blood-stained day than those of the royal family. The Swiss Guard stood, to a man, at their post. Yet, after the King and Queen were gone, seeking the questionable protection of the People's Assembly, for whom must those brave men fight, were they attacked? The answer was soon given. Who has described the scene with as flaming a pen as has Carlyle?

O ye staunch Swiss, ye gallant gentlemen in black, for what a cause are ye to spend and be spent! Look out from the western windows, ye may see King Louis placidly hold on his way; the poor little Prince Royal "sportfully kicking the fallen leaves." . . . The poor Swiss know not how to act; one duty only is clear to them, that of standing by their post; and they will perform

[1] A bust, in the lower gallery at Versailles, gives this pose of the Queen's head with realistic effect.

that. . . . Think ye, staunch Swiss, whether it were good that grim murder begun, and brothers blasted one another in pieces for a stone edifice?—Poor Swiss, they know not how to act; from the southern windows some fling cartridges, in sign of brother-hood; on the eastern outer staircase, and within, through long stairs and corridors, they stand firm-ranked, peaceable and yet refusing to stir. Westermann speaks to them in Alsatian German; Marseillais plead, in hot Provençal speech and pantomime, stunning hubbub pleads and threatens, infinite, around. The Swiss stand fast, peaceable and yet immovable; red granite pier in that waste-flashing sea of steel. . . .

Who can help the inevitable issue;—Marseillais and all France on this side; granite Swiss on that? The pantomime grows hotter and hotter; Marseillais, sabres flourishing by way of action; the Swiss brow also clouding itself, the Swiss thumb bringing its firelock to the cock. And hark! high thundering above all the din, three Marseillais cannon from the Carrousel, pointed by a gunner of bad aim, come rattling over the roofs! Ye Swiss, therefore; Fire! The Swiss fire; by volley, by platoon, in rolling fire. . . .

At last, written order from his Majesty to cease firing! O ye hapless Swiss, why was there no order not to begin it? Gladly would the Swiss cease firing; but who will bid mad Insurrection cease firing? To Insurrection you cannot speak; neither can it, hydra-headed, hear. The dead and dying, by the hundred, lie all around; are borne bleeding through the streets, towards help; the sight of them, like a torch of the Furies, kindling Madness. Patriot Paris roars as the bear bereaved of her whelps. On ye Patriots; Vengeance! Victory or death! There are men seen, who rush on, armed only with walking-sticks. Terror and Fury rule the hour.

And the brave Swiss, hired out by their rapacious government for sixpence a day to this foreign power, gave that priceless lesson to all the world—better to be cut down to the last man than fail in obedience or honor.

THE MARCH OF THE ROYAL FAMILY TO THE TEMPLE

Facsimile of a German print

VI

Among the many accusations hurled at Talleyrand during the last months of his stay in France, was the following: his contemporary, the publicist Michaud [1]—a venomous writer, from whose history some of the most defamatory actions in Talleyrand's life record are asserted with no other proof than affirmation—thus describes Talleyrand's participation in the culminating drama of the exodus of the King and Queen from the Tuileries, August 10th, 1792:

Having arrived in Paris only a month ago, (Talleyrand) kept himself carefully hidden, and only saw in secret, the chiefs of his party, even the duc d'Orleans who was dying of fear in his palace—in deadly fear at the approaches of a revolution of whose programme he was the author, and whose actors he had paid. During the decisive day (August 10th) however, the ci-devant prelate was seen by the side of Roederer . . . *procureur général* of the department of which he himself was a member. He kept by his (Roederer's) side, following the royal family, and not wishing to be remarked, he did not open his mouth during the whole of that terrible séance. However, when the overthrow (of the King) was pronounced—when he perceived the embarrassment all were in as to what, at once, was to be done with the unhappy King, he (Talleyrand) drew from his pocket the address of a letter which he passed to the President, after having written these words: *"Send them to the Tower of the Temple"* (Envoyez les à la tour du Temple). Herault de Séchelles, who presided, made an affirmative sign, and at once it was decided that the entire family should be imprisoned in the old Palace of the Templars, which became the State prison.

This accusation is unsupported by any evidence whatever. Roederer, in his *Chronique des Cinquante Jours*, has no

[1] L. G. Michaud, *Histoire politique et privée de Ch.-M. de Talleyrand*, Paris, 1853, p. 25.

record of so dramatic and important a fact: not one of the other writers of the period mentions this curious bit of paper which was said to have passed from hand to hand— "de main en main," jealously preserved as a precious relic.[1]

[1] *La Vie Privée de Talleyrand*, Lacombe, p. 11.   Plon Nourrit, 1910.

CHAPTER XX

I

FOR some weeks after the imprisonment of the royal family, Talleyrand's movements were veiled in mystery. Pleasure of any sort had given way to a pressing sense of danger.

As the Terror spread its net wider and wider, as the massacres of priests and innocent women became the entertainment of the true "patriot's" day, Talleyrand felt the situation becoming far too dangerous for a moment's hesitation.

Constitutionalists were now tracked; certain had been guillotined. None had been more prominent among the members of the party than Talleyrand. He had reason to fear, for the second time, for his life.

Talleyrand's position in Paris, at this outbreak of the fury of the Revolution, had indeed become acute; danger faced him on every side. He was hated by the Jacobins, was distrusted by the Girondins, and was rated as a deserter of his own order by the Royalists and the Church. His negotiations with London were not only all but ignored, the results obtained were held up to ridicule. He was openly named as a "suspect." Delation was in the air: every gesture was open to suspicion; every visit was reported as being a rendezvous of "conspirators."

Talleyrand was, indeed, under no illusions. As an aristocrat, by birth the bearer of a great name; as a former Bishop, and now an unfrocked priest; and as he who, with Mirabeau, had been the most celebrated of all other Constitutionalists,—Talleyrand knew himself to be a marked man.

The tide of favor, he fully realized, had turned against him. His numerous enemies had not been idle. Every scandalous story connected with his past was cried to the four winds of storm-tossed Paris. The sincerity of his adherence to the Revolution was ridiculed. A true aristocrat, he had merely posed as a democrat to be rid of the Church. Every one knew he had sold himself to the Orleans party. Such were the stories afloat relating to the ex-Bishop of Autun.

True or false, any one of the above facts, or surmises treated as facts, was black enough to send a man to the road which led to prison—and later, to the scaffold.

His one hope and desire was to be able to leave France.

There was still a chance for escape—he could emigrate; but even emigration now presented grave difficulties. On the 28th of July the Assembly had decreed that only "those citizens charged with missions by the government, sailors, and merchants would be entitled to a passport."

The most difficult object to obtain in Paris at that time (1792), save a reprieve of one's life, was a passport. Every known subterfuge was used. Every device was exhausted. Even for one who, so recently, had diligently served France, as had Talleyrand, carrying off difficult diplomatic missions with every obstacle in the way of achievement,—even to Talleyrand, the Civil Tribunal was inexorable. A peremptory refusal met Talleyrand's urgent demands.

What could an aristocrat bearing the name of Talley-rand-Périgord now expect, in these days of the Terror, as his own doom? Courage to face denunciations, scandalous tales or outrageous insults is one form of courage; the highest comes to fine natures in moments of heroic exaltation. The soul may be strong enough to sustain such high altitudes. But how many characters can stand prolonged apprehension?—can endure with serenity the daily, hourly terror of possible imprisonment to be followed, perhaps, by death under the guillotine? Talleyrand would have marched up the too-long steps of the scaffold with his grandest air. The manner of laying his head beneath the glittering knife would have been a lesson in the fine art of an aristocrat's disdain of death. But Talleyrand, walking the streets of Paris in fear of his life; Talleyrand hastening from one friend to another, to seek help and security from any quarter; Talleyrand pleading with the very members of the Convention who, he was certain, were only longing to accuse him—here was a situation which shook with a tremor of fear that soul of Talleyrand as nothing in all his previous life had had power thus to convulse.

II

Now that he knew his life to be in danger, Talleyrand lost not a moment in prosecuting his insistence for a passport. If one door would not open to him, he would try another. The Civil Tribunal having shut its door in his face, there still remained the Minister of Justice. "Let us see if he realizes the meaning of the word"—may very well have been the astute diplomat's semi-amused, semi-cynical, inward murmur.

Danton was then Minister of Justice. Talleyrand, with the sure instinct of the born statesman, knew Danton to be his man—the one, and the only one, who could open the door for him, to safety. For the moment, Danton was supreme. He had the compelling power which comes with the instinct of leadership. Minister of Justice in the provisional executive council which had replaced the royal government on the 10th of August, he was soon the only one of the six members of the council who inspired, controlled, and dominated the other five. His magnetism, his fiery eloquence, his audacity made him as masterful in debate as in the Tribune. This "Mirabeau des Halles"—the Mirabeau of the Market, as Danton was called in contradistinction to "Mirabeau the Constitutionalist"—had charmed and subjugated enemies and friends alike. Though he was the guiding genius of that confused, disorganized, vacillating period immediately following the imprisonment of the royal family in the Temple, Danton's powerful mind was illuminated by one clear conviction: he knew little or nothing of the intricacies of diplomacy.

Among the several essential qualities which were lacking in him, he at least fully recognized his ignorance of foreign affairs. He was too intelligent not to seek guidance, and too ambitious not to utilize any knowledge which could enhance the glories of his brief reign.

He had not far to seek. The right man was close at hand. Danton realized that in Talleyrand he had found the one man who was able to carry out his negotiations with foreign Courts—particularly with England. The two men had had ample means of testing each other's capabilities and talents; both had been co-members of the Department of Paris. Danton had had many intimate talks with the ex-Bishop on all the grave and great topics of those agitated days. Since Talleyrand's return from England, the leader of the Gironde had constantly sought his advice on foreign affairs. When Danton, in his turn, became a "suspect" in 1794, Danton's enemies accused him before the Civil Tribunal of "having been constantly with the Bishop of Autun." Dissimilar as were the two men from the point of view of ancestry, breeding, in all that classifies a man as a gentleman, yet in ambitious designs, in a certain breadth of political outlook, Talleyrand found in Danton many of the same intellectual traits which had drawn him to the giant above them both—to Mirabeau.

Singular, indeed, was the contrast physically between the two men. Danton was cast in the mould of an athlete, physically impressive as are all men of robust, muscular massiveness. The features were markedly plebeian, "the head of a Medusa"; the face was pock-marked as was Mirabeau's: the nose was abrupt; the lips were sensuous but expressive—the true lips of an orator, and, as such, were aids to impassioned speech. The lack of harmony in the features reflected the discordance in Danton's powerful personality; the statesman warred with the demagogue. If Danton's eloquence was stirring as a battle cry in its impetuous ardor, irruptive as it was rich in imagery, he was equally capable of nursing action in the calm of serious reflection.

Before Talleyrand's enigmatic, impassive countenance, its pallor enhancing the disquieting impression of one's facing a mask rather than a human face—in the grand manner which was already so markedly that of a past period—Danton was not to be disturbed by either the diplomat's guarded reserve nor by his *grand seigneur's* courtly grace. The two men had need of each other. And the times were charged with dynamic potentialities.

The uses to which Danton proposed to put Talleyrand's recognized abilities would have seemed insurmountable to a capacity less plastic than Talleyrand's was now known to be, for dealing with foreign Courts and Embassies.

Danton's keen, semi-contemptuous estimate of Talleyrand's peculiar sense of honor, as well as of loyalty, was revealed by the first injunctions given to the ex-Bishop. If Talleyrand above all things in life wished to secure a passport, Danton felt European Courts and the Court of St. James' must be influenced to accept the fall of the monarchy and the establishment of the present Provisional government.

Talleyrand agreed to execute the treacherous task demanded of him.

In a Memoir, written entirely in his own hand, Talleyrand forced himself to prove to Europe that the unhappy Louis XVI was a tyrant and a traitor, the murderers of the Swiss "Guards" as heroes, the Assembly, immutably faithful to its principles, as the saviour and the guarantor of order and peace.[1]

Monsieur Lacombe, Talleyrand's indulgent historian, attempted to condone this shameful act as being that of a lawyer pleading a case rather than that of one advocating personal convictions. Such casuistry cannot perform the miracle of turning black into white. Lacombe states that "he" (Talleyrand) "was guilty of the weakness of consenting to appear, before Europe, as the lawyer of the crime— lawyer and not partisan." Europe, and most certainly England, spun no such fine webs of facile reasoning.

Talleyrand's direct address to England, in this note to

[1] *La Vie Privée de Talleyrand*, Lacombe, p. 16. Plon Nourrit, 1910.

DANTON

the Powers, is replete with that accent of finesse so peculiarly the characteristic touch of the statesman;—and yet, singularly enough, this past-master in the difficult art of treading with feet winged with tact, when approaching delicate ground, committed a most egregious error. In his note to England he urged, insistently, that "A misunderstanding must not take place between England and France: George III and his Ministers must not take as a menace and an insult to all the other kings the overthrow of the King of France, and declare war on the Revolution." The note goes on to affirm the "frank expression of the friendship of the Provisional government for the English government." After similar protestations of "esteem and confidence" the phrase at the end of the circular—a masterpiece of adroit insinuation—states:

the writer invites the English nation to remember that when the English people, in circumstances far more stormy and during events even more terrible [than these through which the French nation was passing], when the English nation recovered its sovereignty, the powers of Europe, and France in particular, did not hesitate to recognize the new government which the nation had accepted.

The reference to the Revolution of 1648 and to the death of Charles I on the scaffold was considered, by the English people, as peculiarly wounding to a nation which had so thoroughly repented of its errors as to commemorate the anniversary of the death of their King as a day of mourning. Talleyrand, for once, had committed a fatal mistake.

His circular produced rather bitterness and indignation, among the Powers, than the desired conciliatory effect.

III

Talleyrand paid, and paid dearly, the price demanded for his passport. Yet, after the delivery of the Note to the Powers, a week passed, and in a panic of fear, he was still waiting for the document. And every day's, every moment's delay might mean imprisonment and death.

On the Place Vendôme, on the 31st of August, 1792, Monsieur Barère mentions in his Memoirs that he met a figure familiar to him. "M. L'Evêque (Talleyrand), at eleven o'clock at night" (dressed) "in a pair of leather knee-breeches, booted, with a round hat, in a little coat, his hair tied in a little queue"—was seen to be ready, in a word, to jump into a posting coach. In spite of being so admirably equipped for his journey, the ex-Bishop must wait a long week before securing the precious paper.

The week had been an anxious one. Talleyrand felt the wide net spread by the Tribunal of the people in which to catch "aristocrats, bishops and priests"—and he had been all three—closing in about him. His solicitations to Danton became more and more urgent. Could he but secure a semi-official passport to England, what might he not accomplish? What errors might he not combat! Diligence, devotion, enthusiasm—all of his powers he would consecrate to keep the English from joining the formidable Coalition forces.

While Talleyrand was so strenuously pleading for his own safety, he was crying to every friend he met: "Leave Paris—leave at once! This is no place for you!" Soon his mistress, Madame de Flahaut, was to heed the warning. Talleyrand, although now not so much an ardent lover as friend—"nothing here below can last forever"—was yet solicitous of her fate.   Morris was to watch over the lady's welfare, after Talleyrand's departure.

Lord Wycombe was in Paris, dining at Gouverneur Morris' hospitable table.   This hospitality continued to be of an extensive order.   Only a few weeks before, Morris had been dining at Madame de Staël's, and, "After dinner, the gentlemen desiring to drink, I send for wine and let them get preciously drunk."   This latter fact is significant; drunkenness has never been a French vice.   But in such days as were those of that frenzied time, when one went about in fear of one's life, even sober Frenchmen must have welcomed a few hours of oblivion.

IV

In parting from Gouverneur Morris, Talleyrand had begged him also to leave Paris, for he "is persuaded that those who rule now mean to quit Paris and to take off the King; that their intention is to destroy the city before they leave it."   As in all revolutions, rumors and the wildest were not only circulated, but were believed by the cleverest and sanest of citizens.

The horrors begun by the "Septembriseurs" were now in full swing.   The prisons were crowded to repletion, as were the convents turned into prisons.   Aristocrats, cheating the gaunt spectre of their coming fate by continuing the frivolous amusements of their old Court life—gossiping, love-making, card-playing—heroically simulated gaiety to hide the gnawing of anguish or fear.   If their name were called, and they must appear before the "Comité," a gallant bow to their partners would precede the one made before the knife of the guillotine.   To the prisoners in the Abbaye, "Monsieur is given his liberty" was the watchword

Monsieur walks out of the dark prison, to be blinded by the daylight, and to face a mob of furies—blood-stained— horrible of mien—whose sharp knives and spikes ready for the victim are as crimson as are the arms which wield them. Refractory priests and nobles were not the only game pursued in this lustful hunt of victims. *Filles de joie* detained in La Salpêtrière, in order "to purify" Paris, were first violated, then killed. The youngest and prettiest suffered most from the first outrage. At Bicêtre, a House of Correction, filled with little boys and girls, these were mercilessly butchered, although the butchers complained that the "youngsters" were more difficult to kill than older people, "as though nature itself protested against such crimes." [1]

Frail, delicate-faced, a little vision appeared in white, eyes starting from the white face. "A bas! A bas!" cry the monsters. And they fall upon their prey like murderous hounds. Madame de Lamballe's lovely head being severed, was carefully dressed by a "patriot" barber. It was paraded on a spike with the other parts of the mangled body, and borne beneath the barred windows of the Temple. On seeing the awful spectacle, a scream was heard and the thud of a falling body. It was the Queen, who had fainted, as she had viewed through her prison windows this terrifying spectacle.

At Versailles, the killing of prisoners went on un- interruptedly. People wandered about the streets of both Paris and Versailles crazed—not knowing what summons might come, were they to remain indoors.

Talleyrand's talent for accomplishing his purpose was to prove anew its magical power. He secured his passport.

[1] *Histoire de France.* Ernest Lavisse. Tome I, La Revolution, p. 405.

He was to be paid, at last, for his Note to the Powers. "Laissez passer Talleyrand—allant à Londres par nos ordres—Danton, 1792—République." (Let Talleyrand pass, going to London by our order.)

Talleyrand's subtle mind had evolved a plan of escape from the dilemma of being classed as an "émigré." He had asked for a passport "to return to London not as charged with any public function, but as having been so charged."

This exceedingly equivocal evasion enabled Talleyrand, when in London, to announce he had not been sent on any mission, and yet to let it be understood that Danton had sent him on a secret mission.

The passport was signed by the six members of the Provisional government. Talleyrand received his passport on the 8th of September. He embarked on the 10th.

We can imagine with what haste the preparations for an immediate departure were made. Leaving a city still reeking with butcheries, yet all along the journey to the coast, the sights of the long lines of refugees were reminders that dangers lurked, like a monstrous beast, in the ambush of every Préfêt's or "patriot's" bureau.

Even with a passport, one signed by the Revolutionary leader, the fugitives were none too sure of escape. At every hamlet, village and town, "patriot guards" must be shown the magic paper. As most of the passports were made out under names of foreigners—of Belgians, Dutchmen or Englishmen, or of Frenchmen of low degree, or merchants —the dread of having to present one's self, if suspected of fraud, before the Mayor of a town, made every stoppage on the route to the coast an added inquisitorial torture. Such was the general terror that even children grew as wise

as though they were grown. Dressed as peasants, they
silently walked beside their disguised parents—showing no
sense of strangeness. Their little white faces might indeed
betray them, since their cheeks had not the burnt-in reds
of the children of the poor, bronzed and reddened by the sun.
And yet—such was the curious state of mind of certain of
the *bourgeoisie*, such power to face danger, even death,
can vanity wield—there were plain men and women who
would join the regiment of disguised nobles in flight, hoping
to be taken for such!

All along his route to the coast, Talleyrand passed such
bands of weary travellers trudging along,—women half-
fainting from fatigue, and children crying with hunger.
In carts and broken-down vehicles, whole families were
packed close, only too thankful to have secured even such
crazy conveyances. To have made use of one's coach
would have brought about the worst of disasters. The
occupants, known to be nobles, would have been apprehended and sent back to Paris. Although for the most
part disguised, and their passports made out under false
names, those who did not seek greater safety by going via
Holland made the journey to the coast in fear of their lives.

V

Once the last post passed in safety, and then to feel
beneath one's feet the balancing, rhythmic motion of the
packet-boat dancing on the sea—what an exultant sense
of relief must have possessed Talleyrand! As the green
coast of France disappeared behind him, and as he gazed,
longingly, toward the safe, white cliffs of England—for safe
he credulously believed them to be—to breathe that tran-

quil September air of England was balm indeed to sense and spirit.

Every object on the journey up to London was a rest to the eyes. The figure of the sturdy English peasant in his drab coat, red waistcoat, tight leather breeches and green, knitted stockings, above which rose the heavy, ruddy features—stolid, impassive—such figures and faces seemed to give assurance that all the world had not gone mad. The thatched, flower-decked cottages; the sweet, homely note of thrifty domestic content which the farms and fields proclaimed—how fair indeed was this England Shakespeare had sung!

Here were no noble Châteaux burning to prove the peasant's rage. Instead, great sweeps of lawn, like a spread carpet of verdure, led the eye to stately seats which seemed as much a part of the landscape as were the hedges; cattle, mild-eyed as were the lads who led them, wended their way to their stalls. The sinking sun poured its tinted rays, transforming earth and skies to the tones beloved of Crome. The still air, which seemed like unto a listening ear, now caught the silvery chimes of the curfew bells. Here was England, and at its best, in this its pastoral calm and content.

CHAPTER XXI

I

NOT long after Talleyrand's arrival in London, he was to experience the shock of an unexpected attack. Among the many compromising letters found in the famous Iron Safe, which had been discovered in the Tuileries, after the King's departure, was one by Talleyrand. In a letter written by Minister Laporte and endorsed by the King, dated April 22nd, 1791, he says:

Sire, I send to your Majesty a letter written the day before yesterday, and which I only received yesterday afternoon. It is from the Bishop of Autun, who desires to serve your Majesty. He wishes me to inform you that you can count on his zeal and his credit (or honorability), and that you can point out to him how you would wish to employ them. The new faction which has arisen among the Jacobins desires the re-establishment of public order, the maintenance of the monarchy, the overthrow of the democratic sect, and the safety of your person.

Talleyrand, as he erroneously supposed, was safe in London, when he learned of his letter having been discovered and read to the Convention. His indignant reply was forthwith despatched. He denied every word of the imputation:

I have never said nor ever done anything of the kind. I have had no direct or indirect relations with the King nor with Monsieur Laporte, I never in all my life have seen Monsieur Laporte more than four times.[1]

The letter is a long one. Its plea of justification did not appeal to the Convention. And in spite of Danton's express command, that Talleyrand was still to be "accredited to the French Embassy," in London, he was classed as a suspect and in Paris as "un Emigré." His papers, in Paris, were searched, and the Commune of Paris decreed seals were to be placed on all such documents.

Talleyrand lost no time in useless laments or recriminations. He proceeded to act as though he were still, if not *persona grata*, at least one whose importance deserved recognition from the English government. With characteristic dignity he offered Lord Grenville his official services:

I greatly desire that you should know that I have no sort of mission in England, that I came solely to seek peace and to enjoy among true friends, true liberty. If however, my Lord Grenville should desire to learn the state of France to-day, which are the parties which convulse her, and what is the true power of the provisional executive—also what possible conjectures may be formed of the terrible and ghastly events of which I have been an eye witness, I should be charmed to render to him an account of the same.

Numerous documents in the Archives of Foreign Affairs apparently testify to the truth of the facts stated in the

[1] Through an intermediary Talleyrand was advised of the desire of the King that he should rally to the support of the monarchy. Knowing Talleyrand's reputation for venality, a large sum was offered him. Talleyrand's reply was: "It is not sufficient. The Revolution offers me larger interests." His "interests" referred doubtless to his finding the earlier phase of the Revolution (the King's offer was made in 1790) more in conformity with his ambitions and reformatory designs.

above letter. Talleyrand had officially no connection with the French Embassy in London. Chauvelin writes, on his part, to the Department in Paris, to confirm the fact that "Talleyrand's mission had ceased to exist since your entry into the Ministry."

The contradictory statements, nevertheless, in relation to Talleyrand's so-called mission, are complicated by Marie-Joseph Chénier's solicitation to the Convention in 1796. The insistent appeals to the poet made by Madame de Staël, to obtain permission for Talleyrand's return to France (the latter was then in America), fired Chénier to become Talleyrand's advocate. "Our diverse Ministries to London attest to his excellent conduct"; Chénier asserts,

and to the services which he rendered. In my hands I have a *Mémoire* whose double has been found in Danton's papers. This *Mémoire*, dated the 25th of November, 1792, proves that he occupied himself in consolidating the Republic, while he was being accused, without motive, etc.

Talleyrand himself states, in a paper he calls an "Eclaircissement," on the 7th of Thermidor, after quoting the words of his passport, ending with the phrase "by our orders": "Thus I left France because I was authorized to do so, since I received from the confidence of the government positive orders for this departure."

Sir Henry Bulwer, in his Essay on Talleyrand,[1] much disturbed by the contradictions between Talleyrand's written statement to Lord Grenville that he had no mission whatever, and his later insistence that he had, asks plaintively:

[1] *Essay on Talleyrand:* Sir Henry Lytton Bulwer, 1867.

How conciliate Chénier's formal declaration with the solemn protestations of M. de Talleyrand to Lord Grenville? How could M. de Talleyrand write Mémoires to Danton, and yet assert his having come to England simply to seek repose?

Sainte-Beuve answers, in his essay on Talleyrand, exultingly, to that question; he is enchanted to find blasting proof of Talleyrand's further iniquitous transactions. "Comment? Comment? c'est se donner bien de la peine pour essayer de concilier ce qui est si simple et si bien dans la nature du personnage"—and he goes on, dosing his phrase with that gloss of delicate irony so essentially Sainte-Beuvesque:

In fact, what must one conclude from all this? the only thing which politeness forbids one to say of people unless they are dead—which is, that M. de Talleyrand lied; and he habitually lied whenever it was to his interest to do so.

In his *Mémoires*, Talleyrand made the not uncommon mistake of convincing himself that he could convince others that his motives always justified his actions, whatever their character might be. His equation does not square with the world's accepted axiom that stainless honorability needs neither explanation, nor commentary, nor justification.

On the same day that Talleyrand offered to present an historic ensemble of the state of France to Lord Grenville, a seemingly inspired communiqué appeared in *The Morning Chronicle*, the organ of English sympathizers with the Revolution. In this we learn:

Messieurs de Talleyrand-Périgord, de Montmorency, d'André, de Jaucourt, Beaumetz, le Chapelier and several others have been obliged to seek here a refuge against the fury of the·faction which now in France violates all principles of justice and humanity. Their sole crime appears to have been to content themselves with abolishing the abuses of the old government and to establish a sort of monarchy, and of their unwillingness to co-operate in establishing anarchy and proscription in the name of the Republic.

In all of the above statements, and in Talleyrand's appeal to Lord Grenville, certain facts stand out with peculiar significance. He wished it *to be thought* he had a mission. On the acceptance of this belief rested, not only his position in England, but also his future in France, when he should be enabled to return. To be considered as one of the innumerable band of *émigrés*, most of whom were penniless, who were either dependent on English bounty, or were working for a precarious living, was to accept for a de Talleyrand-Périgord a most humiliating position. To be classed as such, would present serious difficulties later on, when the time came to re-enter French territory.

Added to the above pressing reasons for desiring to be accepted as having been entrusted with a mission by Danton, was the very human desire of a proud nature to assert its dignity and importance. Talleyrand could not endure the thought of entering the stage of London life as a person of no importance whatever, after having played the rôle of negotiator in so difficult a task as was that of ensuring England's neutrality.

II

That which Talleyrand so strenuously desired, and that which he was forced to accept, in his two years' residence in England, marked the distance between longing and realization.

To his courteous suggestion to Lord Grenville, there was

no reply. Pitt was more than ever hostile. Court doors were definitely closed—and with them, doors of the more conservative aristocrats—doors whose hinges work in obedience to royal signals. English aristocracy was not only horrified at the ever-growing excesses of the French Revolution; even its advocates were beginning to fear its contagion. Burke was to lead the war-cry against the mad, wild "new French doctrines." England rose in rebellion against the growing dangers of French propaganda—that inevitable product of all revolutionary movements. Passionate was the tone of the speeches in the House of Parliament. Burke fulminated: "It is my object to keep the French infection from this country: their principles from our minds and their daggers from our hearts." The great orator did not disdain to make use of a melodramatic gesture: having mentioned the fact that three thousand daggers had been "bespoke at Birmingham, by an Englishman," some of which were for export and others "for home consumption," Burke drew out a dagger which he had kept concealed, and with a theatrical gesture threw it on the floor. "This," he cried, pointing to the dagger, "is what you are to gain by an alliance with France." Fox had been opposing, with his usual vehemence, the introduction of an Alien Bill (December 28, 1792). The Bill was to control the actions and was to authorize the supervision of foreigners in England. The power given to Ministers to exile undesirable aliens was seriously to affect Talleyrand, in the year 1794.

III

So far from leaving England alone, the revolutionary passions in France were leading "patriots" to act like madmen. When France is victorious she is apt to lose her head. France shouted across the Channel: "We'll rouse Ireland! We'll inflame Scotland! We'll arm pirates—your multitude of vessels, so rich in cargoes, will be the prey of our cruisers —we'll revolutionize England." This was wild Kersaint's cry—no statesman, as one perceives, but having been a Breton Captain, at least he knew how to command. He was one of the Committee of twenty-four members, in the Convention, of the Comité de Défense Générale. The government was more temperate: "It will be with regret that we shall war with England whom we esteem; but we shall fight her without fear."

IV

With London filled with French refugees; with the advent of such revolutionary leaders as Talleyrand, as the ex-Minister Narbonne, and such members of the National Assembly as de Jaucourt and Montmorency, London's former hospitable attitude was changing to one of veiled hostility. Talleyrand-Périgord was openly accused of being a "suspect," many of the French royalists being the most venomous in their accusations against the ex-Bishop.

In spite of finding London's reception as hostile as it was disappointing, Talleyrand was to lack neither friends nor entertainment. He established himself in a small house in Woodstock Street, in Kensington—among the gardens and sparse houses of the Kensington of that earlier eighteenth century period. This dwelling was soon to be a centre of mild gaiety and movement.

Talleyrand's house in Kensington became a sort of friendly refuge for several dear friends who had escaped

the horrors and dangers of the Terror. Narbonne, Jaucourt, Mathieu de Montmorency and Beaumetz—those
chosen companions of his youth and manhood were to be
offered such hospitality as lay in his power. The house in
Kensington Square was kept by Madame de la Châtre,
Jaucourt's Egeria and his *amie de cœur*, whom he was later
on to be able to marry. One can imagine something of
the excitement and passionate interest with which those
who had just escaped from imprisonment and certain death
would narrate their experiences.

Narbonne, Montmorency and Beaumetz owed their
lives to Madame de Staël's courage. What a story
of adventure, of thrilling, heroic action, and of lofty self-
sacrifice was this to tell and to which to listen! The very
walls in that small London house must have rung with the
tremors of grateful feeling, as these men gave the tale of
their escape from the knife of the guillotine.

Servants, in the few great houses still open in Paris,
were almost as much of a danger as were the death lists of
the Tribunal of the People. Delation, in this Paris of
crime, had become a favorite pastime among the lower
classes. A man-servant, one morning, early, announced
to Madame de Staël that the Comte Louis de Narbonne's
name was listed, and that the order of his arrest was posted
at the corner of the rue de Bac. The servant must have
enjoyed watching the effect of his news, for in the Swedish
Embassy, Narbonne, together with Montmorency and
Beaumetz, had been in hiding for some days.

Madame de Staël had offered her lover and her two
friends this gracious and, for her, dangerous hospitality.
She knew quite well that the Swedish Embassy was now
no longer a safe refuge for proscribed nobles. Lord Gower,

the English Ambassador, had been stopped, at the moment of his departure from the English Embassy, and was asked to report at the bar of the Assembly. Madame de Staël knew full well, therefore, the serious risk she was running in thus harboring French aristocrats under her roof.

Certain that soon a domiciliary visit would be made, she awaited the dreaded visitors in her room. She did not have long to wait. Soldiers could be heard ranging themselves about the outer door of the Embassy. The Commissioners who demanded entrance were a terror to look upon. They were composed of the lowest orders of the people. Madame de Staël saw, in their ignorance of geography, a chance to save her friends. First of all she attacked them for daring to trespass on foreign soil. She played on their ignorance of frontiers. She boldly announced that Sweden, being a near State to France, would swiftly avenge the insults to its King and to its Ambassador.

The trick was brilliantly played. And it won. The half-frightened, half-dismayed patriots slunk away. Madame de Staël, in accompanying the boorish creatures to the door, jokingly questioned how they dared to suppose her guilty of harboring "the enemies of the people"—but she was careful to have the outer doors of the Embassy tightly closed on such dangerous visitors.

The three hidden guests had been saved, for a brief space, by Madame de Staël's sang-froid and her ready resourcefulness. But every moment the friends spent under her roof was fraught with the gravest peril. Narbonne must quickly make his escape. The situation had been aggravated by the fact that Narbonne had been a Constitutionalist and a Minister of War under Louis XVI. Where could such a marked man find hope of sure rescue?

A young German—Bollman by name—at the risk of his own life arranged a hiding place for de Narbonne. He managed his escape so skilfully that both he and Narbonne arrived in England in perfect safety.[1]

V

Narbonne and Bollman were both warmly welcomed in England by Talleyrand. In his modest dwelling in London, he greeted his friends with a degree of enthusiasm rare in Talleyrand's commonly restrained manner, and with the same exquisite courtesy with which, as Prince de Bénévent, he was to receive his guests later, in his varied career, at his princely Château of Valençay.

Narbonne narrated the story of his escape in his brilliant, effective manner.   How prolonged must such *causeries* have been: far into the London night, the talk would stretch on to the faint dawn, when the roll of carts on their way to market warned the group of eager listeners that they faced the new day.

In M. Bollman's Letters an interesting description is given of both Narbonne and Talleyrand.

Narbonne's appearance had changed considerably since the days when he was a slim youth tripping along the green aisles of the Versailles alleys.

Narbonne is rather a big man (notes friend Erick Bollman), he is a bit heavy, vigorous, and his head strikes one as having an arresting, a superior air. His mind is furnished with in-

[1] Dr. Juste Erick Bollman, a graduate of Göttinburghe, having gone to Paris as a young man of twenty-two, from interest and curiosity, became an habitué of Madame de Staël's salon during the early days of the Revolution.   After effecting de Narbonne's escape, Bollman on his arrival in London was fêted as a hero.   His picturesque career and further heroic exploits prove him to have been one.   Leaving

exhaustible riches of ideas. He possesses in a supreme degree
all the social virtues. He communicates to the most arid of
subjects an incomparable grace. When he wishes, he can attract,
irresistibly, and even intoxicate one person as well as a roomful
of people.

There was only one other man in France who is worthy from
this point of view to be compared to him, one who, in my opinion,
greatly surpasses him: this is his friend, Talleyrand, ex-Bishop
of Autun. Narbonne pleases but in the end, he tires one; on the
contrary, one could listen to Talleyrand for long years. Narbonne seeks to please, and makes one conscious of the effort;
Talleyrand speaks without the least effort and lives constantly
in an atmosphere of perfect contentment.   Narbonne's language is more brilliant; that of Talleyrand is more gracious,
is more incisive, more *coquet*. Narbonne is not the man for every
kind of man; sentimental people cannot endure him, over them
he has no hold. Talleyrand, no less corrupt morally than is
Narbonne, can move to tears even those who despise him.[1]

Talleyrand's habitual manner, in society, was distant,
guarded, inscrutable. Englishmen were at a loss to "class"
Talleyrand.

The manners and turn of mind of a Court prelate who had

London for Vienna, on learning of Lafayette's imprisonment, Bollman practised as a
doctor in that city: his design was to liberate the general. This he did, but both
Lafayette and Bollman were caught and the latter, after being imprisoned, was forced
to leave Austria. He took ship for America. He came under the fascinating
influence of Aaron Burr. Implicated in Burr's wild Mexican enterprise, Bollman was
arrested, and after outrageous treatment, before being tried, was finally imprisoned
in Baltimore. His trial was sensational. Congress, the Courts, the Supreme Court
with Justice John Marshall as Supreme Judge, were at war over the vital question
"as to the legality of suspending the privilege of the writ of Habeas Corpus"—the
privilege having been refused Bollman. Twice, during his trial, Bollman was offered
his "pardon" which he refused. He stoutly asserted his complete innocence of the
charges against him. In the end he was released. (*Life of John Marshall*. Albert
J. Beveridge. *Madame de Staël et son Temps*. Lady Blennerhassett. Houghton,
Mifflin & Co., Boston.)

[1] Letters of Juste Erick Bollman, September 14th, 1792.

become the apologist of a Revolution, confounded most Englishmen; in him they found nothing which corresponded to their common prejudices against Frenchmen, neither frivolity, nor gossip, nor indiscretion, nor the national gaiety. His was a sententious manner, a freezing politeness, a scrutinizing air which formed a kind of defence around his diplomatic personality.

He gave the impression in society of "a man remarkably silent and remarkably pale." He reserved all his seductions for intimacy. It was then he revealed himself "familiar, caressing, attentive, taking infinite pains to please, and amusing in order to be amused." Sorel has given few more lifelike portraits. Talleyrand's society began to be courted by many of the foremost Englishmen belonging to the Opposition.[1]

Talleyrand's actions, whatever their nature, appear to have had little or no power, substantially, to affect his social relations. He was not, it is true, received on this third visit at Court. But Monsieur de Périgord was more than made a welcome guest at many of the great English houses. The errors, mistakes and vices—if he really could be reproached with the practice, at this period of his life, of any vice save that of gambling—tales which tracked him through life—all were ignored among certain of the leading English aristocrats. They recognized in him one of their own caste. The Constitutionalist was forgotten in the *grand seigneur* who was never more seductive than in his own social world.

The Englishmen of the latter end of the eighteenth century were fit antagonists for the delicate, yet pointed wit of the wittiest of Frenchmen.

Their own distinction of manners and of mind delighted

---

[1] *l'Europe et la Révolution Française.* Albert Sorel: Dumont, p. 361, 362.

in a turn of phrase which had the polish of Greek verse.
No one had a tact as subtle as had the scholar who had had
his lesson taught him in tact and in finesse by his Sulpician
masters and at the French Court.

Lord Lansdowne, Lord Holland, Samuel Rogers, the
poet, and the greatest of them all, Charles Fox, were to seek
Talleyrand's company. In Lord Lansdowne, Talleyrand
was to find one of those rare friends who were indifferent
or superior to venomous gossip. A Liberal, a man of wide
and highly cultivated tastes and a great admirer of France,
Landsdowne found in the brilliant Frenchman's society the
charm of intellectual affinities and the graces of delicate,
pungent wit.

VI

In several of the beautiful and great English houses
Talleyrand found himself to be entirely at home. His two
missions to London had given the leading English statesmen
the measure of his talents, as diplomat and negotiator.

Talleyrand was to find in the houses or in the company
of George Canning, of Bentham, of Priestley, of Samuel
Romilly, of Lord Holland and of Lord Hastings—the famous
former Governor-General of India—congenial and brilliant
minds.

Lord Lansdowne remained faithful to his friend. An
interesting letter written by Talleyrand to his Lordship
dated "Kensington Square, 3 October, 1792" reveals the
ever-continuing semi-intimacy between the two friends:

MILORD,

I had hoped since a long time to profit by your goodness to me
and to go and pass in your society some days of wit, of reason, of
instruction, and of tranquillity, but some of my French friends,
devoted to the cause of liberty and chased away by pikes, have

arrived in England and I wished to offer them their first shelter. By the middle of next week they will, I think, have arranged their winter quarters, and thus I will have the honor of paying my court to you at Bowood. . . .

Englishmen of the latter part of the eighteenth century were many of them connoisseurs in art. "Those Italian engravers who dedicated their ponderous volumes to Roman Cardinals and Princes found their most numerous, and certainly their most liberal customers, among Peers and Squires," Trevelyan[1] states. He goes on to note that when Robert Adams, the King's architect, brought out his great book on Diocletian's palace at Spalatro in Dalmatia, that costly work found its chief subscribers among men such as Lord Shelbourne, Lord Bute and others of the peerage.

Talleyrand and those of his friends who found favor among cultivated Englishmen were to enjoy a hospitality which has become synonymous with the word English—a generous and gracious practice which, with the English Pilgrims, traversed the Atlantic.

The great English houses were then adorned with those pictures and family portraits, tapestries, and works of art so many of which, in our own century, have also crossed the seas.

The Italian workmen who travelled from one end of England to the other left many an English ceiling in Hall and Manor decorated with their peculiar style of plaster mouldings. This fanciful style was agreeably suited to the Italianate architectural style which prevailed in the seventeenth century; for in and long after Shakespeare's day, the Italians brought to England their Renaissance models in architecture.

[1] *George III and Charles James Fox.* Trevelyan. 2 vols.

In such beautiful houses, Talleyrand felt entirely at home. The large-hearted hospitality, practised by the owners of such seats, recalled the lavish entertainment of Saverne, of Hautefontaine and of the de Choiseuls, at Chanteloup. Visits here in England were also prolonged *ad infinitum.* "I have fixed no time for my return. . . . I like everything here so much I have no inclination to leave the place," writes George Selwyn to the Earl of March, from a house which is not named.

If Talleyrand's incomparable conversational powers could have made Madame de Staël exclaim: "If the conversation of Monsieur de Talleyrand could be bought, I should ruin myself," what must it have been to have heard him give his experiences to his new friends, of all the scenes in which he had been a participant. True diplomat that he was, he would have told them just so much as he wished them to know. But the great tragedy had been played on so great a stage, and the actors had succeeded each other with so swift a change of character and costume, there was choice enough of scenic presentment.

English peers were no idlers, whether at home or in Parliament. They were conscientious landowners, and diligent politicians. Though their greatest out-door pleasure was taken in the hunting field, to which they devoted much time, money and thought, yet in moments of relaxation at home, the favorite companions of the more cultivated classes would be Livy, or Lucian or a French classic.

Charles James Fox and many other clever Englishmen spoke French and knew French literature. Fox also spoke and read Spanish and Italian as easily as he did French. Horace Walpole, when he was in Paris, at a time when everything English was the rage, and where, as Walpole humorously wrote: "I was as much run after as though I had been a celebrated criminal," also knew French well. Such eminent men set the taste and the intellectual fashion of the day.

CHAPTER XXII

I

THE King's trial before the Convention, begun on October 4th, 1792, in January, 1793, was approaching its fatal conclusion. Those royalists who still called themselves Constitutionalists had been busy with one effort after another in their attempt to save the King.[1]

Narbonne, from the very beginning of the King's trial, acted in the noblest manner. He announced to the Civil Tribunal that he was willing to answer in person to the accusations—to those directed towards the monarch, during his, Narbonne's, ministry. The only reward of this fine action was Narbonne's being prohibited from returning to France.

Malouet and Lally-Tollendal published defences of the King. Madame de Staël's touching tribute to Louis XVI is an instance of the talent of this woman of letters in finding the right words to fit a great occasion: "He was the only King of France who seriously desired the liberty of his people.

---

[1] The King had not lost hope. Although from the month of October he could only see his family at meals and during the brief hour of exercise, his life went on with singular regularity. His phlegmatic character helped him to accept his life of captivity; he read and prayed, his faith becoming more and more the guiding light of his days. He, at least, did not suffer, as did the Queen and the Dauphin, from ill-treatment. His meals were served with care, the *menu* was abundant, his appetite never failed him. Books and clothing were supplied whenever desired. The King, physically, did not suffer from either ill-treatment or deprivation. (*Histoire de France:* La Révolution, Ernest Lavisse.)

MARIE–ANTOINETTE ON HER WAY TO THE SCAFFOLD

This sketch was made by the artist David, who drew it as Marie-Antoinette was passing below the windows of his friend Julien, in the cart which was taking her to the scaffold.

The heroism of philosophy is surpassed by the simplicity with which this former favorite of destiny submitted to his hopeless fate."

Neither the devotion of the hundred royalists—for there were still royalists in Paris who presented themselves to co-operate for the defence of the King—nor the willingness of those who longed to "lay down their lives" for their monarch, nor such brave hearts as was Narbonne's, nor touching eloquence could avail. "If Louis XVI is innocent, we are all rebels; if he is guilty, he must perish,"—was the dread sentence of the party of the Montagnards, in the Assembly. Robespierre's phrase: "Louis is not to be judged; he is judged. He is condemned, or the Republic is not absolved," was the death sentence the people of Paris applauded.

The end came soon enough. One heard from afar, as Sainte-Beuve wrote: "As heavy and hurried as the noise of oars on a still lake, were the sounds of the regular strokes of the knife of the machine on the scaffold."[1]

After the 10th of August, 1792, England joined the Coalition. With Louis XVI's trial before the Convention in January, 1793, and later, his execution; with the continued grinding of that knife of the guillotine on the necks of the hated "aristocrats"; with the setting up of a Tribunal of the People in French towns, and with the butcheries of "suspects" throughout France, England read the lesson of the hour with kindling, horrified eyes. The reign of the people in France and the reign of Terrorism they had brought in, with their assumption of sovereignty, were to be condemned, England decided, by armed force.

When the news of the King's decapitation reached London, first stupor, then horror, and finally hot-headed

[1] *Nouveaux Lundis,* Vol. 12, Sainte-Beuve.

anger seized the public. "War with France! War with France!" were the cries leaping from the throats of the men in the streets. Theatres were closed. The Court and Parliament went into mourning. "Every man," wrote Maret to Lebrun, "who had a black coat, or was able to procure one, put it on." No tragedy since that of Saint Bartholomew had so shaken England as did the murder of Louis XVI. He, as King, stood for what was the rock foundation of English government. Dead, the French King was crowned with the aureole of a martyr. His weaknesses, his fatal errors were forgotten.

Talleyrand mourned his sovereign, as did every other French patriot. His black coat was no hypocrite's garment. A passionate lover of France—the only lasting passion of his long life—monarchist at heart, however deeply inspired with a love of liberty and of the new ideals which had animated him, in the earlier days of the Revolution, Talleyrand's political policy was founded on the principle of constitutional law and order. To these principles Talleyrand was true—under whatever government he may have served—or was to serve.

In putting the King to death, Talleyrand foresaw the future shipwreck of the revolutionary movement. The period of the Terror had already disabused him of all hopes of real reform or of the reign of law.

He ceased, for a time at least, to take further interest in the Convention. He felt relieved from its "abominable yoke."

II

Talleyrand's attitude, while in England, was at once politic and patriotic. He openly proclaimed his longing for the success of French arms, as did every French patriot. Yet he was always held by those in power as being dangerous to English interests. Pitt, from the beginning of his sojourn, continued to consider him "as a deep and dangerous man," *un homme profond et dangereux*, as Lord Grenville had called him.

The execution of Louis XVI changed the attitude of the English government towards France. Former sympathy with the revolutionary movement turned to bitter hostility. Burke led the war-cry; and moreover, so heated was public opinion by the massacres of the 10th of August and by the execution of the King, that Pitt was being angrily charged with purposely delaying military preparations. Revolutionary France soon had the whole world to fight. England's gold was to be emptied from its deep strong boxes in order to supply the armies of the Coalition.

With England's later declaration of war on France, plots and counter-plots were thickening about Talleyrand. In France he found himself denounced by Robespierre and Marat. In England, the royalist *émigrés* were continuing their accusations of his being a spy in the pay of the Jacobins. To these denunciations William Pitt and Lord Grenville were beginning to listen, with open ears.

Talleyrand had the prescience of coming events. This intuitive gift, particularly in political foresight, was almost feminine in its acuity. He realized the thickening clouds which were beginning to gather about his head. He was living in an atmosphere the reverse of that which he had sought to find. Suspicion, denunciation, perfidy were in the air.

For a time at least, however, the English authorities left the ex-Bishop in peace. His occupations were those of all clever men with no active outlet for talent or energy. He read all the books he could lay his hands on. There were visits to be made: certain English houses were open to him, and while many of his French friends were leaving England for other more hospitable countries, there were notable gatherings every evening, among the *émigrés*. Narbonne was still in London. He had now a house of his own, and was accused of "extravagance," since he kept two servants and a coach. There were gatherings where Talleyrand met the Duc de Broglie, the Abbé Louis, "the deacon of the famous Mass in the Champ de Mars," and the visionary Duc de Liancourt. Among the ladies were Madame de Flahaut, Madame de Genlis with her two "pupils"— Pamela and Mademoiselle d'Orléans—the latter to be known as she who governed, in her turn, her brother, King Louis-Philippe, after having been "governed" by the mistress of her own father.

The sparkle and gaiety of such meetings were largely due to Talleyrand, to whom the society of congenial friends was the flint that struck fire to his most brilliant wit. Matters of personal interest were soon to force Talleyrand, however, to a painful resolution. The growing poverty among his more intimate friends; his own diminishing funds; the urgency of finding some help for his needs and, if he were fortunate, for alleviating the situation of others, these pressing necessities finally ended in Talleyrand's coming to a decision. He would be able to meet expenses, he decided, through the making of a great sacrifice. He had managed to save his library; he had transferred it from the rue de l'Université to his Kensington Square house. Only those who have made great sacrifices to secure valuable books; only those who have pursued the delectable game of hunting down a rare volume; and only those who have surrounded themselves finally with the visible proofs of their relentless chase and of their pecuniary sacrifices to secure a prize, can realize what a pang it must have cost Talleyrand to look at his beloved books, and to know that they were to be his no more. To part with them was to tear at the very vitals of this true book-lover. How far away were the gay mornings when, as a young man in his poor lodgings at Bellechasse, he could show, proudly, his last acquisition to the men about him! There was, however, no alternative. This library was his only asset. It must go. Once the decision made, the sale was ordered. The pro-ceeds—seven hundred and fifty pounds—temporarily re-lieved Talleyrand from pressing want. This fund was also to help others. Comparatively small as was the benefit resulting from the sale, Talleyrand gallantly shared some of his newly acquired resources with Madame de Genlis, and others of his friends in distress.

The prudish "governor" of her lover's—the Duc d'Orléans'—children Madame de Genlis repaid Talley-rand's offer of assistance, at this time of her great need, in recording his generosity, in fulsome phrases. Women, at least, were ever ready to render to Talleyrand an appreci-ative recognition of his fine traits.[1] Madame de Staël's statement that "he was the best of men, a misunderstood character" was one no man has ever endorsed. Sorel alone among historians has rendered a just and generous, if im-partial, view of the great statesman. Madame de Staël's own verdict was one she probably would have modified after the rupture, during the Napoleonic period, of her

---

[1] Madame de Genlis states in her Memoirs that Talleyrand offered her 12,000 frs. which she refused.

friendship with Talleyrand. A woman who has been half in love with a man, sees through optics which change color, when deception succeeds an amorous attraction.

III

In spite of the temporary alleviation of their straitened circumstances furnished by the sale of Talleyrand's books, the friends surrounding him decided a change must be made in their manner of living.

The choice of the new dwelling was a most fortunate one; it had been determined by the generous proposal of an English gentleman—Mr. Locke. He offered to loan his fine estate of Juniper Hall, to the refugees.

Historians differ as to the exact date of this change of residence, and as to who were the real hosts at the charming house in Surrey. French writers assert that Juniper Hall was lent by Mr. Locke to Madame de Staël. As hostess it was she who proffered generous hospitality to a whole colony of her French friends. This was in February, 1793. Other historians state that the friends who had lived with Talleyrand in the Kensington house "emigrated" to Juniper Hall in January, installed themselves therein, and that it was there Madame de Staël joined them after her adventurous journey from Switzerland.

In the lovely county of Surrey, near Mickleham, in Juniper Hall, these émigrés had found a dwelling which seemed to fill their every want. While in no sense comparable to any of the great English seats, or fine houses, Juniper Hall had a certain air of luxury. The interior had the style of decoration which had come into fashion with Adam; there were graceful garlands on walls and ceilings and finely sculptured fireplaces.

According to Fanny Burney's Diary,[1] Talleyrand appears to have made frequent visits to the little colony at Juniper Hall. He seems to have maintained his house, in Woodstock Street, however, as his permanent residence.

With the arrival of Madame de Staël in England, as a comet trails its illumined robe along its path, came an added brilliance to the lives of those friends she was to find already assembled at Mickleham. With the quick rebound of the French nature, this group of refugees welcomed Madame de Staël with an enthusiasm colored by the sense of regained security. Her power of conveying strength, her optimism in inspiring hope, and her unfailing generosity were tonic to strained nerves and depressed spirits. The atmosphere generated by her mere presence was soon to restore to life the lost French standard of living, to recapture gaiety, to make France and its horrors seem but a bad dream. Even London, so near, seemed far away. Far away were even the echoes of the venomous gossip, of the perfidy, and of the rancorous jealousies that disgraced the social relations of some of the French royalists; forgotten were such outrageous insinuations indulged in, by former Court ladies, as that the Queen had appeared, after certain absences in her apartments, with "a crumpled dress." Here, at least, for a time, at Mickleham, reigned happiness, peace, and harmony.

Juniper Hall was exceptional among most of the other colonies in that no one, save the richest of all the group, appeared to find any form of labor a necessity.[2] The friends gathered there were to have a brief respite from the remembered horrors of personal danger and want. The two men

[1] *Diary and Letters of Madame D'Arblay* (1778–1840). Edited by her niece, Charlotte Barrett, with preface and notes by Austin Dobson. 6 vols, 8vo. Macmillan & Co.

[2] Madame de Staël wrote continuously during her stay in Surrey.

Madame de Staël had saved—Narbonne and Jaucourt—were her daily companions, both eager to attest their gratitude by every possible attention. There were also Mathieu de Montmorency, Lameth, d'Argenson, General d'Arblay, Madame de la Châtre, and, prince of them all, there was Talleyrand.

It was no light source of relief to the more impecunious, that Madame de Staël was as generous as she was rich. Her purse furnished the Pactolian stream which turned many a friend's eating anxiety into an assured, if temporary, comfort.

IV

Madame de Staël had left Paris in 1792 for Switzerland. She was driven thither not only to seek safety, but also because of an imperative necessity which even women of genius must occasionally obey. She was about to be delivered of a child. Her recent experiences in Paris had convinced this courageous woman that that city of dreadful night was no longer safe.[1] Coppet, her father's residence, was naturally the chosen refuge. There her second son, Albert, was born, in 1792.

One wonders if the reason for Madame de Staël's appearance at Juniper Hall was as clearly understood as it is in our day?

Neither a new-born son, nor the sweetness of family life with her beloved and idolized father, and with her gifted and now invalided mother, could hold, for long, so restless a spirit as was Madame de Staël's. The comparatively calm air of Switzerland was no Capri for one whose inner ear heard, from afar, the roar of the European conflict.

[1] Madame de Staël had been under temporary arrest, in Paris, having foolishly driven through the streets in her Ambassadorial coach. *Madame de Staël et son Temps.* Tome Deuxième. Lady Blennerhassett.

There was yet another magnet drawing Madame de Staël nearer to the theatre whereon such tragic scenes were still enacted.

Narbonne, she knew, was in London, as was also Talley-rand. In those days, women appeared to have won their full and complete freedom without fighting for it. No historian seems to consider that a journey undertaken from Coppet to England in war-time, by a married woman, one only recently a mother, was either strange or unusual. Necker, Madame de Staël's father, however, presents the lamentable figure of a parent destitute of authority. He might have been the modern father. In writing to his friend Meister, he says:

I cannot hide from you how much this journey distresses us. I have done all in my power to prevent its being under-taken, but in vain! My daughter cannot avoid passing through France: this circumstance augments our anxiety, although she will not go near Paris.

But then—Narbonne and Talleyrand were in England. When a woman's body is in one place and her heart and mind are in another, if she be of determined character and her purse be her own, mere distance is only a matter for time to compass. Madame de Staël had taken her flight, undaunted, from dull Coppet to the storm-centre of Europe. She crossed France. She brought to her friends at Juniper Hall the latest news of the anarchy reigning across the Channel.

Such tragic experiences were not the only topics listened to. There were hours so gay and joyous one might have imagined here was a company of friends gathered together for purely festive enjoyment. Through the still green Surrey hedgerows, a dilapidated cabriolet took, each day, two or three of the house-guests at Juniper Hall on interminable drives. Some of the gayest hours were those passed in this rickety cabriolet. There were but two seats in the interior of the vehicle, and one outside for a groom. This latter was soon requisitioned by each one of the male guests in turn. As Madame de Staël was always in one of the front seats, in order not to lose a word of the talk going on between her and her neighbor, the one on the back seat had soon made of the intervening glass window a mass of fragments. Narbonne, Talleyrand, and Montmorency each in turn disputed the honor of seizing the groom's seat. No conversations were ever gayer, more brilliant, more profound, at times, than were those heard in the little English cabriolet. What is a coach and six with dullness seated therein compared to the keenest wits in Europe, in a crazy vehicle?

V

Among the guests who frequented Juniper Hall was a company of clever women whose eyes gradually began to be opened to the irregular relationships existing between certain members of this interesting French colony. Juniper Hall, before the arrival of the distinguished French refugees who now filled it, had been a desert. With the arrival of Madame de Staël, of Talleyrand, of Narbonne and their friends, a Pleiades of wits and intellects had arrived sufficient to enliven a whole neighborhood.

Among the near neighbors of the colony were Miss Fanny Burney and her sister, Mrs. Philipps. The delight and enthusiasm of these ladies, at first, had been roused to a lyrical state of admiration and appreciation of the character and charm of these distinguished French men and women.

Fanny Burney, in writing to her father, comments on the warmth and ardor of the friendship of Madame de Staël for her friends—for de Narbonne, for Talleyrand, and for de Montmorency:

Madame de Staël treats de Narbonne with so much frankness, with so much simplicity, with so little affectation, with such an absence of coquetry that their affection, it seems to me, could not be more frank if they were two men or two women. She is very plain and he is not handsome. The superior intelligence of Madame de Staël constitutes her sole attraction.

And the author adds:

Monsieur de Talleyrand is of their society. She appears to be equally attached to him. She loves Monsieur de Montmorency . . . in fact all this little colony live together like brothers and sisters. You cannot live twenty-four hours in their society without perceiving that their intercourse is of the purest, the most elevated, the most elegant friendship.

Of all the *émigrés* who frequented Mickleham, the most charming, according to Fanny Burney, was Talleyrand.

It is inconceivable [she writes] the impression that Monsieur de Talleyrand had made on me. I consider him now as being the first and the most delightful of the members of this exquisite company. His turn of thought is as remarkable as the ideas which he develops, as well as the wit with which he presents them.

Suddenly, an icy wind blew over the warmth of these sentiments. Certain disturbing rumors reached the ears of Mr. Burney, father of the authoress. Madame de Staël was quick to feel the chill in the atmosphere; but her character was built on large lines; she was great enough to pass over even personal affronts.

Even here, at Mickleham, the serpent which enters every Paradise, with its malicious tongue, worked mischief. The discussions and turmoil in the Convention, like the sounds of the falling knife of the guillotine, appeared to send the echo of their quarrels across the water to envenom such intimate relationships as existed between friends.

For all was not now *couleur de rose* at Juniper Hall. Some of the guests, as well as the leading spirit, were to encounter disapproval from their English friends and neighbors. The cause of some harsh criticism and ill-feeling was due to the fact that England was a very different soil in which to attempt to transplant certain French customs and French immorality. In Juniper Hall and the immediate neighborhood, there were three more or less admitted liaisons. Lally-Tollendal was intimate with the Princesse d'Henin. Madame de Staël had come to be with her lover, Narbonne. Madame de la Châtre was the mistress of de Jaucourt.

To the charm of intimacy succeeded coolness, and eventually a withdrawal from all intercourse between the group of talented French friends and the Burney trio. With their father, the two sisters had been said, by the clever refugees, to unite "knowledge, wit, grace and talent." One element, however, that of indulgence, was lacking.

Miss Fanny Burney should have shown, at least, a more generous spirit. She had been lucky enough to find a husband at Juniper Hall. General d'Arblay fell in love with the somewhat mature charms of the author of *Evelina*. When the marriage took place, after Juniper Hall was again a "desert"—the group of the refugees having left—Madame de Staël sent warm and even affectionate congratulations to the pair. "Sweet memories of Norbury," she wrote, "come and remind me that happiness pure and keen can exist on earth."

Madame de Staël's elevation of mind was, indeed, wholly undisturbed by the criticisms to which she had been subjected. In the pages which she devoted later on to the country of Burke, Wilberforce, Pitt, Fox and other great men, and in which she gave her impressions of England, she states that the country "whose greatness rests on the solid basis of liberal institutions seemed to her as the most complete expression of European civilization."

VI

With Madame de Staël's recall to Coppet—her husband appears to have possessed some remnant of authority—the delightful life was at an end at Juniper Hall. One by one— or by two's, more likely—the group broke up. Narbonne eventually followed his Egeria to Switzerland. Madame de la Châtre soon became de Jaucourt's wife, having obtained her divorce.

Talleyrand wrote from London—from his house in Woodstock Street—the following despondent letter: "I don't know what to do,—I am bored here, and worn out with having no news from those I love or know, in France. There is no one here absolutely in accordance with my mind and heart." This was at the end of August, 1793. Yet Madame de Flahaut was in London, and de Narbonne not yet gone.

That Talleyrand sincerely mourned his separation from his brilliant friend is proven in every letter he writes her, at this time. "It is true to the last degree that I know no

way of being decent or good-tempered except in our union—
and you know what I mean by *our*."

Had Talleyrand really been the favorite at Juniper
Hall?[1] Had earlier relationships been renewed? or was their
intimacy begun there? Talleyrand's letters to Coppet
breathe love, avowed intimacy, an eating loneliness and a
passionate longing for reunion. He had the wild impulses
of a man in love. He was all on fire to leave England and go
to Switzerland. And Madame de Staël opened wide doors
to the desire. It was the Bernese authorities alone who
barred the road which might have brought a very different
fate to the ex-Bishop. Alarmed at the stories of Talleyrand's irreligious attitude and his democratic spirit, an
entrance to the Canton of Vaud was forbidden to Monsieur
l'Evêque.

VII

Before the rupture between the French coterie and the
Burneys was final, Mrs. Philipps related a singularly interesting conversation which took place in her presence between
Narbonne and Talleyrand, one night in May. At that date
the Gironde and the Mountain were engaged in a death

[1] Whether de Narbonne's suspicions of Talleyrand's intimacy with Madame de
Staël during the year 1789 in Paris were or were not justified; or whether Talleyrand
had renewed his devotion to her at Juniper Hall, the recently published love-letters
to Comte O'Donnell in *La Revue de Paris* reveal Madame de Staël as possessing singular ideas in the delicate matter of fidelity. For some six years she more or less
persecutes a man many years younger than herself—the Comte O'Donnell—with her
lamentations at his coldness, ringing all the changes on the dolorous notes of anguished despair; and yet, during the earlier, most heated moments of her passion for
him, she writes to Benjamin Constant: "I return to you with the same attachment, an
attachment that no homage can alter, an attachment which makes it impossible
to compare you with any creature on earth; my heart, my life, all is yours, if you
wish, and as you wish." This gifted lady's heart seemed to be not unlike certain
Chinese boxes, the smaller fitting into the larger ones. (*Revue de Paris*, 1 Janvier,
1926, p. 199.)

struggle; at war with la Vendée and with Europe, the Convention was tottering to its fall. "In a week from now," said Narbonne, "it seems to me that things will be clear enough for us to form a plan." "Before making up our minds," said M. de Talleyrand, "we must know whether the party which would suit us would be strong enough to justify a hope of success; otherwise it would be folly to join it. Personally," he continued laughing, "I long to fight, I admit it."

Narbonne expressed surprise, and Talleyrand replied: "Yes, I assure you it would please me very much to give all those horrid wretches a good beating." "Oh no!" cried Narbonne, with a mixture of gentleness and sadness, "tell me what pleasure it would be to kill these poor wretches, whose greatest crimes are ignorance and stupidity. If we could make war only upon Marat, Danton, Robespierre, M. Egalité [Prince d'Orleans] and a few hundred other infamous rascals, I should, perhaps, find some satisfaction in it also." Talleyrand made no reply. A few moments later he rose to go, and said, very coolly: "I am going to leave my house in Woodstock Street, it is too dear."

CHAPTER XXIII

I

ONE last gleam of hope, before Talleyrand was forced to leave London, danced before his despairing political vision.

The astounding news came that Toulon, the French port, had rebelled against the Convention. The insurgents, believing their courageous stand would fire the whole country to put down the tyrant rule in Paris, boldly proclaimed Louis XVII, the Dauphin, King.

On learning of this amazing movement, Talleyrand's fertile brain began planning a whole scaffolding of projects, dreams and possibilities. Writing to Madame de Staël he announced grandly: "The Constitutionalists are the only ones through whom things can be done and undone" (28th September, 1793). "The Constitution is the only word capable of rallying men's spirits." So inflated was Talleyrand's balloon of hope that he had named the Prince de Conti as Lieutenant-General of the (new) kingdom. Narbonne and Sainte-Croix were to be entrusted with portfolios, and he himself would immediately reappear on the great political stage.

Fate, in the shape of a certain hitherto unheard-of young Captain of Artillery, who was heading an attack on

rebellious Toulon, and who was to win his first victory,
decided otherwise. The fall of Toulon brought Talleyrand's frail scaffolding to earth. The name of the Captain,
unknown save to a few cognizant of his precocious military
capacity, was Napoleon Bonaparte. There seems an in-
dicating finger of fate pointing to the future association
of Talleyrand and Napoleon, in this brilliant victory of the
one, and in the smashing of the hopes which the former had
caressed. After Waterloo, Napoleon's brilliant ex-Minister
was to use his powerful influence to ruin Napoleon and to
seat a Bourbon on the throne. Thus, from the very beginning of the dawning knowledge, on Talleyrand's part, that
so insignificant a creature as Napoleon Bonaparte—a little
Captain of Artillery—could, by his military prowess, thwart
Talleyrand's great hopes of a general insurrection in France,
up to the moment when Napoleon's star fell to earth, the
destinies of these two men were to be intermingled.

Talleyrand's fears that Toulon would fall are proven in
his letter written to Madame de Staël two days before the
victory of the Convention.

I am in a hateful state of mind [he wrote]. I do not know
what to hope for. Here is Moira's attempt turning out useless,
and he will probably put into Portsmouth at the first opportunity.
This will animate the Republicans against the unfortunate
Vendée; and then—countless massacres! One hears news of
battles in which 20,000 or 30,000 men have perished; and yet
things are fundamentally unchanged. What are *your* hopes?

Talleyrand's "hateful state of mind" was to be increased
to hot and impassioned indignation.

He was to receive news of an alarming nature: the

thunderbolt was to descend from an unexpected quarter. The manner of conveying the command of the English government for his immediate banishment was singularly brutal.

II

On the 24th January, 1794, Talleyrand, at five in the afternoon, was sitting in his room. He was apprised that two men—one of whom announced himself as "a Messenger of State"—wished to see him. The Messenger ordered Talleyrand to leave the country, within five days. No reasons were given.

Talleyrand did not accept this humiliating decree without making passionate protests. He wrote to Lord Grenville;

I came to England to enjoy peace and personal security under the shelter of institutions protecting liberty and property. I have been living here, as I have always lived here, a stranger to all discussion, and to all the interests of parties, and having no more to dread from just men in the publicity of a single one of my political opinions than in their knowledge of any one of my actions.

The assertion made by Talleyrand that he was "a stranger to all discussion and to all interests of parties" again raises the question—had he or had he not been entrusted with a mission by Danton? Whether or not Pitt and his government were confident that Talleyrand's activities were employed in secret ways—possibly to England's detriment—the results were such as to confirm the supposition. Pitt exercised his right of the expulsion of undesirable foreigners given by the Alien Bill which had been passed in December, 1792; under this act of Parliament only four foreigners were exiled—M. de Talleyrand-Périgord, a Comte Zenobia, a Comte de Vaux, and a saddler from Brussels, named Simon. Lord Grenville turned a deaf ear to Talleyrand's supplicating letter. Talleyrand made a personal appeal to the King as well as to William Pitt. Receiving no answer to his applications, he bowed to the inevitable.

Talleyrand's final attitude, since his fight with the powers ranged against him had proved futile, was in conformity with his nature. He showed not only the dignity of sustained fortitude—he could even indulge in gleams of gaiety. Narbonne asserted: "Nothing can equal his calm and courage, he is almost gay." Narbonne's letter to Mrs. Philipps is a prolonged lament.

Beaumetz, who was eventually to join Talleyrand, offered to go with him to the ends of the earth. The man whose "arid nature" is so decried by some of his historians, appears to have had a singular power of awakening powerful attachments in friends and dependents. Purely selfish men, men with dried-up sympathies and unlovable traits, singularly enough, do not evoke such proofs of passionate attachment as Talleyrand aroused, up to the last moments of his life.

Where could he go?—Russia—Prussia—Switzerland?—in any one of these countries he might have hoped to find a refuge. But even Switzerland, where Madame de Staël would have welcomed him eagerly, was forbidden territory. The only two countries where he could be safe were Denmark and America. He chose the latter.

In this choice, it is not impossible that his long connection with Gouverneur Morris, their lengthy talks about

America, its financial situation, its opportunities for making money, and its rapid development since its Independence, greatly influenced Talleyrand's decision. He felt—he confessed—he must re-make his fortune.

Talleyrand's pecuniary position at the moment of his departure was a serious one. What remained to him from the sale of his library, after the aid he had given to certain compatriots, was a very small sum. A few hours before embarking he wrote to Madame de Staël:

I have made up my mind. . . . I sail on Saturday. At thirty-nine I begin a new life, for I desire life; I love my friends too well to have any other idea; besides, I have still to proclaim, and proclaim aloud, what I have wished for, what I have done, what I have prevented, and what I have regretted. I have to prove that I have loved Liberty; for I love it still. . . .

A last letter dated from London to General d'Arblay reads:

Good-bye, dear d'Arblay, I am leaving your country until such time as it shall belong no more to the petty passions of men. Then I will return, not, indeed, to busy myself in public affairs— I have long since forsaken them for ever—but to visit the excellent inhabitants of Surrey. . . . I do not know how long I shall stay in America. If anything stable and reasonable should be done for our unfortunate country, I will return; if Europe is engulfed by the approaching campaign, I will prepare a refuge in America for all my friends. Good-bye! . . . I ask of you and promise you friendship for life.

One looks in vain for proofs of bitterness or anger in such a calm philosophic acceptance of the banishment—of the disgrace—which had befallen him.

An unjust persecution has its sweetness [he remarked at a later date]. I have never quite realized what my feelings were, but I certainly felt a kind of satisfaction. It seems to me that, in those days of general misfortune, I should almost have regretted it if I had escaped persecution.

CHAPTER XXIV

I

HOWEVER deeply Talleyrand may have felt the turn of fate which had sent him forth from England as an undesirable alien, he continued to prove the proud front of courage which his friend de Narbonne had eulogized. He was leaving behind friends, some impoverished, and others in dire distress. His country was in the convulsions of the Terror. Every hope, political or reformatory, all his ambitious designs, all the soaring idealism which had built up the fairy structure of a redeemed and purified France—all his work of the past four years, in a word, was struck down to naught, as an iron hand sweeps remorselessly the fragments of a broken idol. At thirty-nine Talleyrand was an exile, an *émigré;* his pockets were lined with but a few hundred pounds; he had before him no fixed purpose, and no certain future.

Talleyrand, during his stay in America, was not to lose, however, he was greatly to gain by his adventure. A newer, a wider horizon was to open before him.

Talleyrand did not cross the wintry Atlantic alone. Beaumetz was as good as his word. Having sworn he would "go to the ends of the world" with his friend whom he so ardently admired, the Chevalier Albert de Beaumetz, on learning of Talleyrand's banishment from England, resolved to accompany him.

The intimacy between the two men has not formed as lengthy recitals in the annals of the time and subsequent histories as have Talleyrand's relationship with de Narbonne, de Montmorency, de Choiseul-Gouffier, and de Jaucourt. Yet Beaumetz and Talleyrand had been associated together in all the social gaieties of pre-Revolutionary Paris. As a Constitutionalist, Beaumetz had served as deputy for the nobility from Artois, in the Etats-Généraux. The political views of the two friends were the same.

From the outset of their journey, the perils of the deep were to assail them. The American merchant ship on which the travellers had embarked was ill-equipped for its long voyage. Having weighed anchor from Greenwich, on February 3rd, 1794, she was buffeted by the great seas in the Channel, being, indeed, in imminent danger of foundering. Some sailors from Falmouth, sighting this vessel in distress, courageously came to her rescue. The ship was ignominiously towed into Falmouth port.

Talleyrand, who, it appears, already had suffered acutely from the tortures of seasickness, took refuge on land. There, in a rude tavern, a rendezvous of sailors, he was confronted with a strange adventure. The landlord of the inn, impressed with the sight of two such distinguished looking guests as were Talleyrand and de Beaumetz, boasted that an American General had been his lodger, for some time. Talleyrand's curiosity having been aroused as to who this General could be who chose so humble a hostelry as was this tavern, sent a courteous message to the American, begging the honor of his acquaintance.

Talleyrand presently saw before him a man prematurely

old, the deep lines in his face and his sunken eyes confessing the havoc wrought by disgrace, sadness, the biting sting of remorse, and exile. There was little or no resemblance to the dashing, brilliant young officer who had charmed Philadelphia belles, in 1778.

The "American General" was Benedict Arnold.

Arnold was dead to even courting distraction. After the interchange of the usual courtesies, he seemed inclined to end the interview. Talleyrand, however, on the alert to make capital out of the incident of meeting one whom he presumed was of some importance in his own country, innocently asked the General if he would kindly give him some letters of introduction to his friends in America.

Talleyrand's own account of the meeting, in his *Mémoires*, reads:

After an exchange of ordinary politeness, I asked him several questions about his country, and from the first, I saw that he was embarrassed. After attempting to continue the conversation which each time he allowed to languish, I asked him if he would not give me some letters to America. "No," he replied, and after some moments of silence, seeing my astonishment, he added: "I am perhaps the only American who cannot give you letters for his own country. All my relations with it are broken off. I must never go back." He did not dare to tell me his name. He was Benedict Arnold.

I must admit that I experienced for him a little pity, for which political Puritans may blame me, perhaps, but I cannot blame myself, for I was a witness of his great distress.

II

Once on the high seas, Talleyrand must again render his tribute to Neptune. The seas, indeed, treated him merci-

lessly. For days and days, his brilliant, epigrammatic wit
was stilled. In his inexhaustible vocabulary, if he found
a new expletive to describe the agonies of seasickness,
history has not recorded it. Yet he bore the capricious
mistress of storm-tossed waves no grudge. He grew to love
the sea's wide expanse, her vast fields of undulating foam,
and her mysterious sources of power.

In that earlier and more glorious expedition, when
Comte Louis-Philippe de Ségur, together with the Duc de
Lauzun, the Prince de Broglie, and the brothers de Lameth,
had left France to join Rochambeau's army in America,
these enthusiasts for liberty had found the seas as unkind
as did Talleyrand and de Beaumetz. Ségur, in his
Esquisses et Récits, narrates: "Broglie and Lameth were
so overcome with seasickness that when I told them we were
in danger of shipwreck, they told me it was all one to them.
I could have beaten them!"

There were other terrors added to those which stormy
seas induce. There was a bare possibility of being captured,
by English or French frigates. Talleyrand's capture
would have been hailed with joy. The Danish Ambassador
to Paris, Comte de Wattersdorff, delighted in recounting
to a roomful of people, in later years, an event which he
insisted actually did take place:

An English frigate, meeting on the high seas the "frail Danish
ship" (the ship in reality was an American vessel), ordered the
Captain to lay to. Arrogating to himself the prescribed English
right of visiting foreign ships, the Captain boarded the ship.
Talleyrand, seized with terror lest he be recognized, was willing to
don the only disguise available—that of the ship's cook's cap and
apron. The trick succeeded; the English Captain, on inspecting
the cabins, could not imagine so great a prize as Talleyrand would

have been, could be discovered in a plebeian costume such as that worn by a ship's cook!

Michaud, the historian, who narrates the incident, whose unrelenting hate of Talleyrand has infected many of his literary successors, in asserting the ship was Danish, places the story in the limbo of apocryphal narratives. The vessel was flying the American flag.

III

One could have hoped to find some mention, in Talleyrand's *Mémoires*, of the attitude of mind with which he fronted this American adventure. This long voyage to America must have been undertaken, by both of these Frenchmen, with a genuine feeling of its being an adventure. It was still the land, to French minds, of wild, untamed and unconquered Indians, of ferocious animals, and of vast forests. The accounts, brought back by the officers and generals who had served in the American armies, had not entirely dispelled this conception of the New World—one so dear to foreigners. Frenchmen, particularly, delighted in the thought of its wide, untilled space; of its coasts and huge tracts of country, as yet unexplored, which haunted their imaginations. In a country as limited as is France, geographically, there is need, if only for purposes of poetic imagery, to creative intellects, of some portions of the earth's surface being an untamed wilderness. For romance to take its flight, there must be a nest in which to build and produce its offspring. Chateaubriand, in his *Atlanta*, gave to French appetite for novelty the very nourishment it craved.

Starting out with such ideas and notions respecting the

"sad country" which they were to visit, Talleyrand and Beaumetz had ample time to prepare their minds to accept any hardship. They had need of such a cuirass of courage in this voyage of thirty-eight days. Courage was a quality in which Talleyrand was never found deficient. What he now lacked was enthusiasm. The days were long since past when he had fronted life as the young, audacious, volatile *abbé de cour*. The years had brought disillusion, embitterment, and soul weariness. The Talleyrand which history has familiarized, as being the cynical man of the world whose witticisms were to reveal his want of faith in man or woman; whose scepticism was to dry up the well of joy; and whose contempt of public opinion turned upon him to blast his reputation as an honest man—this cynical, sceptical, scoffing, indifferent Talleyrand was not yet fully born. Early sufferings, the period of his loathed priesthood, his political deceptions in the evolutions of the revolutionary movement, and, only recently, the disgrace of his banishment from England—such were the causes which were slowly changing the gay, debonair man of the twenties into the disabused Talleyrand of his fortieth year.

"He who goes often to the well must not drink too deep," is an Arab proverb. Talleyrand had drunk too deep. His well was all but dry. Was it Truth—Truth with her wide-open eyes, her knowing smile, the naked reality of all things—staring at him, from the bottom of life's well?

IV

Talleyrand's supreme indifference extended to the lack of any eager longings to touch American shores. This he openly avowed.

The thirty-eight days of the hard voyage ended, Talley-

rand recounts in his *Mémoires*, he was more than ready to
begin another, and longer, voyage:

After several weeks of navigation, I was awakened by a cry
which I dreaded to hear, "Land! Land!" The Captain, the crew
and the passengers, all were possessed with the most impatient
joy. . . . Alone, I was not happy in seeing land. The sea
had a great charm for me, at that moment. The sensations
which I had experienced on board had increased my predilection.
. . . Upon going on deck, I perceived a pilot who was to convey
us up through the River Delaware. A vessel was on the point
of leaving. I asked the Captain what was the destination of
the ship which I saw close by. He told me it was sailing for
Calcutta. I sent at once to the Captain of the departing vessel
a rowboat, to ascertain if he would take another passenger.
I was indifferent as to the destination of the ship. The voyage
might be long; what I wished was not to quit the sea. The
number of the passengers being complete, I was obliged to go
on to Philadelphia.

V

Once landed at the Philadelphia docks, with what
wondering eyes must the two Frenchmen have viewed the
capital of the new United States! Here was the chief city of
the new world before them, in all its sharp contrasts.

Philadelphia was then a city of eighty thousand inhabitants. In 1794, it presented certain aspects of the greater
Philadelphia of to-day. The streets were laid out at right
angles, with wide sidewalks, the latter mostly paved with
bricks. The houses lining the thoroughfares had the white
and reddish pink colors we associate with the Quaker City.
These red brick homes, trimmed with their marble window-
casements and door-jambs, had then, as now, their prim air of
decorous circumspection. It was a matter of pride among

housekeepers to maintain their "front doors," and the pinkish sidewalks, in speckless cleanliness. A few fine houses were conspicuous among the somewhat unvarying aspect of the Quakerish-faced dwellings.

The most imposing of all the residences was the house occupied by the President. The Government buildings, Independence Hall—the cradle of the Union—and the houses of the Foreign Ministers could only accentuate, by their modest aspect, the fact that the American capital was essentially a city of homes, rather than one invested with the air of grandeur supposed to characterize a seat of government.

Outside of Congress, the true life of the city was in its bustling streets and crowded docks. Shops were filled "with every luxury of Europe." Country folk came to gape and buy. Merchants from all the Thirteen States travelled to the metropolis to transact their business.

The contrast in types presented an interesting study. There were the sharp-faced, keen-eyed men from the North, the Southerner with his indolent swagger and urbane air, and the Quaker, whose calm features, beneath the broad-brimmed Quaker hat, proved the serenity developed by the faith he practised.

Gliding past hurrying merchants, sturdy countrymen, well-to-do citizens, negroes and the passing Quakers, whose sober greys and headgear lent a curiously religious aspect to street life, a young Quakeress would pass "in her white dress and close muslin cap looking rather like a nymph than a mortal"—as Comte de Ségur put it when he saw such lovely creatures, on his campaign of a few years before. Such a vision would add a startling note—a new type to foreigners—of feminine beauty.

After the first hours of their inspection of the town, it must have seemed to the two French *émigrés* that the city of Brotherly Love offered but meagre material of either amusement or interest. The city itself, with its plain-faced houses, streets laid out at right angles, and wooden docks—what could such a city offer to eyes used to the irregular charm of the picturesque streets, to the palaces, and to the great hôtels of Paris? The massive splendors of London, its Court life, its superb country estates were still the images dancing before the eyes of the two strangers.

CHAPTER XXV

I

TALLEYRAND had not come to the New World to inspect docks, nor to study street life. He had come, as he openly confessed in a letter to Madame de Staël, "to perfect his political education." The man who had thrown over his own order; who considered himself as "secularized," his priesthood no longer the bond of a hateful past; a Constitutionalist who, with Mirabeau, had been the most conspicuous among the members of the earlier Revolutionaries—this curious, eager-minded Talleyrand was to study the workings of principles for which he had fought, and which he and his co-workers had failed to carry into effect.

He now wished to meet the men who had successfully achieved their political ends. Talleyrand's method was always to seek those highest in command. He felt an imperative desire to know, personally, and as soon as possible, the famous men who were guiding the destinies of the New World. The President,—General Washington,—Alexander Hamilton, the brilliant Secretary of the Treasury, and Jefferson—with such great minds he felt he could indeed "perfect his political education."

Almost immediately on his arrival Talleyrand had met,

and grew to know well, Alexander Hamilton.   Talleyrand
himself states:

I profited during the two winters I passed both in Philadelphia
and New York to see the principal personages which the American
Revolution had placed in history, and particularly General Hamilton who, by his mind and his character, seemed to me, even during
the life of Mr. Pitt and Mr. Fox, to have attained to the height
of the most distinguished statesmen of Europe.

Through Hamilton's influence, Talleyrand had hoped
to secure an audience with the President, General Washington.   Talleyrand may have suspected that Gouverneur Morris' appreciation of him might not be altogether favorable.   He had, therefore, armed himself with a letter from
Lord Lansdowne to Washington.   In that epistle, his kind
friend had represented the ex-Bishop as an ecclesiastic of
great merit who had sacrificed his clerical interests and his
career in the Church to his devotion to the larger interests
of France.

General Washington had already had advices from
Gouverneur Morris; when in London, in the early part of
1792, the latter indited a long letter to General Washington,
in which Talleyrand is mentioned in connection with Comte
de Choiseul-Gouffier, and de Narbonne.   Talleyrand was
then in London, on his mission to that country.

These three are young men of high family, men of wit, and men
of pleasure.   The two latter were men of fortune, but they
spent it.   They were intimates all three, and had run the career
of ambition together, to retrieve their affairs.   On the score of
morals, neither of them is exemplary.   The Bishop is particularly
blamed on that head.   Not so much for adultery, because that

GOUVERNEUR MORRIS

was common enough among the clergy of high rank, but for the variety and publicity of his amours, for gambling and, above all, for stock-jobbing during the Ministry of Monsieur de Calonne, with whom he was on the best of terms—and therefore had opportunities which his enemies say he made no small use of. However, I do not believe in this, and I think that except his gallantries and the mode of thinking rather too liberal for a churchman, the charges are unduly aggravated.

General Washington, it appears, on receiving Lord Lansdowne's letter, was desirous of meeting the "illustrious stranger." Lord Lansdowne's letter to the President was couched in the most eulogistic terms. His Lordship states that apart from the flattering request of "Monsieur Taillerand-Périgord"[1] for him to indite a letter of introduction to the General, he himself "is impelled by a still more imperious reason to write to you—which is to render justice to a very honorable man who had suffered from a combination of persecutions." The whole letter breathes unstinted admiration of Talleyrand's gifts and capacities, especially emphasizing his perfectly correct conduct during his two years' residence in England.

To such a letter there could be but one answer. Fauchet, the French Minister Plenipoteniary, however, prevented the President's acting on his expressed wish to accord Monsieur de Talleyrand-Périgord an audience.

The Minister, appointed as such by the Comité de Salut —the temporary government then in power in Paris— violently opposed Talleyrand's reception. Citoyen Fauchet, as Minister, addressed his fierce attacks on "L'Ex-Evêque" to the American Secretary of State. He asserted

---

[1] The name is thus spelt by Lord Lansdowne, and Napoleon never succeeded in pronouncing it otherwise.

that he could not continue his own mission were such a "suspect" as Talleyrand received by the President of the United States. He represented Talleyrand as "anti-patriotic."

"If Talleyrand is received at the President's Palace," he stated, "I will never set foot in it again: you must choose between an *émigré* and me."

Such violence must have been as offensive to General Washington as the attitude, thus enforced, must have been repugnant to his courteous nature. Washington, however, had no alternative left him. America had recognized the Convention. She was a neutral State. The President, as President of neutral America, could not run the risk of furnishing capital for discussion by receiving an *émigré* listed as such.

Fauchet's name might have been considered for centuries as being one of very secondary interest to historians, save for its association with the above incident.

General Washington, evidently against his personal inclination, found himself forced to reply in the negative, to Monsieur de Talleyrand-Périgord's request. The President had no choice. He must sacrifice his inclination to his duty. He could not endanger relationships with a friendly power. Minister Fauchet's representations of the ex-Bishop's intrigues in London and Paris must be accepted.

Talleyrand's reputation as a distinguished orator, as an advanced and courageous liberal, during his career as a Constitutionalist, and his successful diplomatic missions to London made him the most notable of all the refugees who had come from France. The arrival of the brothers of the King—Comte de Provence and Comte d'Artois—together with their cousin Louis-Philippe, could not arouse the same degree of interest which the brilliant qualities of Talleyrand excited, from the point of view of such a statesman as was Washington.

In the letter which Washington wrote a few weeks later, to Lord Lansdowne, he refers to Talleyrand in the most courteous, as well as in the following flattering terms:

It is a matter of no small regret to me that considerations of a public nature, which you will easily conjecture, have not hitherto permitted me to manifest towards that gentleman the sense I entertain of his personal character, and of your Lordship's recommendation. But I am informed that the reception he has met with in general has been such as to console him, as far as the state of society will admit of it, for what he relinquished in leaving Europe. Time must naturally be favorable to him everywhere, and may be expected to raise a man of his talents and merit above temporary disadvantages which, in revolutions, result from differences of political opinion.

II

The refusal of General Washington to receive Talleyrand produced in him a sensible distaste for his surroundings. He reverts in his *Mémoires* and *Letters* to his longings for the sea; he confesses to finding himself in the midst of "an immense country which said nothing to me."

Villified, persecuted, spied upon by Jacobins, and distrusted by the majority of the royalist *émigrés* who had sought shelter in America, Talleyrand felt himself to be intolerably isolated. It is certain General Washington's refusal to receive him had cut him to the quick. Pitt had always been his enemy. Yet, had not Talleyrand openly boasted, in Paris, before starting on his first mission to London, that "he would have Monsieur Pitt dismissed from office"? Such an attitude does not induce friendly feeling. To have been expelled from England by Pitt might have been regarded, therefore, as actuated by a touch of personal enmity. But Talleyrand had not come to America on a mission. He had approached the country in all amity.

Talleyrand's life and training had not fitted him for embracing, quickly, the many opportunities offered by a new country in process of formation. An aristocrat, in soul and feeling, his sympathies with the reforms he had attempted to effect in the state and condition of the oppressed people of France sprang from his sense of justice and personal interest. In America, the principles he had advocated were already before him, achieved and in full activity. Here were a free people. The rights of man had been gloriously fought for;—liberty, equality, and freedom were established. He found an industrious, intensely energetic population engaged in two pursuits—in the business of the building up of a nation, and in the making of their private fortunes. Such men as Alexander Hamilton and Washington stood out from the mass as giants overtop ordinary mortals.

The renewed energies of the people, released from the long struggle of their War for Independence; their superb courage in furthering the development of the newly-born nation; their passionate ardor in opening up educational opportunities, in broadening every avenue leading to progress, enlightenment and State unity; the fermentation animating men, women and children to develop the spirit of true Americanism—this aspect of a free people building up a free State left Talleyrand, at first, singularly cold. Between America, no longer under English rule—independent, self-sufficing—and his own efforts to free France from corrupt

Bourbon despotism there was all the distance which lies between a dream and its realization.

Born and brought up to Court life, how could Talleyrand find stimulus for imagination in a people as plain and primitive as seemed to him the Philadelphians of 1794 and '95?

There was, indeed, a small, exclusive, social world encircling about the President's Court, and the equally exclusive one, whose leader was the talented Mrs. Bingham. The gaieties which British officers, under Lord Howe's administration, had found so delightful, were still a marked feature of Philadelphia's higher social life. All the beauty among women of that city famed for its beauties had not fled to England with lovely Peggy Shippen, who, as Mrs. Benedict Arnold, was to charm the London world, and who shared with her husband the ignominy of his disgrace and oblivion.

In these close circles of the more notable Philadelphia families, and in the President's diplomatic receptions and dinners, Talleyrand would have found a certain distraction and amusement. That Philadelphia society lost much in not having widely opened its doors to Talleyrand is equally certain. The President's enforced refusal to receive Talleyrand produced its inevitable consequences. Certain houses were, indeed, only too eager to know and to entertain Talleyrand. Foreigners were welcomed warmly then, as now, in America. This aristocrat who was "cousin to Bourbon kings"; this former vicious *abbé de cour*—a priest, at twenty, "confessing" girls and young married women; a Bishop turning traitor to his clerical and social order, in his fight against privilege in the Assembly; the clever statesman sent on missions to London, now a proscribed *émigré*—this famous ex-Bishop talked of openly in every drawing-room in

Philadelphia as "a dangerous and profound man" (for Pitt's stinging accusation had followed Talleyrand)—with such a reputation preceding him, society was on the *qui vive* to see as interesting and "dangerous" an individual.

III

Talleyrand and de Beaumetz at first went about in certain Philadelphia circles. The social flavor of this New World does not seem to have been found either stimulating or amusing to the two Frenchmen. If Talleyrand gratified the insatiable American curiosity for novelty, the staid and narrow conventional life of "respectable Philadelphians" was as dull as it was provincial to one brought up in the Courts of Louis XV and Louis XVI. With the memories of Versailles, Marly, Fontainebleau, and Paris, of the brilliant salons and the regal Château life in France, the Philadelphia Mr. Bowers paints for us in his recent work—"in the glamorous days of Federalist supremacy, Philadelphia with its wealth, its fashion and princely houses"—the city thus described does not seem to conform to the effect produced on critical French nobles.

Talleyrand, on his second visit to the city, signed his own social death warrant. He outraged public opinion, which, all his life long, he flaunted with audacious contempt. He appeared on the streets of the city, in the company of a beautiful mulatto girl, hanging on his arm. Whether this unseemly act was one actuated by bravado, or in ignorance of the strictures born of slavery—relating to the rigid observance of the color line in America—remains a matter of doubt.

Fauchet's persistent and unrelenting attacks, for he saw plots, treason and "infernal plans" in the actions of every *émigré*—his letters to his government being filled with incendiary accounts of their conspiracies, of their efforts to induce their countrymen to establish themselves in America, and of the outrageous speculation indulged in by those already in America—such attacks may have had their retroactive effect in accentuating Talleyrand's cynical indifference.   Fauchet thus wrote to his government:

The speculation of these stock-jobbers and their hope of success are founded solely on the misfortunes of their former country.   They hope that the lack of good laws and the impossibility of establishing tranquillity in the bosom of the Republic will make a considerable portion of the population of France desert her in search of peace, and they are preparing to receive them.   These disastrous conjectures are expressed almost word for word in a letter lately addressed to Bishop Talleyrand by an ex-Chevalier de Grasse, at present an *émigré* in London.[1]

Fauchet's attacks continued, with no more ground of reality than his own suspicious animosity.   There was no plot, no ringleader, no conspiracy.   Talleyrand became interested in quite other plans and projects.

The vitalizing, electrical air of America little by little stung Talleyrand to renewed activities.   Brooding over misfortune was not in conformity with his moral or mental composition.   All newcomers to America are insensibly seized by the intensive national frenzy for action, for work. After a few months of dining out, of finding Philadelphia society insipid, of rising to philosophic reflections on the character of the American people and of the government, Talleyrand suddenly makes an illuminating discovery.   He

[1] Fauchet's letter of the 9th November, 1794.   *Correspondence of French Ministers* . . . , 466.

confessed to Madame de Staël that he too "wishes to re-make his fortune."

There are revelations, as time goes on, of this new spirit animating Talleyrand. If he writes philosophic reflections on America and her prospects and destiny, to Madame de Staël, he also turns amazingly practical. He was to be seized with the American mania—he longed "to make money." The spirit of enterprise, of audacious speculation which was in the very air of the new Continent, was too strong. Talleyrand was swung into the vortex of money-making America.

A mind as alert, as occupied with reflections on grave themes as was his, had the receptivity which reflected conditions. As in his youth he had been morally debased by the corrosive influences of the Court, in this stirring period of the new American nation, then struggling to establish permanent political stability—to work out its salvation, in a word—Talleyrand was caught and captured by the intensive passion for work, characterizing all classes.

IV

There was a feverish activity amongst all the French refugees, to replenish their diminished incomes by ventures in any sort of plan or project. Talleyrand and de Beaumetz were soon to follow the general movement. The Duc de Noailles and a friend had conceived the idea of founding a town on the banks of the Susquehanna. The French Consul-General, Monsieur de la Forest, had made a good thing in purchases and subsequent sales of hundreds of acres in Virginia. The impetus given to speculation throughout the States, among the inhabitants and the

French exiles, was a noticeable feature of the post-war period. Wild accounts were given of success in such ventures. It was the native American, however, whose "yankee cuteness" captured credulous customers rather than the *émigré*, and whose speculations were remunerative.

Talleyrand's letters to Madame de Staël prove the sharp difference between American methods, and the conservative French ways of approaching a business move. But then the Americans had conquered the wilderness, had fought and conquered England, and Talleyrand had been bred at Courts, and the training in his case had been that of a priest—one vowed to live by rule, the rule of Rome.

Writing from Boston to Madame de Staël, August 4th, 1794, Talleyrand states:

I perceive a chance to give useful work to all of us who, after this campaign, should wish to put away all chimeras from their mind and believe no more either in France or in any foreign powers. There are more chances to re-make one's fortune here than in any other place. I am arranging to get commissions from Europe, and all such as are given me will be useful to me. If some of the friends of Monsieur, your father, would send ships to America, if some Swedes sent over here objects for sale, either to New York or to Philadelphia, I am in a position to do good business for those who would trust themselves directly to me. I beg of you to use a little of your activity in order to procure me some commissions. It would be too stupid to be here and not to be able to accumulate enough of a subsistence to shelter one against future need; and in a little time, one can make a great deal of money, either by commissions in public funds, or by commissions in the purchase of land. The reputations of American merchants are so uncertain that European merchants are always handicapped to find some one to represent them. It is for that I propose myself, having some qualifications.

Talleyrand had learned at least one great secret of self-advertisement—that of decrying the business capacity of competitors.

One tries to imagine an American approaching a business enterprise in this stately fashion—even a hundred or more years before the appearance of the "hustler." Again he writes from Boston, on the 14th of August, 1794, addressing himself in as positive a manner, in another long letter to his devoted friend, to whom he says that she alone is beloved by him and with "all his soul."

My reason tells me that I must re-make a little fortune so that when I am older I shall not be in want or in continual dependence; this idea occupies me, but up to the present moment, I do not see clearly any big thing. If you know people who have any desire to invest in the purchase of farms here, I would willingly attend to their affairs. If I had a large enough number of persons who would charge me with their affairs and who would give me an interest, they and I would greatly gain thereby; they, because American merchants are not very much to be trusted in business, and I, because I would have no motive to have any interest in such speculations. Pray interest yourself in this matter.

It was entirely in accordance with Talleyrand's gambling instinct that his first effort to better his fortunes should have been of a speculative nature.

One of Talleyrand's earlier speculations was in land. He and de Beaumetz purchased some untilled territory in the State of Maine, from General Knox, who was Secretary of War. On this land was a certain establishment which Talleyrand proposed should be divided into lots, to provide dwellings for indigent *émigrés* and for his friends.

His latest enterprise had been to send a ship laden with American products to India. Talleyrand's standing with certain Philadelphia firms was sufficiently good to enable him to freight the ship with a cargo furnished by his new friends. The purpose of the venture was to sell such goods at enormous profits, and to realize a fortune. Beaumetz having married an impecunious widow, with two children, set sail with hopes as gilded as Talleyrand's friend, a Mr. Law, had painted the certain success of the enterprise. There had been a moment when Talleyrand himself entertained the idea of landing on the banks of the Ganges. India paled before the rising sun of his longing for Paris. "Either there will be a general earthquake in Europe or I shall return next May." This was in a letter written to Madame de Staël on the 8th of September, 1795. The stars in their courses were to see that assertion become a certainty.

The success of Talleyrand's business ventures does not appear to have been great. It is known he left America, eventually, carrying fifty thousand francs with him, as his entire fortune, to Holland. But were these fifty thousand francs the result of his successful ventures?[1]

There are other letters to Madame de Staël in which Talleyrand confesses his more personal feelings. He touches on the impatience with which he awaited news from France. He narrates his daily impressions, his hopes for the morrow, his many troubles, the services which she might render him.

. . . Since I have been in America, I have only received two letters, one from Mathieu [de Montmorency] and yours. How much good they did me! How long a time had elapsed since anything so dear had touched my heart! For a long time I have been distracting myself with mental occupations, with ideas of making

[1] A letter of Benjamin Constant written to Monsieur Eugenet states that Madame de Staël had lent Talleyrand money while he was in America. See p. 379.

a fortune, and with speculative combinations. All that is good for a quarter of an hour, but that is all. Beaumetz appeals very little to my heart. He has a restless vanity which renders him dry, and which explains why, at forty, his oldest friends are only acquaintances of about eighteen months.

(The date of this letter is the 12th of May, 1794.)

The human side of Talleyrand in such letters is given with an abandonment rare in so secretive a nature. The above letter breathes loneliness, sadness, and the various efforts made to escape from the depressing influences of exile, in a foreign land.

Talleyrand spent many long evenings alone in his dingy lodgings in Third Street North. His mind would fly to his unhappy country. He would dream of what the future might bring. He felt acutely his impecunious situation. He states, with philosophical fortitude, which is to be admired: "I profited by the arrangement of my little room to indulge in plans of great political significance and to re-arrange the world; for nothing embarrasses the man, who, far from his country, is in an Inn or in a poor apartment." He beguiled his loneliness also by writing long letters to his two friends—to Lord Lansdowne and to Madame de Staël. Certain of his confessions to the latter reveal the depth of his feelings—feelings of isolation, of what, in more common phraseology, we term homesickness. Many were the grey days, days of sadness and despondency.

CHAPTER XXVI

I

THE impressions Talleyrand records of America's religious and political development, and his prophecies concerning the future of our country are of even more value to-day than when written, in his old age in 1830. To Americans, there are few pages as interesting in his *Mémoires*, mutilated as they unquestionably have been, as those in which he describes his stay in America, and his record of a journey to its forests.

Three gentlemen and a servant were to start forth from Philadelphia, on an adventurous trip. The purpose of the journey was to make a bold dash for the wilderness. Talleyrand, his friend de Beaumetz, and a gentleman from Holland named Heydecoper, were the adventurers. A servant of Talleyrand's completed the party.

The outlying country about Philadelphia with its lakes and the Delaware River, its undulating hills and rural aspect, might have furnished a sylvan frame, as well as recreation grounds, for the capital. The quite impracticable roads made access to the countryside all but impossible. Talleyrand and his friends were to find conditions as they left the city, exactly the same as had La Rochefoucauld-Liancourt before them:

All the roads leading to Philadelphia are bad, because the carts drawn by four and six horses, coming from all points heavily laden with produce for the market, create deep ruts, especially near the city, where they meet. There were certain roads which were so thick with mud, and the holes were so deep, that there was danger either of sticking fast, or losing a wheel, or seeing one's load topple over into the slush.

Every object the eye rested on attested to the still primitive habits and customs of the people. The coaches which rattled into town, from the countryside, were brilliant in their yellow, red or blue bodies, yet they were encrusted with mud. The passengers, to European eyes, seemed more like peasants than prosperous farmers. Carts, wagons, gigs were the vehicles of people more interested in the carrying quality of their equipages than in the style or beauty of their conveyances.

Talleyrand proposed that the party should travel into the interior of the country. His companions accepted the proposal, "and I must confess that from the very first the early days of my enterprise delighted me. I was struck with astonishment," was Talleyrand's verdict. "Not more than fifty leagues from the capital, I perceived no traces of the hand of man. I found a Nature brutal and savage" (*toute brute et toute sauvage*).

There were also traces of old tempests which had destroyed everything in their passage. . . . It is a novel spectacle for the traveller to leave some large town in which the social state has reached perfection, and pass through every successive degree of civilization and industry, watching their gradual decrease, until in a few days he comes to the rough and shapeless hut built from the trunks of newly-felled trees. Such a voyage is a kind of practical and living analysis of the origin of states and

nations. We start from the most composite whole and arrive
at the simplest elements; every day a few of the inventions which
our multiplying needs have rendered necessary, vanish from
sight. It seems like a journey backwards through the history of
human progress. Though such a journey appeals strongly to the
imagination, though it is pleasant to find in the succeeding regions
what would seem to belong only to the succeeding ages, we must
be prepared to find very few social ties and no common characteristics among men who seem hardly to belong to the same
genus.

The forests were as old as the world. The *débris* of plants
and dead trees encumbered the earth. . . . Others were growing to succeed them, and later, were to perish as had they. Vines
often opposed our passage. The borders of the rivers were
decorated with a fresh and vigorous verdure. Sometimes, there
were flowers new to me. Having attained a little elevation, I
was lost in looking upon a view as varied as it was agreeable.
Tops of trees, the undulations of the ground which alone broke
the regularity of the immense spaces, produced a singular effect.

Our imaginations began to work before this great extent of
country. We placed villages, cities, hamlets; forests were to be
left on the heights of mountains. The sides of the hills were to
be covered with houses and already droves of cattle coming to
feed in the pastures of the valleys, passed before our eyes.

Consider these populous cities of English, Germans, Dutch
and Irish, as well as the indigenous inhabitants; the straggling
villages lying so far apart; the vast stretches of uncultivated
country, traversed rather than inhabited by men who have no
nationality. What common bond can be imagined to unite all
this disparity?

In spite of his talent as an observer, Talleyrand failed
to grasp the influences which, even in his day, were soon to
knit into a nation these "disparate" nationalities. The
common love of freedom, the appeal made to the adventurous spirit of man, in a vast continent to be explored and sub-

dued, and the late War of Independence, such were the material and spiritual forces which were to mould "English, Germans, Dutch and Irish" into what was to be the true United States.

Talleyrand's analytic perception did not carry him far enough into discerning the essential character of the inhabitants—nor of their true relation to each other.

On certain superficial aspects he shows a better understanding. In a letter to his "noble friend" Lord Lansdowne, one dated February 1, 1795, he writes as follows:

The attitude of America proves "une forte inclination pour la Nation Française" (a strong inclination for the French Nation)—that all Americans still talk with enthusiasm of those generous brothers-in-arms who crossed the Atlantic to fight with them in favor of liberty! . . . Yet, in spite of the fact that the very name of England is mentioned with aversion, America is entirely English, that is to say that to England belongs all the advantage over France that one country can derive from another country. This preference rests on the two causes which alone can produce such a desire:—inclination and interest.

"America is quite English," he reiterates to Lord Lansdowne: "that is to say, that England has still every advantage over France to benefit by the United States as much as one nation can benefit by the existence of another."

II

In these letters to Lord Lansdowne and in the pages devoted to his impression of America in his *Mémoires*, Talleyrand gives a series of vivid pictures of the moral, political and religious state and condition of our people and country in the years 1794–96.

Talleyrand found

that there were both Republican and monarchical principles involved in the American Constitution—such as the power vested in the chief executive.

He considered that this marriage of the two conflicting principles would only endure as long as Washington was in power. So short-sighted a view, in one possessed of as far-seeing a vision, in political and governmental matters, as Talleyrand was to prove in his career as statesman, is scarcely to be wondered at. Soon after their independence had been won, the true union of the States was to pass through several phases of dissension before the truly United States of America were cemented into a nation.

In so subtly discerning the two warring principles involved in the American Constitution, Talleyrand demonstrated his probing instinct—the instinct of the born statesman. Yet the two principles lived in seeming harmony, neither warring on the other, until the year 1918. President Wilson was the first President who attempted to "carry out his policies" according to monarchical principles.

III

Much of the journeying of the French travellers was through seemingly endless tracts of forest. The forests of America were still, in Talleyrand's day, sufficiently infested with mosquitoes and monster flies, with wolves, bears and foxes to make travelling therein, if not actually dangerous, at least distressing to personal comfort. There are, however, no petulant outbreaks in the record of the journey, at any such annoyance. The spirit of adventure animated the travellers. If later, the depression of the worn worldling settled down upon Talleyrand, and he could confess "the immense country awakened no curiosity," in the earlier days, the relief of getting away from cramping town life, the living amid great open spaces, and the novelty of exploring virgin forest induced gaiety and a boyish sense of the comic. The party were lost, one night, in a great wood: Talleyrand cried out to one of his friends, "Hola! are you there?" "Mais oui, Monseigneur, je suis ici!" Reunited, the ex-Bishop jokingly taunted his friend with remembering his former title—when the latter felt himself to be in danger.

The travellers had a diversified experience in modes of travel. At times they took to the lumbering stage-coach, over incredibly rough roads; they were ferried across rivers on a rude raft; they slept in log-cabins; they were even of a mind to turn trappers, after passing some days in a trapper's hut, and hearing his tales of the fortune that could be made by luring wild animals to the death-trap.

Talleyrand's experiences are noted with that caustic humor which was characteristic of him:

Being obliged to ask of a native hospitality near Frenchmen's Bay, I asked the man, with whom I lived for a short time, some questions. He lived in the best house in the district. He was a man of great respectability, as they say in this country. I dared to ask him if he knew General Washington. "I have never seen him," he replied. "If you went to Philadelphia, would you not be very glad to see him?" "Oh, yes, certainly, but above all else," he added, with an animated air, "I should like to see Mr. Bingham who, they say, is so rich." Throughout America, I found this same admiration for money, and often as grossly expressed. Luxury has come here too quickly. When the first needs of man are barely satisfied, luxury is shocking.

America, as a nation, was barely eighteen years old. Such "luxury" as it could display was wholly derived from

English models. A few travellers to France had brought
with them, as did Gouverneur Morris, French porcelains,
French silver, bibelots, and examples of French furniture.
In passing, it may be noted that Morris, on his return to
Morrisania, brought, among his many boxes, several cases
of Imperial Tokay. This wine had been a wedding present
from Marie-Thérèse, Empress of Austria, to Marie-
Antoinette. Each bottle bore the seal of the double-headed
eagle. Gouverneur Morris had bought the wine for twenty-
five *sous* a bottle, in a common wine-shop, in Paris, during the
Revolution. This would have been a "luxury" for which
Talleyrand would have had only complimentary phrases.

In writing of these experiences in later days, Talleyrand
proves himself rather the keen observer, the philosopher
and the statesman than either the sportsman or the lover
of adventure. His reflections bear the stamp of opinions
in which impressions are passed through the alembic of a
contemplative mind. There was one aspect of American
development which drew from this former novice at Saint-
Sulpice, from this ex-priest and Bishop, a ringing note of
amazed commendation.

Talleyrand's commentary on American religious freedom
was the warmer, in praise, since he himself had hoped to
promote a similar liberty, by his Bill, for the appropriation by
the State of clerical privileges and properties. In as in-
rootedly a Catholic country as is France, religious liberty
may be tolerated—it can never be exercised save in defiance
of public opinion.

With what surprise does the traveller behold all [the religious
sects] co-existing in a perfect calm, which appears forever
unalterable; when in the same house father, mother, and children

peacefully follow, without opposition, the form of worship which each one prefers! I have seen this myself more than once, and nothing I had ever seen in Europe had prepared me for such a spectacle. On the days consecrated to religion, the members of one family went out together, each one sought the minister of his own form of worship, and they all returned to share the same domestic interests. This diversity of opinion caused no discord in their feelings and other habits; there were no disputes, no questions were even asked on the subject. It seemed as if religion here were looked upon as a personal secret which no man thought he had any right to question or penetrate. Thus, when some ambitious sectarian arrives in America from any European country, anxious to secure the triumph of his own doctrine by exciting discussion, instead of finding, as elsewhere, men disposed to engage themselves beneath his banner, he is hardly noticed by his neighbors; his enthusiasm neither attracts nor disturbs; he inspires neither hatred nor curiosity; each man keeps to his own religion, and goes about his business.

An impassibility such as the most fiery proselytism cannot shake, which it is not my purpose here to criticize, but to explain, has undoubtedly for its immediate cause, the liberty, and above all, the equality of all forms of worship. In America not one is proscribed, not one is imposed, hence religious agitations are unknown. . . . [Talleyrand concludes] The liberty, and above all the equality of all forms of worship, is one of the strongest guarantees of social tranquillity; for where consciences are respected, other rights cannot fail to be respected likewise.

One of Talleyrand's most discerning estimates of American character was the following:

The American, of all people on earth, is he who is least given to passions and is the least governed by them; and in such a people, sentiments and inclinations are only habits. All American habits make of him an Englishman. . . . The similitude alone of language constitutes a proprietary English right over

American inclinations. When Englishmen and Americans travel in the country of the other, they will always feel at home.

The interdependence of America and England, from a commercial point of view, is outlined at length:—there are prophetic views of the undeveloped forces in the country which reveal the clairvoyance of a master-intellect.

The conditions of supply and demand in America, of all objects pertaining to the manufacturing of clothing, etc., also interested this intelligent observer:

The population of America which is actually 4,000,000—and it augments rapidly—is in the infancy of manufactures. Some few glass factories, many tanneries, although imperfect, some looms of cloth and cashmere in Connecticut, cottons in different places, prove the insufficiency of the efforts made more than the desire to furnish the country with articles for its daily needs.

Talleyrand proclaims his economist's ideas in the above review of the infancy of American manufactures. His belief in the necessity for America to turn its energies into agricultural channels serves to show that, as he had travelled only in New England, and as far into the interior as Ohio, he knew little or nothing of the soil, from the point of view of productivity.

A new people who have modelled themselves upon the refined customs of Europe without passing through the slow evolution of civilization, have need to study nature in her greatest school; and it is by agriculture that all great states must commence. I say, and all economists are with me, that it is agriculture which lays the first foundation of society, teaches respect for property, and warns us that our interests are blind if they are too strongly opposed to those of others. It is agriculture which teaches us, in the most intimate manner, how indispensable is the connection between the duties and the rights of men. By attaching the laborer to his field it attaches man to his country; it teaches him, with his first attempts, the need of division of labor, the source of all the phenomena of individual and public prosperity. It moves the heart and interest of men to call a large family a source of wealth, and also by the resignation which it teaches, submits our intelligence to that supreme and universal order which rules the world. From all this I conclude that agriculture alone can put an end to revolutions, for it alone can usefully employ the whole strength of man, calm without discouraging him, teach him respect for experience, by means of which he may measure fresh attempts, and set constantly before his eyes the grand result of mere regularity of labor; and finally because it neither hastens nor delays anything.[1]

[1] *Mémoires de Talleyrand*, I, 236–237.

The letters of Talleyrand to Lord Lansdowne, and his reflections noted in his *Mémoires*, many of which he developed in the address which he gave at the Institute in Paris, on his return, 1796, are worthy of careful study, in the light of the extraordinary development and greatness to which our country has attained, in the growing of wheat, cotton and tobacco in the Western and Southern States.

CHAPTER XXVII

I

DURING his stay in America, Talleyrand journeyed not only into the wilderness, but also to New York and to Boston, and up the Hudson to Albany. In New York he was to meet and to know Aaron Burr. The latter's personal attraction and brilliancy of mind do not appear to have made a deep or a lasting impression on Talleyrand. Slight mention is made of the acquaintance in his *Mémoires* and yet one would have thought that the extraordinary fascination Burr appears to have exercised on all those whom he wished to charm, as well as his varied and adventurous political career, one which made him one of the most picturesque figures in the American political life of the time, would have captured Talleyrand. In those days psychological affinities or repulsions were not as defined nor as subtly analyzed as is the fashion in our more scientific era. There were certain traits of character in Burr's composite moral or immoral equipment in which Talleyrand may have recognized a certain family likeness to some personal peculiarities he preferred to ignore. Burr's aptitude for the machinery of politics Talleyrand could not fail to admire. Burr's unscrupulous methods may have been

335

divined by the future great statesman as being unpleasantly suggestive. Burr's career ended in disaster and ruin. He lacked the mental weight and that political genius which carried Talleyrand, in spite of his moral obliquity, to heights of lasting fame.[1] At an historic breakfast given by Aaron Burr at his attractive country place, near New York, besides Talleyrand, Volney, Madame de Genlis and other distinguished foreigners, was Louis-Philippe. Burr's beautiful daughter, Theodosia—the idol of his life—did the honors with a grace and dignity whose charm still irradiates the pages of every "Life" of her too-famous father. This memorable festivity must have been given during the year 1796—Louis-Philippe having started for America in 1795. His wanderings, since leaving Paris, had taken him to Norway, Sweden and as far as the North Cape; geography was one of the future king's passions—a passion which had been agreeably varied by his boyish adoration of his "Gouverneur" Madame de Genlis, and a later more romantic episode, in Holland, with Madame de Flahaut.

II

Richmond Hill, in the village of Greenwich, where Aaron Burr lived, was in the country. Burr, who had aristocratic tastes, had embellished his property with a handsome gateway; he had planted many beautiful trees and shrubs, and had made an ornamental pond. It was from that delightful dwelling that Burr went out, on a July morning, in 1804, to

[1] An interesting story is told by one of the descendants of General Schuyler's family relating to a visit paid by Aaron Burr when in Paris. This journey was made some time after Burr's having killed, in a duel, Alexander Hamilton. Talleyrand was not at home when Burr called on him. On seeing his card, Talleyrand said to his major-domo: "You may tell Monsieur Burr that the picture of Alexander Hamilton hangs over my mantelpiece." Burr took the hint and did not attempt a second visit.

fight his duel with Alexander Hamilton—to earn unending reproach and contumely thereby, and thus eventually to end his own political career.

In the New York of that day the city presented startling contrasts to Quakerish Philadelphia. The streets were narrow, so narrow that sidewalks in Pearl Street were forbidden. As late as 1789, "New York was a dull and dirty little town. It was a city without a bathroom, without a furnace, with bedrooms which in winter lay within the Arctic Zone, with no ice during the torrid season, without an omnibus, without a moustache, without a latch key."

The early Dutch influences in the style of buildings were still a marked architectural feature of the city which, in its earlier period, had been known as New Amsterdam. The picturesque gabled houses greatly added to the more attractive aspects of New York. There were a few interesting old (for a new country) Dutch taverns, with their huge ovens and solid tables and chairs. The Presidential Mansion in New York, built by William Walton, said to be, in 1752, the finest house in the colonies, was still, in Talleyrand's time, one of the chief show houses of the town.

III

Talleyrand is reported as having passed the better part of the summer of 1795 in New York. One great attraction in drawing Talleyrand to this city was his intimacy with Monsieur de la Forest.

In the French Consul-General, Antoine-René-Charles Mathurin, Comte de la Forest, Talleyrand had found a friend as well as counsellor. Monsieur de la Forest had entered the Diplomatic Corps in 1774. As Secretary of Legation at Geneva, he had followed his Minister to the

United States in 1779.   Named as Vice-Consul to Savannah, in Georgia, afterwards head of the Consulate at Charleston (August 26, 1783), and Vice-Consul-General for France in America, he was also Consul in New York when the French Revolution broke out.   De la Forest had the good luck to realize his property in France.   He bought huge tracts of land in Virginia; his overseer was a citizen named Cooper—the father of Fenimore Cooper.   It was therefore in the untamed Virginian wilderness of the de la Forest estate that Cooper's childish mind was to receive its first impressions of the wild country which was to excite the imagination and capture the fancy of the millions of the future readers of his famous novels.

When Talleyrand and the Consul-General de la Forest met, the acquaintance was soon to ripen into a close friendship.   The Consul-General's speculations in land greatly interested the ex-Bishop.   De la Forest's counsel and experience were sought and followed.   That the Consul's purse, also, helped Talleyrand, at certain difficult turnings of pecuniary corners, is more than certain.

His manner of proving his gratitude for such friendly offices shows the finer, nobler side of Talleyrand's nature. It is only the richly endowed, in mind or nature, who are lofty enough in spirit to show gratitude—or the very poor. Talleyrand, as Minister under the Directoire (July 18th, 1797), confided to his helper and friend a place in his Ministry; the latter became Head of a Division in his department. Talleyrand's gratitude did not end there; from "Directeur de la Comptabilité et des Fonds aux Affaires Etrangères"; later "Directeur des Postes," de la Forest was to be Minister to Berlin and Ambassador to Madrid.   He further figures in the Congress held at Lunéville, in the Diet of Ratisbon, and was the negotiator of the deposed King Ferdinand VII, at the signing of the Treaty, at Valençay.

We may thus note the successive advancement of the former Consul-General in New York, concurring with the gradual and continuous rise of Talleyrand's own power. The friendship begun in America continued as long as life lasted. In all of his most secret negotiations, Talleyrand must have his tried friend as chief aid. In his headship of the Provisional Government in 1814, the Prince—now so called, his title as Prince de Bénévent being no longer his, since it lapsed with Napoleon's fall—the Prince de Talleyrand named his friend Minister of Foreign Affairs. When the Comte d'Artois became King, the sovereign made de la Forest Minister of State and Member of the Privy Council.

In the case of the unceasing care and devotion for the advancement of his son Charles—by Madame de Flahaut—and in the protection shown to de la Forest, the tender, persistent and tenacious efforts for the career of those dear to Talleyrand are proven.

IV

During the summer of 1795 the pest—doubtless yellow fever, brought from the Islands of the West Indies—was raging in New York. Although the ex-Bishop appears to have been immune from this contagious malady, the epidemic and dispiriting tropical heat, prevalent at that season on our Eastern seaboard, may have suggested a trip to cooler regions. An agreeable journey took Talleyrand and his friend of that day—an eccentric Englishman named Law—to Albany. On their way thither they were to have revealed to them the contrasting beauties of the Hudson, its uprising, rocky Palisades, its inland lake aspect at Dobbs Ferry, the foliaged heights of the mountainous region at West Point, and beyond, the level of pasture-lands and peaceful farms.

The travellers were received at General Schuyler's hospitable mansion, at Albany. General Schuyler, the father of the clever and talented hostess, Mrs. Van Rensselaer, and his famous son-in-law, General Hamilton, were of the party. The latter had left the Cabinet, having resigned his post as Secretary of Finance. He expected to pass some time with General Schuyler.

In that city and at Troy an agreeable surprise—if the encounter was a surprise—awaited Talleyrand. He was to meet old friends—Monsieur and Madame de la Tour du Pin—a few days later, at the sister city.

A fantastic account of a previous meeting of Talleyrand with Madame de la Tour du Pin, at the Philadelphia market, is recorded by Madame de Genlis, in her *Mémoires*. The writer imagined the vaudeville setting of a pretty woman, young, with a certain air about her which attracted Talleyrand's gaze, driving her cart, filled with vegetables, to market. To Talleyrand's amazed delight, as the charming market-woman came nearer, in her he discovered an old friend—Madame de la Tour du Pin. This was the story of Madame de Genlis, who was a writer of stories.

The account of this meeting with the ex-Bishop d'Autun is quite differently given by Madame de la Tour du Pin in her own interesting *Journal d'une Femme de Cinquante Ans*. As the readers of that fascinating journal have learned, Monsieur and Madame de la Tour du Pin fled from the horrors of the Terror in Bordeaux, to America. Shortly after their arrival, they bought a fine farm near Albany, where they lived and worked for three years or more, making it a paying success.

Obliged to wait until spring to establish themselves in this new domain, they were fortunate in finding a modest wooden house with a big yard, in Troy. There, as Madame de la Tour du Pin recounts;

One day at the end of September, I was in my yard, hatchet in my hand, busied in cutting the bone of a leg of mutton which I intended to roast on a spit for dinner. . . . All at once, behind me, a deep voice made itself heard;—"It is impossible to thrust a spit through a leg of mutton with a greater air of majesty." On turning around quickly, I perceived M. de Talleyrand and M. de Beaumetz. Having arrived the day before at Albany, they had found out where we were from General Schuyler. They came to ask us, in his name, to dine and to pass the following day at his house. These gentlemen were only to stop in town two days . . . However, as Monsieur de Talleyrand was greatly amused at the sight of my leg of mutton, I insisted that they should come back the next day and eat it with us.

Throughout these famous *Mémoires*, whenever Talleyrand is mentioned, Madame de la Tour du Pin's comments are invariably bitten with the acid of her unrelenting animosity. She portrays herself as incarnating all the virtues —domestic, conjugal, maternal; she is *par excellence* the finished woman of the highest world, as she also pictures for us her heroism in surmounting any and all difficulties. That she was admirable in adversity must be admitted. Her gratitude, however, was not as ardent as was her appreciation of her own capacities.

The wives of the Puritan Fathers—many of whom were equally well born—exchanging luxury and country for the American wilderness in its wildest aspects, confronting the horrors of Indian massacres, underwent hardships which make this French lady's trials seem trivial—yet these heroic women did not consider it necessary to recount their experiences in hundreds of pages in two octavo volumes.

When Talleyrand sent to his hostess of a few hours, a fine lady's saddle, bridle, horse-blanket and other accessories, as well as medicaments, Madame de la Tour du Pin's praise of so generous an action is just sufficient to free her from the reproach of gross ingratitude. Her estimate of his character is the superficial one of a narrow nature whose opinions are tinctured with the personal point of view. A fervent Catholic, she abhorred in Talleyrand the renegade ex-Bishop. A passionate royalist, she could only sneer at the "absurdes théories des Constituants que M. de Talleyrand sacrifiait volontiers."

Monsieur de Talleyrand was kind, as he always has been, without any variation, with that added agreeability of conversation none possessed as did he. He had known me since my childhood, and because of this circumstance assumed towards me a sort of paternal and gracious attitude which was full of charm. One secretly regretted so many reasons for not esteeming him.

The message Talleyrand brought to Monsieur and Madame de la Tour du Pin, was an invitation from General Schuyler to pass the remainder of the day of their visit at the Schuyler mansion, in Albany.

On the way thither how fast the hours must have sped! There was all the later news of Europe to interchange. And the news was more dreadful than ever. The royal Princesse Elizabeth had paid for her devotion to her brother the King, and to the Queen, by death on the scaffold. The guillotine was never busier; blood flowed as a river in the

streets of Paris. Relatives and friends had been brutally
sacrificed to the cold cruelty of Robespierre. Gloomy visions of still greater losses oppressed the minds of the four
friends.

V

On arriving at the hospitable Schuyler mansion, they
found the General on the porch. He was waving his hands,
frantically.

"Come, come quickly! There is great news from
France!" he cried.

The "great news" was the death of Robespierre. The
river of blood was about to be staunched. Samson's tireless arm must, perforce, take a rest.

The émigrés, grouped together in the drawing-room,
were soon devouring the Gazettes. After reading of the
merciful deliverance of France from the pitiless fury of
Robespierre, they turned to the more recent lists of his
victims.

Talleyrand and de Beaumetz were rejoicing in the news
that several of those whom they dreaded to find included
in the records, had escaped. Talleyrand's joy, at first, was
great at finding that his sister-in-law, Madame Archambauld
de Talleyrand, had not perished on the scaffold. His
brother had emigrated as early as 1790. As the fortune of
the family belonged to his wife, the Comte had coolly
insisted that she should remain in Paris, lest the property be
confiscated. As a faithful wife to a prudent but selfish
husband, she had obeyed.

Later on in the evening, Talleyrand picked up a news-
paper he had not, as yet, seen. And there, to his horror, he
read that on the very day of Robespierre's arrest, the 9th

Thermidor, among the victims condemned by that arch-assassin, Madame de Talleyrand had been hurried to the scaffold. She mounted the dread steps of the guillotine during the very hour when Robespierre himself was condemned to pay for his crimes by the drop of the knife. Never did it fall, with greater justice, on any neck it severed.

Talleyrand was an economist of his emotions; yet like all powerful natures, the current of his passions ran strong; his affections were not shallow pools, they flowed in deep channels. He was greatly afflicted by the death of a sister-in-law for whom he had always entertained feelings of affection and admiration. She left three children, one girl, who, later, was to be Duchesse de Poix, and two sons. Louis, the elder, was to die in one of Napoleon's battles; the second son, Edmond, was to be a much-beloved nephew of Talleyrand. He was to wed the great heiress and famous beauty, the Princesse Dorothée de Courlande, better known as the Duchesse de Dino, the last of Talleyrand's more enduring passions.

Grief could not long claim too pronounced an outward aspect. During Talleyrand's stay at General Schuyler's he was to find one whom he was proud to call his friend—General Hamilton.

Another confessed element of surprise was the culture and refinement which Talleyrand found in this circle of intimates. The grace, the breadth of intellectual comprehension and the judgment with which Mrs. Van Rensselaer, in particular, discoursed on men, governments and the trend of events, amazed the brilliant diplomat. At thirty, this talented woman was at that period of mental development which may be likened to the meeting of summer and autumn. The fresh, spontaneous graces of youth were not yet lost;

Alexander Hamilton

From an etching by Jacques Reich

Alexander Hamilton
From an etching by Jacques Reich

A Hamilton

yet experience, wifehood and motherhood, and her intimate
intercourse with the most talented man, save Washington,
which the American War of Independence had produced—
General Hamilton—had developed in her a ripened maturity
of character and intellect.   Talleyrand was to see in this
clever woman one who "might well have passed any number
of years in Europe."   One did not have to wait for Mr.
James Russell Lowell's famous essay on a "Certain Con-
descension in Foreigners" to find its delicate irony as true
in 1794 as it is even to-day, in 1926.

Talleyrand's attitude towards Hamilton was one of
profound admiration.   Their acquaintance, begun in Philadelphia, was to develop in Albany, and in New York, into
intimacy.   Talleyrand states that "in the two winters I
spent in America, either in New York or in Philadelphia, I
availed myself of the opportunity this afforded me to see
the chief personages whose names the American Revolution
handed down to history, especially General Hamilton whose
mind and character placed him, I thought, on a par with
the most distinguished statesmen of Europe, not even
excepting Mr. Pitt and Mr. Fox."

The later history of the attempted far-reaching doctrines
of the French revolutionaries—doctrines which were to
subvert Americans—was a subject Talleyrand and Hamilton
must frequently have talked over, before meeting at Albany.
The former's stay in New York was unquestionably influenced by Hamilton's residence in the city, after his
resignation as Cabinet Minister.   It was in New York
Hamilton was to practise law.   It was no venal ambition,
but necessity which had changed Alexander Hamilton from
exercising the functions of a Cabinet Minister to the duller
routine of a New York lawyer.   The needs of a growing

family—Hamilton was the father of six children—and other
pressing family affairs had forced the decision. Griswold, the
historian of "The Republican Court," goes so far as to state:
"it is true that Hamilton was something of a roué."
Hamilton at the close of his career could write in a saddened, depressed state of mind: "What can I do better
than withdraw from the scene? Every day proves to me
more and more that this American world was not made for
me." [1] The whole fabric of his toil, his superhuman efforts
to mould and form a nation seemed to have gone down into
the abyss of failure. His party had gone to ruin—democracy, which he hated, was seated in triumph with Jefferson's
election to the Presidential chair; his own life was blighted
by blasted hopes, by attacks—not undeserved—on his
private character—attacks which followed him until Aaron
Burr's pistol turned enemies and friends alike into mourners.

To Hamilton, Talleyrand was drawn by the attraction of
intellectual sympathy. There was the same breadth in
their mental outlook. There had been a like training in the
making of a Constitution, in guiding the birth of a nation
to new conditions, and in filling difficult and commanding
posts. Hamilton's knowledge of the French language,
which he had spoken as a child in the Isle of Nevis—his
mother, though of Scotch birth, was of Huguenot descent—
was a further cementing link in their friendship. With
Hamilton's French blood, an atavistic strain as well as a
kinship in their natures enabled him to understand, and
even to sympathize with the amorous excesses of which
Talleyrand was accused. Hamilton himself was to show a
weakness not uncommon in great men. His susceptibility
to the charm of women, his frequent lapses from the stern

[1] Hamilton's Works.

rule of conjugal fidelity, his passionate, if brief liaisons, his public confession of his relations with one of his mistresses—Mrs. Reynolds—have furnished his biographers with chances of presenting the various stages of this great man's career in dramatic setting.

In their previous talks at Philadelphia, Talleyrand and Hamilton had unquestionably canvassed the attitude and sentiment of America relating to the tragic revolutionary outbreak in France. Since they had last met, opinion in the States had sensibly stiffened into abhorrence of the violence, anarchy and revenge of the later phases of the movement. Cold-blooded murder, rapine, wild disorder and wholesale confiscation of property have never appealed to the descendants of English law-abiding Puritans, to those of stolid Dutchmen, nor to chivalric Southerners.

The earlier beliefs preached by the great leaders who attempted to save the monarchy, to institute a Constitution, to give freedom and liberty to France, had been hailed with enthusiasm in America.

The glowing future presented by the ideals of the National Assembly of the country which had helped to free America from England's yoke had seemed a renewal of the bond between them. But first, the steady grind of the guillotine on innocent women's and even on youthful necks; then the prolonged horrors of the "Red Terror"; later the excesses of Genêt, the new Minister sent as the representative of the French government to the United States—these successive developments had turned sympathy into open hostility of feeling and sentiment. The policy of General Washington and of Hamilton had been to preserve strict neutrality towards both France and England, then at war. This policy had not been easy to enforce. Genêt's act

of fitting out privateers at Charleston; the capture of prizes
of English vessels by these privateers; the redress demanded of such outrages by the English government; the foment-
ing of political trouble by Genêt in forming Revolutionary
clubs patterned on those of Paris—all the essential features
of red cap processions, inflammatory speeches by so-called
"patriotic" Frenchmen, many of whom were Jacobin
émigrés—such attempts to foment anarchy and insurrection
in New York had armed the government at Washington
with all the power Jefferson had attempted to thwart.
Genêt's recall was demanded; the incipient rebellion was
crushed, and Jefferson sufficiently humbled to consider,
seriously, resigning from the Cabinet.

The new Republic could now continue its strict neutrality, in relation to foreign affairs, fully supported by public
opinion. The episodic outbreaks of threatened disorder had
been a salutary lesson to the foreign elements in our midst.

There were, indeed, not only the more recent history of
the mistaken policy of French agents in America, but all
the more dramatic and tragic scenes in which Talleyrand
had taken part in the pre-revolutionary and revolutionary
days in France, as subjects of discussion between these two
famous men.

Hamilton was to know, and to listen later on to, the
suave voice of temptation, and alas! to pay for his fall with
his life.

The contrast between Hamilton and Talleyrand, physically and temperamentally, must have been of keen interest
to those who saw them together. Hamilton was of small
stature. His well-shaped, clean-cut features were illuminated by eyes which seemed the very windows of his soul, so
revealing were their fire and depth. When strongly moved,

Hamilton rose, in spite of his inches, to a seemingly commanding presence. His flaming passion, his burning eloquence, his stately periods carried all audiences to enthusiastic rapture. The conviction which his words imparted that he was the impassioned *porte-parole* of strongly-fibred sincerity was, above all else, the vitalizing quality which carried his audiences captive.

Hamilton's ardent nature flamed into passionate speech which his reasonableness tempered, whenever a subject interested him. Talleyrand's powerful armor of self-restraint could be loosened, in sympathetic intercourse, but never could he wholly abandon a certain guarded reserve.

Hamilton's mobile countenance reflected the quickly moving, easily stirred soul within. Talleyrand's strength lay in his superb control over passions and emotionalism. Hamilton's impressive eloquence, his great gifts as orator and debater earned Talleyrand's unstinted praise. He unquestionably gave him his confidence, as he gave it to few, in his long life.[1]

The attraction which Talleyrand exercised over such widely different characters, as for example Mirabeau, Napoleon, the Czar Alexander and Hamilton, was not alone due to what we now term the "complex" of his many-sided nature.

[1] Talleyrand is reported to have observed in casual conversation, that he had known many of the most remarkable men of his time, but that he had never, on the whole, known one as great as Hamilton. (*George III and Charles James Fox.* Trevelyan, Vol. 2, p. 414.)

CHAPTER XXVIII

I

WITH the death of Robespierre, the complexion of political events in France had begun sensibly to change. The prisons delivered up those who would have been the victims of the morrow had not the fall of the tyrant brought about the return of more humane feelings. The French people were wearied with tyranny; they were satiated with the entertainment of watching heads fall under the glistening knife of the guillotine. They were tired of their own brutality. The cry was Peace—and better government.

The great news of this change had quickly spread. Timidly at first, and then in larger and larger numbers, the *émigrés* nearest France dared to hazard a return to their beloved country. Such was the news that was carried to those who were far away in America. With what emotions must those we have followed to that distant land have heard the glad tidings! Loss of property, confiscation, pillage of great châteaux—even prospective poverty—what were these compared to the ineffable joy of touching French soil, of once more being in the one and only country in the world for Frenchmen?

In Talleyrand's small room in Philadelphia, he had soon

matured his plans. The results of his labors in the fields of speculation, his vast projects for giving work to "all refugees in America," such hopes and aspirations paled before the rising sun irradiating the prospect of a return to Paris.

Talleyrand applied himself at once to work upon the sensibilities and generous nature of Madame de Staël. His cry, that rang across the seas, "I shall die if I remain here another year," was as a trumpet call to the responsive sympathies of that large-hearted woman.

Talleyrand appealed to the one friend whose affection and whose disinterestedness could be counted on. Madame de Staël was now in Paris; she had re-opened her salon. The Baron de Staël, reinstated as Swedish Ambassador under Gustavus IV, lent the aureole of his official post as an added appendage of power to the most famous woman in France. Apart from his sincere friendship for his gifted friend, Talleyrand gravitated as naturally towards those who sat in the seats of the mighty as the needle follows the magnet.

In this new world of the Directoire, there were new faces, new names, new fortunes. There were courtiers of the time of Louis XVI who elbowed deputies who had voted for the death of their King; there were financiers whose fortunes and whose sudden emergence from obscurity were tales told in whispers; there were courteous but frigidly distant *grandes dames* who gazed, shocked and amazed, at the insolent new beauties of this new world parading their nudity.

Madame de Staël proceeded to throw her net, cleverly, into these troubled social waters. Talleyrand's appeal roused all the latent fires of her capacity for devotion. This new world was as a recovered field of operations to

Madame de Staël's active spirit. For her disconsolate friend, languishing in a land of semi-savages, what would she not do? She rushed to the battle of pushing his interests with all the zeal and cunning of the experienced mover of men that she was. Tallien, Barras, Chénier [1]—these her new friends were left no respite. Talleyrand's talents as negotiator, his genius for statecraft, the great services he had rendered in the Assembly,—these rare gifts and acts were cited with an eloquence which forced indifference to turn to partisanship. Tallien was moved to the point of declaring from the Tribune that "justice had not been done to Talleyrand-Périgord"; he quoted Roederer who had advocated that a distinction should be made between *émigrés* and fugitives, citing Talleyrand as one "who had been included in the list of *émigrés*, though he left the country on a Government mission." Tallien at least seemed sure of his facts, viz.: that Danton had sent Talleyrand to London on a mission.

Meanwhile, the work done behind the scenes by Madame de Staël was unremitting. Chénier, the poet, one of the most eloquent of the Deputies, must be won. To excite his powers, or his interest, he must be moved and he must be convinced; he was somewhat unique, among his colleagues— he was sincere.

Talleyrand also had been "sincere," was Madame de Staël's impassioned outburst, in the courageous stand he had taken, against his order, against the clergy, in the Assembly. And where find a negotiator as successful, proving the highest statesmanlike qualities, as he who had forced England to remain neutral? Madame de Staël warmed to her work. The future author of *Corinne*

[1] Marie-Josèphe Chénier, brother to the more famous poet André.

was furnished with a theme, in thus reviewing Talleyrand's life work (with some notable acts omitted), suited to her talent for embellishing character.

It was a matter of supreme interest to learn that Chénier was in love. Here was a chord to touch. Feeling and sentiment must be aroused. The charming woman who was Chénier's divinity, was induced to sing some verses suitable to excite compassionate emotion. The result was such as might have been foreseen.

In his speech in the Convention, the poet, during the sitting of the members of that body on the 18th Fructidor, the year III, stirred his hearers by his enumeration of the services that "Talleyrand-Perigord, ex-Bishop of Autun, had rendered the Constitutional Assembly."

He hurled the facts, acts and services of Talleyrand, "who had busied himself to consolidate the Republic," as soldiers wave a victorious flag. Chénier flourished, in the teeth of certain inimical members, Danton's passport, proving that "Talleyrand had left on a governmental mission"; he quoted the brilliant report Talleyrand had sent to Danton on the relations of France among European nations (25th November, 1792). He enlarged upon "the great services he had rendered the Republic, in the diverse missions entrusted to him, in London."

In the days when he was proscribed in France by Robespierre and Marat, Pitt proscribed him in England. It was in the heart of a Republic, in the country of Benjamin Franklin, that he contemplated the impressive spectacle of a free people, awaiting the time when France should possess judges and not assassins, a Republic and not an Anarchy.

His report ended with an eloquent appeal to have Talleyrand given permission to re-enter France:

I call upon you for Talleyrand—I claim him in the name of his many services: I claim him in the name of national equity. I claim him in the name of the Republic to which his talents may be of service and in the name of the hatred you bear to *émigrés* of whom he would be the victim, like yourselves, if cowards could triumph!

Among Chénier's assertions of Talleyrand's services to the revolutionary movement were, "that he was one of the founders of liberty"—he had never taken up arms against his country: "he left France on a government mission." Here again the wording of Danton's passport to Talleyrand plays its rôle; Talleyrand's Essay of November 25th, 1792, on the "Relations of France with the European States," is cited as proof that Talleyrand was sent by the Provisional Executive Council, then in power, on a secret mission,— a so-called "Mémoire," it was triumphantly stated, which was found among Danton's papers.

Chénier's eloquence won the day. Some lighter armed partisans rushed to complete the victory. Brivals, Génisson, Boissy d'Anglas were ready to defeat Deputy Légendre's hostile suggestion; he had moved an adjournment: "Let the petition" (Talleyrand's petition sent to the Convention 16th of June, 1795) "let it be referred to the Committee of Legislation to make a report." Madame de Staël's troops were well drilled. Boissy d'Anglas saw the danger; he hurled: "This is no question of friendship but of justice. Talleyrand is not an *émigré*." The call upon the sense of justice found its response in Chénier's motion being put to the vote. Amid enthusiastic applause, Talleyrand, it was voted, was to be once more a French citizen.

Talleyrand's petition, sent to the Convention, on June 16, 1795, read:

I am not an *émigré* and I ought not to be treated as one. One condemned in his absence must not be likened to an *émigré;* flight due to an accusation, and still more, absence prolonged for such a cause, bears no resemblance to voluntary departure which constitutes the misdemeanor of emigration. The National Convention has admitted that all those convicted by warrant of arrest, of denunciation, since the 31st of May, are authorized to return. The case of Talleyrand is absolutely identical.

Talleyrand in his petition states positively that he was sent to England after August 10th—and this for the first time. The petition was passed, through des Renaudes' friendly offices, to the Convention. His ex-Grand Vicar, in whom Talleyrand, when Bishop of Autun, had found an able administrator, had remained faithful to his former Bishop. Des Renaudes, never having been arrested, was able to prove his friendly zeal to further Talleyrand's interests.

The decree of annulment read:

The National Convention decrees that Talleyrand-Périgord, ex-Bishop of Autun, is authorized to re-enter the territory of the French Republic and that his name shall be erased from the lists of *émigrés*. In consequence, the Convention recalls the decree of accusation formerly launched against him.[1]

II

With the precious document in his possession, for he received the decree of the Convention in the beginning of November, 1795, why did not Talleyrand start for France at once? No records exist which satisfactorily explain his delay of seven months in taking ship.

[1] Procès-Verbaux de la Convention Nationale, lxix, 38.

Assured now of his right to return to France, Talleyrand nevertheless appeared to be in no haste to take passage. He spent the whole winter in Philadelphia in his "small house in a back alley." His chief occupation seems to have been writing to his friends.

Talleyrand's gratitude to Madame de Staël was not dealt out in niggardly phrases. That Madame de Staël's devotion and her zeal in procuring the repeal of the banishment had deeply affected him is evidenced by the tenor of his letter to her. His later ingratitude was to take another form.

So the business is ended, thanks to you [he wrote her on the 14th Nov., 1795]. You have done everything that I desired. . . . I shall leave in the Spring for whatever port you may point out, and the rest of my life shall be spent near you, wherever you may be. . . . Will Monsieur de Staël give me a small room? [Talleyrand was now used to small rooms.] It is to your house that I should like to come on arrival.

And he adds, after sending messages to friends—to Mathieu de Montmorency, to de Castellane, etc., "Dear Friend, I love you with all my heart." Talleyrand meant every word of the love and affection which he professed then. Madame de Staël died comparatively young—at the age of fifty-six years. Yet she was to survive many years the death of her friendship with Talleyrand who "wished to spend the rest of my life with you."

Now that the Convention had given up its ghost of power to be succeeded by the Directoire—were the times ripe for departure? During the long cold winter, Talleyrand's thoughts must have been turning daily, perhaps hourly, over the question—"Are the times ripe?" One of his reasons for delay, given in a letter to Madame de Staël had been, "I shall wait until the equinoctial gales are over." The memory of his thirty-eight days' voyage to America had not been dimmed. Then, as autumn merged into winter, Talleyrand wrote he would take passage in the spring. Yet it was June before he eventually took ship.

Conclusions are obvious. Talleyrand was waiting for the new government to prove its capacity. Would it last? If it lasted, could he hope to enter the lists? Among the Five Hundred he had friends—Constitutionalists—members, as he had been, of the Assembly. Through the Consul-General, Monsieur de la Forest, Talleyrand doubtless had more news from France than he had had during the Terror. Talleyrand's letters to his two friends—to Madame de Staël and to des Renaudes—prove he kept in close touch with the moving political changes in Paris. He must have had frequent meetings with his friend Monsieur de la Forest, the Consul-General, in New York. Still he lingered in Philadelphia; his reasons for delaying his departure must be largely conjectural. Talleyrand's decision to watch events, to follow from a distance the course taken by the Directoire may be ascribed to his philosophic attitude of "letting time do its work"—which is one of the most interesting proofs of his staying power, and is the mark of the born statesman's capacity for taking long views.

Talleyrand saw the chances once more drifting towards him of remaking a place, a career, in the new France of this new Republic. The great theatre of action, he was persuaded, was once more to offer him his longed-for opportunity. He was ready now, armed, equipped, seasoned, as never before, for playing the rôle which he had always felt he was destined to make a great one. Genius has such

moments of the insight we call second-sight. The consciousness of unusual powers is like the head-light of a ship—
intuition blazes its light across the sea of destiny. Talleyrand found ample time for maturing his plans. The manner
of his entrance on the Parisian scene proves such plans had
been painstakingly elaborated. In reviewing the political
situation in France, he quickly discerned that among the
Ministers there was no trained diplomat. There was a
place for one. Some Minister would be named; mistakes
and errors in the management of the difficult relations of
the Directoire towards European nations would be made.
It was the part of wisdom to allow the ineptitude of bunglers
to be proven. "Let time do its work."

The new government was still in a fluctuating state.
The Directoire, in succeeding the Terror, had inherited the
ruins the Terror had left—a sinister legacy. One of the
greatest difficulties of the Ministers was to find money to
meet expenses. The Treasury was empty.

Two appalling facts stared the Directors in the face—
facts which must be faced—a solution for which the most
ingenious mind seemed to find no remedy. The immediate
one which must be met was the want of bread.

Morris notes in his Diary as early as April 13, 1795,
"Paris is far from quiet, and the scarcity of food becomes
daily more sensible." On April 13th Madame de Flahaut,
whom Morris meets at Altona, informs him that as early as
March 27th, Parisians were reduced to four ounces of bread
a day!

The cry that rang up in the Paris streets in the long hard
winter of 1795–96 was "Bread! Bread!" How could the
Five Directors, or the Ancients, or the Five Hundred, how
could any government find bread where there was none? How

provision the city? The country was in ruins;—there were the ruined churches, ruined châteaux, ruined lands, much of the latter untilled because of ruined ploughs and farm instruments;—there was much of the same confusion in the interior as the Terrorists had sown; there was the war still going on with the Powers;—and the funds to pay the armies —where were they? The Treasury was empty! The Five Directors could appoint Ministers, there was no money even to pay their salaries. How find the millions necessary to supply an army with food, cannon, and clothes?

Talleyrand's letters, at this period, prove him to have been in full possession of all these difficulties confronting the Directoire. He enters into minute details of the advantage of the export of American harvests—of surplus rice, flour, salted meats and salted fish. There is no record of Talleyrand's services having been accepted.

If Talleyrand's insatiable ambition, if his passionate longing to play a part in the new government—if such ambitious designs haunted his fertile mind, his natural caution, that quality of his genius which acted as a balance wheel to his most audacious projects—this cool calculating prudence kept him in America.

An empty treasury!—No, the times were not yet ripe.

III

From certain points of view, as the winter went on into the spring, the news was more encouraging. The Directoire was gradually establishing a better order. The two legislative powers—the Council of Five Hundred, and the Council of the Ancients, these two Assemblies, in reality the cradle of the present Chambre des Députés and of the French Sénat—these powers had delivered a proclamation to the people; royalist counter-revolutions were to be suppressed; all ideas of vengeance must be combated; abundance, credit, confidence, social order must be the watchword of the future. Such programmes are the usual political house-cleaning of newly-formed governments.

There must have risen, like a burning sun, in the mind and soul of Talleyrand, the orbed belief that his dark days were over. Beyond and above the hope of amassing a fortune, loomed the shapes, not only of material, but of immaterial possibilities. There was born in him the exhilarating consciousness of power, of the chance of playing a great part in this re-born France. Such beliefs, hopes and possibilities during all that long, cold, dreary winter, must have been like unto a great light blazing ahead. America itself, in its joyous optimism, in its sober yet exalted faith in the future, and in its untiring labor to secure the triple prize of happiness, fortune and liberty, was the unconscious joint partner in a building up of fairy castles. The ferment of belief in success was a part of the very soil of America. It vibrated with energy.

With better news came better spirits. The certainty of taking ship sooner or later; of re-entering France not as an *émigré*, but as a loyal French citizen; hope coloring every plan made, visions of possible advancement, of high place, of power—dancing before one's eyes—with such thoughts and projects warming the mind, Talleyrand experienced a re-birth of the gaiety that had made *l'abbé de cour* sought in every salon in Paris.

In a small room, at the back of a stationer's shop, a company of Frenchmen, during this winter of waiting, met nightly. The place of meeting was hardly one of the most distinguished, as a French phrase would put it. One of the members of the circle had set up a stationery and book-seller's shop, in the little house. The enterprising shop-keeper was Moreau de Saint-Méry. The circle of intimates were de Noailles, La Rochefoucauld-Liancourt, Talon, the idealist Moreau de Méry, Volney, and other friends now living in the Quaker City. Among these friends, French *joie de vivre* now found its voice; old habits, old tastes were revived. In making a common purse of purses lightly lined, there could be a cosy supper-table laid. A bottle of the famous Madeira, warranted to have passed the Cape, would be opened, and under the stimulus of such hosts and guests the hours would fly as they had flown when King Pleasure reigned at the Court of Versailles.

"How many times, Talleyrand"—wrote Moreau in his Journal—"having reached the little court-yard in front of my shop, would turn around, run up the stairs, to sit out the night." In that French milieu, with his old friends about him, Talleyrand once more would exericse the old, gracious, incomparable social charm. Talks on every known subject would fill the all too short hours. Every scrap of news from France would be narrated, criticized, and enlarged upon. There were no darkening shadows of prolonged exile, of dreaded horrors, of further losses of friends or property. These were hours when camaraderie became friendship, and warmth of sentiment induced inti-macy. "We opened our hearts to each other, our most intimate sentiments, our thoughts were avowed, our experi-ences were confessed," wrote Moreau de Saint-Méry. Though Talleyrand could afford to sit out the night, Mad-ame de Moreau de Saint-Méry would remind her guest that her husband must be up at seven in the morning "to open shop." Her guests were warned also not "to talk so loud," as Philadelphia customers fought shy of a shop where excited French voices, many of them raised in loud tones, sounded not unlike violent outbreaks.

Talleyrand came to dinner with us, and from my house took ship for Hamburg in the Brig *Den-Frie-Prove*. Thus am I deprived of one of my dearest joys . . . [the date given is June 13th, 1796]. Every day since October, 1795, he came to my bureau at eight o'clock at night. There, alone, uninterrupted, except when Beaumetz, Talon, Noailles, Volney, Payen, de Boisneuf, Demeunier, Boislandry came all together or separately, we opened our hearts to one another, we interchanged openly our sentiments, and our most intimate thoughts became common property. . . . Talleyrand did not take supper . . . I had some excellent madeira which Talleyrand greatly liked and he drank some at supper.[1]

Spring had turned her bright face to summer, and it was in June, as M. Moreau states, that Talleyrand took ship for Hamburg.

[1] *Journal of Monsieur de Moreau de Saint-Méry.*

CHAPTER XXIX

I

ON landing at Hamburg, Talleyrand received an unexpected form of welcome. Monsieur Ricci handed him a letter from Madame de Flahaut. After a series of adventures, the lady had reached Hamburg. In her missive, in the most impassioned phrases, she implored her ci-devant lover not to land but to return to America; were his presence to be known in Hamburg, her hoped-for and soon-to-be-solemnized marriage with Monsieur de Souza, Portuguese Minister to Paris, might not come off. If Monsieur Ricci had been a physiognomist, it must have been an entertaining study for him to have watched Talleyrand's countenance. It is to be presumed that the latter's habitual facial mask was more than usually impenetrable. Talleyrand's instantaneous decision proved his cynical indifference to as naïve an appeal. He forthwith promptly proceeded to land. During the month of his sojourn in Hamburg, the wedding of Madame de Flahaut to the Portuguese Minister was postponed. It took place in Paris in 1802. No disturbing reminders of the past—of the lady's somewhat richly colored experiences—appear to have clouded her new venture.

On his way to Paris, Talleyrand went to Brussels,

possibly to Berlin. As he was in direct communication with La Revellière-Lépeaux—one of the five executive Directors of the new government—there is unfounded but interesting evidence that he may have been sent to the Prussian capital on a secret mission, as the city offered a wide field of observation.

Once in Paris, Talleyrand found himself in a city transformed. The former picturesque grandeur with which Court life, its costumes and great coaches had embellished streets and squares, was gone. Many of the old ancestral hôtels had been turned into warehouses (one may still see such transformations in the Paris of to-day—in the Marais); wines and vegetable shops masked sculptured façades, and portraits of ancestors stared at returned *émigrés* from shop windows loaded with the loot of palaces. The tones of voices heard in the streets echoed the new life; a gayer, less restrained note rang through lips and laughter. Through blood and murder, through horrors unspeakable, France had won its longed-for liberty. The people of the Directoire clamorously celebrated its independence—its release from monarchical tyranny. The old world of centuries was dead; from its tomb the triumphant figure of Democracy arose—for good or ill, to trumpet its birth to future unborn generations. In the semi-nude dress of the "Les Merveilleuses" as through the lorgnettes of "Les Incroyables," this new world proved it had outgrown conventionality. Extravagant fashions in dress symbolized the extravagant passion for amusement. Young and old, the new rich, and the new poor, the ruined aristocrats, and the members of the Directoire, turned to dancing, to supping as though pleasure were a rite. Public balls were the rendezvous of all this world which had survived the guillotine, emigration and confiscation. Private balls were not in favor; they and the salons were considered to be nests of intrigue and conspiracy.

II

Talleyrand soon found his milieu in this new, strange world. He had the quick instinct of how and where to make his presence known and felt to such disparate elements. A four years' absence from a city as changed as was Paris, made the return of one who proposed to play a part—and a notable one—on the stage the Directoire had set, a matter of serious calculation. Such an entrance on the field of action must be impressive.

Two days after his arrival, he was offered the chance of making his bow before the élite of the Paris world. While in America, he had received a particularly gratifying honor. The National Institute of Paris had elected him a member of the second class of Moral and Political Science. Immediately his presence was known in the city, his fellow members requested him to give them an address. Here was an unlooked-for opportunity to make his return heralded—to hear his name once more acclaimed, and under the most favorable auspices.

When Talleyrand made his bow before his French audience, they looked on a man astonishingly young for one who was forty-two years of age. His tall, slight figure, his erect, dignified bearing, an expression at once suave yet noticeably self-contained on his pallid face, made an impressive effect. The secret of his distinction was revealed in voice, manner and gesture. Those who had lived in the world of the later years of the eighteenth century saw imaged before them a day that was dead; those of the new world looked wonderingly on one who, in himself, mirrored the already legendary past. Some among those in the audience knew of Talleyrand's all-but unrivalled reputation as a conversationalist. His success as a debater and as a promoter of bills in the Assembly was already a matter of history. This professional assemblage of scientists demanded qualities in an orator of a different, of a more critical and philosophical order.

The subject of Talleyrand's discourse was a general description of America. The American character as a whole, its curious religious liberty, its respect for law, its sentiment for France, and its deep, English-inrooted traditions, were presented in a remarkably original and striking manner. Sir Henry Lytton Bulwer's *Essay on Talleyrand* is the more valuable since he states that while not a contemporary, he had the advantage of knowing many friends and contemporaries of the great statesman; added to his fine historical talent, he possessed a rare critical faculty. Sir Henry rates this Essay of Talleyrand's very high:

Few writings of the kind contain as many right ideas in as limited a frame. The author gives a general description of the state of American society, its calm character, its varied and original habits, its Saxon laws, and the religious sentiments of this recently born community.

He goes on to state a fact, then little understood:

that England had gained more than she had lost by the separation; and that the needs of America attached her to English interests, while their language, their education, their history and their laws inspired sentiments which, rightly directed, were and would remain English.

III

Success in scientific and literary circles was not the real goal Talleyrand had set out to win. His place, he felt, was plainly designated. The new government had no experienced diplomatic statesman—no one trained to the difficulties and management of foreign affairs. He must be named Minister of that department. Among the Five Hundred, he had many friends—Constitutionalists as he had been, in the earlier Revolutionary days. He could be sure of only one friend among the five Directors—La Revellière-Lépeaux. Carnot hated him with a deadly hatred; to Reubell, the obstinate and narrow-minded Colmarian, he was the incarnation of Bourbon vices and Machiavelian trickery. On Barras—the only "elegant" among the Five, with his southern love of pleasure and his hereditary traditions—it was on Barras that Talleyrand had fixed his cool and discerning gaze. Barras must be attacked, pursued, seduced, entrapped.

Of the five Directors, the executive chiefs of the Directoire—La Revellière, Le Tourneur, Reubell, Carnot and Barras—the latter was the only one with an ex-title. The four *bourgeois* were either lawyers by profession, or had held rank as captains in the army before the Revolution. Barras, the ex-Vicomte, had been a captain in the engineer corps. He had been chosen not so much for his talents, but as being a man of the world,—one who could best organize a democratic Court and who could receive ambassadors with distinction and grace. He was a man who could be reached.

Before forcible methods were resorted to, Talleyrand attempted to accomplish his purpose by a more indirect route. A club he had joined, together with some of the members of the Directoire, brought him closely in touch with the government circle. There were Sieyès, Treilhard, Chénier, Montesquiou, Maret, Benjamin Constant, Roederer, and others in this so-called Constitutional Club. With his customary address and that suppleness which made him the friend of any political adversary he felt must be won, whether it were a Danton, a Robespierre, a Mirabeau, Talleyrand soon became one of the motive powers in the club. He was once more in the front rank for political preferment. A Treaty of Peace with England necessitated a negotiator. Barthélemy was chosen as Minister Plenipotentiary. The names suggested had been Le Tourneur, Talleyrand and Maret. Reubell had launched a violent attack against the "ex-priest." "If you want honesty and capacity," he had cried, "guard yourself against thinking of Talleyrand."

Defeated, Talleyrand lost no time in vain regrets.

IV

The friendships which Talleyrand formed among the new comers were noticeably Montrond, Dorinville, André d'Arbelles, and among his "ancients" there was de Narbonne. Soon Barras was to prove his devotion, by pushing Talleyrand's political fortunes. Copying the costume of the period, the latter donned the short breeches, the cut-away coat, the rich vest, with the lawn cravat, wound like a scarf beneath the powdered curls and high-held chin. There is a legend that Talleyrand wore earrings. Whatever may have been the details of the costume, one may be assured that it was in the highest fashion.[1]

[1] On Talleyrand's return to Paris, Chénier, from having been impassioned advocate and liberator, was to turn to a hate of Talleyrand and of all his ways. In commenting on a letter of the ex-Bishop's, in which Talleyrand asserted "my most ardent wishes have been, and are constantly for the happiness and glory of the French

On his return to Paris, Talleyrand's intimacy with
Comte Casimir de Montrond began, one which was to last,
with a brief interval of coolness, until his death. Montrond
was an interesting, if depraved, type of eighteenth century
capacities and immoralities. His wit, his talent for intrigue,
his all but incomparable charm, placed him among the
notable figures of the age. His learning rested on a solid
base:—Pascal, La Fontaine, Voltaire, Rabelais, and the
classics were his literary familiars. This serious side of
his tastes was, however, kept in the background. As a man
of the highest fashion—as one who gave the *ton* to the cut
of a coat or of a cravat—Montrond posed as a clever man.
Talleyrand alone was his rival in wit. His successes with
women furnished the salons of the day with endless gossip.
He was the perpetual lover of Fortunée Hamelin, the famous
Directoire beauty and intriguante; Lady Yarmouth, Pauline
Borghèse (Napoleon's sister), Madame Junot (Duchesse
d'Abrantés) were among his conquests. For a brief period
he was the husband of Aimée de Coigny, Duchesse de Fleury,
whose passion for intrigue could match his own.

For many years, Montrond was Talleyrand's chief aid
and negotiator in difficult affairs. Montrond was called
"Talleyrand à cheval" (Talleyrand on horseback). He was

Republic," Chénier writes, in a spirit of unconcealed contempt: "The letter of L'Abbé
Maurice" (as Chénier now derisively calls him) "proves that after having been
monarchist, Orleanist, and not having been able to be Robespierrist, since Maximilian
would have none of him, he now is turning Directorist, waiting for whatever will
be the power a little later on. That b—" (the word is untranslatable) "wanting in
respect for the episcopacy, is like a sponge which absorbs all the liquids into which
one plunged it, with this difference that, if pressed, the sponge renders back what it
has taken in, and that in this instance all things are good booty for our friend."
Chénier is chiefly remembered as a poet: Talleyrand, since his death in 1838, has
never been more quoted, his statecraft as carefully studied, and his life and character have never furnished more material to more historians than at the present time
of Europe's distressful condition. How often one hears the wish echoed in the
France of to-day: "Had France but a Talleyrand!" (June, 1926).

in close relations with the Embassies of London, Berlin and Vienna. Talleyrand made use of his supple and subtle arts to convey to foreign Ministers his own secret designs, and to learn the secrets of Cabinets through Montrond's rare skill in extracting information from those in authority. All such matters were carried out through personal inter-course—letters were compromising: Montrond's instruc-tions were conveyed through the medium of direct speech. He played an important rôle in the Coup d'Etat of 18 Brumaire. His negotiations with Comte de Nesselrode and Metternich were determining causes in the decisions made at the Council of Vienna. He was offered, by Napo-leon, on his return from Elba, an income of two hundred thousand francs if he could detach Talleyrand from Louis XVIII.

To the question asked Talleyrand at the Council of Vienna: "Could he consider making war against France?" his contemptuous answer was: "It is not a war against France that is under consideration, it is one against the *man of the Island of Elba*." Talleyrand's long nourished revenge for the insults to which Napoleon's justifiable anger had subjected him, rings in the last line.[1]

V

Having failed with men, to secure his post, Talleyrand now turned to women. Madame de Staël had already begun her siege on Barras' apparent or feigned indifference. On her return to Paris, after her temporary exile,[2] she had brought the powers of her eloquence and her turbulent intensity to agitate opinion, to electrify her circle and to

[1] *Le Beau Montrond*, by Henri Malo, 1 Vol., 1926. Emile-Paul Frères. Paris.
[2] The Directoire had considered her salon to be a nest of intrigue.

push the fortunes of her friends. Benjamin Constant, being the god of the hour, through her activities was already in the foremost rank for government advancement. Talleyrand's aims were more difficult to explain. His enemies were on his track. The old taunts, the old criminatory attacks were hurled against the "vile, the unfrocked, the licentious priest"; he was a Jacobin to the Girondist, he was an Orleanist to Revolutionaries, and he was a traitor to his order and to Rome, to all royalists.

The task Talleyrand had imposed on his friend and advocate was no light one. Madame de Staël, however, with the light of battle in her fine eyes, began her siege. Barras had been her chief conquest, among the members of the new government. Madame de Staël may be said to have been a judge of a fine man. Barras pleased her. He had distinction and grace; he was clever without being brilliant, possessing courage and energy in decisive moments, yet he was lacking in the intensive power of continuous effort. He was one of those men who, in political crises, emerge on the top wave of circumstance and, by some magic of equilibrium, manage to maintain a footing to the end. In Madame de Staël's frequent visits to the Director, she continued to sing, in eloquent strains, the talents, the capacity for managing difficult situations, the knowledge of courts, kings, foreign ministers and embassies possessed by Talleyrand as no other man in public affairs, in the fluctuant state of the Directoire, could even approach. What was a Delacroix—the present Minister of Foreign Affairs—from the point of experience and intellect, compared to a de Talleyrand-Périgord?

Madame de Staël poured forth her rapid phrases with the eloquence which was to conquer Europe. Yet Barras remained unmoved. The counter-attacks of Carnot, of Reubell, of all Talleyrand's enemies—towards those who seemed in favor of the ex-Bishop's cause—had sensibly cooled any warmth he may have felt. Barras finally showed temper. He admitted he could grant no more interviews to hear Talleyrand's praises sung. Why was Madame de Staël so importunate? What was her real motive—had she a personal interest in pushing Talleyrand's fortunes? At all times, and in all ages, no Frenchman can be made to believe in the naïveté of disinterestedness. There was indeed, a hidden motive in the famous lady's advocacy of her friend's desires, in her enthusiastic pleading for her friend's promotion to ministerial honors.[1] Were Talleyrand Minister, out of the graces of gratitude he would be bound to secure to her the return of the two millions of francs which her father, Monsieur Necker, had left in the State Treasury when he made his hasty exit from ministerial power, under Louis XVI.[2] For the past ten years, Madame de Staël had made appeal after appeal to each succeeding government, for the reimbursement of the sum, without success. Barras' stern refusal to advance Talleyrand's aims, therefore, could not be accepted as final.

On learning the pass to which things had come, Talleyrand's inventive resourcefulness came to the rescue. With the skill of an artist he arranged a scene of dramatic intensity. Such a comedy as he proposed to play, would, he knew, stir Madame de Staël, who was a lover of drama, to make a last and moving emotional appeal. On entering her salon, he threw his purse on a table.

[1] *Madame de Staël*, Joseph Turquan. Emile-Paul Frères, 1926.
[2] *Histoire Politique et Privée de Charles-Maurice Talleyrand*. L. J. Michaud, Paris, 1853. P. 30.

My dear child [he cried in ringing tones], I have only twenty louis d'or left: there isn't enough with which to go to the end of the month. You know I cannot walk, that I must have a carriage. If you do not find me the means of securing a remunerative post, I must blow my brains out. . . . If you love me—you see what you must do.

Madame de Staël felt herself to be before the footlights of the European stage; had she not made de Narbonne Minister of War? In forcing Barras' hand, among her other claims to immortality she would also be immortalized as the maker of ministers. Talleyrand's cause was won.

In her turn, she prepared herself for her own great scene. Barras, in his *Mémoires*, shows us Madame de Staël in the throes of her emotional climax. After recounting her late interview with Talleyrand, she cried:

Oh my friend, it is possible that at this moment he no longer exists. He told me only a few moments ago, that he would throw himself into the Seine unless he was made Minister of Foreign Affairs. He is so poor—he has only ten louis left. If only you would receive him.

In recounting the singular interview, Barras lingers dotingly on its spectacular climax. He paints Madame de Staël as being so wrought upon by her emotions, as to be on the point of falling into his arms. Barras was from the Midi; he could invest a scene with the elements of drama. According to his version, Madame de Staël resorted to extreme measures. Clasping Barras' hands, the tears pouring down her cheeks, she told the pitiful story of Talleyrand's neglected childhood, of his abhorrence of being forced into the priesthood; through choking sobs she

admitted her sorrow at his sceptical attitude and his having
been accused of certain vices prevalent during the former
régime, perhaps having practised them; regaining strength
to voice her friend's brilliant services during the Revolution,
she recounted his further successes in England, as negotiator;
and finally, carried away by her own eloquence and her
agitated state, she all but flung herself into his arms.
Barras indeed would have us believe in a scene ending in a
Potipharesque climax.[1]

VI

Madame de Staël's own version of the assistance given
her friend does not tally with either that of Barras or of
Talleyrand:

The friends of the Directoire hoped that the Directoire would
consolidate constitutional measures, and to forward that end,
Ministers would be chosen which would sustain the government.
M. de Talleyrand seemed the best possible choice for the department of Foreign Affairs, since he was willing to accept the post.
To an accomplishment of this purpose I effectively served him, in
having had him presented to Barras by one of my friends, and in
having forcibly recommended him. Monsieur de Talleyrand
needed help to arrive at a commanding position: but, on having
attained to power, he could quite well dispense with the help of
others.

The bitter note at the end of the above statement, which
one may find in the talented author's *Considérations sur la
Révolution*, was made after the rupture of the friendship
between the two friends—a coolness largely due to Bonaparte's hostility to Madame de Staël. Talleyrand was not

[1] See *Mémoires de Barras.*

as ungrateful as Madame de Staël would have the world believe. While Minister of Foreign Affairs, under the Directoire, on the first occasion of Bonaparte's visit to the Ministry, after the Italian victories, among the few nobilities asked to be present to greet the hero of the day, was Madame de Staël. She was one of the distinguished guests at the ball given at the Hôtel Gallifet for the General and Joséphine de Beauharnais, then Madame Bonaparte. The ball, in its magnificence, was a reminder of former Court splendors: "It must have cost a lot, Citizen Minister"—said one of the parvenu guests. "Not the Peru," replied Talleyrand. It was at this ball that the oft-quoted and supposed-to-be-cruel reply of Bonaparte to Madame de Staël was given. Seeing the General so surrounded as to be unapproachable, irritated at not having received from him the homage she felt to be her due, she addressed herself to a friend, to M. Vincent Arnault: "One cannot get near to your General; you must introduce me to him." Knowing Bonaparte's often expressed abhorrence of learned ladies, Arnault attempted to evade the request. But taking his arm, Madame de Staël pushed her way through the press, and at last, confronting Bonaparte, awaited what she expected would be a public tribute to her genius. Bonaparte, annoyed, visibly hurried, strove to end the interview with a bow. But the lady had her way; in finely turned phrases she made him understand she considered him to be "le premier des hommes," and then she asked the fatal question which brought upon her the fatal answer. "And you, General, whom do you consider to be the first among women?"—"She who has borne the most children," and this time the General won his release. He bowed, kissed her hand and left the group.

VII

Talleyrand, in his own *Mémoires*,[1] gives a very different version from the one Barras depicts, of the manner of his appointment as Minister of Foreign Affairs, as well as of the circumstance of his meeting with Barras. Throughout this account, Talleyrand carefully veils the real facts of the case, as revealed by the Memoirs of his contemporaries. After stating that he had "paid his debt as an Academician" he goes on to narrate:

Having paid my literary debt and perceiving no element of order and no guarantee of stability in the various political factions whose struggles I witnessed, I took care to keep aloof from active politics. Madame de Staël, who had already resumed a certain influence, insisted on my going with her to Barras, one of the members of the Directoire. I demurred at first: I could not call on a member of the Directoire, without asking to see all the other Directors, and chiefly those who had been my colleagues in the Constituent Assembly. The reasons alleged to justify my refusal did not seem valid. Besides, they had to be conveyed through Madame de Staël, who, being anxious I should be personally known to Barras, so managed affairs that the Director sent me a note inviting me to dine with him, at Suresnes, on a certain day. I had no alternative but to accept. On the appointed day I was at Suresnes at about three o'clock in the afternoon. In the dining-room which I had to cross to reach the drawing-room, I noticed covers laid for five persons. Much to my surprise, Madame de Staël was not invited. . . . Two young men came in to ascertain the time by the drawing-room clock. [Barras not having as yet returned, Talleyrand went on reading a book.] . . . When twenty minutes after the two young men had left

[1] *Mémoires du Prince de Talleyrand.* Vol. I, p. 188. Edited by the Duc de Broglie. Translated by Raphaël Ledos de Beaufort. London, 1891.

BENJAMIN CONSTANT
By Mauchieson

the room, the horrifying news came that one of the two—named Raymond—had been drowned.   The friends had gone in bathing, and a whirlpool the Seine formed at a certain spot, had swept Raymond to his death.   All efforts to rescue the young man had been unavailing.

On learning of his young friend's death, Barras, on his arrival, was so overcome by grief that he begged Talleyrand to excuse him from appearing at dinner.   Talleyrand was left to dine alone.   Unable to partake of the feast prepared, Talleyrand was requested, presently, to mount the stairs to the Director's room.   There "he took hold of both my hands and embraced me; he was weeping.   I said all the kind things which the position in which I saw him and that in which I was myself, could dictate."   Talleyrand's sympathy conquered weeping Barras.   Whether, therefore, it was through Madame de Staël's or the Director's tears that Talleyrand became Minister of Foreign Affairs, under the Directoire, his entrance into the government appears to have been due to an emotional crisis.[1]   Such is the dignified manner in which Talleyrand, after his long and brilliant career, would have the world and historians believe, in writing the story of his life, that the door was opened to him by a gracious Minister, to become his colleague. Between Barras' presentment and Talleyrand's, there is the difference which exists between the way things are really accomplished and the manner in which we desire they should appear to be done.   Talleyrand, at eighty, did not wish to record the painful fact that his first post as Minister he owed to a woman.

[1] *Mémoires du Prince de Talleyrand.*

VIII

With Talleyrand's entrance on the European stage as Minister of Foreign Affairs under the Directoire, the first part of this historic record of his earlier years comes to an end. To present, adequately, his further prolonged official and diplomatic career, in a single volume, is an impossible task.

During his ministry under the Directoire the event which was fraught with consequences of the most momentous importance to Europe and indeed, to the history of the world, was that he "divined" Napoleon. His letters to Bonaparte during the Italian campaign were couched in language calculated to convince the hero of Arcole that Talleyrand was the master-mind of the Directoire. For subtle flattery, for furtive, but insinuating, suggestion of the part to be played in other fields than in those of military prowess, these letters are all but unsurpassed. On Bonaparte's return from Italy, it was largely through Talleyrand's influence that the command of the army of Egypt was awarded to Bonaparte.[1]

When the young General paid his visit to the Minister of Foreign Affairs, the very morning after his return from his victorious campaign in Italy (Bonaparte reached Paris in December), Talleyrand, on seeing him for the first time, fell under the spell of his charm. "The victory of twenty battles goes so well with youth, with a bright glance, with pallor, with a sort of exhaustion," he stated.

IX

An interesting letter of Benjamin Constant's to Monsieur Euginet in the year 1807 throws a disagreeably lurid light

[1] Talleyrand's Letters. "Sous Le Directoire." Pallain, 1 vol.

on the final chapter of the famous friendship of Madame de Staël and Talleyrand.[1] The letter relates to certain monies loaned by Talleyrand to Benjamin Constant. The loan appears to have been covered, in singular fashion, by Madame de Staël. The bitterness revealed in her statements to Constant, regarding Talleyrand, is sufficiently revealing of one cause of the estrangement. The letter is as follows:

I have the pleasure of asking a favor of you, my dear Eugène, it concerns some explications which you can perhaps give me, by reviving your memory. I do not know if you remember that in 1798, Monsieur de Talleyrand, who had just been made Minister, and you know by whom, was at St. Ouen with Madame de Staël, lent me 18,000 frcs, for which amount Madame de Staël made herself responsible by a letter to Talleyrand of 24,000 frcs, on my part. When M. de Talleyrand quarrelled with her and with me I did not care to give that man the advantage of boasting that I was his debtor. I spoke about the matter to Madame de Staël who told me that he was indebted to her for several sums of money much larger than the one lent to me, lent to him either in England to help him to live, or before his return from America to pay his debts, to preserve for him his books and his furniture, or up to the time she had him named Minister. I also remember that she wrote him after their rupture, when he would not receive her in that Hôtel of Foreign Affairs where she had placed him, she retraced his conduct reminding him of I do not know what fictitious payments he pretended had been paid by him to M. de Staël in bad *assignats*. She concluded by telling him that she considered me to be her personal debtor, for sums which he owed her far in excess of my debt. Since then I have not thought of the matter. I have at this date reasons for clearing up this affair. Please let me know if, with your knowledge of Madame de Staël's affairs, you know whether Monsieur de Talleyrand is

---

[1] Monsieur Euginet was the Secretary of the Duc d'Orléans.

still in her debt. The question rests entirely on a moral basis, and I give you my word of honor in this letter, that I will not make any use either legal or public of such knowledge. And that Madame de Staël shall not even be named. It is only for the matter of personal satisfaction that I wish to know it.

Adieu my dear Euginet. You will oblige me by sending me a prompt reply. Accept my salutations.

BENJAMIN CONSTANT.

le 25 8bre 1807.

Defamatory in character as is the accusation made in this letter, it is to be remembered one hears only one side of the question. When he was a poor man, on receiving his first settled income, Talleyrand repaid to L'Abbé Huet the debt, owed by his parents, for his instruction at the College d'Harcourt. In London, he came repeatedly to the assistance of his poorer friends. Madame Genlis, in her *Mémoires*, records, with the deepest gratitude, his proffered loan to her.

The ex-Bishop who, in London, and later in Paris repeatedly came to the rescue of several Constitutional priests in distress, and to some of the Professors of the Sorbonne when in want, was scarcely the man to repay a debt to a woman in "bad assignats." One should learn at what period Talleyrand repaid his debt to the Ambassador. Assignats were good money, when first issued, backed as were the issues by the capital of State Funds, in 1790.

Madame de Staël was angry, and presumably, with the best of reasons. Yet again, of the cause of the quarrel between the friends, no satisfactory reason is given. Talleyrand may well have found the burden of his indebtedness to his exacting friend to be too heavy a load. Given Bona-

J'ai eu plaisir à vous demander, mon cher Eugène, ce tout des éclair-
issements que peut être vous pourrez me donner d'après votre
mémoire. Je ne sai si vous vous rappelez qu'en 1798 étant à
St Ouen avec Mad. de Stael, M. de Talleyrand, qui venoit
d'être fait Ministre, vous savez par qui, me prêta 18000
frs. sur un billet de 24000 que Mde de Stael lui envoya
de ma part avec une lettre. Quand M. de Talleyrand
se brouilla avec elle & avec moi, je pensai à ne pas donner
à cet homme l'avantage de me dire son débiteur, j'en parlai
à Mde de Stael qui me dit qu'elle lui étoit redevable de plu-
sieurs sommes beaucoup plus fortes, prêtées soit en Angleterre
pour le faire vivre soit avant son retour d'Amérique pour
faire payer ses dettes & lui conserver ses droits à ses meubles,
soit jusqu'au moment où elle l'avoit fait nommer Ministre. J'ai encore dans mon souvenir qu'elle lui écrivit
après leur rupture, quand il ne vouloit pas la recevoir,
dans cet hôtel des relations extérieures, où elle l'avoit
fait entrer, elle lui retraçait sa conduite, & en lui
parlant de je ne sai quel remboursement fictif préten-
du fait par lui à M. de Stael en mauvais assignats,
elle finissoit par lui dire qu'elle me regardait comme
son débiteur à elle à compte de beaucoup plus qu'il lui
devoit. Depuis ce tems je n'y ai plus pensé. J'ai des
raisons aujourd'hui de désirer éclaircir cette affaire.
Dites moi autant que vous le pourrez si, dans votre con-
naissance des affaires de Mad de Stael, vous savez si M.
de Talleyrand est resté son débiteur. C'est tout à fait une
question morale, & je vous donne ma parole dans cette lettre

FACSIMILE OF LETTER OF BENJAMIN CONSTANT

parte's animosity towards her, and Talleyrand's official position, as his Minister, under him as First Consul, Madame de Staël may, nay, unquestionably did demand of the man who owed her so much, favors and a pre-eminence which he was powerless to confer. Madame de Staël's "passionate letters" to General Bonaparte, during the Italian campaign, were the true explication of Bonaparte's earlier repulsion. With her customary effrontery, when intent on subjugating a victim, in her enthusiasm for Bonaparte's genius, as well as in her unconcealed design to attach so great a man to her train of admirers as was the young hero, she wrote: "that a union with a little insignificant Creole, unworthy of appreciating or of understanding him, was a monstrosity." In another letter she states that "they (he and she) were made for each other." Such insolent overtures, such extravagance of expression, disgusted the then love-sick General. He cried to Bourrienne, on receiving one such letter: "Bourrienne—that woman is mad! Well—yes—a woman *bel-esprit*, a maker-up of sentiment to compare herself to Josephine! Bourrienne, I will not reply to such letters!"[1]

Madame de Staël's persistent and daring attack in public, at Talleyrand's ball, is the better understood, as well as Bonaparte's oft-repeated phrase, cutting short the interview, in the light of the impassioned, and rather vulgar character of the lady's letters to the hero of Arcole.[2]

The unrelenting hate of the Emperor which Madame de Staël carried later, as part of her travelling equipment, to every country she visited—to Germany, to Saxony, to Russia, to Sweden, during her ten years of exile from Paris—unquestionably helped to prepare the way for Napoleon's

---

[1] J. C. Bailleul, *Etudes sur Napoléon*, 11–55.
[2] *Mémoires*. Bourrienne, IV, 217.

fall. Her eloquence could hold, could stir, and could delight kings, as well as men of the highest intellect. As Napoleon's conquest of Europe advanced, one might figure Madame de Staël as sowing the dragon's teeth before his mighty tread, which were to turn the silent rage, the fury of revenge among the conquered into the Allied armies which overthrew the Conqueror.[1]

X

Talleyrand was responsible during his Ministry for sending the warlike and sanguinary Augereau to Paris, whose ambition for a military despotism resulted in the reign of what is called "la Terror Sèche"—a Terror guiltless of bloodshed, but the cold-blooded deportations to Guiana were only sure death, in another form. Talleyrand had then feared the Bourbons might be recalled. He tried, by absentism from active association in the event of the 13 Vendémiaire, to keep his own hands clean. The evening of the Coup d'Etat of 18 Fructidor he passed with Madame de Staël and Benjamin Constant. The latter was started from fear of a royalist uprising and its possible success; Talleyrand had everything then to fear from Bourbon rule, as a Constitutionalist during the early Revolutionary days. The Coup d'Etat of 18 Brumaire was largely due to Talleyrand's belief in Bonaparte as being the only man who could rally leaders and the nation behind him, and who—above all others—had the genius of organization which could wield order out of chaos. His admiration for Bonaparte's capacities was then genuine, and his belief in the young General's desire for constitutional reform was deeply grounded.

[1] *Madame de Staël.* Joseph Turquan, p. 150–154. Emile Paul Frères, 1926.

XI

Talleyrand was at the theatre with his friend Monsieur de Castellane when the news of his nomination as Minister was conveyed to him. The friends leapt to their feet, left the play, and rushed for a vehicle to convey them to Barras' house. Talleyrand's exultant joy found expression in tones which proved his sense of triumph—and of relief. To be swept from a state of eating anxiety to power and to possible riches, was to experience one of the great moments in life when soul and mind rise to wingèd heights. Talleyrand's recorded, rapturous outburst, "Riches—yes immense riches will be mine!" seems prophetic of the fortunes he was indeed to reap through his various Ministerial posts.

The memory of Calonne, and of this Minister's methods of increasing his own and his friends' fortunes, may have risen to dazzle Talleyrand's vision of what power might bring.

This, Talleyrand's first post as Minister, offered him the means of realizing his dream of acquiring riches, if not "immense riches."

It was while he was Minister of Foreign Affairs that he began his systematic practice of extortion. After a few weeks in office the treaty with Portugal brought with it eight millions in payment for certain concessions. The four Directors pocketed a million apiece.

Talleyrand sent Barras three millions which "were gratefully accepted." It is presumed that the million Talleyrand pocketed was the sum deposited later by him in Hamburg or London banks. He never made any secret of his transactions with the foreign powers. If his talents and the interests of the State secured advantages for foreign countries, such concessions must be paid for. "Principles are all very well for the schools" was one of his later maxims, a bald statement he covered by adding, "States are governed by their own interests"—and Talleyrand's, he might have added. Venality was to be the blight on Talleyrand's reputation—one which darkened the brilliance of his great gifts. Napoleon knew this trait of the Minister whom he at one time had caressed. "Come now, Talleyrand, your hand on your conscience, how much have you made out of me?" was one of Napoleon's playful attacks. On another occasion he asked: "How have you managed to become so rich?" "Sire," was the flattering reply, "the means was very simple: I bought bonds on the 18 Brumaire and I sold them on the 19th—the day after." This piece of flattery was all the more delicate in that it was the expression of a great truth.[1]

His transactions with the powers were rarely conducted personally. He had in his pay certain corrupt and confidential agents who did the work for him. Talleyrand had his own ideas of honor, in such matters, strangely strained as the sense of honorability may have been. In a transaction with the magnates of Warsaw four millions of florins were given to Talleyrand, then all-powerful as Minister. The bribe, it was hoped, would influence Talleyrand to favor the restoration of their country. Owing to the retreat of the Minister, after Tilsit and Erfurt, Talleyrand's influence no longer being all-powerful, the sum was restored.

One reproach has never been levelled at Talleyrand. In

---

[1] Talleyrand's residence as Minister of Foreign Affairs was l'Hotel Gallifet. He had a crowd of servants whose wages he was unable to pay, and who used "costly Sèvres dishes because there was no money to buy earthenware." One of his first appointments was that of d'Hauterive, whom he had known at Chanteloup, and who worked with Talleyrand during the latter's successive posts as Minister of Foreign Affairs. *Talleyrand*, Lady Blennerhassett. Translated by Frederic Clark. John Murray, 1894.

all such nefarious negotiations, he would never accept, nor would he listen to terms, however advantageous for himself, which might effect or which might tend to the destruction of France.

It was during his Ministry that the dispute which had arisen between the Directoire government and the United States—a difficulty which had begun in the year 1794—was brought to an abrupt close. The seizure of American vessels by the Directoire as an answer to England's pretension that neutrals were not to be treated as such, resulted in the American President, Mr. Adams, sending as negotiators Generals Pinckney and Marshall and Mr. Elbridge Gerry, the distinguished lawyer, to France to ransom the ships. In order to satisfy the demands of the American government, Talleyrand advanced, as a preliminary, his favorite plan. To the amazement of the Envoys Extraordinary sent by the President, he suggested that an offer of £50,000 to the Directors would bring the negotiations to a happy termination. On learning of this attempt at corruption, the American envoys, revolted at such outrageous demands, promptly refused, and shortly afterwards left Paris.[1] Hamilton, who had suggested the mission, hoping doubtless for Talleyrand's special interest in facilitating the conditions of the settlement, must have experienced further enlightenment as to Talleyrand's methods of conducting public affairs.[2]

The noise of this scandalous offer having gone the rounds of the Paris salons, Madame de Staël rushed to the Ministry. Talleyrand must clear himself of the attacks made upon him; his enemies would have their longed-for chance to force

[1] *Talleyrand*, Lady Blennerhassett. John Murray, 1894.
[2] See Addendum No. II, p. 512.

him to resign. He listened, quietly, to the impassioned appeals made to his "honor"—to the necessity of clearing the Directoire from such calumnious attacks as would be made. Excusing himself, finally he left the room, and did not return. On relating the tiresome scene his friend had inflicted on him, he remarked: "Madame de Staël has only one fault: she is insupportable."

XII

The years during which Talleyrand was Minister of Foreign Affairs under the Consulate; later, during the Empire, filling the same post under Napoleon; called upon by the Emperor as diplomatic negotiator and treaty-maker at the Council of Erfurt; utilizing the period, during his disgrace, after his fall from power, to undermine and intrigue against the conqueror of Europe;—considered as being the head of the Provisional government during the occupation of the Allies in Paris; his influence paramount in placing the crown of France on the head of the Bourbon King —Louis XVIII; his nomination under the latter sovereign as Minister of Foreign Affairs and as Minister Plenipotentiary at the Council of Vienna—on to the ending of Prince de Talleyrand's official career as Ambassador to the Court of Saint James, at the age of eighty (in 1834)—to present these forty years of crowded life in detail would entail the survey of the history of France and Europe during that period.

PART II

STORY OF TALLEYRAND'S MARRIAGE—THE LATER YEARS—CONVERSION AND DEATH

MADAME GRAND, PRINCESSE DE TALLEYRAND

From the painting by Mme. Vigée-Lebrun, formerly in the Jacques Doucet collection

CHAPTER I

I

WHILE Talleyrand was in England, in the autumn of the year 1792, occupied in writing his serious Essay, "Un Mémoire sur les rapports actuels de la France avec les autres Etats de l'Europe"[1] (the Mémoire he addressed to Danton in November of that year), he little dreamed that the birth of a girl, at the other end of the world, was to precipitate the second fateful tragedy of his life.

Talleyrand himself had laid down the axiomatic truism that certain blunders may be counted as crimes. The sequence of events which was to bring about a marriage between Catherine Noël Worlée, known by her married name of Madame Grand, and Talleyrand, was more than a mistake on the part of the latter. At the time of his marriage, Talleyrand, though secularized by a papal decree, had not been officially absolved from his vows as an anointed Bishop. In contracting marriage he committed the crime, not only of outraging good taste and of offending public opinion, but of defying the rigid rules of his Church.

In that hour of revolt, of despair, prior to his taking the priestly vows—in his early manhood—Talleyrand's

[1] "A Mémoire on the actual relations of France with the other States of Europe."

character had been tested: that fibre of virility to risk all, to gain all, by refusing to bind himself to a hated vocation, was lacking. In his forty-eighth year the same weakness broke down his defences. The new fetters marriage was to forge, perhaps, were to grind more deeply than had those which had bound him in accepting priesthood.

II

Catherine Noël Worlée, having been born on the 21st of November, 1762, at Tranquebar, in India—a Danish possession—was rapidly growing into girlhood. Though born in a Danish colony, Catherine was of French birth. Her father was a French official. He was a Chevalier de Saint-Louis, acting as a functionary, at the Port of Pondichéry, under King Louis XV. Catherine had been duly baptized four days after her birth, at the parish church of Tranquebar. The fact that Catherine saw the light of day in a Danish colony, was to prove to be a happy accident in the later developments of her precarious existence.

The Worlée family removed in the year 1777 from Pondichéry to Chandernagor. At the latter town, where her father had been advanced to be captain of the port, under the new King, Louis XVI, Catherine's extraordinary career began. She was to enter upon a series of more or less disreputable adventures through the portals of a reputable marriage. An Englishman, George Francis Grand, was to give his name to one of the most successful adventuresses in Europe.

Grand was, also, in the Indian civil service. Having met the captivating Catherine, he succumbed to her charms, and asked her in marriage. He was accepted by the parents, for while not a brilliant match, he offered, at least, a suitable home for the bride of fifteen. His young wife brought a more than modest dot—12,000 rupees (sicca), some linen, a few jewels and her trousseau were not riches. Catherine's charms were her real dot. Her beauty and her power of seduction already, at the age of fifteen, had won for her the fame of being the fairest and the most alluring of her sex, in the little foreign colony of Chandernagor. Having secured as rare a prize, George Francis Grand proposed to take no chances. What a double marriage service could do to rivet the chain of fidelity, the two churches, the Church of Rome and the Protestant Episcopal church—Grand's parents were Protestant—were to cement by the most solemn of vows.

Grand was in love, but he was heavy, dull of humor, to be proved venal, possessed of neither physical attractions nor mental qualities which could excite admiration in a vain, coquettish, unscrupulous, and ambitious woman of sixteen. Women, like fruit, mature quickly under tropical skies.

Grand's credulous infatuation lasted almost a year. His duties, as did his fate, took him and his young wife to Calcutta. In that city Catherine was to be courted and fêted; she was the toasted belle, as she was the cynosure of all eyes.

III

A highly placed Englishman, Sir Philip Francis, Councillor in the King's Council, was among the first to note the arrival of the new beauty. Madame Grand's flexible southern grace, the slim perfect shape, the contrast between the masses of her blond hair and black eyebrows and eyelashes, a skin as transparent as a child's and as freshly tinted, the snow of teeth revealed by a smile as natural as it was seductive—where find another such paragon of physical perfection?

Sir Philip's attentions culminated in a ball given to Grand's wife. This honor completed frail Catherine's conquest. Sir Philip was an uncommonly clever, even brilliant King's Councillor: his reputation for intellectual capacity was such as to convulse England, for years, with the exciting query—was it he who was the author of the mysterious *Letters of Junius?* For so clever a man, Sir Philip had one unfortunate habit, he set down, in terse, brief phrase, the chief episode, act, or incident of his day. In this his daily journal he noted, triumphantly, on November 24th, 1778—*omnia vincit amor.*

The Fates, however, were busy. They were to have their revenge on the ever over-active son of Venus. Again, with an official brevity, but in unofficial language, Sir Philip records in his diary (the date being December 8th):—"This night, the devil to pay in the house of G. F. Grand, Esq." It was not, as it turned out, the devil, but Sir Philip Francis himself who was to pay. The various accounts, given in the Memoirs of the time, touching on the nature of the incident, agree in noting the chief details of what would seem to be pure comedy.[1] There was a perfect mise-en-scène;—a dark night; a husband's absence; a stealthy entrance into a mistress's window by means of a ladder; prying servants; capture of the lover; threat of a duel by the outraged husband—and the semi-tragedy to end before a judge in a court-room, and a "satisfied" husband.

Sir Philip had trusted to the fair Catherine's assertion,

---

[1] *Memoirs of William Hickey* (1749–1803). Edited by Alfred Spencer. 4 vols. 8vo. Hurst & Blackett.

on a certain evening, that her husband was to be absent, and that her maid would be dismissed. Sure of his prowess, the enterprising lover had used the darkness of night as a cloak, and a bamboo ladder as his means of penetrating into the window of his mistress's room.

Servants, in all countries, of whatever nationality or color, have one instinct in common—that of curiosity. Intrigued by the unusual appearance of a ladder, on the *qui vive* to learn its use, the appearance of a figure of a man groping his way down the bamboo steps—such proceedings fired the peering group below, in the garden, to action. Seizing the intruder as he descended, recognizing in him Sir Philip Francis, the redoubtable Councillor of the Queen's Council, a frequent visitor at the house—the over-zealous servants, undeterred by the Councillor's high rank, secured him. They seated him in a chair where they held him. With a zeal not always shown in more important crises, one of the serving-men ran to announce to his master the exciting news. George Francis Grand seems to have been cast, by the great *impresario* nature, for the very part of a betrayed husband. He might have been supposed to be in conspiracy with his betrayer, since he gave him ample time for a fortuitous flight: Sir Philip, it appears, had prepared an escape from possible ambush. The servants guarding the prisoner heard a shrill whistle, a bevy of unknown men ran in, and behold! when the tear-dimmed husband appeared, he found a certain unknown Mr. Shee seated in the chair, and no sign whatever of Sir Philip Francis.

The sequel to the sorry adventure was aired in the law courts. The outraged Grand had sent his seconds to his betrayer, as should a man of honor, in those days before

Queen Victoria decreed no man's honor was worth the cost of a possible death by duelling.[1] When questioned, Sir Philip haughtily and insolently declared he did not know of what the matter in hand treated. The Supreme Court of Calcutta decreed that Sir Philip must refresh his memory. He was ordered to pay 50,000 rupees to G. F. Grand for trespassing alike on his domain and on the field of his affections. In view of the handsome sum, G. F. Grand declared himself to be "entirely satisfied." There are certain men and husbands cast in that peculiar mould.

IV

Madame Grand, homeless and dishonored, betook herself to her parents' house at Chandernagor. There Sir Philip found her, disconsolate, sitting amid what she considered to be the ruins of her young life. Her lover, in persuading her to return to Calcutta, to brave gossip and averted eyes, held a trump card in reserve, were she to lack the necessary courage. The lovely Catherine was not only to be received at his house, Lady Francis, Sir Philip's wife, was to welcome her! The latter lady appears to have been either the most credulous of women, or one wilfully blind; for Madame Grand lived for a full year, protected and admired, under the shadow of her possibly trusting hostess. And day by day, with that habit of entrusting secrets to paper, Sir Philip's entry in his Diary, in terse, brief phrase, was to tell all his world and ours the true nature of the tie existing between the fair Catherine and a king's highly placed functionary—under his indulgent wife's roof. Had

[1] In 1844 an Act was passed by the Queen forbidding duelling among officers in the Army.

the wife possibly learned certain secrets of marital diplomacy, in her long residence abroad?

The "friendship" which Lady Francis insisted, on all occasions, had been purely platonic, came to an end at the close of the year.

The cause which armed Catherine Grand to launch forth, literally, into a sea of further adventure, is lost in the mists of conjecture. Even the revealing Diary enshrouds the departure of the ex-wife of the "old, horrid, sordid Frenchman" as Sir Philip called G. F. Grand, in mystery. Whether the traveller took ship for England or France, we have only Lady Francis' testimony; it was she who asserted her guest embarked for an English port.

V

This was presumably in the year 1782. To follow the wanderings, to describe the various liaisons, and the numerous houses occupied and deserted by this frail votary of pleasure would demand the space of a separate volume. For fourteen long years—years that saw the last days of "the delights of life," under Bourbon rule—years burdened later with the horrors of the Revolution and the Terror— the latter to end its surcease of tyranny under the Directoire—these years stretching from 1782 to 1796 saw Catherine in Paris in the spring of 1791. Her lovers were known: they were neither obscure nor poor. Valdec de Lessart, Minister of the Legislation, loved her "to distraction"; a Louis Monneron, a banker, and "le beau Dillon" the Comtesse de Boigne's nephew, are named as having been among her conquests or lovers. She led the life of every other adventurous woman of her type, having fine houses, and buying pictures and jewels. Her boxes at the Opera and at the Comédie Française were frequented by her lovers and friends.

She contributed, through a vanity backed by louis d'or, at least one work of art to posterity. In the portrait painted of her, at this period, by Madame Vigée-Lebrun, the talented portraitist transmitted to our day the secret of much of the charm and beauty that made men go down before Catherine Worlée's loveliness as worshippers bow the knee to a divinity; it was a loveliness which was to enchain for at least a year one of the cleverest men in India, and for four years the most adroit statesman in Europe.

From whatever source the money came which paid for lavish entertainment, for the wardrobe of a princess, for costly books and for a writing-master—the lady's orthography being hardly on a plane with the perfection of her gowns—Madame Grand had, at least, in Paris, attained to a certain height on the steps of the social ladder. She gave a ball and a ball implies ladies. Masson quotes the *Moniteur Universel* as publishing a paragraph (18th December, 1791) in which Madame de Lessart and Madame Grand reclaim a package containing letters which had been mislaid, sent from India by M. Grand. The several names cited together appear to proclaim that once again Catherine Worlée Grand had found a friend in the wife of one of her adorers.

The protection of both a Minister and of his wife were not sufficient to avert curious-eyed suspicion. The 10th of August, 1792, brought all strangers before the bars of revolutionary control. Madame Grand having seen one of the brave Swiss guards massacred, below her windows, by the infuriated mob coming from the Tuileries, on August 10th, took to flight, from mingled horror and fear. Her destination was England.

VI

On arriving at Dover her plight was more than serious. With but a dozen louis in her purse, knowing no one, she might have had to face the merciless front of official enquiry. Once again, a rescuer was at hand. Beauty such as hers was as good as a queen's retinue. A young naval officer, one Nathaniel Melchise by name, struck by the pitiful melancholy and helpless appearance of this stranger, on learning her story, vowed he and a friend would come to her rescue. True knights that they were, after confronting a hundred dangers in Paris, the two chivalric young men presented their new-found friend with her jewels, her money, her gold service, and her bonds.

Mirabeau's agents had requisitioned, already, certain valuables found in one of Madame Grand's rented apartments; an inventory of costly porcelains, silver service, furs, odds and ends of all sorts had been made. Under the Directoire, later on, Madame Grand reclaimed possession of her books, taken from her Library.[1]

In London, then filled with French *émigrés* and notabilities of the great French world, Madame Grand found herself confronted with closed doors and hostile faces. She was not to be received. Gossip had crossed the Channel. Indian society also, in that day of sailing ships, far away though it was, was in close epistolary touch with all the English world of fashion and of the Court. Madame Grand's past, she discovered, was too well known. Posing as a "royalist and an *émigré* of distinction" was of no avail; thumbs were turned down. Admirers, it is said, there were indeed, who extended the glad hand of welcome and of a

[1] Archives of the Seine.

questionable courtesy. Madame Grand having experienced the agreeable warmth of governmental recognition under Lady Francis, and of ministerial social favor under Madame de Lessart, felt the chill of the arctic English social atmosphere to be too penetrating.

The Terror having been succeeded by the Directoire, she took packet for France.

VII

Madame Grand did not cross the Channel alone. She travelled in company with a diplomat—Christopher Spinola. This gentleman was attached to the Ministry of Genoa. He was venturing on a hazardous enterprise; he was returning to France hoping to secure possession of his wife's property, for the lady's father, the Maréchal de Lévis, had been guillotined, during the Terror.

Both travellers were to have the unpleasant surprise of discovering that Paris, during these early days of the Directoire, was no safer than had been the Terror. The police was eager to prove its efficiency. Every new arrival was suspected of being a conspirator. Christopher Spinola and his companion were immediately under suspicion: the Genoese government had sent not a diplomat but a spy, it was asserted, to scent out intrigues; or, if not under Genoese direction, Spinola was at least, it was whispered, an agent of Malmesbury's.

Almost immediately on their arrival in Paris, the two travellers knew they were considered to be suspects: a half dozen men tracked every step they took. Their modest furnished apartment in the rue Niçaise, night and day, was watched by the over-zealous Directoire police.

The reward of such vigilance came on the 10th Messidor. Walking in the Luxembourg Gardens, to see the triumphant return of General Sérurier, who came laden with the trophies of the victorious Italian armies, Christopher Spinola and Catherine Worlée Grand were duly arrested. A decree of immediate expulsion—one merited, perhaps—sent Spinola back to London.

The accusation against Catherine was that she was in correspondence with the *émigrés*, which was an ironic turn of fate, since in London they would have none of her. During the weeks which elapsed between her arrest and the fateful meeting with Talleyrand—if a first meeting it was—she lost no time in supine acceptance of her fate. The woman who has been held up to ridicule as being as ignorant as she was stupid, whose errors in speech, whose comic mistakes, and whose Malapropisms have furnished biographers with unending copy—this supposed-to-be dull-minded and ignorant woman showed, at all times, during the various crises in her astonishing career, a resourceful spirit as intelligent as it was commonly triumphantly successful.

Realizing the danger of her ambiguous situation, Catherine began her campaign for deliverance from suspicion. She made the boldest bid for her release. To no less a person than to Talleyrand, Minister of Foreign Affairs, at this time all-powerful in matters relating, at least, to those not in direct conflict with the tyrannous rule of his superiors —it was to this Minister Madame Grand determined to plead for safety.

Her approach to as important a personage was facilitated through the Marquise de Sainte-Croix—a sister of the Avocat Général and aunt of Mme. du Cayla. It is also stated that she met Talleyrand through his "familiar"— through that subtle, unscrupulous, *rusée* personage—Monsieur de Montrond. Whoever obtained for her the coveted introduction, the story of the meeting between this seductive adventuress and the Minister is subject to doubtful accuracy. The story is as follows:

Talleyrand, after a long day's harassing work at the Ministry, having finished the night by his habitual prolonged game of whist, on returning home, received the annoying announcement that a lady was awaiting him, in the salon. The servant forthwith presented a letter of introduction. Tired and weary, his late hour of rest having come, far more ready for bed than for an interview with a pushing visitor—were she the incarnation of all the virtues and charms —Talleyrand bent his steps to the salon, in the worst of bad humors.

Seated in a deep fauteuil, close to the fire, was the indefinite shape of a woman. Was she old—was she young? An enveloping wrap, such as was worn by the beauties of the day, with its hood screening head and face, made conjecture futile. The mysterious lady was fast asleep. The relaxed figure suddenly came to life. Awakened by the sense of Talleyrand's presence, Catherine started to her feet. Caught thus in this her moment of embarrassed surprise—her long hours of waiting having ended in benumbing sleep—roseate as a child after rest, the blue eyes wide with semi-fright, the adorable face animated by mingled amazement, delight and an appealing eagerness—before such a startling apparition, Talleyrand was confronted with his doom.

The result was of a piece with the surprising adventures of Catherine's past life. Talleyrand forgot his fatigue. Although, at first, he refused to listen to the passionate pleadings of the lady, before her tears the stern Minister melted; he was only a man, and presently that guarded reserve of sensibility so rarely allowed to play its rôle opened its gates. The promise of protection was given. The scene had lasted fifteen minutes. Its consequences were to stretch on for thirty-eight long years.

VIII

The solid ground on which historic accuracy can rest is at least established in all essentials relating to the affair.

Talleyrand arrived in the month of September, 1796, in Paris via Hamburg, Amsterdam, and Bruxelles. Madame Grand's correspondence with an *émigré*—Count Lambertye, who was residing in London—was read, and she was immediately arrested.

In a rare volume—*L'Album Perdu*—by Henri de la Touche, the assertion is made that it was the Marquise de Sainte-Croix who introduced Madame Grand to Talleyrand. This statement gains weight from the fact that the Marquise was the aunt of Madame du Cayla, the favorite of Louis XVIII.

Talleyrand and the seductive Catherine may have met at Amsterdam, at Strassburg, or at Hamburg. Lady Blennerhassett affirms it was in New York or Philadelphia that the two had known each other. Mr. Bowers, in his brilliant volume, *Jefferson and Hamilton*, asserts that Talleyrand, "whose Philadelphia immoralities shocked the French Minister, and whose affair with a lady of color excluded him from the Bingham drawing-room," adds in a note "probably Madame Grand."[1] In Barras' *Mémoires*

---

[1] Neither Lady Blennerhassett in her *Life of Talleyrand* nor Mr. Bowers cite authorities for the meeting of Talleyrand and Madame Grand in America. Nor are there any records of Mme. Grand having crossed the seas. "The lady of color" is noted by Loliée as being a pretty mulatto—a far more probable supposition.

it is simply stated that Talleyrand met Madame Grand abroad, *à l'étranger*.

However short or long may have been the duration of the liasion between Talleyrand and Catherine Grand, before it was openly acknowledged, it is certain the attachment was strong enough on his side, for him to appeal to Barras, the latter at that time being one of the most influential of the famous Five.

On the 3rd Germinal, in the year VI (23rd of March, 1798), Talleyrand interceded effectively in favor of the woman whose beauty had conquered him. The letter he wrote to Barras is no historical novelty.[1]

CITIZEN BARRAS:

Madame Grand has been arrested as a conspirator. Of all people in Europe she is the farthest removed from, and the most incapable of mixing herself in any kind of an affair; she is a very beautiful *Indienne*, very indolent,—the most indolent of all the women I have ever met. I beg you to take an interest in her. I am sure that not the shadow of a pretext can be found not to end this little affair, one which I should regret being made public. I love her, and I attest to you, as man to man, that in all her life she has never been and is not capable of ever having been mixed up in any affair. [This is repeated in the text—de se mêler d'aucune affaire.] She is a veritable *Indienne* and you know how far removed from any sort of intrigue are such kinds of women.

Salutations and attachment,

CH. MAUR. TALLEYRAND.[2]

[1] The authenticity of this letter has been disputed. It has been suggested it was a forgery of Perry's—Talleyrand's dishonest secretary whose imitation of his master's signature and handwriting deceived experts.

[2] Michaud cited this letter as having been sent the 3rd Germinal IV. This is inaccurate. Talleyrand did not arrive in Paris until September, 1796—nearly two years after the above date.

IX

In *Les Mémoires de Barras* there is a singular and lengthy account of the author's serious difficulties with his colleagues—the other four members of the Directoire. The trouble arose on the request made by him, to his co-Directors, for the release of Madame Grand.

This act would seem to have been one simple enough to grant. One of the five members at the head of the rather insecure Directoire government asking, as a favor, the release from prison of a pretty woman against whom nothing more serious could be proved than that she had corresponded with an *émigré*—surely as easy a matter to grant would be dismissed with smiling acquiescence, and the mighty Five could pass on to weightier matters.

Barras found, on making his request, that he had aroused as passionate an opposition as ever Mirabeau had faced in the Assembly.

The first to rush to the attack was Reubell, the fiery Alsatian. The knowledge that Barras was aiding and abetting that "unfrocked—that vile libertine"—Talleyrand, was enough to rouse all the ferocity in Reubell whose quarrelsome nature was as a scourge to his fellow members. On this occasion, at least, Reubell knew well, or thought he knew, he was riding to victory; for all save Barras, who was a friend of Talleyrand's, had been of Reubell's soured mind. The Directors had turned rebellious under the Minister's grand, would-be autocratic manners: they were suspicious and jealous—suspicious of Talleyrand's growing intimacy with Bonaparte, and jealous of the preference and the deference shown to the Minister of Foreign Affairs, by the rising military star. When jealousy, suspicion, and resentment are yoked together, the roads that lead to angry invective, to insulting suggestion, are quickly attained. "Talleyrand wouldn't be happy unless there was a screaming scandal," shouted Reubell. "He must go to England—to those the English export from India—for his pleasures." "I demand that the nomination of this impudent priest be revoked . . ." in like strain he fulminated for hours.

Merlin took up the strain, with a Puritanical air of scandalized horror. In his softly hypocritical voice he purred. If Talleyrand had need of such, there are beautiful women in France—why go to English India?" Then came the accusation:—"In all this there is something, I confess, which seems to me to be beyond the domain of private life and to touch politics." And he subtly suggested an abominable treachery of Talleyrand's—that he was sold to England—that his liaison had a political motive, and that Madame was the "paquebot intermédiare" for furthering the same. François de Neufchâteau, who hated Talleyrand, in his turn "declaimed and shouted," until Barras, weary of the shouting, closed the tumultuous meeting by stating that the "affair" had best be sent to the Minister of Police, which was done.

What secret influence worked upon the Minister of Police? Certain it is that prison doors were opened, mysteriously, and the manner of their opening is never to be looked for in the records of the Ministry of Police.[1]

[1] One of the many reasons for the various and seemingly contradictory statements relating to Talleyrand's intimacy with Catherine Grand, prior to their marriage, is a simple and a sufficiently plausible one. The scandal to which his marriage gave birth resulted in the suppression, possibly, of all official documents and statements concerning the act, during his posts under various governments, as Minister of Foreign Affairs.

The violent attack on Talleyrand by the members of the Directoire had, as a result, that of enforcing the conviction, possibly, in Talleyrand's mind, that a Directoire headed by men of such intemperate minds was unfit properly to govern France.

Madame Grand took immediate precautions to ensure her full liberty. The lucky chance of having been born in a Danish colony, at Tranquebar, served as a pretext for her to demand naturalization as a Danish subject. Talleyrand's influence, doubtless, was expected to facilitate the act. Once a subject of the Danish King, Catherine Grand could neither be classed as an *émigré*, nor as an English subject. There was still one more formality to be undertaken to secure even more complete liberty. Divorce was as much the fashion under the Directoire as was re-marriage, or the choice of no marriage at all—of free-love, in a word. Whatever may have been Catherine's ambitious designs, the fact that she sued for an annulment of her marriage to G. F. Grand almost immediately after her liberation, is proof that as Minister of Foreign Affairs, Talleyrand doubtless judged that his liaison with a divorcée would be less open to harsh criticism than if Madame Grand were still tied to a living husband. The fact that Madame Grand could testify that she had had no news of her husband for the past five years, made her demand for freedom the more readily granted.

After the annulment of her marriage, Talleyrand's liaison with Madame Grand was openly proclaimed. At the Hotel de Gallifet, the official residence of the Minister of Foreign Affairs, as at the charming villa Talleyrand bought at Neuilly, Catherine Grand received her lover's guests at the balls, fêtes and official dinners given, as though she were the legitimate wife of the Minister, in lieu of being his mistress.

Immorality, it is true, was another of the fashions of this, as yet, unorganized society of the Directoire. Immorality and dissolute habits had been the reproach, as they had conduced to the charm and gaiety of the Court of Louis XV, and of the earlier years of the reign of Louis XVI. In those days of a past era of manners and customs, however, certain codes of decency were as strictly observed as good manners were the rule. If the husband were a profligate and the wife a woman of one or many lovers, the screen of the marital tie was considered to cover the amours at least of the wife.

The Revolution had opened wide doors on unknown worlds, customs, beliefs, manners and morals. The soldiers of the Revolutionary armies, as did their officers and generals, brought back to Paris, and to the most obscure villages and hamlets, stories of the way men and women lived, moved, and had their being in other countries— stories as startling as they were subversive of old habits. The *émigrés* had been shaken, for a time, out of the corselet of old French tradition. The nobility, who had believed the true world—the only one truly civilized—to be the one bounded by the Palace of Versailles, by the forests of the hunter, at Fontainebleau, or Chantilly, or Saint-Germain, had seen the great English life, or the stiff German officialdom, or the lax and alluring Italian modes of life, or had experienced the generous, yet cold-tempered Swiss reserve; and others still, like Volney, de Noailles, La Rochefoucauld, Talleyrand and how many others, had learned what space meant in the forests of America, and had looked on the happy faces of a free people.

Fear of the guillotine had had one result never dreamed of by its inventor:—it had sent thousands of French men and women to the school of the world.

The Revolution, and the Terror in its turn, had broken up the shell of conventional morality. Nearness of death, as does the lust of blood, loosens passions; it breeds a thirst for immediate enjoyment, for the quick kiss of satisfied desire, lest the end comes before the cup of life has yielded up its fill of delight. The Marseillais cut-throats snatched their longing for a gay moment, from the brimming wine-cup, lacing the Paris streets with their mad carmagnole, before they butchered Swiss Guards. Tallien caught the most fascinating woman in France at Bordeaux, Madame de Fontenay, by the waist, and carried her to Paris, where she was to be acclaimed as queen of all revels. Joséphine de Beauharnais, with her insinuating grace and indolent southern charm, was to forget her prison and a husband's death under the knife, in the arms, it was said, of both Barras and of General Hoche, before the lean, olive-complexioned Corsican won her.

The times and the spirit of the Directoire days lent themselves to an utter disregard of the unwritten laws of good taste. To live, to the fullest, was the order of the hour. Any excess was forgiven, were enjoyment its excuse. Divorce, re-marriage, free love—these were incidental, episodic conditions. That which must not suffer change or interruption was the dance of life—that wild Bacchanal of fêtes, dinners, balls, which were to make the horrors of the Terror a forgotten nightmare. The example set by the women of the day was typical of a world gone mad. The divorced wife of the Marquis de Fontenay, the wife of Tallien—the fascinating Thérèse Cabarrus—set the fashion

of gossamer gowns and loosened bodices. She undressed
the Directoire. Phryne's descendant—citoyenne Hamelin—who chose to parade her charms, uncovered to the
waist, on a famous walk she took from the Luxembourg
to the Champs Elysées, was boo-ed, it is true, by Parisians
not yet prepared to reward such a generous display: but
Juliette Récamier, Joséphine de Beauharnais, and Madame
Tallien—in "transparent gowns," à la Grècque—"Thérèsa"
in "bare feet covered with jewels"—could dance a quadrille
which evoked murmurous applause from a circle of admirers.

The society of the Directoire was, indeed, virtually that
of a *demi-monde*. If the Revolution opened all doors to
ambition, its successor was the new carmagnole, where,
at the public balls, the daughters of guillotined fathers
clasped hands with the revolutionaries who had sent the
latter to the scaffold; where actresses of notorious amours
were swung into the same mad whirl with *émigré* duchesses,
and where the new-rich of yesterday elbowed ministers,
deputies, foreign ambassadors and royalists.

In such a world, all standards were abolished. Family
life no longer existed. "In cutting off Louis XVI's head,
the Revolution had cut off the heads of every father of a
family." With parental authority gone, license reigned.
The lovely bared feet of Thérèse Tallien had pressed down
rules and social customs it had taken centuries to establish.

X

Talleyrand, on his arrival in Paris, proved how clearly
he read the meaning and the lawlessness of his time. With
this new world, he was to show the same manner, but a
new indulgence. He had been quick to seize the fact that
with the Directoire, the social world was as undressed, in

point of manners and decorum, as were its women.   In
the comedy of this pell-mell of aristocrats of finance, many
of whom had sprung from the gutter, of parvenus holding
the reins of social power, of political leaders whose knowledge of affairs had been gained as clerks, or as shopkeepers—
in this upside-down world of the Directoire, his suppleness
could bend to the command of circumstance.   Talleyrand
was perhaps the first opportunist of our modern times.

Among his new colleagues, Talleyrand's air of impressive distinction produced, however, its usual effect.   With
his regained authority, his inherent dignity imposed on the
mixed elements of this curiously mixed world.   "I was Minister under the Directoire; all the iron-shod boots of the Revolution strode across my ante-chamber, yet not a single individual ever attempted any familiarity with me," he said,
in speaking of this experience, in later life.

Madame Grand could hardly be cited as being excep-
tionable, among the more prominent women of the Directoire social world.   In placing her at the head of his establishment, Talleyrand's daring act throws a blazing light on
the accepted immoralities of the day.   Talleyrand's grand
air and manner suffer from his loss of prestige as a patrician.
For a Tallien or a Barras to offend, in matters of decorum,
one may proffer the excuse of the milieu.   Why should a de
Talleyrand-Périgord lower himself to their level?   Why forget to remember that one was a great gentleman?

XI

A description given by Madame de Casenove d'Arlens
of one of Talleyrand's receptions, in his Hôtel de Gallifet,
presents some lifelike pictures of the change from the
"room in a dark alley," in Philadelphia, to the splendors of

a fête at the Ministry of Foreign Affairs. In the rue de
Bac so great was the crowd, the coaches and carriages formed
compact lines. On finally reaching the court, before the
open Hôtel doors, an army of lackeys, in the livery of the
de Talleyrands-Périgords, was ranged in the great hall. A
flood of light lit up the flowers adorning the marbles of the
stairway, the gowns, uniforms, and jewelled orders of those
mounting upwards.

It was a scene of enchantment. A stately figure, tall,
slender, composed, stood at the top of the long stairs. As
host, Talleyrand received his guests with a courtesy as finished as his dignity was a barrier to the familiarity of this
heteroclite world. It was a lesson in the gracious manner
of a vanished world. Talleyrand's face, the observant
Madame d'Arlens noted, so blanched was its pallor, was in
marked contrast to the brilliant reds of his Ministerial
costume.

A fête given in honor of the hereditary Prince of
Parma and his wife, the Infanta of Spain, was held at the
Villa at Neuilly. The preparations were on an extensive
scale. The guests might have imagined themselves as being in the city of Florence itself. In the illuminated Park,
the Pitti Palace rose up, its painted façade glowing dimly
under the soft lights; peasants in costume danced their National dance; the poet, Esménard, recited verses, to recall
the idyll of the Decameron; music charmed the ear the live-
long night. Supper was set out three times in succession,
from midnight to the small hours. The dancers—the
couples who sought the discretion of the faery-lit gardens—
or the unwearied old, and the tireless young, were alike surprised, at dawn, by the presence of an uninvited guest—the
sun.

NAPOLEON BONAPARTE
By Girodet
Versailles Museum

XII

At one of these receptions given by Talleyrand, his time of reckoning came. Some of the high-born wives of the Ambassadors in Paris protested, and loudly, at having to make their courtesies to a Madame Grand, whose antecedents, and whose relation to the Minister of Foreign Affairs, were no secret.

Bonaparte, at this time, was all powerful as First Consul. Learning of the outcries made by the distinguished ladies, considering their remonstrances as being justifiable, he acted with his usual promptitude. Talleyrand made, perhaps, his first experience with Bonaparte's rude, hot temper. In brusque, harsh tones he ordered his Minister to "break with his mistress, or to marry her within twenty-four hours." There is no record of Talleyrand's answer.

As Consul, Bonaparte was as despotic as he was to be when Emperor. The true nature of the born Dictator and of the future imperious conqueror of Europe was asserting itself. Reforms were commanded to march—as Bonaparte had forced the marches of his ofttimes weary but victorious troops—to the martial commands conveyed through the Code, and the Concordat.

This superhuman work of reorganizing a world out of chaotic conditions possessed him. He must have order, and orderly relations in all the most intimate social and personal matters.

In that golden age at la Malmaison, where Bonaparte was enjoying a hitherto unknown domestic and intimate social life and felicity, he determined that his Generals and Ministers must be good husbands, as well as good citizens. Like all impressionable natures, with the instinct of sovereignty peculiar to Italians—when in power—in attempting to regulate the matrimonial arrangements of his subjects, Bonaparte carried his would-be control to excess.

At this period, as has been well said, "Everything was conducted from a military point of view. Orders were given that one must love—one loved." Strangely enough these forced marriages seemed to have ended in happy unions. One hears, even after the Napoleonic end of Empire, of neither divorces nor of milder forms of separation. Among those whom the despotic ruler married as authoritatively as he ordered an attack, mutual interests doubtless played their egoistic part in cementing such marriages.

In giving Talleyrand his ultimatum, relating to his mistress, even Bonaparte could not have imagined its far-reaching results.

XIII

On learning the First Consul's appalling decision, Catherine had shown those remarkable powers of resourcefulness which never seemed to desert her, in a crisis. The type of woman to which she belonged would never become successful adventuresses were such not gifted with the quickened instinct of expediency, in moments of peril. Fearsome possibilities opened up before Catherine Grand. Must she return to a precarious, uncertain livelihood? Was there to be no security for her in the future? Were all her hopes, her glorious dreams of greater grandeur, to vanish into thin air before the dictatorial blast of Bonaparte?

At la Malmaison a more touching scene was enacted than the heated one which Talleyrand had had to endure. Before a sympathizing Joséphine, Catherine exposed her

pitiful, her desperate state. Amid passionate tears she
begged her friend—for friends the two had become—to
intercede for her. Were the First Consul to consent to
hear her cause, she was certain of accomplishing her purpose. For Catherine, apparently, knew Talleyrand better
than he knew himself.

Bonaparte, in this instance at least, was as helpless
before a woman's tears, as weaker men are apt to prove
themselves. Catherine had the art of weeping without her
lovely features being distorted. Such moving beauty as
was hers, enhanced by real emotion and passionate cries,
produced the desired effect. "Well—let Talleyrand marry
you, and all will be well. Only you must bear his name, or
not again be seen at his house." Bonaparte, perhaps,
thought to be giving Talleyrand a desirable gift;—he was
to be among the first to realize that he had destined him to
Promethean torture.

There are various theories relating to the pressure exercised by Madame Grand to force Talleyrand to marry her.
To theorize is easy—not so to probe the true motive of a
man's yielding. Grave historians, in searching for the
reasons of Talleyrand's accepting union with a woman of as
notorious a past as was that of Madame Grand, have suggested that she was in posssession of secrets which would
ruin him. A threat of her's is cited. "Unless you marry me
at once, I'll make you a foot shorter."[1] Another theory
advanced was that she was the depository of his fortune.
More sentimental, Pasquier[2] sees in the Minister's acquiescence nothing more unusual than the eloquence of a woman's
tears, of a desire for peace, and for the continuance of an

[1] *Mémoires du Baron Thiébault*, V, 335.
[2] *Mémoires de Pasquier*, I, 251.

existence with a beautiful creature whose facile nature, indolence and charm made home life restful and attractive.

Such theorizing proves nothing. The facts are clear enough. Talleyrand agreed to marriage. Immediately, a thorny path was to open before him, and to lead to the recognition of the irreparable error he had committed.

XIV

The decision of marriage once taken, annoying as well as insuperable difficulties barred the way. As though to present themselves as living reminders of Catherine Grand's past, both Sir Philip Francis and G. F. Grand came to Paris. It might have seemed a concerted plan. Sir Philip's presence was embarrassing to a newly divorced lady, seeking remarriage, and Grand himself was to give all Paris the joy of flinging its contemptuous innuendoes at the Minister of Foreign Affairs. In the salons, gusts of delighted laughter followed each move in the game deftly played by Talleyrand to rid Paris of such eloquent reminders of his Catherine's past. There was less difficulty in disposing of Sir Philip than of the troublesome ex-husband. The former Councillor having asked permission to pay his respects, on Madame Grand's assurance that she was leaving for the country, the ex-Councillor made no further effort to see his former mistress.

The attempt to persuade the ex-husband to shorten his stay in Paris was a more serious matter. If it be true, as Napoleon affirmed at Saint-Helena, and as Madame de Rémusat also states in her *Mémoires*, that, venal as ever, Grand was attempting to extort money from Talleyrand, the prolongation of his stay in the capital is understood.

Talleyrand had recourse to a stratagem.   Through a friend,
the Dutch Minister, Monsieur Van de Goës, he obtained a
lucrative place for his predecessor, in the Cape of Good
Hope.   Grand again declared himself "entirely satisfied"
at the idea of exchanging a precarious existence in Paris
for a post yielding 2000 florins a year.   He continued to
find the flesh pots of Europe, however, also entirely to his
taste.   Although he removed his obnoxious presence as far
as Amsterdam, Talleyrand found Amsterdam too close to
Paris and its gossips.   Through a possibly dictated letter,
written by Madame Grand to the Minister of Holland, she
expressed her hope that his Excellency should demand
"that M. G. shall embark without delay, it being in the
highest degree inconvenient that he should prolong his stay
at Amsterdam."   The demand had its due effect.   M.
Grand departed, and save that it was known that he remar-
ried later on, he was heard of no more.

XV

Having successfully removed both the ex-husband and
Sir Philip Francis, Talleyrand was face-to-face with a far
more delicate and embarrassing situation.

With Bonaparte, with the Pope's emissary—Monseigneur
Spinola—and with the other clerical and laïcal members of the
Council, Talleyrand had been solemnly engaged in negotiat-
ing the formula of the Concordat with Rome.

Talleyrand was one of the most efficient, as well as one
of the most influential negotiators of the Concordat.   With
admirable clairvoyance, the First Consul, once he was in
the seat of power, had discerned the imperious necessity of
reconciling France with Rome.   The ravages of the Revolution must be repaired;—its murderous horrors, its impi-

ous sacrileges—Robespierre and his impudent creation of a
l'Etre Suprême—its killing of the King and Queen to prove
the cry "Vive la Liberté" to be a reality—its tempestuous
violence in every department of civil and social life—all
the torrential fury of the Revolution issuing from "the vol-
cano which had spit out its lava"—such destructive forces
were to be replaced by civic order and by religious unity.

This conception of the law that the rôle of a ruler is to
govern was not one acquired, but was inborn in the very
nature of Napoleon. At his budding Court, he must have
the note of "*bon ton*, of decency, of correct manners."
He had told Talleyrand, among other disagreeable truths,
that the days were gone when free-love could be counte-
nanced. He had offered Talleyrand, at an earlier period,
the cardinalate. As Cardinal the scandal of Talleyrand's
earlier life would be smothered under the voluminous robes
of scarlet silks. His superior abilities would be welcomed
and appreciated at Rome. He would be a controlling influence in the Church. Who knows—he might possibly be Pope.

Talleyrand refused. He had no taste for as exalted a
prospect. He preferred freedom—and a woman's arms.
Did he reason that from the latter it would be easier to
escape, did he so wish, than to break away, a second time,
from the too-close constraint of Rome? He may also have
reasoned that to accept as high an honor from a Church
he had practically deserted, might lead to a new scandal.

Meanwhile, at work on the Concordat under Napoleon,
together with the representatives of the Holy Synod, Monseigneur Spinola and other negotiators, Talleyrand was diligently using his influence to free himself, as well as others,
from their vows as priests. Tenacious, resolute, indomitable, he pressed and kept on pressing his point. His argu-

ment was that the secularized clergy—the priests and bishops secularized under the Constitutionalist law of 1789—should be absolved from their vows.   Many of the priests and some few bishops had married; it would be only just, under the new conditions of an orderly government, to regularize their status.   Talleyrand's arguments were forcibly reiterated and enlarged upon; all the more passionately did he plead them since he did not attempt to conceal the fact that the freedom he urged for others, should be conceded to him.

Bonaparte, for his part, was willing enough to agree to a proposition which seemed to him but clear justice.   The papal representative was at once up in arms.   Bonaparte's formula was:—"Ecclesiastics who have contracted marriage since their consecration, or who by other acts have notoriously renounced the ecclesiastical state, shall become simple citizens and as such shall have rights to laïcal communion." Monseigneur Spinola hotly asserted that the clause—"or who by other acts have renounced the ecclesiastical state"— this clause would never be acceptable to Rome.   He perceived the hand of Talleyrand in the above subtle phrase.

Thus the trouble began.   There must be sittings and sittings; there must be notes—interminable, endless notes exchanged between Cardinal Consalvi at Saint Peter's, and Monseigneur Spinola, in Paris; ecclesiastical history must be ransacked to find arguments to support Talleyrand's point of view.   Pius VII himself found in the decision of Julius III, in the reign of Mary Tudor, a reënforcing instance of papal inflexibility.   The Pope of that more rigid day would grant no freedom to the English infidel clergy.   Pius VII had this as a precedent on which to stand firm.   Yet was Rome anxious, and its tremors were justi-

fied. For it was Talleyrand who, more than anyone, had
encouraged Bonaparte to make peace with Rome. Talleyrand, after having been, perhaps the most able, save Bonaparte, of all the negotiators of the Concordat; having in
more than one instance shown a skill, a dexterity in solving
difficult and knotty questions, involving ecclesiastical law
and precedent, superior to all the Roman negotiators—
here was Talleyrand turning ugly, as Rome proved to be
more and more fixed in its opposition. He was showing not
only temper; he raised difficulties instead of solving them;
he was indifferent or caustic, encouraging discussions sure
to invite dissension. From aider and abettor of Bonaparte's
propositions, he was constantly putting spokes in the wheel.

In only one direction was the line of his attack unalter-
ably persisted in; he never lost an opportunity to touch
on the burning question which came to be called, derisively,
"the cause of Madame Grand." Even during his annual
cure, always taken at Bourbon-Archambault, his friend
and colleague, Blanc d'Hauterive, was empowered to continue the assault.

In this first prolonged and fiercely waged attack on the
Church's irreconcilable attitude, both Bonaparte and Talleyrand were defeated.

The Concordat was signed on the 15th of July, 1801.
No mention was made of "unfaithful" priests: sadly but
firmly Rome pronounced its *non possumus.* Talleyrand
was not to be downed; he and his Divisional chief and ally,
d'Hauterive, by their outcries, recriminations, and manœuvres succeeded in softening the final decision.

By a measure of exceptional clemency [Pius VII] finally issued his last word. His Holiness absolved the deacons and sub-

deacons and priests of the secular clergy who had married or who had renounced their charge: but no pardon was extended to those who had taken religious vows, nor to former Bishops.

As a signal act of papal indulgence, the edict of excommunication was annulled. Talleyrand was again among the faithful.

In Talleyrand's vocabulary, once his mind was made up, there was no such word as *no*. He had the sure instinct of the subtle diplomat. He undertook his second and more successful attack on papal inflexibility, at a propitious moment. Great as was the rejoicing in France at this her return to the bosom of the true Church, it was not more jubilate than were the rejoicings in Rome. In this time of softening influences, Talleyrand, as the powerful Minister of Foreign Affairs of this repentant if erring France—now brought back to the fold—made his last, effective plea. Talleyrand humbled himself; he made his confession of repentance. He begged the Pope's pardon for the grave errors he had committed; he declared he had always adhered firmly, devoutly to the Catholic, Apostolic and Roman religion; he implored the Pope's mercy—to be absolved from his sins and his vows. Such touching humility wrought upon the susceptibilities of the Papal Council. Still, there was delay in the sending of the answer, and protracted delay. Laws, rules, decisions must be consulted and discussed. Rome's two thousand years of Christian domination had accumulated more than two thousand *pros* and *cons* on every and any question. And the present matter presented innumerable difficulties. After weeks of decision, of revising, of discussions, a Brief was at last concluded and despatched. It was addressed to Jean Baptiste Cardinal

Caprara, "our legat à laterie, to the First Consul." In
the Brief, Talleyrand was made to say everything he had
carefully abstained from saying. "Tu avoues spontané-
ment avoir tombé dans les plus graves erreurs; tu gémis des
crimes que tu a commis: accuillant de sages conseils, tu
demandes pardon à ton Père bien aimé et tu rougis." There
were many such imaginary mental, moral and spiritual postures and states of mind attributed to a Talleyrand who
only existed in the pages of the Papal Brief:

Not only dost thou solemnly promise to be, in the future,
very submissive, proving a filial obedience and docility to the
Apostolic Throne, but even to work with all thy energy for the
amplification and the aggrandizement of religion and its Church.

Because of this—"Thy many sins may be forgiven thee."
A Talleyrand groaning over his crimes: blushing at the
thought of them; a submissive and docile Talleyrand, devoting his best energies to serve a religion and a Church from
whose vows and fetters he was exercising every faculty he
possessed to wrench himself free—such a Talleyrand as
Rome imagined to be possible was as far away from the real
Talleyrand as is a Machiavelli from a Cardinal Newman.
Rome's conception of the clever and brilliant Minister, in
the posture of a penitent, was a being seen through the
mist of distance and the mirage of papal imagination.

On the 27th day of May, 1802, a certain Monsieur Le-
fèbre—chief of a squadron—was seen rushing along the
road from Paris to Rome. If all roads lead to Rome, the
one taken by Bonaparte's messenger was to be shortened
by an intemperate haste and quick changes of relays.

The First Consul, personally, was to make an attack on

Rome. The State, as it was conceived by Bonaparte, was to enter the lists. State *versus* Church—which was to win?

Bonaparte's message, carried by his courier, to the ecclesiastical Council, was to announce that he himself requested the secularization of his Minister.

This Minister has rendered great service to the Church and to the State. He has publicly and irrevocably renounced clerical functions and dignities. He desires that this renouncement should be consecrated by a formal avowal of the Supreme Chief of religion. . . . Since France has become again a Catholic nation it is not seemly that a Minister who shares, in large part, the confidence of the government, should be an object of uncertainty and of controversy relative to his former state.

Bonaparte enlarges on certain concessions granted by former Popes: of Camille Pamphile, a Cardinal, who was secularized and died a laïc; of Cæsar Borgia, Archbishop of Valence, who became Duc de Valentinois and who married a princess, and of other secularizations by the Holy Father. The letter of the First Consul was a long one.

On the arrival of this important and alarming document, consternation reigned in the Council of the Church. Such a request from the French government to the Holy Synod placed the whole question of Talleyrand's secularization on a different footing. The official document must be answered, not as an indulgent Father to an erring son, but by the stern rule of strict ecclesiastical law.

The Brief which the First Consul's messenger carried back to Paris was anything but favorable to Talleyrand. He was not to be absolved from his vow as Bishop. "Never a dispensation from celibacy has been accorded to anyone whomsoever who previously has been invested with the character of Bishop." Such examples as those cited by the First Consul from the rule:—"neither Camille Pamphile nor Cæsar Borgia had ever received episcopal consecration, nor even sacerdotal ordination."

The character of a Bishop can never change. In eighteen centuries—not once, in spite of ardent prayers, in spite of imperious motives—not once has the Church consented to the marriage of a Bishop. . . . There is no reason to accord the dispensation asked for.

In the Brief sent to Paris, after a long and, to Talleyrand, an interminable delay, the above reasons, instances, and decisions, conveyed in Latin phrases, were beautifully expressed. Rome has always had the secret of saying unpleasant things in subtle ways. Talleyrand's tact was met by one superior to his own, since it was Rome, through the lips of the Sulpician Fathers, that had taught him the art. He was to be permitted "to enter into the laïcal communion, with the right of wearing the secular habit, and to fulfil the great offices of State." Of permission to marry—not a word.

Rome had spoken.

And now for the State. There was to be no subtility in its response. The words would strike as hard, and their objective would be as unerringly attained as shell, properly directed, shoots from cannon. Rome's power was to be estopped. The powers of the State were to protect its citizens, and their temporal rights, from intrusion of Roman decree.

No Bull, Brief or decree, mandate, provision, signature serving as provision, nor other expeditions from the court of Rome,

even those pertaining only to individuals, can be received, published or printed, nor otherwise executed without the authoriza-
tion of the government.

Such was the mandate of the State.   It holds good to
this day.   It was indeed one which had already been
made legal, being the first article of the law promulgated
on the 18th Germinal.   On that memorable day (19
August, 1802) this law, read out in a Council of State, by
the Councillor Portalis, was the reminder to Rome that its
authority stopped at the confines of the temporal rights of
French citizens.

Bonaparte's answer to the Pope's Brief was as follows;
it was inserted in the *Bulletin des Lois:*

The Consuls of the Republic, in view of the Brief of Pius VII
given at Saint-Peter's, of Rome 29 June, 1802, on the report of
the Councillor of State charged with all matters pertaining to the
cult—the Council of State having heard—

Attest: Brief of Pius VII given at Saint-Peter's at Rome the
29 June, 1802, by which the citizen Charles-Maurice Talleyrand,
Minister of Foreign Affairs, is returned to secular and laical life,
will have its full and entire effect.

"Le tour est joué!" says Lacombe.   The trick was
indeed played.   What Rome would not grant, was to be
granted by the State.   Talleyrand, to all intents and purposes, was to be free—at last.   The public was to see in
him a citizen, like any and all other citizens—free to live
his life—free to marry, among other rights.   And to this
our day of so-called liberty, the world has seen in Talleyrand the renegade, the perjured priest, the unfrocked
Bishop—untrue to his vows.   Behind the richly embroidered Minister's coat as behind the Ambassadorial fineries,

there looms the shadowy robe, the Bishop's Mitre, and the Bishop's Crozier.

The State, though nominally governed by the Three Consuls, was, in reality, Bonaparte. He had interpreted the Pope's Brief to suit his own will and desires. By the Pope, Talleyrand had been rendered back to the secular life, but he was not absolved from his vow as Bishop—of chastity. Bonaparte decided otherwise. Talleyrand having been secularized as citizen, his secularization was "to have full and entire effect." Twenty days after the Brief recorded by the French government (20th of August, 1802), Talleyrand's marriage took place (10th September, 1802).

Comte Molé, in his recently published *Mémoires*, gives an extraordinary version of a conversation held with Napoleon relating to Talleyrand and to his marriage[1]:

On returning from America after the Terror, he succeeded in lowering his reputation by attaching himself, publicly, to an elderly prostitute devoid of cleverness. I wished, in spite of him, to get him out of that filthy situation, during the Concordat, by requesting the Pope to bestow upon him the Cardinal's Hat, and I nearly succeeded in obtaining it. Well—he never would acquiesce, and *in spite of me*, he married his shameful mistress, scandalizing all Europe—and by whom he could not even hope to have children. He is certainly, and none are ignorant that he is of all men, he who stole the most, and he hasn't a penny, and I am forced to keep him going from my privy purse and at this moment to pay his debts.

This account of Comte Molé's differs in every particular from the one that history has accepted in regard to Talleyrand's marriage. It was Napoleon who forced the marriage.

[1] *Le Comte Molé—Sa Vie et Ses Mémoires*, 1781–1855. Tome Premier, p. 193.

Finding the marriage of the ex-Bishop had aroused a scandal far in excess of his liaison with Madame Grand, Napoleon then denied his own act.

The Emperor's anger at Talleyrand (1814) was at its height at the time of his talk with Molé.   He knew Talleyrand had been in secret correspondence with the Royal Princes—in a word had been conspiring against him.

CHAPTER II

I

TALLEYRAND was married in the Mairie of his quarter, the Hotel de Gallifet being in the city's Xth arrondissement. The Mayor's office was in the rue de Verneuil. In the two buildings numbered respectively 13 and 15, one may still find what was formerly the Mairie, in the year 1802. The street has not lost its sad-faced aspect. Even in its better days, when some of the now dispirited looking houses were fine hôtels, there was never enough breadth nor sunshine to give to the rue de Verneuil an air of gaiety.

The bridal couple and their friends, the latter the witnesses of the marriage, made a glittering mass of color as they entered the Mayor's office. Talleyrand's corpse-like pallor, in the startling daylight, seemed to mock the very nature of the ceremony. The richness of his costume accentuated his too apparent indifference. On Madame Grand's radiant countenance was written the triumph of the hour.

Among the friends and signers of the marriage register were Pierre Louis Roederer, the President of the section of the Interior of the State; General Pierre Ryel Beurnonville, Minister Plenipotentiary of the (French) Republic to the Court of Prussia; Vice-Admiral Bruix, Councillor of State;

the Prince of Nassau Siegen, François Nicholas Henri Othon, Grand d'Espagne de la Première Classe, lieutenant-general in the service of his Catholic Majesty, and Admiral in the service of the Emperor of Russia; and Pierre Claude Maximilien Radyx Sainte-Foy. The latter, as was the Prince de Nassau, were friends of the bride. [1]

The Councillor of State, Roederer, had been one of the conspirators with Talleyrand, in the Coup d'Etat of the 18 Brumaire; Radyx Sainte-Foy had been Secretary to the Comte d'Artois; and the Prince de Nassau—"the paladin of the XVIII Century" as he was derisively called—had had a more or less parti-colored career.

II

In the marriage registry, now destroyed, but painstakingly copied by Jal in 1867, there is no mention made of Talleyrand's two brothers having been present. Monsieur Lacombe, in his long chapters on *Le Mariage de Talleyrand*, affirms their having witnessed the marriage contract at Talleyrand's house at Neuilly, for the formalities of the bride's dot, which she was supposed to bring, as her part of the marriage fortunes. Talleyrand doubtless had conveyed to his former mistress certain properties, enabling her thus to make a suitable appearance of being possessed of a comfortable maintenance.

Monsieur Lacour-Gayet, in his history of Talleyrand, recounts in a somewhat exultant tone, the discovery that in the marriage contract Talleyrand *signed* the fact that both his parents were dead. The *copy* of the marriage contract reads:

[1] Of Sainte-Foy Talleyrand said, one day, laconically: "His name is one which cannot be proposed, if a matter of confidence is to be debated" (Foy being French for good faith).

Acte de mariage de Charles-Maurice Talleyrand-Périgord,
agé de quarante-huit ans né à Paris depart. de la Seine le 2
Fevrier 1754; profession: Ministre des relations extérieures, de-
meurant à Paris rue du Bac, à l'Hôtel du Ministère des Relations,
fils de Charles-Gabriel-Talleyrand-Périgord et d'Alexandrine-
Victoire-Eléonore-Damas d'Antigny son épouse, *tous deux décédés*,
etc.

Talleyrand's father had died in November, 1788. His
mother, at the time of his marriage, was alive. She did not
approve of her son's marriage. She was neither at his house,
with her two sons, nor at the civil marriage ceremony, at
the Mayor's office. Devout, sincerely attached to all the
rules and laws of her Church, she was deeply grieved at her
son's act of defiance to the dictum of Rome. As an anointed
Bishop, he had never received, nor could he receive, absolution from his vows. In contracting marriage, he was placing
himself outside of the pale of the Church. Madame de
Talleyrand had spent the day in which the marriage was
made legal, in tears. Her death is recorded in the Registres
de Présentations, of the church *de la Madeleine*, Paris, as
having taken place in Paris in the rue d'Anjou, no. 34, on
the 29th of June, 1809. Seven years after her son had
declared her to be dead, she was still living. The above
accusation stands on what appears to be somewhat friable
ground.

First of all, the marriage contract quoted by M. Lacour-
Gayet is a *copy* of the original, the actual act itself having
disappeared. The document cited is copied from the
"Dictionnaire critique de biographie et d'histoire," which
based its documentation on a reconstitution made in 1873
of such acts "d'après les archives notariales." A copy can
never replace an original document.

At the Villa de Neuilly, Talleyrand's two brothers, Archambauld and Boson de Périgord, as has been stated, were present together with Bonaparte, Cambacérès, Joséphine de Beauharnais and others, for a signing of the contract of marriage regulating the fortune of the bride. This was on the 9th September, 1802. On the day of the marriage ceremony the act in question would have us believe Talleyrand had declared his mother to be dead, though still living. Such a statement made by as clever and as prudent a statesman as was Talleyrand is inconceivable. He never lied, if we accept Sainte-Beuve's assertion that he made use of the subterfuge of mendacity whenever such practices served his purpose—he never lied, unless a lie served a purpose.

What could be gained by stating the demise of his living parent? As he was forty-eight years of age, he did not need the authority of his mother's consent to marry. The old French law, it is true, stipulated that the demand of the consent of the parents at any age was a legal necessity. Under the new laws—under the Code—a marriage under the Civil law was valid without the consent of the parents, provided that either party contracting marriage was twenty-one years of age. There seems no proven motive for as stupid an act. A singular mystery hangs over the actual place of burial of Madame de Talleyrand. Neither in the cemetery of the Château de Valençay, nor in the Archives of the Seine, nor, apparently, in the records or letters of the family now living, is there any proof of where the body of Madame de Talleyrand was laid.[1]

[1] In my desire to clear up, if possible, the mystery of the supposed death of Mme. de Talleyrand, I wrote to one of the most distinguished descendants of Talleyrand's family now living in Paris, to ask if any documents could be given me which would throw light on the actual facts recorded in the copy of the Talleyrand marriage register. The answer given was that there were no authentic documents either to refute or to sustain the statements made therein.—Author.

During the entire length of Talleyrand's remarkable career, the years stretching from 1775 to 1836, there was ever an army of spies, detractors, political enemies ready to snatch at any fact or act which could blacken his character. Would as grave a charge have passed unnoted, unnoticed, as the one cited in the copy of the marriage register? Michaud, the royalist, a contemporary, would never have missed gloating over so rare a proof of Talleyrand's infamy. Nor would Sainte-Beuve have refrained from casting one more stone at the man he calls "venal and corrupt"—the statesman to whom he dedicates one hundred and twenty pages in the *Nouveaux Lundis* to prove Talleyrand's being one of the most depraved of men.

III

Was there or was there not a religious ceremony of the marriage? Authorities differ. Pasquier, the future Chancellor, records in his *Mémoires:*

The marriage was celebrated furtively somewhere at Epinay in the valley of Montmorency. Monsieur de Monville, ex-Councillor of the Parliament of Paris, who had an estate in that village, arranged the matter with the Curé. This complaisance on the part of M. de Monville (I think it was arranged by M. Louis) brought him a peerage in 1815, when M. de Talleyrand was president of the Council.

The parish register having disappeared, Pasquier's statement, unsupported by an official record, is considered doubtful, in view of other inaccuracies in his *Mémoires*. Two other statements relating to the religious ceremony rest on equally unfounded authority. One records that the religious ceremony took place at Saint-Gratien where his friend Admiral Bruix had a country place—the Curé d'Epinay officiating; and still another authority endorses M. Pasquier's statement that the Curé d'Epinay, a Constitutionalist priest, gave the bridal couple the nuptial benediction, in that parish, Madame Grand having passed several summers in a house near the church. Religiously married or not, Talleyrand was tied for life to a woman whom he could not respect, yet for whom his sense of form exacted that respect should be shown by others. The yoke was to be borne without a murmur; Madame de Talleyrand was neither to hear a reproach for her extravagance in expenditure, nor for her foolish speeches, nor for her laughable mistakes which furnished the Paris salons and European Courts with weapons of ridicule with which to sting Talleyrand. As his mistress he had given her first place; as his wife, she was a figure-head, of no consequence save that she bore his name, was at the head of his house, and therefore the formality of polite consideration must be rendered her. There are several ways of putting away from one a wife, when one lives with her: a separate existence can be maintained, though man and wife live under the same roof. Frigid silences, a manner which discourages familiarity, a crowded life rendering intimacy impossible—and the freezing process accomplishes its purpose: Talleyrand married, in his own house, was the most solitary of men.

Bonaparte, in attempting to render the Consulate respectable, to give to manners a certain tone and prestige, had made a useless sacrifice of Talleyrand's liberty. The Directoire had had its orgy of indecency and libertinage. A society based on at least an outward form of morality, was to succeed a society which had known no law. This passion for order, and Talleyrand's weakness in yielding to a woman's tears—and possibly to her threats—was to darken the succeeding years of Talleyrand's life.

For thirteen years, "this woman, in whom everything must shock him, and who beside him, is like unto the visible sign of his vices" as Châteaubriand says—for years Talleyrand endured his bondage. Relations, of an intimate nature, it is true, almost immediately after the enforced marriage, had become more and more strained. Madame de Talleyrand received at the Hôtel d'Anjou, during the time of Talleyrand's disgrace, after his dismissal by Napoleon, as Minister of Foreign Affairs. The Emperor, however, having admitted her once at Court, during Talleyrand's Ministry, to prove her right to such presentation, appears to have had a tacit understanding with Talleyrand that thenceforth she should not appear at the Tuileries. The Prince bore her occasional lapses from grammatical purity, as he did such amusing proofs of ignorance as her confounding the works of a distinguished savant with those of the author of *Robinson Crusoe*, with the same front of assumed phlegm with which he met stinging calumny. Yet, had she not borne his name, with what relish he would have been the first to announce to delighted salons Madame de Talleyrand's now historic answer to the question as to her birthplace—"Je suis d'Inde."

IV

From the Consulate to the Empire, up to the year 1808, Talleyrand, as Minister of Foreign Affairs, as the Duc de Broglie well says:

went on from treaty to treaty, like his master from victory to

MGR. LE PRINCE DE BÉNÉVENT

victory, imposing the law of the conqueror on the conquered, until the day when he himself fell into disgrace because of his having advised the Emperor to halt half-way in his foolish enterprises in Spain.[1]

The Emperor, shortly after the capture—and betrayal —of the Spanish Princes at the close of the Spanish expedition, learned that Talleyrand had written to a friend a disparaging letter, one couched in a sarcastic tone, relating to the whole enterprise. The Emperor's fury knew no bounds. He chose his moment. It was before a group of the dignitaries of the Court, before his Ministers—that the vials of his wrath were poured forth.

In ringing tones, anger flashing from his eyes, he accused Talleyrand of "betraying him":

You have told people—and you have written that you had gone down on your knees to prevent my going into the Spanish expedition, whereas you have been urging me to undertake it for the last two years!

This and much more abuse was flung at Talleyrand. The Emperor's fury, flaming to passionate excess, was so uncontrolled, the bystanders feared he would proceed to personal violence. Talleyrand, blanched, but unflinching, listened with no outward sign on his impassive face. Leaning against the mantelpiece, he faced the Emperor with imperturbable calm. Of all the Court he was the least embarrassed, the most perfectly self-controlled. As Napoleon's outburst ended, waiting for the sign of dismissal, he bowed, with his accustomed grace. On the way down the Palace stairs, his only comment to the one nearest him was

---

[1] *Personal Recollections of the Duc de Broglie*, Vol. II, Raphael Ledos de Beaufort.

—"What a pity that so great a man should have been so badly brought up!"[1]

This scene had ended Talleyrand's post as Minister of Foreign Affairs under Napoleon. He was in semi-disgrace; yet, Napoleon could not wholly sever relations with as important and as valuable a statesman. The Emperor named him Grand Chamberlain. His generosity, or his secret liking, urged him to still further concessions. Learning that Talleyrand's lavish entertainments at the Ministry of Foreign Affairs had crippled him with debts, the Emperor paid them. He also gave him a million francs, with which to purchase the Hôtel Monaco, in the rue de Varenne—his residence, after having left the Ministry. Such gifts, however, were to be paid for; and for one in whom pride of race and of caste was stronger than the pride greater men place in the sanctuary of honor, the payment demanded was peculiarly wounding. After having "ruled Europe" together with Napoleon, to be gaoler to the Spanish Princes was disgrace indeed.

There may well have been a hidden malice in Napoleon's motive in imposing the Princes as "guests" in Talleyrand's Château. The latter, alone among the Emperor's Ministers, had the courage to confront him, at times, with ugly-faced truth. "He indulges in the pleasure and the risk of being sincere with the terrible Napoleon," as Jacques Sindral well says.[2]

After Talleyrand had ceased to be Minister of Foreign Affairs, under Napoleon when Emperor, the balls given for children in his house in the rue d'Anjou, and in the rue de Varenne, in the house named the Hôtel Monaco—such balls

---

[1] *Mémoires de Talleyrand.* Edited by the Duc de Broglie.
[2] *Talleyrand,* Jacques Sindral, Libraires Gallimard, 1926.

for Charlotte became famous. Who was Charlotte? During the earlier days of his marriage, Talleyrand announced to his wife and to his intimates that a specially dear friend in England had begged of him the greatest of favors: would he accept as a ward, a little girl to be brought up under his roof, to be treated as one of the family?

Talleyrand accepted the charge. Sceptics and the gossips gave a different version of the supposed adoption. Whatever the nature of the claim, Charlotte was treated as a beloved child in the household. Her education was carefully supervised; the *bals d'enfants* given for her were the talk of Paris. Talleyrand finally married her to a cousin, Baron de Talleyrand.

In the Hôtel Monaco, the festivities given were on such a scale of magnificence that the reunions were called "the little court."

CHAPTER III

I

AFTER Austerlitz, Napoleon had turned his eyes towards Spain. With a Bourbon King on the Spanish throne, he announced he did not feel safe. He therefore made war on Spain—against Talleyrand's advice; a disastrous war entered into by Talleyrand's advice, was Napoleon's reiterated assertion, in his *Mémoires* written at St. Helena.

The Spanish war was a prelude to the Russian disaster. Napoleon's intrigues to capture both the King, Charles IV and his sons—the Royal Princes—remain as a tarnished leaf in the Conqueror's victorious crown. He had trapped the King and the three Spanish Princes at Bayonne, after having sworn to respect their rights and independence. He lured them across the border. Having captured them, he imprisoned them. The King was sent as a prisoner to the Château de Compiègne. The Emperor reserved a softer fate for Ferdinand, Prince of the Asturias, for Prince Carlos, the second son, and for their uncle, Don Antonio.

Napoleon did not ask, he ordered Talleyrand to receive the Princes at the Château de Valençay. The ex-Minister was to be made to drink some bitter drops out of the cup proffered him by his master who, in concluding his "orders,"

Napoleon First

From a color plate

Napoleon First
From a color plate

added, in his letter from Bayonne: "For yourself, your mission is sufficiently honorable; to receive three illustrious persons and amuse them is quite in the character of the nation's and of your rank." No longer Minister of Foreign Affairs, having been in semi-retirement after his disgrace, still, however, Grand Chamberlain, Talleyrand read the true meaning in the insulting order—for insulting indeed was the following indelicate suggestion in the letter: "You might have Madame de Talleyrand there, and four or five pretty women. If the Prince of the Asturias should fall in love with some pretty woman, and the fact were known, there would be no objection to it, as it would be one more way of keeping a watch on him." The tap on the drum, commanding Talleyrand to "march," was more authoritative than ever. The stroke struck, intolerably, its insolent note:

See that the rooms are ready, prepare the beds and table linen. I wish these Princes to be received without exterior pomp, but decently and with attention, and that you should do your best to amuse them. If you have a theatre at Valençay there would be no harm in having some comedians down.

Enamored of grandeur as was Napoleon, yet the lack of early training in a grand style of living had left its narrowing impress. Talleyrand had bought the Château de Valençay, five years before. In its furnishing, with its tapestries, its Beauvais and Gobelins salon sets, its long picture gallery with its rare collection of antiques and bibelots, and the *meubles* signed by the great artists of 18th century art —the Château was a princely residence. The gardens and fountains were a fitting frame to the great house. "See that the rooms are ready, prepare the beds and table linen."

Talleyrand could smile at as naïve a command. Beneath
the richly embroidered mantle of assumed royalty there
were revealed the signs of the former narrow Corsican bourgeois life.

Talleyrand's reply to the monarch was in the correct
tone of perfect courtesy: "I will respond with my best
endeavors to the confidence with which your Majesty hon-
ours me. Mme. de Talleyrand left last night to give the
preliminary orders. The Château is amply furnished with
cooks, china and linen of all kinds." Unlike royalty, who
must send its cars ahead filled with beds, cooks and furniture, when changing from one State Château to another,
Talleyrand's house was mounted as private mansions should
be—ready for occupancy.

II

If Napoleon had captured the King of Spain and the
Princes by an abominable treachery, Talleyrand proposed
to prove how a *grand seigneur* of an older France could
render captivity an illusion.

From the first moment of the entrance into the Valençay
grounds, the Princes were made conscious of the magnificence of their reception. By their host, they were received
with the deference due to their rank and to their misfortune.

On the 19th of May, they made their entrance into Valençay
[Talleyrand writes in his *Mémoires*]. This moment has left on
my mind an impression which will never be effaced. The Princes
were young, and over them, around them, in their clothing, in
the liveries of their servants, was seen the image of bygone centuries. The coach from which I saw them alight might have
been taken for a carriage of Philip V. . . . They were the first
Bourbons that I saw again after so many years of storms and dis-

tress. It was not they who were embarrassed, it was I, and I am pleased to say it.

The Princes were received indeed, with royal state. The Spanish flag floated on the Tower. Lackeys in Spanish liveries were in attendance. Royal Princes, they were to be treated as royalty. No one was to be admitted to their presence, unless permission were granted. Those who approached them must be in Court dress.

The captivity of the Princes was to be a continuous pleasure performance. They were taught to shoot—some of them never having shot before; they rode perfectly trained mounts through groves and wide forests; they could fish, or loaf. At night, with charming ladies in Court dress, they danced. There were the Duchesse de Gênes, Mme. de Brignole, and the wife and sister-in-law of an Austrian Field Marshal—Mesdames de Bellegarde. And there was the hostess—still beautiful, in spite of increasing embonpoint, still flirtatious, though under the all-seeing eyes of a husband whose wary glance—guarded, enigmatic—saw everything. San Carlos,[1] who only saw what foolish courtiers are trained to see, quickly discerned the nature of the light in the Princess's black-fringed blue orbs. Princes, guests, and host and hostess were alike in captivity. They met morning, noon, and night, as fine birds in fine plumage must meet, in a cage. At Mass, making music or listening to it; walking, dancing, riding, the comedy, edged with tragic consequences for Madame de Talleyrand, went on.

Madame de Talleyrand, like Penelope, had found a lover in her house. Unlike the faithful Homeric heroine, her nights were spent in weaving plots for the morrow's illicit

[1] The Princes were accompanied by a Spanish nobleman—San Carlos—reputed to be a lady-killer.

meetings, rather than proving her fidelity to her lord.
San Carlos was to be the facile prestidigitator who changed
the Princesse de Talleyrand into her original rôle of courtesan.

The news of the liaison had flown, and swiftly, as far as
the Tuileries. Madame de Talleyrand suddenly left Valençay. She was never to see the Château again. She had
signed her own social death-warrant. Her punishment did
not come at once. But the lean hand of fate and Talleyrand's implacable resentment had marked her for their
own.

Incorrigibly imprudent, Madame de Talleyrand kept
up a correspondence on her return to Paris, with her lover,
through Canon Escoiquitz, a Spaniard. The latter was
constantly to be seen at her Hôtel.[1]

In Madame de Chastenay's *Mémoires* she states that
Madame de Talleyrand, on her return to Paris, not only
"received le Canon Escoiquitz, wearing the grand cordon
of Charles III of Spain," but her admirer, the Duke of San
Carlos, was a constant visitor.

Did Talleyrand consider that in receiving the Spanish
nobleman, he could disarm criticism? Gossip had run a
swift course from Valençay to the Paris salons. The liaison
of the Princesse de Talleyrand was so open a secret that
Napoleon could cry out, to Talleyrand, at his levée: "You
never told me that San Carlos was your wife's lover, at
Valençay." The reply was as cuttingly incisive as was the
brutality of the question. "For the glory of your Majesty
as well as for mine, it is better that the question of the
Princes of Spain should never be mentioned." Napoleon

---

[1] The imprisonment of the Spanish Princes was to last five years. Don Carlos
was imprisoned in the Fortress de Bourg-en-Bresse. Later the Prince and his
brother, the Prince of the Asturias, were to be confined at Compiègne—and later
still, they were again to be in captivity at Valençay.

received the rebuke in silence. "But from this moment dated the rupture which, more or less marked, took place between him and me. Never after did he pronounce the name of Spain, of Valençay, or mine without adding to it some injurious epithet," Talleyrand stated in his *Mémoires*.[1]

Napoleon asserted in his *Mémoires* that it was M. de Talleyrand who had counselled him to confiscate the Spanish throne; M. de Talleyrand frequently repeated that, on the contrary, he wished to dissuade him from the project. What is really probable is that the King's Minister counselled an arrangement which would have given France the territory to the north of the Ebro, and that Portugal should be ceded, in compensation, to the Spanish monarchy.

Count Beugnot, in his *Mémoires*, affirms:

Prince Talleyrand knew all the details of everything that had passed at Bayonne and he appeared to me to be very indignant. "Such victories," he said, "do not suffice to efface such actions, because in all that which has been done there is *je ne sais quoi de vil, de la tromperie, de la tricherie.* I do not know what will become of it all, but you will see that no one will forgive the Emperor for what he has done."

III

While Talleyrand had been shooting, riding, amusing and fascinating the young Spanish Princes at Valençay, Napoleon had conceived his great plan. In his further designs on world conquest, he realized that a pact with the Czar was the imperative sign to be written in the peace he now deemed necessary, with which to blind Europe. The signing of the pact must have the world as spectators. All Europe—all the vanquished kings, and all

[1] *Mémoires de Talleyrand.*

those to be vanquished, must be assembled at Erfurt.
Hand in hand, the sovereign of Europe and the ruler of
all the Russias would present to a "parterre of kings" an
historic picture such as would immortalize the century,
and one which would be the prelude to Napoleon's vast
plan of the conquest of the East.

Napoleon had caressed the longing, after his victories
of Eylau, Tilsit and Austerlitz, for world domination. After
Prussia's submission, Austria must be conquered. Hun-
gary, Bohemia, Poland—these easily would be overcome.
Russia must serve as a roadway to the conquest of the East
—to India—after Constantinople. Napoleon foresaw another possible opening of the road through Russia, without
being forced to a reasonable quarrel with the Czar, before
declaring war. Such were his full-orbed dreams. Two
disastrous defeats had seen this vision of Eastern conquest
fade into uncertain outlines. General Junot, Napoleon's
beloved general, had lost, in Spain, the battle of Cintra.
The defeat greatly affected the Emperor. His plan for
"dazzling Europe" at Erfurt was more than ever important.

For the third time in a year a revolution had broken out
in Constantinople. "This catastrophe distressed me," was
the Emperor's confession to the French Senate, before he
had realized, to the full, the necessity of a meeting and
of coming to an understanding with the Czar. More than
ever, after Cintra, and the insurrection in Constantinople,
was an amicable treaty necessary with Russia.

Now that Prussia, after the victories of Eylau, Tilsit
and Austerlitz, was crushed, the future submission of Austria became imperative. Austria must be rendered impo-
tent; Russia must be made to see she could not expect peace

in Europe if Austria were free—free to join Russia in case
the latter needed her, in a possible assault, on Russia's
part, on Constantinople.

Austria and her fate, were, indeed, the pivotal point
about which were to turn all the intrigues at Erfurt.

This interview of the Czar with Napoleon at Erfurt
"was sought only with the idea and upon the condition
that the position of Turkey should be settled previously,
and that the object of the interview should be simply to come
to a thorough understanding in carrying out the said
partition."[1]

IV

Talleyrand left Valençay before his wife to join Napoleon at Nantes, on the 9th of August, 1808. It was there
the Emperor confided to him his great secret. "We are
going to Erfurt. I desire on my return to be free to do as I
please with Spain. I must be assured that Austria will be
anxious, but restrained; and I do not wish to be bound in
restrictive measures with Russia in regard to the Levant."
That was what Napoleon said: what Talleyrand read into
the avowal was altogether different. His conclusion was:
"To finish with her also, reducing her to the state of Prussia: and then, the Alliance with Russia having accomplished
its purpose, Napoleon will finish with Russia and constrain
her to obedience." For such a plan to succeed the co-
operation of Alexander I was essential. For its execution,
Talleyrand was to be the scene-shifter.

Before Talleyrand set forth on his journey to Erfurt,
a second scene had occurred at Nantes, one which was

[1] *Mémoires de Talleyrand.* Edited by the Duc de Broglie, translated by Raphael
Ledos de Beaufort, Vol. I, page 396.

to have a decisive influence on the relations between Napoleon and his Grand Chamberlain.

The Emperor proceeded, on a certain evening, to boast of the successful termination of his Spanish campaign, and how all difficulties which had been feared had been surmounted:

Well, you see what all your predictions as to the difficulties I should encounter in regulating the affairs of Spain according to my views have amounted to; I have overcome these people here: they have all been caught in the nets I spread for them, and I am Master of the situation in Spain as in the rest of Europe.

Talleyrand records, in his *Mémoires:*

Provoked by this boasting, so little justified in my eyes, and above all by the shameful means he had employed to arrive at his ends I replied that I did not see things under the same aspect as he, that "I believed he had lost more than he had gained by the events at Bayonne." "What do you mean by that?" was the Emperor's angry query. "Mon Dieu," I said, "it is very simple and I will show by example. If a man of the world commits follies, has mistresses, conducts himself badly towards his wife, does even grave wrongs to his friends he will doubtless be blamed: but if he is rich, powerful and clever, he may still expect to be treated with indulgence in society. If he cheats at gambling, he is immediately banished from good company which will never pardon him."

The "cheating" in Napoleon's game of imprisoning the Spanish King and his sons, after luring them to Bayonne on false promises, was, not only to get rid of a Bourbon King —his *bête noire*—but the trick also was played so as to enable him to place his brother Joseph on the Spanish throne.

In choosing Talleyrand as his negotiator at the Council

of Erfurt, after Austerlitz, Napoleon had need of him both as a statesman and as aristocrat.

Napoleon might fiercely resent his ex-Minister's plain speaking; he might brutally insult him, as he did before his full Court; but in all his Court, Talleyrand alone had a triple value as statesman, aristocrat, and as being the friend of kings and monarchs; his presence could not be dispensed with, even though he were to outrage the "Sovereign of Europe" by accusing him of cheating at cards.

When it came to such a "parterre of kings" as were to be assembled at Erfurt, no one in all his Empire could impress as would the Prince de Bénévent. Napoleon must have Talleyrand where the Czar of Russia, where the King of Prussia, lesser Kings and such Ministers as Metternich were to watch the great game played by Napoleon and the Czar. At that time the Emperor was in need, or thought he was, of Russia's friendship. Remembering Napoleon's treachery with the Spanish Princes, Alexander put the price high. Austria, it was agreed, under Talleyrand's persuasive argument, instead of being crushed, as Napoleon had thought would be wise, was to be let alone —a decision which, among others, was to cost Napoleon his crown. In yielding, the Emperor believed, as never before, there could be nothing to fear—from mortals—this after Austerlitz, the Homeric victory which was the defeat of England's supremacy and the news of which killed Pitt. [1]

[1] He was at Bath when he received the news. Tradition says he was looking at pictures in a gallery when he heard the furious gallop of a horse. "That must be a courier," he exclaimed, "with news for me." When he opened the packet, he said, "Heavy news indeed," and asked for brandy. He hurriedly swallowed one or two drams; had he not, he must have fainted. He then asked for a map and desired to be left alone. A few days later, his eyes resting on the map of Europe, he said: "Roll up that map, it will not be wanted for ten years." (*Pitt:* Lord Salisbury. Pitt's prophecy came true in just nine years.)

V

Before "the comedy of friendship" which was played at Erfurt, between Napoleon and the Czar, the latter, during the negotiations at Tilsit, had been greatly impressed by Talleyrand. "In him," as so admirably states Etienne Lamy,[1] "he had been charmed by all the seductions of race; in him he had recognized the traditions of that older France which judged with a sense of measure the unconsidered designs of genius."

Napoleon's "designs," from his recorded orders to Talleyrand, prove they were not wholly "unconsidered." They were in point of fact, elaborate; they embraced, with a theatrical sense of effect, not only the glamor of as an impressive a personality as was Talleyrand, but also his known cordial relationship with the Czar.

My dear Talleyrand, you must be at Erfurt a day or two before me. You know the Emperor Alexander well. You will speak to him in that language that suits him. You will tell him that in the benefit our alliance may prove to mankind, one recognizes one of the great purposes of Providence. We are both young; we need not hurry. The welfare (or interest) of the Continent—that is understood: seven millions of Greeks made free—there's a fine field for philanthropy to play its part; in all I give you *carte blanche*, only I must have a distant philanthropy.

The philanthropy Talleyrand proposed to preach was of a quite different order.

VI

The Council of Erfurt is of special significance in the history of Europe. The tri-partite contest to be played by

[1] Preface de Etienne Lamy, *Souvenirs de la Duchesse de Dino*, publiés par La Comtesse Jean de Castellane, page 27.

Napoleon, the Czar of Russia and Talleyrand, in the little city of gardens, was to have cataclysmic results. The Emperor, the Czar and Talleyrand each went to the eventful meeting with a definite, clear purpose; but the designs and intentions of each were veiled by the consummate art with which each was to weave the web of intrigue in disguising their separate intentions. In the end, the Czar and Talleyrand were to find that their plans more or less coincided: they were to understand each other—and this understanding was to come about not through open confidence, nor by explanation; but because the finesse of Talleyrand could place a vague phrase which the Slavic ruse of the Russian sovereign could clearly interpret.

The game to be played in the future destinies of Europe might well have aroused the envy of the Fates. The results were to be momentous. Napoleon, who believed himself to be the arbiter of Europe, was to see, shortly after the meeting at Erfurt, this arbitrage pass into the hands of the Czar. Talleyrand was largely instrumental, through his intrigues, and his hostility towards Napoleon, in placing the sceptre of power in Russia's hand.

On Talleyrand's part, his purpose in going to Erfurt was to unite humiliated and discontented Europe—Prussia, Austria, Russia—for the decisive moment when Napoleon's power, being on the wane, would yield before armed Europe. In preserving Austria from conquest, in earning her gratitude, Talleyrand saw the key of the arch assured.

The Czar's plans and ambitions coincided with those of Talleyrand; they were, however, on a grander scale. Alexander I, esteemed to be timid, hesitating, irresolute before the danger of Napoleon's ambitions, found himself armed with courage, and with the subtle Russian power of dissembling his policy. His Majesty felt that he must disengage himself from his promises made at Tilsit, and must prevent Austria being destroyed that she might be reserved as an ally for the eventual coalition of Europe against France.

When the Emperor ordered Talleyrand to prepare a treaty "which will satisfy Alexander—which above all else shall be directed against England, and in which I shall be at ease, in regard to everything else"—"Etre à son aise!" —"Le gêner" was Talleyrand's thought—and hinder his Emperor, in his plans and projects, he most successfully did, during the coming six years. It was to be a success crowned with the Czar's aid; but the great *coup* was Talleyrand's—the diplomatic feat which, in 1814, put the crown of France on a Bourbon King's head and exiled "Bonaparte" to Elba.

Napoleon's explosions of anger, his stinging insults before a full Court, were dangerous methods to indulge in, with such a man and such a character as was Talleyrand.

The Emperor forgot to remember that Talleyrand was no weakling King of Prussia who could bend the knee— nor a King of Spain, who could be trapped.

I committed a great mistake [he said, later]: as I had driven him [Talleyrand] to the point he had reached of discontent, I should either have shut him up, or have kept him always beside me. He could not escape the temptation to avenge himself; a mind as acute as his could not but foresee the approach of the Bourbons—that they alone could assure the success of his vengeance.

This clear perception of the effects of his own ungovernable anger, came too late to the greatest living genius of the day.

PORTRAIT OF TALLEYRAND
Taken after the Council of Erfurt, by Prud'hon

Talleyrand, on his part, "nursed his rancor, watched all that was going on, took pains to know everything, worked to aggravate embarrassing situations, without compromising himself too much, and held himself in readiness to strike the last blows."

It was in such a spirit that the Emperor and his ex-Minister went to meet the kings of the earth.

VII

Before Talleyrand's departure from Nantes, Napoleon avowed to Talleyrand his imperialistic designs. "I wish my journey to be brilliant. . . . It seems to me we have not any very aristocratic names: I must have some. . . ." To Rémusat he said: "I must have a play—send for Dazincourt—is he not the director? I wish to astonish Germany by my splendor."

The scenes which were to be set at Erfurt, by Napoleon, were carefully planned and on a spectacular basis. The eyes of the world and of future ages were to be fixed on the meeting of the two sovereigns of the world. When the news came to Erfurt that the Czar of all the Russias was at Weimar, "Napoleon, followed by his aides-de-camp in full dress, rode up to meet him. When within sight of each other, the two sovereigns rushed to each other's arms, in the most friendly fashion."

The narrow streets of Erfurt were crowded with Napoleon's marshals, generals and officers, whose jewelled orders and gold embroidered uniforms lit up the little city's old house façades. Through the larger garden-trimmed thoroughfares, princesses and duchesses trailed their brocaded gowns.

At night, at the play, Napoleon sat between his conquered vassal kings and grand dukes, assisting at his own apotheosis, while behind him were the sixty odd other grandees you may find named in Talleyrand's *Mémoires*, "and I have not named them all," he added. Two uncrowned kings, whose fame has outlasted the Prussian dynasty, were among the Conqueror's guests—they were Goëthe and Wieland.

"It will not do you any harm to see some good French tragedies," was Napoleon's advice to the genius of Germany, whom he honored with a long discourse.

On Sunday, at the church at the top of the long hill, the same multitude, on their knees, would be praying each one for that which hate and envy, malice and treachery had warmed into passionate life.

On the first visit the Czar paid to Napoleon, when His Majesty introduced Talleyrand, Alexander said: "He is an old acquaintance—I am delighted to see him again. I had hoped he would be of our party."

VIII

The very night of Talleyrand's arrival at Erfurt, he began his artful spinning of the web of intrigue. Had Napoleon known what momentous projects were to be formulated with what tragic results to his own fortunes, in the meetings held over certain tea-cups, he would have devoted his energies to more fruitful results than dazzling the Czar with his splendor.

Talleyrand had paid a visit to an old friend, the Princesse de Turn et Taxis, the evening of his arrival. The Czar was announced. His Majesty expressed his pleasure at meeting his "old acquaintance." On requesting the Princess to give him a cup of tea, the Czar said she should give

him one, "every evening after the Play." Every evening
thereafter, Talleyrand held, with the Emperor of Russia,
the most informal and most charming of tête-à-têtes.
Talleyrand, with the tact and finesse of which he was master, talked to the Czar, indeed, "that language that suits
him," as Napoleon had commanded. Approaching Alexander with an apparent indifference to the weighty matters
in the affairs of nations to be decided, Talleyrand at first
talked frivolities. From touching lightly on light matters,
there was a more trenchant note struck when Talleyrand
thought the time ripe to say: "If I had not seen Monsieur
Vincent to-day—I should have believed the interview at
Erfurt was purely a pleasure party."[1] "What did M.
Vincent say?" The door being opened to allow Talleyrand
to pass on the very word *he* had come to Erfurt to say he
answered, softly "very reasonable things, Sire, for he hopes
your Majesty will not allow himself to be dragged by the
Emperor into issuing menacing measures, or at least offensive ones, towards Austria. And if your Majesty permits
me to say so, I have the same desire." This was Talleyrand's plan—the one he had not confided to his Emperor,
at Nantes. Such were his methods, the most subtle, the
most insinuating. In erecting a screen—Austria's representative or another—and using such, in a voice as soft
as a cooing dove to venture to thrust one's face forward to
deliver words which were to strike at the very foundations
of Napoleon's prodigious fortunes, such was Talleyrand's
way of pushing his ends. The next evening Talleyrand
had no need of a screen. The conversation being continued, Talleyrand struck a more pointed, a pathetic note.

[1] Monsieur Vincent was the Austrian envoy—no Austrian Minister having been
sent to Erfurt.

"Sire—what are you doing here? It is for you to save Europe." And daring all, he added:

You will only succeed in so doing in holding your own against Napoleon. The people of France are civilized, her sovereign is not; the sovereign of Russia is civilized, his people are not; it is then the duty of the sovereign of Russia to become the ally of the French people. The Rhine, the Alps, the Pyrenees are France's conquests. The rest is the Emperor's conquest for which the people do not care.

No argument for sustaining Austria's, cause, against Napoleon, could be more forcibly presented. For it was "the rest" which was essential to Russia's ambitions: the Allies would unite to crush Napoleon—once he had conquered Europe, and once the Rhine passed, France would be crushed in her turn—"vanquished, ravished, disorganized—decapitated—out to the most ancient limits."

Such was the language talked, insinuated rather, to the Czar—the language "that suited him," by Napoleon's trusted negotiator.

Lady Blennerhassett records Metternich's "insinuations," to the effect that as early as 1809 Talleyrand contemplated a change of régime. This was, presumably, premature. Intrigues were on foot; certain meetings in Passy, at the house of the Duchesse de Duras, a year or more before Talleyrand became "the King-maker" of the Bourbon Restauration in 1814, were held. After the Russian disaster, Talleyrand's dictum "c'est le commencement de la fin" being born of his own conviction, he was not one to remain idle with the upturning of all Europe as a certainty. Talleyrand has been accused of treachery towards Napoleon, not only during the interviews he held with the

PORTRAIT OF TALLEYRAND AS AMBASSADOR
By Julien

Czar, but in his plotting with Fouché, before the Erfurt meeting.

IX

It was at Erfurt, among so many other fateful projects, that the word *divorce* was first pronounced before Talleyrand. "He tried to speak to me, he wanted to say something than that which he did say," was Talleyrand's version of his learning, from the Emperor, of his intention for the safety of France—of Europe—of divorcing Josephine, to re-marry and to continue, through the birth of an heir, the Napoleonic dynasty. The Czar had a daughter. A Russian Princess as Empress of France—was such a throne not high enough? There were plays within plays and dramas outside of theatrical boards being enacted at Erfurt.

On October 5th the two sovereigns had had one of their long secret sessions. The Czar, who now felt himself to be sustained in his views by Talleyrand, had shown a new spirit. His consent to any of Napoleon's proposals was halting, illusive. "I've done nothing . . . I haven't advanced a step," the Emperor confessed to Talleyrand. The latter attempted to reassure his sovereign: "On the contrary, I consider your Majesty has accomplished a great deal since he came here, for the Emperor Alexander is completely under your charm." "He shows it to you —you are his dupe. If he loves me so much—why doesn't he sign?" Sorel well says: "Napoleon saw clearly enough, yet he yielded. He was also a dupe, but a willing one." Alexander had, Napoleon thought, all but acquiesced when he had broached the subject of the marriage. It was at Weimar that the Emperor had first touched, tentatively, on the great project. The Czar smiled his suave smile; he had appeared to consent. Napoleon saw only what he wished to see in the amiable smile. Talleyrand was instructed to push matters. "My destiny and the peace of France demand it," said Napoleon, authoritatively.

Talleyrand's interview with the Czar can only be described as perfidious in its deliberate treachery. Ostensibly serving his sovereign, he betrayed him. His own words condemn him, in more blasting fashion than can any censure:

I confess [he recounts] that I feared for Europe the forming of another alliance between France and Russia. From my point of view the idea of this alliance should be sufficiently admitted to satisfy Napoleon, and yet that there should be certain reserves which would render it difficult. All the art I believed I must practise with the Emperor Alexander was useless. At the first word he understood me and he understood exactly what I wished to say.

The Dowager Empress of Russia's possible refusal to such a marriage was the convenient "difficulty" the Czar could proffer, as a reason for the whole question to be deferred until his return to Russia. When the matter came to be discussed in Paris, Alexander now knew he had an ally: Talleyrand saw as clearly as did His Majesty the danger of such a "nightmare" as the Russian marriage becoming a possibility.

Talleyrand had definitely ranged himself on the side of Europe, in this battle of the Emperor for world supremacy.

He no longer believed in the magic of the star. He had noted its paling after, and even during, the war with Prussia. Napoleon's vaulting ambitions surely marked him for a fall. Alexander the Persian, the really Great—Cæsar— Louis XIV—had any one of the great Conquerors completed their work—attained to the summit of their dreams? Talleyrand, after Tilsit, believed that Napoleon had reached the summit of *his* power. Europe, half vanquished as it was, would end in an alliance with Russia and England to combat such monstrous designs as were the rosy visions of world supremacy which floated before Napoleon's fascinated gaze.

The time was ripe for wise men and for subjects to pierce such veils. Talleyrand realized to the full his own precarious situation. He must ride two steeds—or fall. Since the Emperor could not do without him—kept him in reserve —must call upon him in difficult moments, he would accept to act a part so useful for watching, at first hand, the future developments of the great drama. Yet the part of wisdom was to plan for one's future. Europe, in the end, and England, would be mightier than one man's genius. Who— what would come after? The Bourbons?—a Regency? Whatever was to come, it behooved a statesman to be on the side of power—to believe in Europe's revenge—and to work for it.

Talleyrand may well have seen, with his clear vision, the imperative need of peace, for both France and Europe; even the peasants, throughout France, after every fresh victory, were crying "Peace!—let us have done with wars!"

Between the Emperor and Talleyrand, therefore, a wide divergence in regard to France's future was slowly forming. Napoleon had arrived at the apogee of his power. Talleyrand had need of the Emperor, not only as the purveyor of place and fortune, but also to further his ends, and those were now more and more centred on his plan of slowly undermining the power Napoleon's victories had won.

X

Such was the part Talleyrand played in the years following his open treachery to Napoleon, at Erfurt.

Talleyrand judged that the interest of France, the interest of Europe, his own interest, which he confounded with the general interest, demanded that he should defeat the plan Napoleon charged him to execute. His views concerning this matter were already of ancient date, and time was strengthening them. He had the feeling of the march onwards being towards the impossible—of the awful paradox of French policy—since he had served it—since 1797. Step by step, he had observed its development. Submissive, interested, frightened under the Directoire; fascinated, for an instant, then startled under the Consulate. . . . And now he would not go any further; he renounced all hope of stopping his master: he decided to woo, in his manner, the force of things, which sooner or later would throw down the colossus, trying his best that France should not thereby be too greatly dislocated, nor himself too crushed. Europe would triumph, and in order that this triumph should not accomplish this dual disaster, he would make France European, and himself European Minister of France in Europe, of Europe in France.[1]

Talleyrand as a statesman, reasoned thus plausibly. As a man he had even deeper personal motives for thwarting Napoleon. To his conscience, none too tender, he could administer soothing potions. Talleyrand had indeed a "case" against the Emperor. On the 18th Brumaire, he had helped more than any one of the conspirators, to place Bonaparte on the steps of the ladder as First Consul—

[1] See note, p. 457.

the steps which led to the throne. His reward had been—
his enforced marriage. What humiliations had that union
and its consequences brought him! The Emperor had
doubly disgraced him:—he insulted him before his Court,
and only recently had brutally blurted out, at his levée,
the outrageous query relating to his wife's infidelity. To
resent such offenses was but human. To play the part of
betrayer, however, to the sovereign whom he still served;
to be made the depository of Imperial plans; to be entrusted
as negotiator for their fulfillment, and to utilize such knowledge to carry out one's own designs—designs which had
but one clear object in view, which was to oppose, to destroy,
to dethrone the man who was his Emperor—for such actions
there is but one name.

Yet Talleyrand was to see his dream of the future of
France and of Europe come true. He himself was indeed
to be Minister of France, before Europe, and Europe's
Minister in France. The astonishing results of his policy
and the success of his work would almost seem to prove
that he was right in his conviction that Napoleon's world
ambitions "authorized his infidelity."

"Between the Cæsar who believed in universal power,
and the Statesman who believed in a balance of power in
Europe, a great gulf was fixed." Talleyrand's avowal to
Gayern: "Je ne veux pas être le bourreau de l'Europe,"
is revealing; his having recalled the Bourbons to the throne
was born of Talleyrand's far-sighted views of Napoleon's
destructive policy.

Monsieur Thiers' praise of Talleyrand is just: "M. de
Talleyrand had a moral virtue which was to love peace
under a master who loved war and he showed it."[1]

[1] L'Europe et la Rèvolution Française, Albert Sorel, Septième Partie, page 301.

XI

The Czar, at parting from Talleyrand, wished to prove his satisfaction for the services he had rendered him. Talleyrand had repaid the Czar's consideration by favoring the latter's insistent desire to have the provinces of Wallachia and Moldavia revert to Russia. "What can I do for you?" was the kindly monarch's query. Talleyrand lost not a moment in reflection. He knew the facile forgetfulness of a monarch's memory. He had his answer ready. For himself, Talleyrand replied, he had nothing to ask. He caressed, however, a secret hope; his greatest desire was that the hand of the young Princesse Dorothée de Courlande should be given in marriage to his dear nephew —the Comte Edmond de Périgord.

The Czar promised to further the marriage. On his journey to his capital, he turned out of his way to pay a visit to the mother of the young Princess. The ladies were at their estate at Löbekau. In the Czar's suite, Talleyrand had adroitly introduced, as Secretary to the French Ambassador to Russia, the Duc de Vicence, his young nephew, the Comte Edmond de Périgord.

On arriving at the Castle, the Czar found an unexpected and enthusiastic ally in the Duchesse de Courlande. The project of marriage, proposed by her sovereign, came at a timely moment. Her daughter, Dorothée, considered herself as being "bound" to Prince Adam Czartorisky, whose mother opposed the match. Infuriated at such an insolent attitude, the duchess, whose husband—Duc de Courlande —had reigned as sovereign over his duchy, threw herself heart and soul into the Czar's demand for the hand of her daughter; to wed her to as great a name as was that of the de Talleyrand-Périgords was revenge enough. The heart of the duchess herself was in a tumult of joy; she was half in love with the Prince de Bénévent, the man considered as only second to Napoleon, in power and influence.[1]

The marriage was consummated through resort to a base subterfuge. Dorothée having announced she was not only engaged to Prince Czartorisky, she loved him, the duchess assured her that the Prince did not consider the engagement to be binding, since he was shortly to marry a wife of his mother's choosing. Stung to the quick, in her moment of outraged pride, the young Princess gave her consent to wed Comte Edmond de Périgord. A month later, the marriage was celebrated at Frankfort-on-Main, the 22nd of April, 1809.

Talleyrand saw his niece, who was to be the idol of his later years, for the first time at Frankfort, at the time of the sacrificial marriage. He is said to have been "subdued" by her beauty. The latter already possessed the quality of charm which captivates and holds. She had a natural haughty bearing, tempered by grace; her beauty, the brilliance of which seemed centred in eyes of rare power and sensibility, was beauty enhanced by the accent of character.

Dorothée de Courlande's marriage to the young Comte is said to have been one of pure form; yet there were three children born, the living descendants being the Duc de Talleyrand[2] (whose wife is Anna Gould), Boson, duc de Valençay, Comte Jean de Castellane, and the Marquis

---

[1] Napoleon conferred the title of Prince de Bénévent on Talleyrand in 1806. The small estate was in the Papal dominions. After Napoleon's fall, Talleyrand was known as Prince de Talleyrand. On being congratulated by a group of courtiers on his elevation to the rank of Prince, Talleyrand cried: "It is not here you should come—go to Mme. de Talleyrand; women are always pleased to be princesses."

[2] Talleyrand-Périgord-Hélie. duc de et Prince de Sagan.

Boniface—known as "Boni" de Castellane—first husband of Anna Gould.

Talleyrand veils his longing to secure for his nephew union with the greatest heiress in Europe with the unctuous phrase, in his *Mémoires:*

I wished to marry my nephew. It was important that the choice of the wife I was to give him should not arouse the susceptibilities of Napoleon who did not desire that the destiny of a young man bearing one of the great names of France, should escape his influence. . . . He would not have permitted me to make a choice in France, for he reserved for his devoted Generals the great matches which were to be found in that country. I looked abroad.

Dorothée de Courlande, though a Russian subject, was Princess in her own right. Young as she was—in 1808 she was but fifteen and a half—since several years she had been mistress absolute of her time, her life, and her desires. On the death of her father—the famous Duc de Courlande—Dorothée became the richest heiress in Europe.

The precocious intelligence of the young Princess, her unusual independence as a mere child, and the peculiar education she had received, all conjoined to fit her for the great part she was to play in the coming years of her famous uncle's career. For years—until Talleyrand's death, in 1838—their interests, their ambitions, their tastes were the same. The larger part of the Princess's great possessions were in Prussia. With the King as one of her guardians, it was but fitting that as important a youthful heiress should fix her residence in Berlin.

The palace in which the Duchesse de Courlande and her daughter Dorothée lived was a palace with two queens.

Although I lived under the roof with her, I knew too well that the palace belonged to me, that the servants who served me were mine, that it was my money which payed my expenses—and that, in fact, my establishment was entirely separated from hers. . . . I was greatly concerned to render my house agreeable, and never have I received or dispensed the honors of my salon with better grace than when I was thirteen.[1]

This astonishing "young queen" could greet her guests in German, Russian, English, or French.

Courses in philosophy, astronomy and science under an accomplished Italian scholar, l'Abbé Piattoli—a Jesuit, but an unbeliever—completed an education whose breadth was to be developed by Dorothée's cosmopolitan outlook; a Russian subject, she had "reigned" as a Princess in Berlin; through her marriage, she was to become a Frenchwoman, and as a young woman she was to be under the influence of one of the master-minds of Europe. At Berlin, she was received as a playmate to the Heir Apparent, at the Palace, the King of Prussia being her godfather. She had seen the tragedy of the Prussian reign—the devouring sadness of lovely Queen Louise at her failure to soften Napoleon's harsh measures. She had also witnessed royalty in exile, at the dismal court of the Comte de Provence, at Mitau—the Bourbon whom Talleyrand was to make King of France. Such was the training of the gifted woman who was to share in all the glories of Talleyrand's later life —to be to him "amie" in the earlier years of their intimacy, and till his death, friend, confidante, companion and best beloved. Talleyrand's rare good fortune in winning such devotion is proof that in his private life, when he chose, he could grapple to him with hooks of steel, those dear to

[1] *Souvenirs de la Duchesse de Dino.* Comtesse Jean de Castellane. Calman Lévy.

him. To certain men and to almost all women, Talleyrand could show—and feel—a gentleness as rare as it was captivating. There is no quality so subduing as gentleness. And this quality, being interwoven among the many fibres of Talleyrand's curiously mixed nature, was the more all-conquering in being in opposition to his commonly cold indifference.

CHAPTER IV

I

TALLEYRAND was sixty when Napoleon's star was seen to lower on the horizon.

After the Peace signed at Valençay with Spain; after the evacuation of Germany, Poland, and Illyria; after the return of the Pope to Rome, and the Allies' advance towards the Rhine, the Emperor did not need Talleyrand's penetrating insight to fix the outlines of the future. "If I am killed, my succession will not pass now to the King of Rome. From the pass to which things have come, only a Bourbon can succeed me." And he asked numerous questions concerning the character of the Bourbons. [1]

Signals of distress were sent broadcast: he wrote to Louis, "You are no longer King of Holland" [2]; to Joseph: "France is invaded—the whole of Europe is in arms against France —but particularly against me. You are no longer King of Spain."

He had sent a negotiator to Fontainebleau; but the Pope felt the crumbling of the Empire and affirmed he would "treat" with Napoleon at Rome and nowhere else. The former Conqueror of Europe could no longer command, he

---

[1] *Souvenirs de Madame de Coigny.* Conversations.

[2] *Lettres à Louis.*

must accede. In his own family there was rebellion, desertion, betrayal. Metternich's policy was to detach Murat, King of Naples, from Napoleon: it was in Austria's interest to win the "pompous, inflated and infantile" Murat and his wife to turn traitor. Caroline, Napoleon's sister, the most ambitious and the cleverest of the sisters, was an easy prey: Metternich had sent the Comte de Neipperg to play on the responsive chords of Caroline's and Murat's grasping natures. Neipperg was to display the same "qualities of perfidy and of seduction" which won Marie-Louise—Napoleon's wife—to such quick capture on her way to exile.[1]

On January 24 (1814) the Emperor made his final arrangements: his brother Joseph was to watch over his wife and son—incapable as he knew him to be; but Napoleon never liberated himself from the obsession of the age-long tyranny of Joseph's being the head of the family, the old clan tradition.[2]

He named Marie-Louise Regent, with Joseph and the Arch-Chancellor as her Councillors. Masson adds, "at three o'clock in the morning after having burnt his most secret papers he left."[3]

The Emperor was on his way to his last encounter with the armies of the Allies.

II

When the fate of France and of Napoleon was hanging in the balance, during the winter and spring of 1814,

[1] Sorel, *L'Europe et la Révolution Française*, Huitième Partie, 1812–1815.
[2] *Lettres à Joseph*, 4–5–7, 1814.
[3] *Manuscripts de Napoléon*. Napoléon Inconnu, Vol. I, page 38. Frédéric Masson. Paul Ollendorf, 1895.

CHÂTEAU DE ROSNY-SUR-SEINE

By Corot

Musée du Louvre

through some remarkable letters, written in Talleyrand's bad little handwriting as he says himself ("de ma mauvaise petite écriture"), we can follow, step by step, the sweeping drama of the victory of the Coalition forces and of the collapse of the Napoleonic fortunes.

The earlier letters are of a sufficiently tender tone, one rising at times to such impassioned accents as to warrant Madame de Boigne's caustic statement: "I do not know whether it was at this time he ended his affair with the duchess and began his intimacy with the niece." There are outbreaks of rapture and passion, succeeded by graver notes of "respect," "hommages," deep regards." Talleyrand had so many quivers in his amorous bow one can never be sure of their exact character. In any case, it is well known that to the duchess he communicated his inmost thoughts.[1]

In this series of letters, written to the Duchesse de Courlande during the most thrilling experience of Talleyrand's life—when he was practically the head of the Provisional government, when he was the arbiter of Napoleon's fate, when Alexander, Czar of all the Russias, was his house-guest, when his phrase, "the Bourbons represent tradition" put Louis XVIII on the throne of France—day by day Talleyrand's *billets-de-matin* took flight to the Château de Rosny-sur-Seine.

He had sent the Duchesse de Courlande and his niece by marriage together with her children and Charlotte, for safety, to Rosny. The Château, one of Sully's seven châ-

---

[1] Talleyrand's tribute to the duchess, after her death, proved the depth of his affection, if not of his love, for her. The Duchesse de Dino, showing him her mother's portrait, one day, the Prince was seized with an emotion he did not strive to conceal. Brushing away a tear, he said: "I do not think there was ever, on earth, a woman more worthy of being adored."

teaux, is still standing.[1] It was in possession of the de Talleyrand family in 1814.

Through these notes of Talleyrand, notes obviously scratched off between a conference with the Powers, or a rendezvous with an Ambassador, his more intimate nature is revealed as in no other document. They show him preoccupied, under the stress of the most stirring and exciting period of his career, for those who are dearest to him. Solicitous of their comfort, of their health, every line of the letters breathes tenderness, love, ardor and a complete absence of self. The gravest national and international affairs, in all of which he was a prime mover—together with the Czar of Russia—are given a line or two: the burden of the daily little letters is ceaseless interest in arranging meetings or dinners, in seeing that the duchess and "Dorothée," as Talleyrand called his niece by marriage, should have places for the entry of the Comte d'Artois into Paris, or that they should be among his guests to meet the Czar.

A new, a surprisingly tender side of Talleyrand's nature is revealed through these hurriedly written lines. Herein we are led into the secret room of his guarded fortress of

[1] Though much changed the Château has still the aspect of a great house. Sully found his king at the Château after the battle of Ivry. Wounded, having had two horses killed under him, having captured four prisoners, Sully was brought from the Château d'Anet, after the battle, where his wounds were dressed, to Rosny. Together with his four Lignière prisoners, Sully, lover of pomp, was escorted by his grooms, his pages, his master of the horse and by his friends, also wounded. Henri IV between his battles always had time for the hunt; hearing his beloved friend was being carried on a litter, strewn with branches, to his Château, he left the chase in pursuit of his "brother." L'Abbé Thomas records the elaborate speech of the King on meeting Sully, and the accolade which was given with the words: "Et parlant en présence de ces princes, capitaines et grands chevaliers qui sont ici près de moi, vous veux-je embrasser des deux bras, et vous déclare, à leur vue, vrai et franc chevalier." On the same highroad where this historic meeting took place, motorists pass daily, since Rosny-sur-Seine lies between Mantes and Evreux.

defence. The mask the world has known, one fixed upon the features of that colorless face, is lifted. In a careful perusal of these letters, it is difficult to imagine the writer as being the Talleyrand of history, the Talleyrand of artifice, of impenetrable, enigmatic subtlety. Given the milieu in which the letters were written, surprise yields place to amazement. He proves the complex of his enigmatic nature. For here, in these letters, he confounds his detractors. The tender, soft, delicate, surprisingly painstaking side of one of the most interesting of historic characters is presented and in the simplest but most touching of phrases, as a loom weaves pictures of tragedies on tapestried backgrounds.

The First Restoration was really due to the work of Talleyrand. It was the apogee of his success as a master-diplomat and statesman. His Hôtel in the rue Saint-Florentin was the central pivot on which swung the future destinies of France. His master-stroke had been to capture the Czar Alexander I as his house-guest. He had installed his Majesty in the luxurious apartments of the first story of the Hôtel in the rue Saint-Florentin. Talleyrand's army of secretaries, under the indefatigable Laborie, as well as all those who came who were possessed of hopes; those who came laden with plans for saving France; emissaries from foreign courts; intriguers who sought Talleyrand's aid in approaching the Czar; generals and marshals with their clinking swords and heady ambitious projects—all that world which filled the entresol—Talleyrand's quarters—it was in such a whirl of conflicting jealousies, of clamorous ambitions that Talleyrand's notes took flight to Rosny.

III

One follows the varying phases of the dramatic movement of those gravest of hours in France's history through lyrical phrases. "I love you, dear friend, with all my soul—each day there is a stronger reason for loving you." There is bad news January 10th (1814). But though "one torments one's self for those one loves, for one's country, for one's self," still the note ends, "I stop: I can only think of sad things—Adieu—I love you with all my heart." The latter phrase, in the ending of the eighteenth century letters, appears to be used more or less as "yours affectionately" is now in vogue in terminating an epistle. In the letter January 25, 1814, we read:—"I find all things supportable when near you—Vous! Vous! Vous! that is what I love best in all the world"; the outburst takes on the complexion of a warmer hue.

In a dozen of the letters, his care is all for Charlotte. "Kiss Charlotte for me," or "I recommend to you Charlotte; finish her education; let her character be modelled on yours"; or "I thank you for all your goodness to Charlotte; her letters are filled with gratitude to you and to Dorothée," or "I embrace Charlotte." "Charlotte's dinner went off well." "Bring Charlotte up with you." This hard-worked statesman, who confesses his fatigue in "conferences which last all night," can descend to such homely details as "I do not know if cows at Rosny are being requisitioned—mine at Saint-Brice are being taken." Noting in the letter dated *1 Mars, 1814, 1 heure du matin* that "the conference for the armies continues," that "matters are so mixed that the cleverest State news, twenty times a day, is as soon proved to be false," he adds at the end of this, one of the longest of the letters: "I should deeply repent me of my too great caution, if I only thought of myself" (he refers to being separated from the duchess by a distance of fifteen leagues), "but I feared you might be too greatly disturbed in this agitated milieu."

On the 15th of February, 1814, Talleyrand adds to his note, laconically: "The Princes" (the Spanish Princes) "have left Valençay."

Later, on the 15th of March, the Princes had gone; "I await with impatience news of the condition of the Château, which I think will be found to be deplorable."

As the Coalition forces approached Paris, "As Prussian and Russian prisoners enter the city" on February 20 (1814) the Prince states: "We know little of what is happening. We are only somewhat re-assured by the great confidence all have in the Emperor."

While the Prussian and Russian armies were passing the Rhine, January 1st, 1814, Talleyrand wrote January 2nd (1814), "The morning has been less stormy than that of yesterday. . . . Faces were like the weather—a little cold. At dinner, dear friend, we shall see each other. I embrace you and love you with all my soul." On January 3rd he writes: "Towards three o'clock I shall be at Dorothée's. To-day, I am still in (the spirit) of New Years. I love you, dear friend, with all my soul, in hard times as in better days. I press you against my heart, adieu." Again, on the 8th, having written daily since the 3rd, Talleyrand announces, prematurely, the Emperor's departure. "I find the times very dark. The Emperor is said to have left Thursday for Verdun." He did not leave until the 25th. The letter closes with: "I shall go and see you before dinner, at Dorothée's. I love you, dear friend, with all my soul. Each day one discovers one more reason for loving you."

Finally (February 26th, 1814) he can announce:

Dear Friend, there is a question of a suspension of arms. Several parliamentaries have come to the headquarters of the Emperor. If there is no suspension of arms, peace will necessarily follow. . . . There is so little agreement in this coalition that each one appears to act in a sense contrary to the others.

On March 1st, he writes: "events go so quickly that 24 hours change the scene."

As the Allied armies approach Paris, Talleyrand suggests that the duchess and her family take refuge at Honfleur "as, if Paris is attacked, men of all parties will rush to the Châteaux which they presume have not yet been visited." The drama takes on a more sombre tone. It has been decided, in council, that the Empress Marie-Louise and the King of Rome should leave Paris and go to Tours. Talleyrand names the suite which are to accompany Her Majesty. As Grand Chamberlain, his post demanded he should be among those who were to follow the Empress. The Prince does not mention in these letters the clever subterfuge by means of which he managed to remain in Paris. Calling for his finest coach, the Prince set out for the barrier gate of Neuilly. On being asked by the Police Guard for his passport, Talleyrand replied he had none. "But it is His Excellency the Grand Chamberlain, Prince de Talleyrand," one of the attendants cried out: "Let His Excellency pass," was loudly voiced by the Police. "Not at all," calmly announced the Emperor's Grand Chamberlain, "I must conform, like any other subject, to the orders given." And his own orders were to return to the rue Saint-Florentin.

The note on the 29th of March, 1814, states, laconically: "The Empress left with the persons whom I named. Many baggage wagons follow. She goes first to Rambouillet. I'll go and see you this morning . . . I embrace you." Talleyrand complains bitterly, in subsequent letters, of the lack of news. "It is shameful that in such circumstances we should be so little informed as we are and as I am."

Presently comes the great news. Prince Schwarzenberg, Commander-in-Chief of the Allied forces, sends his historic Proclamation to be placarded on the walls of Paris. The most important sentence in the Proclamation reads: "The Allied Sovereigns seek in good faith a salutary authority for France. . . ." In the Czar Alexander's Proclamation of the same date, the people of Paris read: "The Allied Sovereigns proclaim: that they will not treat with Napoleon Buonaparte nor with any of his family. . . ." April 2nd the next Proclamation reads:

The 2nd of April, the Senate had pronounced the fall of Napoleon and of his family and had created a provisional government thus composed.

> Le Prince de Talleyrand
> L'Abbé de Montesquiou
> Le duc de Dolberg
> Le général Comte de Beurnonville
> Le Comte de Jaucourt.

On the very day Talleyrand is made virtually the head of this Provisional Government—the "King of Paris"—he writes to the Duchesse de Courlande:

Dear friend, at midnight there will be at the Saint-Germain

Post, a detachment of Cossacks who will escort Dorothée [to Paris]. To arrive she must take the route of Aubergenville, Flin, Fresnes—straight to Saint-Germain. Read my letter carefully, for the other road is not a good one. Je vous aime de toute mon âme.

Vaulabelle, in his *Histoire des Deux Restaurations:* "The elegant and beautiful Comtesse de Périgord (since Duchesse de Dino) rode during the evening seated *astradelle* behind a Cossack." This was, of course, a pure invention. Talleyrand sent the detachment of Cossacks to ensure his niece's safety.

With the return of the Bourbons, Talleyrand's work was ended. On the 30th of May, 1814, he signs the Treaty of Peace.

I have finished my peace with the four great powers—at four o'clock peace was signed; it is a very good (peace)—made on the basis of the greatest equality and, in spite of France's (soil) being covered by foreigners, my friends and you above all others, you should be pleased with me who loves you with all my soul.

Care is taken that the ladies shall miss none of the historic events in Paris. On the 11th of April "the Comte d'Artois arrives to-morrow—you will have your seats," he writes. "At the *carrefour* de Bondy" the Comte d'Artois was to make his triumphal entrance into Paris, preceding his brother Louis XVIII. The Comte d'Artois was to be harangued by "Son Altesse Sérénissime le Prince de Talleyrand" at the barrier of Paris, before the first Bourbon to enter Paris since the Revolution bent his knee, on the following day, to render thanks at Nôtre Dame. The dinners given by Talleyrand to the Czar were presided over by

Madame Edmond de Périgord. "Come and dine with Dorothée—the Emperor dines." Three days later, April 23rd, 1814. "I have finished my armistice. It was a good thing." Dinners with "Kings and Emperors" after the entry of the King Louis XVIII into Paris, end with "I shall do better than that—for I shall dine with you in the little entresol of the Princesse."[1]

[1] Alexander I, during his sojourn in Paris, said one day: "When I entered the capital of France, my Allies and I, our only aim was to overthrow the despotism of Napoleon: we desired to leave the choice to France to choose the government which might suit her. I became Talleyrand's guest: he held Napoleon II in one hand and the Bourbons in the other; he opened the hand he wished to open." *Souvenirs Intimes Album Perdu.* Henri Delatouche, p. 104. E. Desster, Editeur, 1870.

CHAPTER V

WITH the marriage of the brilliant young heiress Dorothée de Courlande with Comte Edmond de Périgord, the fate of Madame de Talleyrand, among that of other mortals, was virtually decided at the Council of Erfurt. In the rich complexity of Madame de Dino's character, one force was paramount—that of aristocratic distinction. Talleyrand possessed the same intolerance toward those inferior to him, in social status, in birth, or in breeding. He, however, driven by passion, could yield to the weakness of being dominated by such beauty as had made the courtesan Madame Grand, the Princesse de Talleyrand.

Madame de Talleyrand was neither so ignorant nor as stupid as some Memoirs of the time assert her as being. Madame de Chastenay, in her *Mémoires*, describes her as being neither above nor below the average intelligence of average women. Michaud states in his *Histoire Universelle*, in his famous article on Talleyrand, that Talleyrand's wife was neither a nonentity nor a fool. She was "not born" and she had had a shady past; she was therefore a target for the ridicule of Talleyrand's aristocratic friends.

Thirteen years after his marriage, Talleyrand's patience

Valençay ce 4 Juin 1816

Mille graces de votre lettre de 2. j'ai besoin de
savoir que chaque jour me portera une
preuve de votre affection. Les deux grosses
lettres que vous m'avez envoyées sont de M. de C.
l'une est de 18 mai, plus fraîche de six jours
que celle dont je vous ai parlé dans mes
précédents numéros ; l'autre n'est qu'une
enveloppe contenant un portrait pour lequel
j'avais écrit. — Il saisit l'occasion de
me l'envoyer pour répéter dans une
grande lettre beaucoup des mêmes choses
désagréables que sa dernière épître contenait.
Du reste le portrait renvoyé m'est fort
agréable, de plus il m'assure généreusement
de son plus profond oubli et ajoute qu'il
tâche d'effacer de son esprit le souvenir
des humiliations qu'il a souffertes et
qui sont chaque jour encore renouvelées

FACSIMILE LETTER OF THE DUCHESS DE DINO

was to be rewarded. Time worked its usual miracle. His deliverance came through a not unusual medium—through a beautiful woman, through the Comtesse de Péri-gord, not yet Duchesse de Dino. Having been "presented to all Europe" at the Congress of Vienna, she had found that her power, after her triumphant success as the head of Prince de Talleyrand's salon, was paramount. Having conquered her place, she proposed to keep it. Refusing to recognize the Princesse de Talleyrand as her aunt, she displayed a tact, a skill, and a resourcefulness, in making the break between Talleyrand and his wife not only inevitable, but lasting.

During Napoleon's tragic throw with the "dice of God," during the Hundred Days, the Princesse de Talleyrand sought a refuge in England. Talleyrand was then at the Council of Vienna. On his return to Paris, in 1815, between the unrelenting enmity of his niece, Dorothée, and the tone of the Court of Louis XVIII which had taken on *ultra* Bourbon airs, Talleyrand was face to face with what he most disliked—a domestic decision. Either he must break with his wife, or, possibly, lose the close companionship of one who had become the dearest object of his existence.

The Comtesse Edmond was quite willing to continue to receive for her uncle in the salons of the Hôtel rue Saint-Florentin, as she had at Vienna. Only, there must be no divided sovereignty. The countess refused even to meet "the parvenu," as she called the Prince de Talleyrand's wife. The break became inevitable.

Talleyrand's mind had been made up for him. He was at last to be delivered from an intolerable burden. He found an amiable envoy in the person of the French Ambassador to London, the Marquis d'Osmond, whom he had chosen to represent France. The Marquis was "to bring her (Madame de Talleyrand) to reason." His task was made the easier by the Princesse de Bénévent—or de Talleyrand, as the lady delighted to be called—accepting her husband's conditions. Madame de Talleyrand could read the writing on the wall; she accepted her fate. In her place, which she had never filled, was enthroned a young and beautiful Princess—one who reigned by right of birth and intellectual ascendency. What power had she, the questionably legitimate wife, one whose marriage to an ex-Bishop had never been recognized by the Church,—what weapons could she wield before such an array of charms and capacity? Her mirror reflected a now reddened face, a figure grown stout and heavy—for "l'âge prend tout." Age, however, did not dim that curious power of discernment which had always been the torch to light difficult situations in Catherine Worlée Grand Talleyrand's adventurous life. She knew her Talleyrand. In an interview with Madame d' Osmond she stated:

I knew the place held by Madame Edmond at M. de Talleyrand's, in Vienna: I did not wish to be a witness of it. This sensitiveness prevented my joining him, as I should have done. . . . Had I gone to Vienna instead of going to London, M. de Talleyrand would have been forced to receive me. I know him well, he would have welcomed me with perfect courtesy. The more he would have been put out, the less would he have shown it. On the contrary, he would have been charming to me.

This avowal, by Madame de Boigne, in her *Récits d'une Tante*, proves that Madame de Talleyrand was far from being as stupid as her detractors assert. Her

Caricature of Talleyrand published in 1815

Caricature of Talleyrand published in 1815
From a color print

VIVE LES NOTABLES!

VIVE LA LIBERTÉ

VIVE LE 1er CONSUL!

VIVE L'EMPEREUR!

VIVE!

VIVE le Roi!

DÉDIÉ À MM^{rs}

LES CHEVALIERS DE LA GIROUETTE.

Se trouve dans l'ell^e du 15 avr^l 1815. & se vend au Bureau du Petit Journal

Caricature sur Talleyrand publiée par le Nain Jaune
en 1815.

knowledge of Talleyrand's manner of concealing annoyance or anger reveals her finesse.

Talleyrand was in a tremor of fear lest, at any moment, Madame might appear at his Hôtel. "Madame Edmond," however, although as far away from Paris as was Valençay, had a will-power which could traverse space. From a distance she could enforce arguments which might have been painful to express.

The famous letter of "le petit Marmousin"—Madame de Périgord's pet name, doubtless given her by Talleyrand —is an unconscious revelation of the character of the writer. The original letter, now yellow with age, whose pages are pasted together, is written in the careless, all-but-illegible handwriting of the period when thought was so clear, wit unexcelled in point and pungency, and such a detail as chirography was considered to be a negligible accomplishment.[1]

In this revealing letter, Madame de Périgord alternately caresses her uncle; she is very solicitous of his sensibilities:—"I will venture to give you a piece of advice which will spare you a public correspondence which will be distasteful to you,"—and later on, she gives a cat-like thrust. She is perfectly mistress of her woman's art of forcible insistence.

I have given a great deal of thought to the answer which must be given to Madame de Talleyrand; more and more she makes me fear lest she make a sudden entrance into your room. She will begin by telling you that she will remain only a few hours—but that she desires to have an explanation with you, in the hope of drawing some more money from you.

[1] This interesting autograph letter is in the possession of the author.

And the clever writer goes on to state that as "money is the motive power of all Mme. de Talleyrand's actions," she suggests that her uncle should send a certain M. Perrey with a letter of credit, but that not a *sou* should be paid unless she remained in England. The advice was only in part followed.

According to the terms of the agreement, Talleyrand was to pay his wife 30,000 francs income. She was to reside at a house he gave her at Pont-de-Sains, near Paris.

Eventually, Madame de Talleyrand made the dreaded visit to the Hôtel in the rue Saint-Florentin. A few days later, the King, Louis XVIII, asked his Grand Chamberlain, at his levée, maliciously, "if it were true that the Princess had returned?" Talleyrand's stinging reply was: "Nothing could be truer, Sire; it seems that I also must have my 20th of March." (He referred to the day when Louis XVIII was forced to fly from Paris, before Napoleon's victorious march up from the South, after leaving Elba.)

Life in common, however, between the Prince and his wife was never renewed. She was vaguely known to be, for a certain time, in a Villa at Neuilly. Finally she took a small house in the rue de Lille. She lived on memories, all that was left her. Few were the friends who sought her society. Occasionally some artists and poets would enliven her dull evenings. Thomas Moore, on a visit to Paris, had seen the Talleyrand arms on cushions, and on the walls— even on a clock. The device *Ré que Dieu* blazoned forth the survival of the puerile pride of the much-talked-of, of the former Madame Grand "whose beauty could best be compared to that of Mme. Récamier as she had preserved an infantile grace in face and figure."

CHAPTER VI

I

DURING his eleven years' reign, Louis XVIII proved the ingratitude of kings. His indebtedness to Talleyrand for influencing the decision of the Czar in his favor was either too heavy a load for a Bourbon to carry, or the favoritism shown to Monsieur Decazes and to Madame du Cayla made a Talleyrand unnecessary. After a few short months as Minister of Foreign Affairs, Talleyrand was relegated to the post of Grand Chamberlain.

Lady Morgan in 1816, who saw Talleyrand at a dramatic representation at the Tuileries seated, resplendent in his costume as Grand Chamberlain to Louis XVIII, behind the King's arm-chair, gives the following portrait of the Prince:

I had often seen this celebrated personage who will figure in the history of the future; I had seen him at court, at public fêtes, at the marriage of a Prince, under the dome of Notre Dame, in the most tragic as in the most comical scenes; but I had always seen him the same, cold, immovable, neither indifferent nor absorbed, always impassive, no changeful color varying the livid pallor of his face, no expression revealing his impenetrable character. Was he dead, was he living? one could doubt, at times; . . . by what one saw, one could hazard the conjecture that one recognized in him the enigmatic sphinx who had said: "la parole a été donné á l'homme pour cacher sa pensée." Neither the tenderest love, nor the most devoted friendship, nor community of interests could force that countenance to speak, one which can only be compared to a book written in a dead language.[1]

Yet, as a man, he was lovable. In the intimacy of his home life, which the Duchesse de Dino and her family made a source of continuous delight, Talleyrand won confidence, love, devotion. As a statesman he was unrivalled in his powers of discernment and in capacity for subtle adjustment of difficulties. As a patriot, he carried the interests of France above sectional partisan views. Ancestral pride of birth was his earliest, last and longest, perhaps his only superstition. To the last he held high above all other achievements, the pride of having "been born." Even the King on whose head he had placed a crown, must treat him as an equal. The Talleyrand which all his later portraits reveal, proves what such a life—what such a soul bereft of a spiritual life or lofty moral aims, can present. It is the face of a cynic, of one completely disillusioned; neither power nor all his success, nor his fame had brought him content. The acid of disillusion had burrowed deep. He made, too late, the |discovery that character outbalances the highest gifts. His intelligence, in his later years, was a searchlight, pitilessly revealing the soul's moral blight. There was no need of Talleyrand's bending the knee in the confessional: he had confessed himself. Hence he wore a mask. "Tout ce qui est profond," says Nietzsche, "a besoin d'un masque." (He who is deep, needs a masque.) Portrait painters are pitiless when they are masters of their

[1] *La France:* par Lady Morgan. T. 11, page 26.

PORTRAIT OF TALLEYRAND
Ary Scheffer
The Musée de Chantilly

art. They tear the mask aside and reveal the inner man—
the workings of the soul which sculpture the face.

Sainte-Beuve presents such a portrait—with *his* consummate art. He represents Talleyrand as still possessing a
"powerful organization" in spite of his growing debility.

He had a masculine voice, profound, coming from a hollow,
though from principle and as a matter of good taste he did not
indulge in bursts of laughter. With his long cane which resembled
a crutch, and with which from time to time he struck at the iron
of the instrument which supported his bad leg—he presented
himself imperiously. Under bristling eyebrows his grey eyes
(shone) in a face marked with blotches—a small face whose
size was further diminished by his masses of hair, the chin lost
in a huge soft cravat, which enveloped it—a cravat, recalling
the Incroyables and the négligé of the Directoire; the retroussé
nose insolently pointed upwards, a lower lip projecting upon the
upper one—a lip which had an indefinably scornful expression—
one which was affixed to the two corners of the mouth.

II

During the six years' reign of Charles X (the Comte
d'Artois) Talleyrand's virtual retreat from active political
life began. In the year 1832, after Louis-Philippe had succeeded Charles X, Talleyrand's zeal in promoting Louis-
Philippe's accession to the throne was rewarded by his
being appointed Ambassador to the Court of St. James.
During the two years of his Ambassadorship, the early
dream he had caressed in his young manhood came true:
he was able to achieve a rapprochement between France
and England;—his and Mirabeau's hope was crowned,
after forty-three years, with success.

A curious and interesting State document reveals the
somewhat asonishing figures of the sums paid to Talleyrand

during the two years spent at his post: 300,000 francs, in those days, represented an almost princely fortune. Was this the usual sum paid to Ambassadors? Or was the amount increased to prove the King's gratitude that, at last, an Orleans Prince was ruling France?

Talleyrand's reflections may well have been tinged at times with the gall of regret—if not of remorse. He may have excused the excesses of his youth: the spirit of the age had set the pace of the world of his earlier day. His concessions to another spirit of the time were the deeper, biting acid. The hounds of calumny which had loosened their foul cries—cries which had never ceased to pursue each rise of his fortune—these yelps of rage and abuse had causes for their hate. As Bishop he had shown too irreverent an attitude; as the officiating priest of the Champ de Mars Fête he was doubly culpable—avowedly a sceptic, he yet had celebrated the Mass. There was that unpleasant affair of his speculations in State funds;—it is true the transaction had paved the way for his future fortunes.

It was an unlucky turn of fate that had kept him in his post as Minister of Foreign Affairs, when the Duc d'Enghien was murdered;—had he really played too high in that intrigue? If he had, there were so many qualifying reasons for his vague suggestions to Bonaparte;—yet, as he remembered his arguments relating to the danger of the Duke's being allowed to continue his own intrigues—why did Bonaparte precipitate matters? The arguments presented had been, really, very vague. Yet Bonaparte, true to his Corsican ideas of fidelity, had laid the plan of the murder on him. The world had accepted the verdict. He would go down in history as co-partner in that crime with the real offender.

Such reflections—and so many other spectres of the past —reflections which were never—could never—be confessed, wrote their betraying signs on Talleyrand's face and soul. The deep lines, the wrinkles, the cynical curves on lip and the saddened, bitter expression one notes on the pallid face deliver up to us, through the painter's art, what these useless concessions had graven on Talleyrand's visage. Useless— for the Revolution had outpaced him, in its Terror-sweeping atrocities; and had he not really shared Bonaparte's fears, at the time, of Bourbon intrigues, the Duc d'Enghien would have lived.

III

It was on his return from London after resigning his post as Ambassador, that Talleyrand settled down to the contentment of old age. And a rare and peaceful end of his varied and tumultuous life was his.

Talleyrand was never more completely master of himself and of circumstance than in these his last years. He possessed all the requirements which, in combination, promote felicity. He was in full mental vigor; he was rich; his reign in his salon, in Paris, was still that of the much-sought and the courted *grand seigneur*. He was completely happy in his home-life: in Madame de Dino's devotion—in her whose mind and character furnished every element of charm, he enjoyed a companionship rare at any age. It was even vouchsafed to him to have a last, and an exquisitely pure and tender passion. He had fallen in love with one of the loveliest of creatures—with his grand-niece Pauline, the daughter of the Duchesse de Dino. She inherited her mother's incomparable grace and charm of manner; and her soul was clear as crystal, and in that purity Talleyrand seemed to bathe as in cleansing waters. Were Pauline absent from Valençay, he was miserable: "the house is quite empty when you are not here. . . . I find it difficult to get used to not having you in the house—dear Minette"—the pet name of the young girl. His letters, in the absence of his "guardian angel"—as he repeatedly called Pauline—are a revelation of Talleyrand's powers of love, of his deep and yearning tenderness. In his letters to the young girl he proves a singular ingenuity in treating subjects which would interest and please a youthful mind: from Paris he writes that "the Arc de Triomphe is superb, it is one hundred and fifty-two feet high, a hundred and thirty-eight feet wide, and sixty-eight feet deep."

There were gay interludes in the more serious life at Valençay. Feasts were given on the master's Saints' days—St.-Maurice and St.-Charles must both be honored. Vaudevilles, plays such as *Les Femmes Savantes*, were acted by the duchess and the younger members of the family; visits of poets and of old friends—of Royer Collard, the Duc de Noailles, and Decazes, and the Prince de Laval— were numerous. On one occasion, the pomp and splendor of the days when the imprisoned Spanish Princes were holding their Court, in exile, at Valençay were revived. The Duc d'Orleans' visit to the Château was made memorable by martial music, by a review of the village national guard, and by a ball.

In these closing years of his long life, Talleyrand received several times a week, in his palace, in Paris. Social potentate that he was, up to the hour of his death, he held his court. His sway was untouched by the accidents of place or post. His undisputed reign outlasted governments and kings. He had lived under five Bourbon Kings, the Consulate and the Empire of Napoleon, and under eight forms of government. The few of his chosen friends still alive clung to the lips of one whose wit and wisdom, whose air and manner of an older day, and whose memory, burdened with the experience of his fabulous career, had become the one link that made the past seem real. To members of the younger generation, to be admitted to the famous salon, in the rue Saint-Florentin, was to gaze upon a legendary fame endowed with life. In his huge fauteuil, tapping his infirm leg with its iron brace, with the cane which was as much a part of his toilet as were his powdered locks, whether the still keen grey-blue eyes were veiled, or were suddenly opened wide to greet a friend, the Prince de Talleyrand was still the Prince—gracious, suave, apparently indifferent, gracefully indolent. Yet would he come suddenly to quickened life. To impress Monsieur de Montalivet, a young man, already cited as among the clever men of his generation, Talleyrand's voice took on its old sonorous, grave, male note:

Your father was an Imperialist, and you owe me a grudge because you think I abandoned the Emperor. I have always remained faithful to anyone only so long as they remained faithful to themselves, according to the rule of common sense. But if you will judge all my actions according to this great rule, you will be forced to recognize that I have been extraordinarily consistent and where will you find a creature vile enough, or a citizen sufficiently unworthy to submit his intelligence or to sacrifice his country to an individual, whatever he may be, however well born or highly gifted he may be?

The whole theory of Talleyrand's policy is embraced—is avowed—in the above statement. His hearer, and others of the younger generation, were to listen to Talleyrand's expositions of sixty years' experience. He exerted himself to charm such.

IV

When Talleyrand was in Paris, in his so-called Palace of the rue Saint-Florentin, he was to learn of his wife's serious illness, in December, 1835.

Madame de Dino entered her uncle's room in the early morning—furtively. She dreaded to deliver the news whose effects, she feared, might bring about disastrous consequences. Talleyrand had had an attack of illness a short while before. He was now nearly eighty-two years of age. With infinite precautions, a month before, the duchess had stated, in the course of a conversation, that she had heard rumors of Mme. de Talleyrand's illness. To her surprise her uncle had taken the news quite calmly. He interested himself in writing out the names of those who must be apprised of her death, as soon as she had passed away—of the mourning to be assumed—the latter no inconsiderable affair, in a great household, with all the family as well as the liveries of servants—even the trappings of horses and harnesses to be thought of.

If long ago all feeling of his former passion had lost its vibrant touch, one other passion was as strong as ever. He had no thought of concealing it: he coolly stated the pleasure he would experience in no longer having to pay the Princess's yearly stipend. There is no atrophy so complete as the deadness of a dead love. It is as though nature took its revenge on man's having substituted sentiment for nature's own more primitive purpose.

10 décembre rochecotte

c'est par vous, mon cher rolland que
j'ai appris le malheur que vous venez d'éprouver
en suis véritablement peiné. les chagrins.
les personnes avec lesquelles on a traversé la
vie deviennent des malheurs personnels pour
trouver quelque consolation il faut souvent
un aux belles qualités de celui qu'on
regrette, et votre gendre passoit pour être un
une excellent
vous êtes bien bon de vous être occupé
ma petite commission, je vous en remercie,
mille amitiés
p. de talleyrand

FACSIMILE OF LETTER OF TALLEYRAND

On learning the news of his ex-wife's death, Talleyrand's calm amazed even the duchess.

"This greatly simplifies my position," was his only comment.

Two years later, these memorable words were to find their full and complete explanation.

V

In these four years before his death, Talleyrand could measure the place posterity must inevitably assign to him. In resigning himself to the life, at eighty, of old age, in full strength of his mental vigor, as a general recalls his victories, the Prince could survey his diplomatic triumphs;— triumphs which were so inextricably interwoven with the history of France.

In these four years of his semi-seclusion, light is poured on one determining feature animating his whole career. As in the revolutionary days he stood for law, order and constitutional authority, so in the years of comparative quiet vouchsafed him, before the end he proved he was to bow to authority—to the authority against which he had rebelled. He was to make his peace with Rome. This act is in itself enlightening; it lays bare the secret springs which worked the whole outward machinery of Talleyrand's political acts. He was a traditionalist—an aristocrat to the fibre of his being. A *grand seigneur* does not die a sceptic; the sacramental oils of the last offices are as essential to the dignified end of a great man and Prince as are armorial bearings on one's tomb. "It is true that there is no sentiment less aristocratic than that of incredulity," was one of Talleyrand's *mots*.

The manner of the aged statesman's approaches to Rome

was in consonance with his former thoughtful, unhurried ways in matters of grave state decisions.

In the quiet of Valençay, his beloved retreat, he had long hours in which to meditate and to plan the great act—the act which was to be, from his point of view, the fitting climax to his end. He began his gradual approaches to Rome through the higher clergy at Valençay. He entertained prelates and bishops. A year before his death, in the year 1837, the marriage of the Duc d'Orleans had drawn him to Fontainebleau. While at court he was reminded of the visit of the Archbishop of Bourges; Monseigneur was to pass through Valençay to administer confirmation. Greatly fêted, Madame de Maintenon's apartment at Versailles having been placed at his disposal, the King and the Princes assiduous in their attentions, yet Talleyrand had but one thought: he must be at Valençay to receive the Archbishop. With his beloved grand-niece Pauline beside him, he made his adieux, and was swept onwards to greet his friend and guest.

In these last days and hours, he who had been dictator of a Kingdom was humbled, was softened; as in months before the end he had envisaged the act—the final act of submission—at the last he showed himself willing to accept —to yield.

Yet to the last, he must dictate—and dictate imperiously—the day, the very hour of his capitulation. He had written out a very long and somewhat obscure political and religious declaration. In it he makes the astounding statement that though "I ceased to be her Minister [of the Church] I never ceased to be her son." The Archbishop of Paris after reading the somewhat verbose document wrote to Mme. de Dino that more full and

Portrait of Talleyrand as Ambassador
By Boilly

complete admissions of repentance, on several points, were required. Another paper was prepared by the Abbé Dupanloup, one destined to be presented in tragic circumstances.

In Talleyrand's Will, dated 1836, he gives a résumé of the guiding principles which he followed in his political career. In conformity with his wish, the Will was read to his family and friends. In this his Will he states he wishes to die in the Roman Apostolic Church; that he "never ceased to be one of her sons."

Above all else, the Prince declares, he had placed first (*il a préféré*) the interests of France. . . . He acquits himself of the reproach of having betrayed Napoleon; if he abandoned him it was when he recognized that he could no longer embrace, as he had hitherto, the Emperor and France in the same affection: this (desertion) was not accomplished without keen sorrow, for he owed to him almost all his fortune; he pledges his heirs never to forget this and to repeat the same to their children and to those who come after them in order that if, at any time, a man bearing the name of Bonaparte should be in want, they will hasten to his aid to give help and assistance.

In answer to those who reproach him with having successively served all governments, he declares he felt no scruple in so doing, and that he acted in this matter, guided by the principle that in whatever situation a country may have found itself, there was always a way of trying to help it to a better state, and that it was the duty of a statesman to apply himself to give such help.[1]

[1] The above is an extract from the *Moniteur* of May 27, 1838, page 1412, cited by Sir Henry Lytton Bulwer in his *Essay on Talleyrand*, page 365. The above is translated from the French edition of Monsieur Georges Perrot. C. Reinwold, Paris, 1868.

The remark that "I never ceased to be her son" proves a fact often contested, that Talleyrand's reconciliation with the Church, just before his death, had not been a matter of sudden impulse or one accepted from pressure of family influence; on the contrary, with that sense of order and method so conspicuous as traits of his character, the Prince had long meditated the manner of his approaching Rome. The deliberation with which he prepared the preliminary steps was in accordance with his whole political career. His first step towards a renewal of intercourse, of a personal, more intimate nature, with the Church, was characteristic. It took the form of an invitation to dinner. He invited Abbé Dupanloup to dine with him. The Prince had heard much good of the young priest; he was the confessor of his youthful grand-niece—Pauline—daughter of the Duchesse de Dino. Abbé Dupanloup and l'Abbé Lacordaire were, at that time, the most eloquent and most zealous among the younger clergy in Paris. Their devotion, their untiring energy, their talents as preachers, had won them the admiration of their order; Abbé Dupanloup's work as Superior in the Convent of Saint-Nicholas was cited as an example to others.

On hearing l'Abbé Dupanloup's name repeatedly mentioned with enthusiasm by the young girl—by Pauline—he had remarked, "I should rather like to know this Abbé Dupanloup." The latter did not at once see fit to accept the invitation tendered him in her uncle's name, by the Duchesse de Dino.

In the remarkable narrative given by Abbé Dupanloup of his relations with M. de Talleyrand, the priest states: "After due consideration I thought it best to refuse the honor he wished to confer upon me." The excuse given was the Abbé's retired life and his multiform duties. The Prince's comment on the Abbé's refusal is enlightening. "I am surprised at this refusal: they told me Abbé Dupanloup was a clever man: if it were true, he does not understand his profession. He would have understood the importance of his getting an entry into this house. *Il ne connait pas son métier.*" If the priest had not seized the importance of approaching so famous a man as was the great statesman, the purpose Talleyrand had in mind was sufficiently urgent for him to repeat the invitation. This time it was accepted.

VI

In a long and remarkable letter, which is known as "The Narrative by Abbé Dupanloup of his relations with Monsieur de Talleyrand," written in February, 1838, literature as well as history is enriched by a work of inestimable value. In this narrative the last days and hours of Talleyrand are rendered with graphic simplicity and precision. The whole story of his reconciliation with the Church, of the elaborate formalities necessary for the acceptance by Rome, of his repentance and submission, can be followed step by step. The impression produced on the Abbé, of the Prince de Talleyrand in his old age, of his striking personality, of his vigor of mind, of his still incomparable charm of manner, is only surpassed by the detailed exactitude with which every phase of Talleyrand's final acts of contrition and humility are recorded. A close study of these pages arouses curious reflection. Whatever may be one's conclusions, there can be but one opinion as to the desire to impress on one the spirit of truth, of deep

sincerity, and the touching piety which this record of the
Prince's reconciliation with his Church affirms.

On presenting himself at the entresol of the rue Saint-
Florentin—an entresol of historic interest as having been
the residence of the Czar, in 1814, as Talleyrand's guest—
the Abbé confesses he went to the dinner with a heavy
heart.   In the letter written by the Abbé to a distinguished
friend in Italy, a narrative written in September, 1838,
which contains a long résumé of Talleyrand's last days and
hours, the priest states:

I was seriously annoyed and even sad at finding myself condemned . . . to leave my pious retreat for Monsieur de Talleyrand's house. . . . Like the rest of the world I had not much
belief in Prince de Talleyrand's good faith. I knew his ability
and my own lack of it, and found all this very embarrassing, yet
my conscience and the duty of my ministry obliged me to go
through with it. . . . In this state I crossed the threshold of
Monsieur de Talleyrand's house, putting my trust in God. . . .
At last I entered.   The Prince received me with the utmost kindness: he was seated in one of those high, wide arm-chairs which
was his favorite seat. He dominated the whole room with his
high glance and his rare, witty, and strongly marked, but always
courteous speech.   No king could be more a king in his immediate circle than was M. de Talleyrand in his salon.

The Abbé goes on to state:

though conversation was at first rather cold and halting, and,
though outwardly respectful, I felt nothing but deep compassion
at the sight of this old man, without the least confusion or embarrassment. I heard later that he affected most people in that
way, and that of the distinguished men of the Imperial Court he
alone sometimes embarrassed the Emperor by his wit, by the

loftiness, promptness and soundness of his views, the coolness and vivacity of his repartees, and by his unfailing calm.

Dupanloup explains his own complete sense of independence in his further prolonged intercourse with so redoubtable a character. From his ignorance of "many things in his life, I did not fully appreciate his great political career. . . . I only knew the bad side of his life. I had always been accustomed to look upon him as a great sinner and a source of grave scandal."

And now this devout Abbé was seated at the "great sinner's table."

There were twenty people at the dinner. Conversation soon grew animated; but imagine my surprise: I had expected propriety, but it was more than that, it was quite religious, all the time. Monsieur de Talleyrand spoke a great deal of sermons and preachers of the present day: he quoted many fine passages and beautiful expressions from preachers he had heard in his youth.

Such was the easy, subtle and gracious way in which Talleyrand prepared his reception into the bosom of the Church he had offended. If a certain place, now somewhat discredited, is said to be paved with good intentions, so accomplished a courtier arranged, by his facile art, and by the simplest of methods, his own deliberate intention of securing access to the opposite, to the more difficult and holier road.

How sincere was Talleyrand's final repentance of his errors and sins? How deep was his confession of religious faith—of his submission to the Holy Father—of his confessed horror of the scandal his life had given the world and the Church—he an anointed Bishop renouncing his vows—

marrying, against all the laws of the Church? Modern
agnostics have scoffed at his sincerity. Protestants consider the Catholic Church opens wide, sometimes too wide
arms to dying penitents, whose lives refute their tremulous
confession: intolerant critics echo Sainte-Beuve's scathing
condemnation.

Science perhaps, and an appreciation of the profound influence of tradition, on French minds and character, may
help to probe the mystery of Talleyrand's reconciliation
with his Church. John Fiske's scientific discovery of the
reversal to type, after fifty or sixty years of age, explains
many of the later acts of men which have puzzled posterity.

For long centuries, Talleyrand's ancestors had been
Catholic; from generation to generation they had been
known as devoted adherents of the cult. His mother was
devout. He himself had passed all of his early years in a
Catholic Seminary. Though never a priest at heart, hat-
ing his enforced vocation, a priest he had been, performing
the offices of the Church as such. In all his later life,
through all the success and fame his talents had brought
him—whatever his place, at all times he had shown a
marked affection for the sons of the Church, coming to
the aid of poor priests, during the Revolution, seeking the
honor of having Bishops and holy men at his house, as
guests.

In old age, the earlier impress of heredity, of tradition,
of youthful influences become directing forces. They are
the voices heard in the silent recesses of the soul. All about
him, these voices found living tongues—ardent, tearful,
appealing, in those who surrounded him. The Duchesse
de Dino and her daughter—Pauline—were exercising, daily,
their pressure on the aged statesman. Pauline's piety, her

youthful enthusiasm for her faith and for her Confessor was a living reminder of the serenity and of the elevating influences that come to those who live through Christ. Madame de Dino's influence in drawing her uncle to the Church was due to more complex motives than was her young daughter's simple faith. The duchess appreciated, to the full, the historic place Talleyrand was to occupy in the annals of France, as in those of the Church; to die unreconciled to the Holy Father would blacken his memory with an even deeper reproach than had certain acts of his life. Once his peace made with Rome, much would be forgiven him: he would receive the consolations and be sustained by the touching ceremonies which the Church administers to the dying. Talleyrand, in a word, would die a Christian death and would be buried with the rites and the pomp accorded to a son of the Holy Roman Catholic Church.

VII

Those not of the faith will be struck, in perusing these moving pages, by the formalities observed in the process of Talleyrand's making a Christian end. After such a life as the ex-Bishop had led, Rome must be approached, not only with due humility, but with all the precision and ecclesiastical form demanded by as portentous a recantation as was the Prince's. Two years before his death, the Archbishop of Paris had been in correspondence with the Sovereign Pontiff concerning Talleyrand's great age and the inevitable approaching end. Monseigneur de Quélen had been true to his promise,—he had carefully, prayerfully, watched over Talleyrand's soul, thus fulfilling the request of his predecessor, Talleyrand's uncle. All arrangements had been made with the Archbishop as early as 1836. His Holiness had authorized the Archbishop "to inform the person in question of the Holy Father's grief and affliction and the consolation he would derive from his return."

On his part, in the winter of 1838, after coming in closer contact with l'Abbé Dupanloup, the Prince handed the Abbé an exceedingly interesting document. It was his recantation, one which was presented in a curious form. In this manifestation of his revealed and earnest desire for reconciliation with the Church, Talleyrand made a number of extraordinary admissions. Written a fortnight before his death, he gave a review of his entire life. It summed up the great political and religious phases in which he had been a political figure. Touching on his political career he states "That in the course of this Revolution which has lasted fifty years [the phrase is his] Society has changed its form and its masters ten times," and Monsieur de Talleyrand claimed that his patriotism consisted in combating the Revolution under every form of government and every master. He called himself "the greatest defender of the French Monarchy." Of Protestantism he said it was "the enemy of unity," and called it "a dangerous auxiliary of the Republic amongst us."

In turning to his own more intimate personal life he declared himself to be "a child of the Church," and his readiness to condemn the Constitutional Schism, if the Church demands it. In touching on certain errors of conduct he stated "The respect I owe to the memory of those who gave me life, does not prohibit me from saying that all my youth was directed towards a profession for which I was not born." The Abbé felicitously notes the delicacy with which this burning injustice was expressed.

Pce Talleyrand
Sketches by D'Orsay

TALLEYRAND AS AN OLD MAN

A sketch by Comte d'Orsay

The document was not considered to be sufficiently satisfactory to be sent to Rome. The phrase relating to the sacerdotal character with which he had been invested— "Dispensed by the Venerable Pius VI"—was not entirely correct; he had never been freed from his vows; the Pope's dispensation was accorded simply to his non-exercise of his ecclesiastical functions. In the Will to which Talleyrand had added the avowal that he desired to "die in the Roman, Catholic, and Apostolic Church" he had changed the sentence, "Dispensed by the Venerable Pius VI, I was free," to "I thought I was free." This admission could not be accepted as sufficient; the Prince de Talleyrand had deeply offended the Church by the grave errors committed in his past life and by his marriage. A full, complete and satisfactory statement, in the ecclesiastical form necessary for as important a document, alone could be acceptable to the Holy Father. This was accepted by Talleyrand as being admissible. The Prince gave much thought and care to the re-writing of the important paper.

For months before his death, l'Abbé Dupanloup was assiduous in his devotion to the Prince. Sacred books were brought to him; prolonged conversations were becoming a daily necessity between the youthful priest and the statesman who was preparing his treaty with God.

VIII

Before the end brought to a climax the reconciliation with Rome, Talleyrand had decided to make his bow to the living and, in a manner chosen characteristically by him— to posterity. He announced to the Institut de France, of which he was made a member in 1795, that he would be pleased to pronounce, in person, a eulogy of the Comte

Reinhard, a close friend, who had often served under him. There was a tie between them which had made mutual understanding rest on a sure base: both had received an ecclesiastical education. In enumerating Reinhard's talents and capacities, Monsieur de Talleyrand in his discourse sums up in review, the different branches of the diplomatic service, and "of the duties which are attached to each one of these branches, and it [the discourse] is a kind of legacy left by the orator to that profession of which he was for so long a time, its ornament."[1]

This last public appearance of the Prince de Talleyrand was attended with something of the solemnity and the pomp which acclaims royalty. The Hall of the Institute was crowded to repletion. There were no ladies, the audience being largely composed of leading political and literary men, and of distinguished members of the diplomatic corps. When "The Prince" was announced, the whole audience rose to their feet. Unable to mount the stairs of the building, two servants in livery had carried him to the door. The Prince made an effective entrance, leaning on the arm of Monsieur Mignet, perpetual secretary. The President, Monsieur Droz, on asking Talleyrand if he would not take time for a little rest, before speaking, was answered in that deep, grave voice which filled the Hall, that he preferred to begin his speech at once. His opening sentence was— *"Messieurs: J'étais en Amérique lorsque l'on eut la bonté de me nommer membre de L'Institut"*; and for over an hour, the aged statesman continued to hold his audience captive by the noble simplicity of the style in which the discourse was written, by the precision of its thought, and by cer-

[1] *Essai sur Talleyrand*, Sir Henry Lytton Bulwer, translated by M. Georges Perrot, 1868, Paris. Vol. I, page 345.

tain daring allusions and assertions. His statement that "diplomacy is not a science of ruse and of duplicity"; and that Monsieur Reinhard's earlier studies in theology "had given him a force and a suppleness" which characterized his diplomatic career, provoked loud applause.

The ovation which followed the termination of the eulogy well proved, as Sainte-Beuve was constrained to admit, "Ah! on that day one saw clearly what power is wielded by a masterly mind in French Society, above all when it is enhanced by birth"—and, or it would not have been Sainte-Beuve, he must add, casting his last stone at the man whom he anathematized; "and—must one say it? when he is decorated with all the vices."

IX

Two short months after this, Talleyrand's last triumphant success, "one which crowned his career," he was attacked by his mortal illness. A chill was followed by fever. Soon, the doctors diagnosed a gangrenous carbuncle. The pain was intense. An operation was pronounced to be urgent. It was long and cruel. There was no anæsthetic in that day to dull prolonged agony. "Do you know you are hurting me a good deal?" was the Prince's sole remark. The operation being terminated, he insisted on being taken to the salon, where, still suffering, in high fever, he continued to converse; he recounted, with amused relish, that one of the physicians—Doctor Marjolin—put his dog who was barking at his calves, during the operation, out of the room. This is his last recorded pleasantry.

The condition of the sick man soon gave rise to the liveliest fears. Not only was the suffering intense, but the

Prince's waning strength awakened alarm, consternation and even despair in the hearts of the entire household. Masters and servants were convulsed with sorrow, and fear. L'Abbé Dupanloup having been hastily summoned, the priest was immediately admitted to the sick room. He found "this old man, this dying Bishop" as the Abbé names him in his recital of the long agony, greatly changed. The face was shrunken, the eyes drooping—seemingly already void of life. The voice, however, in greeting the priest, was still clear and strong. "Monsieur L'Abbé—it is a long time since we saw each other—I am very ill." Ill unto death though he was, no time now must be lost in fufilling that grave, momentous duty which devolved on the priest. The document which had been so carefully prepared, which the Holy Father was anxiously awaiting, which the Archbishop of Paris was breathlessly expecting, —this, Talleyrand's full and complete recantation, had not been signed. The priest went on to the performance of his task with the ardor of one who knew he was fighting an enemy who had already marked the stricken sinner before him with his fatal sign. "I did not wait," the priest confesses. . . . "I presented perhaps with too much haste the thoughts which his sad comments on his grave condition had inspired." Dupanloup made his approach to the great question with abrupt directness. He wished to reach the two pages which, modified by the Prince, in several points, had been sent to the Archbishop of Paris—unsigned.

He answered me, on the spot, with a firmness which surprised me, and I confess it, which almost discouraged me. "Monsieur L'Abbé, I had carefully reflected on what I had written. I put everything into those two pages, and those who know how they should be read, will find in them all that is necessary."

Embarrassed by such an explicit rejoinder, yet the Abbé found the courage to urge the sufferer before him to acknowledge that though "those who knew would indeed find in the pages all that was essential—but you cannot ignore the fact that in this country, there are many people who do not know how to read"; and with subtle art, the priest added, "Permit me to add, people will be very difficult toward you: they will not wish to read well. . . ."

The sick man saw the force of such argument. "Give it to me—I will read it myself," and the pages were read, carefully.

This concession was only the beginning of the battle which was to be waged about the sick-bed. Under the canopy of the wide bed, beneath its silken curtains and stately ornamental plumes, for two days and nights Talleyrand sat, at times on the edge of the bed propped by pillows and supported by two lackeys who, every two hours, were relieved by two others. The lower part of his body was paralyzed; the pain from his wound was too excruciating to permit of his assuming a recumbent position. If sleep came, to dull the agony of the pain his shrunken lower limbs and the recent operation caused him, Talleyrand's head sank upon his chest. When he awoke, it was to find about him the anxious faces, to hear the pleading voices of those dearest to him, convulsed, it is true with sorrow, but voices also laden with the anguish of fear. Hour by hour, the forces of life were lessening. Yet, the document—the all important pages which were to prove the Prince's pious recantation of his errors and sincere repentance of his sins—this document was still unsigned. As the pulse-beats marked the declining vigor, as prolonged palpitations awakened the anguished fears of priest and of the family lest the end might come, as the heart ceased its heightened pulsations, priest and family were possessed by one dominating thought. Pressure must be exercised: and it must come in a form which would so touch the dying sufferer that the appeal could not be refused. Pauline—Talleyrand's "guardian angel" as he lovingly called his saintly grand-niece— was to wring the promise which neither the pleading of the priest nor of the duchess had effected. "My daughter," the duchess said to Pauline, "you know what you owe to the love of your uncle—this is the moment for you to prove to him your gratitude." The young girl, bursting into tears, knelt at the feet of the priest, to implore his blessing. Passing into the sick room, the door closed. When it opened, Pauline could announce that she brought with her the longed-for promise. Her uncle would see the Abbé—the final arrangements for the solemn act would be concluded.

To the last, however, Talleyrand made the terms of his complete submission to Rome bear the impress of his cool, inflexible independence of character. He would sign— yes—but the signature was not to be made until the following morning, "between five and six o'clock." Why at that hour? Conjectures were many and conflicting, the sanest supposition being that the early hour was chosen when the friends, the frivolous worldlings and the unbelieving political sceptics who crowded the salons during the day and evenings, would be absent.

The decision of the Prince not to sign until early morning awakened fresh and agonizing fears. Would he last until then? The night was peaceful. As the fateful hours approached, those who were to witness the solemn act met in silence. "We talked by signs," writes the Abbé, in his touching record of the moving scene.

The Prince, lifting his head, seeming to come to renewed life from out of a deep sleep, opened his eyes, looking each of those surrounding him full in the face. His morning salutation was kindly, warmed with feeling. "What time is it?" was his next utterance. "It is six o'clock," said one of those about the bedside. The priest, however, could not allow, at such a moment, even a pious falsehood to remain unrebuked. "Prince—it is only five o'clock." "Good," replied the Prince. And, "dominating others as he dominated himself," he remained, silent— waiting.

At the door of the apartment, a white-veiled, white-robed vision appeared. It was Marie de Talleyrand, the daughter of the mysterious Charlotte, the Baronne de Talleyrand. The young girl was to make her first communion. The child knelt at the bedside—at Talleyrand's feet. "Uncle, I ask your benediction." "My child, I wish you much happiness in your life, and if I can in any way contribute to that end, I will do it with all my heart." "By giving her your blessing you can," said the Duchesse de Dino. Extending his hands, the dying man gave the child his blessing. All were in tears.

Six o'clock now struck. The last great scene in the life of the Prince who held the stage to the very last hour of his astonishing career, was to be enacted. Supported by his nephew, the Duc de Valençay, and by Monsieur de Bacourt, the Duchesse de Dino and Pauline kneeling at his feet; in the salon, peering over a screen, Monsieur le Duc de Poix, M. Molé, M. de Barante, M. E. Royer-Collard, and M. de la Rochefoucauld—the witnesses to the signing— the Prince—after a clear reading of the Act by the Duchesse de Dino, who now stood beside the drooping figure—Prince de Talleyrand having received the declaration, in a firm hand, without a moment's hesitation signed,

CHARLES-MAURICE PRINCE DE TALLEYRAND

The date chosen by the Prince to be affixed to the document was the 10th March—the week in which he had read his eulogy of Comte Reinhard, before the Institut. There was to be no misconception possible, in the declaration of the Prince's full and complete desire of his intention to recant, and to make his submission to Rome. The date chosen was to prove him to be in full possession of his intellectual faculties.

At eight o'clock still another scene was to succeed the deeply moving religious act. The whole hôtel was in a state of commotion.

The King was announced.

The Prince had fallen into a state of lethargy. Great difficulty was experienced in awakening him, in making him comprehend the importance of the coming visit. Once fully alive to the ceremonious nature of the moment, the Prince rallied his forces. As the King entered the room, followed by the Princesse Adelaïde, seated on the edge of the bed, lifting his head, Talleyrand was once more the perfect courtier. It was the King who was visibly embarrassed. In a low, trembling voice, His Majesty said, "I am distressed to see you in such suffering." "Sire, you have come to assist at the sufferings of a dying man—and those who care for him can have but one desire, to see them soon end," answered the Prince in his old, deep, sonorous voice—tones so strikingly in contrast to his shrunken shape.

As the King was about to bring the brief and painful

visit to a close, the Prince was again the Grand Chamberlain who remembered the etiquette of Courts: he named all those present to His Majesty—not omitting to name his old valet whom he had chosen to represent the other servants at his bedside. Slowly raising himself, with infinite pain, Talleyrand made his last and fitting bow to earthly pride and pomp of circumstance.

"Sire, our house has received an honor to-day worthy to be inscribed in our annals, an honor which my successors will remember with pride and gratitude."

One last glimpse of the more worldly Talleyrand is given us before the curtain drops. In the salon, close to the chamber of death, the élite of Parisian society was gathered. There were old friends, grey-haired men, talking softly, and sadly, in one corner. In another, younger men, of the modern world, were waiting for the end—gleaners of news and gossip. On a certain sofa sat two beauties of the day, their wide skirts billowing about them; and below, at their feet, on cushions lolled some of their adorers, gaily chattering, as though at a comedy rather than assisting at the tragic end of a great Frenchman.

At a certain moment, near four o'clock of the afternoon, a servant, with swollen eyes, red from weeping, tiptoed to the doctor, who was waiting. Conversation stopped. The rustle of death's wings silenced even the foolish. The doctor, rushing to the open door, was the signal for all present to follow him—to crowd about the entrance.

Still seated on the edge of the bed, still upheld by the arms of his secretary, a sudden concentration of the forces of life—of that vigor that had animated his whole being, seemed to have returned to the Prince. Casting his eyes about the crowded room, with an amazingly brisk movement shaking his grey locks away to gain a better view, he surveyed the friends and the world who had assembled to see him die, as he had lived—honored by royal pomp, in full court.

When the end came, the fluttering, as of a flight of birds, filled salons and the stairways. The crowd of friends, of sceptics, of political detractors, of indifferent social puppets took wing, each rushing to tell Paris how the last act had been played—to a finish.

The Church remained to perform its pious offices. After the signing of the recantation, the exultant pious Abbé Dupanloup hastened to convey the pious document to the waiting—to the praying Archbishop.

After the King's visit, the Prince's confession was given. The last sanctifying acts of purification, the prayers for the dying, were rendered.

In the chamber of death a priest, one hired for the occasion, recited prayers for the repose of the soul the Church had re-won. The funeral was attended by all the pomp and splendor then still possible in days when great funeral ceremonies were at once a spectacle and an honorary tribute. Prince de Talleyrand was laid at rest in the Chapel at Valençay. Of those who had knelt at his feet, who had wept oceans of tears, of those numerous members of his family who had received riches and pleasures at his hands, and who were to inherit his great fortune, not one followed him to Valençay.

His world, however, had not yet done with him. "I can never forgive him for denying the eighteenth century"— cried one of those who was outraged at certain clauses in the Prince's recantation.

"*Il est mort en homme qui sait vivre,*" was a more

kindly verdict. And history? History has not yet said its last word, since in Talleyrand's mind and character there were the eternal elements which dispute with the God-like in man that baser nature which has given us the story of the Fall.

ADDENDA

I

THE history of the debt to the French government in money incurred by the Americans in their War of Independence is fully given in two remarkably clear and impartial articles contributed by the celebrated French historian Alphonse Aulard to the *Revue de Paris* published successively May 15th and June 1, 1925.[1]

The following résumé of his article is a literal translation of his valuable record.

Aid in money sent to the American revolutionaries was given before any accredited American emissary came to Versailles.

In May (2nd), 1776, Vergennes, French Minister of Foreign Affairs, requested the King to authorize the "furnishing of one million livres for the English Colonies." Vergennes added that this sum would be passed "aux Américains, de la main à la main, par M. de Montaudoin, armateur de Nantes," who having a treaty with Franklin, exported ammunitions of war, (an act) tolerated by the French government. The fear of England's knowledge of this sum given to Beaumarchais was openly acknowledged by the Minister to the King.

This first million was a gift, pure and simple. The King gave

---

[1] "*La Dette Américaine.*" Alphonse Aulard. *Revue de Paris*, May 15 and June 1, 1925.

outright another two millions—three millions having therefore
been given before the entrance of France into the war, and before
the Treaties between France and America were signed.

There followed a series of gifts and loans.

In 1781 another gift of six millions was forwarded. A generous gift of Louis XVI.

After the Treaties had been signed came the following loans:

In 1778, 3 millions of livres.
In 1779, 1 million paid in quarterly payments.
In 1780, 5 millions paid in five payments.

In 1781 the French King borrowed from Holland five millions
of florins, equivalent to ten millions of livres. This was to enable the King to furnish the monies required by the American
armies to continue the war. This sum was eventually loaned in
entirety to the Americans.

In 1782–3, another loan was negotiated of three millions.

In all, these loans amounted to 28 millions. In 1783 another
loan of six millions was awarded, and still three millions more
were due to certain "particuliers en France," and another million
to the *Fermiers Généraux*.

Thirty-eight millions therefore was owing, at the end of the
war, by the American government to France or Frenchmen.[1]

In all of these gifts and loans the King Louis XVI "was more
disposed to generosity than was his Minister, Vergennes, for at
that time the King was much more under the influence of his
people than was his Minister. If the Ministers of Louis XVI
saw in the insurrection (of the Americans) a serious embarrassment for England—an opportunity perhaps to avenge the humiliation of 1763—the French public, more enlightened, was moved by
nobler sentiments. A quickened sympathy was aroused for these
courageous insurgents who hated despotism, who wished to live
as free men or die." It was at this time that Lafayette avowed
"que son cœur fut enrôlé"—that his heart was enrolled.

Throughout the whole transactions of France's inestimable
help rendered to the American cause, Louis XVI showed himself
as a generous and even enthusiastic friend to the American people.

[1] See French estimate, page 143.

He was continually in conflict with his Minister Vergennes who, as a perfervid Royalist, saw with fear and dismay the triumph of Republican principles.

It is a positive and uncontrovertible fact that not only would the colonies never have been able to gain their independence had it not been for Louis XVI's courageous generosity, but it is equally undeniable that the gifts and loans, given to the Americans, accelerated the ruin of French finances. This ruin was intensified by the enormous expenses incurred by French participation in our war. Monsieur Aulard well says: "If the American Revolution prepared the French Revolution by its example and the contagion of its principles, it also prepared it (the French Revolution) by the disastrous situations into which the assistance given by France plunged French finances. Had such assistance not been given, the *ancien régime* would perhaps have lasted a few years longer."

II

Silas Deane, a political agent sent by the American Congress to France, in the first days of July, 1776, was commissioned to buy arms, clothing and ammunition for 25,000 men, and 100 cannon. Mention is made in the Archives of the Ministère des Affaires Etrangères, Paris, in a document entitled *Décisions du Roi*, 1760–1792 (7th December, 1780) under the entry *Affaires de l'Amérique* that Deane had received a *secours extraordinaire*, of 24,000 livres drawn from the secret funds.

Talleyrand's demand for a gift—though also extraordinary, and in this case excessive—found its precedent in Deane's acceptance of 24,000 livres from the King's privy purse.[1]

[1] Page 385.

BIBLIOGRAPHY

HISTORY

Histoire de France. J. Michelet. 7 Vols.

Histoire de France. Louis Madelin. 1 Vol. Paris.

Marie-Antoinette Dauphine. Pierre de Nohlac. 1 Vol. Paris, 1900.

La Reine Marie-Antoinette. Pierre de Nohlac. Paris, 1900.

Les Massacres de Septembre. J. Lenôtre. 1 Vol. Paris, 1907.

La Captivité et la Mort de Marie-Antoinette. J. Lenôtre.

Histoire de Dix Ans—1830–1840. 5 Vols. Louis Blanc. Paris.

La Mère Dieu et Robespierre. J. Lenôtre. 1926. Perrin.

History of European Morals. 2 Vols. William Edward Hartpole Lecky, M.A. D. Appleton & Co., New York. 1884.

La Révolution. Louis Madelin. 1 Vol. Paris, 1911.

Louis XIV. Histoire de France Contemporaine. Ed. Ernest Lavisse. Hachette.

Louis XV. Histoire de France Contemporaine. Ed. Ernest Lavisse. Hachette.

L'Ancien Régime. Henri Taine. Paris, 1887.

L'Ancien Régime. Funck-Brentano. 1926. Fayard.

Histoire de France Contemporaine. Ernest Lavisse.

La Révolution. Tome Premier (1789–1792), par P. Sagnac.

La Révolution. Tome Second (1792–1799), par G. Pariset.

L'Europe et la Révolution Française. Albert Sorel. 8 Vols. Paris, 1922.

Essais d'Histoire et de Critique. Albert Sorel. 1 Vol. Paris, 1883.

The French Revolution. Thomas Carlyle. London, 1887.

Pitt. Lord Rosebery. 1 Vol. Chapter III.

Mirabeau. Louis Barthou. 1 Vol. Paris, 1920.

Monseigneur Dupanloup. Emile Faguet.

Lauzun. Duc de la Force. 1913. Hachette.

La Mission de Talleyrand à Londres en 1792. Les Lettres à Lord Lansdowne. 1 Vol. G. Pallain. Paris, 1889.

La Mission de Talleyrand sous le Directoire. 1 Vol. G. Pallain. Paris, 1891.

Correspondance inédite du Prince de Talleyrand et du Roi Louis XVIII pendant le Congrès de Vienne. 1 Vol. G. Pallain. Paris, 1881.

Napoleon, from the Tuileries to St. Helena. Louis Etienne St.-Denis. Translated from the French and Notes by Frank Hunter Potter. New York and London, 1922.

Napoleon Intime. Arthur Lévy.

Histoire Politique et Privée de Charles-Maurice Talleyrand. L. J. Michaud. 1 Vol. 1853. Paris.

Madame de Staël. 1 Vol. Joseph Turquan. Emile-Paul Frères. 1926.

L'Album Perdu—M. de Talleyrand. Par Henri Delatouche. 1 Vol. Recueilli par Amédée Pichon. E. Dentu. 1870.

George III and Charles James Fox. G. Trevelyan. 2 Vols.

Histoire de France. Jacques Bainville. 1 Vol. Arthème Fayard. Paris.

The Greatest American, Alexander Hamilton. Arthur Hendrick Vandenberg. 1 Vol. G. P. Putnam's Sons. New York and London, 1921.

The Italian Renaissance in England. 1 Vol. Louis Einstein. Columbia University Press. New York, 1903.

Historic New York. Edited by Maud Wilder Goodwin. G. P. Putnam's Sons. New York.

BIOGRAPHY—ESSAYS—SOCIETY

Nouveaux Lundis. Monsieur de Talleyrand. Vol. 12. Sainte-Beuve. Paris.

Portraits de Femmes. C. A. Sainte-Beuve. 1 Vol. Paris, 1886.

Le Prince de Bénévent. Monsieur de Lanzac de Laborie. *La Revue Hebdomadaire.* April 7, 1917.

Ninon de Lanclos. Emile Magne. Paris, 1925. Emile-Paul.

Les ci-devant Nobles et la Révolution. La Comte G. Mareschal de Bièvre. Paris, 1914.

Le Duc de Lauzun. Gaston Maugras. Paris, 1911.

La Cour de Lunéville. Gaston Maugras. Paris, 1911.

Le Comte Molé. Ed. Marquis de Noailles. 3 Vols. Paris, 1924.

Journal d'Une Femme de Cinquante Ans. Marquise de la Tour du Pin. 2 Vols. Paris, 1920.

Les Femmes de l'Emigration. I and II Series. Joseph Turquan. Paris, 1911.

Souvenirs. Madame Vigée-Lebrun. 2 Vols. Paris, 1869.

The Chevelier de Boufflers. Nesta H. Webster. London, 1920.

Essai sur Talleyrand. Sir Henry Lytton Bulwer. Traduit de l'anglais par M. Georges Perrot. 1 Vol. E. Reinwald. 1868. Paris.

Scènes et Portraits. Duc de Saint-Simon. 2 Vols. Perrin & Cie. 1903.

Talleyrand et la Société Française. Frédéric Lolie. Emile-Paul. 1910.

The Secret of the Coup d'Etat. Introduction by the Earl of Kerry, and a Study by Philip Guedalla. G. P. Putnam's Sons, New York and London.

Madame de Maintenon. Madame Saint-André Taillandier. 1 Vol. Paris, 1923.

Le Duc de Morny. Marcel Boulenger. Librairie Hachette.

Le Beau Montrond. Henri Malo. Emile-Paul Frères. Paris, 1926.

Letters of Horace Walpole. Ed. Charles Duke Young. 2 Vols. New York, 1890.

Talleyrand Intime. Correspondance avec la Duchesse de Courlande. La Restauration en 1814. Paris.

Chanteloup. Jeanne d'Orliac. *La Revue Hebdomadaire,* 13 May, 1920.

Beaumarchais. André Hallays. Paris, 1837.

Madame de Sévigné. André Hallays. Paris, 1821.

Les Lettres de Madame de Sévigné. Didier et Cie. Paris, 1866.

La Fin du XVIIIième Siècle. Lucien Perry. 1 Vol. Paris, 1891.

Belles du Vieux Temps. Vicomte de Reiset. 1 Vol. Paris, 1909.

Beaux Jours et Lendemains. Vicomte de Reiset. 1 Vol. Paris, 1922.

La Société Française du XVIième au XXième Siècle. Victor du Bled. Paris, 1909.

La Société Française au XVIIième Siècle. Paris, 1905.

L'Ancien Clergé de France. Abbé Augustin Sicard. Paris, 1912.

Autun—Les Monuments. Harold de Fontenay et Anatole Charmasse. 1 Vol. Dejussieu Père & Fils. Autun, 1889.

Talleyrand, Metternich et Chateaubriand. Par Maurice Paléologue. 1 Vol. Librairie Hachette. 1924.

Walpole. John Morley.

Diderot. John Morley.

Talleyrand. Translated from the German by Frederic Clarke. Lady Blennerhasset. 2 Vols. London, 1892.

Madame de Staël et son Temps. 3 Vols. Lady Blennerhasset. Paris, 1890.

Prince de Ligne. Mlle. Oulié. 1926. Hachette.

De Goncourt. 10 Vols. 1881–1895. Charpentier.

Alexander Hamilton. Henry Cabot Lodge. Boston, 1883.

Jefferson and Hamilton. Bowers.

Seven Ages of Washington. Owen Wister. New York, 1907.

The Life of John Marshall. 4 Vols. Albert Beveridge. Boston and New York, 1916.

The Life of George Washington. Jared Sparks. 1 Vol. Boston, 1844.

The Life of Voltaire. S. G. Tallentyre. 1 Vol. London, 1910.

Talleyrand, Evêque d'Autun. 1 Vol. Bernard de Lacombe. 2ième Edition. Perrin & Cie. Paris, 1903.

La Vie Privée de Talleyrand. Bernard de Lacombe. 1 Vol. Paris, 1910.

Souvenirs du Congrès de Vienne. Comte Fleury. 1 Vol. 1901. Paris.

La Rome de Napoléon (1809–1814). Louis Madelin. 1 Vol.
Librairie Plon-Nourrit, 1906.
La France. Lady Morgan. Tome II, p. 26.
Mémoires Baron de Vitrolles. 3 Vols. 1884. Charpentier. Louis
XIV. Louis XV.

LIVES AND MEMOIRS

Mémoires d'Outre-Tombe. Chateaubriand. Paris. 6 Vols.
1898–1900. Garnier.
Mémoires sur M. de Talleyrand. Ch. Place et J. Flourus. Paris,
1838.
Mémoires. Duchesse d'Abrantès. 10 Vols. Paris, 1893. Gar-
nier.
Mémoires. Comtesse de Boigne. 4 Vols. Paris, 1921.
Mémoires du Prince de Talleyrand. Ed. Duc de Broglie. Paris,
1891.
Mémoires sur la Vie de Marie-Antoinette. Madame Campan.
First Edition. 1823.
La Maréchale de Luxembourg. Hippolyte de Buffenoir. 1 Vol.
Paris, 1924.
Mémoires de la Reine Hortense. Tome Premier. Publiés par
Le Prince Napoléon, avec notes de Jean Hanoteau. Librairie
Plon. 1927.
Diary of William Hickey (1749–1803). 4 Vols. Ed. by Alfred
Spencer. G. P. Putnam's Sons. London, 1925.
Mémoires. Barras. 4 Vols. 1895–1896. Hachette.
Mémoires. Baron Thiébaut. 5 Vols. 1893–95. Plon.
Mémoires. Chancelier Pasquier. 6 Vols. 1893–95. Plon.
Personal Recollections of the Duc de Broglie. Vol. II. Raphael
Ledos de Beaufort.
Memoirs of the Prince de Talleyrand. Edited by the Duc de
Broglie. Translation by Raphael Ledos de Beaufort.
Souvenirs de Madame Aimée de Coigny. Conversations. 1902.
C. Lévy.
Souvenirs de Napoléon. Napoléon Inconnu. Frédéric Masson.
Paul Ollendorf. 1895.

Journal de Monsieur Moreau de Saint-Méry.

Souvenirs d'Enfance et de Jeunesse. Ernest Renan. 1883. C. Lévy.

Souvenirs de la Duchesse de Dino. Publiés par la Comtesse Jean de Castellane. 1 Vol. Preface par M. Etienne Lamy. Calmann-Lévy. Paris.

Le Duc et la Duchesse de Choiseul. Gaston Maugras. Librairie Plon. 1924.

La Disgrace de Choiseul. Gaston Maugras. Librairie Plon. 1903.

INDEX

A

Abrantés, Saint-Martin Permont Duchesse d', wife of General Junot, 369

Academy of Moral and Political Science, 37, 39, 334, 365, 497, 498, 504

Adams, Robert, architect, 278

Adams, John, 2nd President of the U. S. A., 385

Adélaïde, Madame, daughter of King Louis XV, 63, 64

Adélaïde, Madame, sister of King Louis-Philippe, 284, 504

Agoult, Comte d', 167

Aiguillon, Duc d', Cabinet minister, 88, 93

Aix, Archbishop of, 166

Albany, Town of, 335, 339, 340 et seq., 345

Alembert, d', Encyclopædist, 84

Alexander I, Czar of Russia, 21, 52, 110, 177, 349, 432, 441 et seq., 445 et. seq., 450, 451, 453, 454, 458, 465, 466, 467, 471, 473, 479, 492

Altona, City of, in Germany, 358

America, United States of, 41, 108, 119, 143, 147, 150, 154, 180, 194, 196, 197, 205, 209, 235, 274, 299, 300, 302, 304 et. seq., 308, 314 et seq., 323, 325, 328, et seq., 332, 333, 335, 336, 338 et seq., 345, 347, 348, 350, 351, 357, 360, 363, 365, 379, 385, 406, 424

Amsterdam, City of, 209, 401, 415

André, M. d', 267

Anet, Château d', 466

Angoulême, Louis-Antoine de Bourbon, Duc d', 159

Angoulême, Marie-Thérèse, Duchesse d', Madame Royale, 177

Anjou, Hôtel d', 432

Anjou, Rue d', street in Paris, 428, 435

Antilles, Islands of, 71

Antonio, Don, 436

Antreignes, Monsieur d', 140

Antwerp, town of, 236

Arbelles, André d', 368

Arblay, Major General d', 288, 292, 300

Arblay, Mme. d', see Burney

Arcole, Battle of, 148, 381

Argenson, Mr. d', 75, 288

Arnault, M. Antoine-Vincent, poet and dramatist, 375

Arnold, Benedict, General, 304

Arnold, Mrs. Benedict, see Shippen

Arras, town of, 161

Artois, Province of, 303

Artois, Comte d', later Charles X, King of France, 33, 101, 103, 138, 151, 159, 166, 167, 178, 208, 218, 314, 339, 427, 466, 472, 479, 481

Asturias, Prince of, see Ferdinand

Atlantic Ocean, 18, 278, 302, 328

Aubergenville, locality, 472

Augereau, Pierre-François-Charles, Duc de Castiglione, 382

Austerlitz, Battle of, 436, 442, 445

Austria, 87, 123, 214, 219, 227, 228, 274, 442, 443, 445, 447, 448, 451, 452, 464

Autun, Bishop and Bishopric of, see Talleyrand

B

Bac, Rue du, Street in Paris, 199, 410, 428

Bachaumont, Louis Petit de, 121

Bacourt, Monsieur de, 80, 216, 503

Bailleul, Monsieur J. C., historian, 381

Bailly, Jean-Sylvain, President of the National Assembly, 164, 165

Bain, scientist, 85

Bainville, Monsieur Jacques, historian, 227

Baltimore, town of, 274

Balzac, Honoré de, author, 73

Barante, Baron de, 503

Barras, Paul-Jean, Comte de, 352, 367, 368, 370 et seq., 376, 377, 383, 401 et seq., 407, 409